TECHNICIANS OF THE SACRED

TECHNICIANS

A Range of Poetries

from Africa

America

Asia

Europe

& Oceania

UNIVERSITY OF CALIFORNIA PRESS

$O F \; T H E \; S A C R E D$

Edited with commentaries

$by \; Jerome \; Rothenberg$

$B E R K E L E Y$ $L O S \; A N G E L E S$ $L O N D O N$

University of California Press
Berkeley and Los Angeles, California

University of California Press, Ltd.
London, England

Second Edition, Revised and Expanded
Copyright © 1968, 1985 by Jerome Rothenberg

Library of Congress Cataloging in Publication Data
Main entry under title:

Technicians of the sacred.

1. Folk poetry. 2. Folk-songs—Texts.
I. Rothenberg, Jerome, 1931–
PN1347.T43   1984   398.2   84-16276
ISBN 0-520-04912-8 (pbk.)

Printed in the United States of America

08 07 06 05 04 03 02 01
12 11 10 9 8 7 6

The paper used in this publication meets the minimum
requirements of ANSI/NISO Z39.48-1992 (R 1997)
(Permanence of Paper). ∞

```
*****************************
*I*love*my ************world*
*****************************
*****************************
*I*love*my ************time*
*****************************
*****************************
*I*love*my*growing*children*
*****************************
*****************************
*I*love*my ********old*people*
*****************************
*****************************
*I*love*my ********ceremonies*
*****************************
```

CONTENTS

PRE-FACE (1984)   xvii

PRE-FACE (1967)   xxv

THE TEXTS   1

ORIGINS & NAMINGS   5

Genesis I (Kato Indian)   7
Sounds   8
Genesis II (Arnhem Land, Australia)   9
Egyptian God Names   11
Genesis III (Maori, New Zealand)   13
Images   15
Bantu Combinations (Africa)   16
Correspondences (Chinese)   17
Genesis IV (Hebrew)   19
Aztec Definitions   20
Genesis V (Uitoto Indian, Colombia)   25
The Pictures   26
The Girl of the Early Race Who Made the Stars
    (Bushman, Africa)   32
The Fragments   34
All Lives, All Dances, & All Is Loud (Gabon Pygmy,
    Africa)   36
Yoruba Praises (Africa)   37
A Poem for the Wind (Welsh)   38
War God's Horse Song I (Navajo Indian)   40
War God's Horse Song II (Navajo Indian)   41

To the God of Fire as a Horse (India)   44

The Stars (Passamaquoddy Indian)   45

VISIONS & SPELS   47

The Annunciation (Tibetan)   49

How Isaac Tens Became a Shaman (Gitksan Indian)   50

A Shaman Climbs Up the Sky (Altaic)   54

The Dog Vision (Sioux Indian [Lakota])   58

From *The Midnight Velada* (Mazatec Indian)   62

The Dream of Enkidu (Mesopotamia)   65

A List of Bad Dreams Chanted as a Cause & Cure
    for Missing Souls (Bidayuh, Sarawak) 67

The Killer (Cherokee Indian)   70

Spell Against Jaundice (Serbian)   71

A Poison Arrow (Hausa, Africa)   73

A Breastplate Against Death (Irish)   74

Ol' Hannah (Afro-American)   76

Offering Flowers (Aztec)   81

From *The Night Chant* (Navajo Indian)   83

DEATH & DEFEAT   87

When Hare Heard of Death (Winnebago Indian)   89

A Peruvian Dance Song (Ayacucho Indian)   90

Death Song (Papago Indian)   90

From *The Odyssey* (Greek)   91

The Mourning Song of Small-Lake-Underneath
    (Tlingit Indian)   94

The Story of the Leopard Tortoise (Bushman, Africa)   95

Nottamun Town (Appalachia, United States)   97

The Flight of Quetzalcoatl (Aztec)   98

The String Game (Bushman, Africa)   104

The Abortion (Santal, India)   105

Improvised Song Against a White Man
    (Malagasy, Madagascar)   107
Psalm 137 (Hebrew)   108
A Sequence of Songs of the Ghost Dance Religion   109

THE BOOK OF EVENTS (I)   111

Lily Events (Arnhem Land, Australia)   113
Garbage Event (Dayak, Borneo)   114
Beard Event (Arnhem Land, Australia)   114
Stone Fire Event (Arnhem Land, Australia)   115
Climbing Event (Sarawak)   115
Forest Event (Hungary)   115
Gift Event (Kwakiutl Indian)   116
Marriage Event (Hervey Islands, Polynesia)   117
Three Magic Events (Sweden)   118
Going-Around Event (Asiatic Eskimo)   119
Language Event (Venda, Africa)   120
Burial Events (Tibet)   122
Friendship Dance (Cherokee Indian)   123
Grease Feast Event (Kwakiutl Indian)   124
Peacemaking Event (Andaman Islands)   126
Wild Man Events (Bohemia)   128
Booger Event (Cherokee Indian)   129
Sea Water Event (Arnhem Land, Australia)   131
Noise Event (Hebrew)   131

THE BOOK OF EVENTS (II)   133

Taming the Storm (Copper Eskimo)   135
Coronation Event & Drama (Egyptian)   140
For the Rain God Tlaloc: A Dialogue for God &
    Chanters (Aztec)   144

AFRICA   147

Ghosts & Shadows (Gabon Pygmy)   149
The Chapter of Changing Into Ptah (Egyptian)   150
The Cannibal Hymn (Egyptian)   152
Conversations in Courtship (Egyptian)   154
The Comet (Ekoi)   157
The Lovers (Ekoi)   158
Drum Poem #7 (Ashanti)   159
Praises of Ogun (Yoruba)   161
Abuse Poem: for Kodzo & Others (Ewe)   164
What Fell Down? Penis! (Ekperi)   166
What Fell Down? Vulva! (Ekperi)   168
The Train (Hurutshe)   169
Speaking the World: Seven Praise-Mottoes (Dogon)   170
Death Rites I and II (Gabon Pygmy)   172
The Praises of the Falls (Basuto)   174
Ika Meji (Yoruba)   181
Little Leper of Munjolóbo (Haya)   185
Voice of the Karaw (Bamana)   191
Gassire's Lute (Soninke)   194

AMERICA   203

Mide Songs & Picture-Songs (Ojibwa)   205
Seven Chippewa (Ojibwa) Songs   208
From *The Wishing Bone Cycle* (Swampy Cree)   210
Three Teton Sioux Songs   213
From Battiste Good's Winter Count (Dakota)   215
Peyote Songs (Comanche)   218
Song of the Humpbacked Flute Player (Hopi)   219
Coyote & Junco (Zuni)   220
The Tenth Horse Song of Frank Mitchell
   (Navajo)   224

A Song of the Winds (Seri) 226
Six Seri Whale Songs 227
Flower World: Three Poems from the Yaqui Deer Dance 229
"To Find Our Life" (Huichol) 231
The Painted Book (Nahuatl, Texcoco) 233
From *Codex Boturini* (Aztec) 236
From *The Popol Vuh:* Blood-Girl & the Chiefs of
    Hell (Maya) 240
Mayan Definitions 243
From *Inatoipippiler* (Cuna) 246
From *The Elegy for the Great Inca Atawallpa* (Quechua) 249
Three Quechua Poems 251
Poems for a Carnival (Quechua) 254
Raising the Mediating Center & the Field of Evil
    (Spanish, Peru) 255
The Machi Exorcises the Spirit Huecuve (Araucanian) 260
Words from Seven Magic Songs (Copper Eskimo) 261
My Breath (Netsilik Eskimo) 262
Eskimo Prose Poems 265

ASIA 269

The Quest of Milarepa (Tibetan) 271
Keeping Still / The Mountain (Chinese) 274
The Marrying Maiden (Chinese) 276
From *The Nine Songs* (Chinese) 278
Song of the Dead, Relating the Origin of Bitterness
    (Na-Khi, China) 281
A Shaman Vision Poem (Chinese) 286
Al Que Quiere: II *pai-hua* (Chinese) 287
From *The Kojiki:* How Opo-Kuni-Nusi Bids Farewell to
    His Jealous Wife, Suseri-Bime, in Song (Japanese) 291
A Song of the Spider Goddess (Ainu) 293

Things Seen by the Shaman Karawe (Chukchee)   301
Praise Song of the Buck-Hare (Teleut)   303
Setchin the Singer (Vogul)   305
Mantra for Binding a Witch (Baiga, India)   309
The Pig (Baiga, India)   310
Two Cosmologies (Sanskrit, India)   312
From *The Guide to Lord Murukan* (Tamil, India)   314
For the Lord of Caves (Kannada, India)   317

EUROPE & THE ANCIENT NEAR EAST   319

The Calendar (Upper Paleolithic)   321
The Vulva Song of Inana (Sumerian)   322
The Battle Between Anat & the Forces of Mot
    (Ugaritic)   324
From *The Song of Ullikummi* (Hittite)   327
From *Theogony* [Godbirths] (Greek)   329
Song of the Arval Brothers (Roman)   333
Birth of the Fire God (Armenian)   335
The Round Dance of Jesus (Syriac)   336
A Song of Amergin (Irish)   341
From *The Red Book of Hergest* (Welsh)   342
Two Poems for All-Hallows' Eve (Welsh)   344
The Fairy Woman's Lullaby (Scottish Gaelic)   345
The Nine Herbs Charm (Anglo-Saxon)   347
From Shakespeare's *Lear* (English)   350
Odin's Shaman Song (Icelandic)   353
From *Kalevala* (Finnish)   355
The Fox (Lapp)   358
Blood River Shaman Chant (Nenets)   359
Bald Mountain *Zaum*-Poems (Russian)   361
A Poem for the Goddess Her City & the Marriage of Her
    Son & Daughter (Serbian)   362

The Message of King Sakis & the Legend of the Twelve
  Dreams He Had in One Night (Serbo-Croatian)   364
A Love Poem with Witches (Rumanian)   366
The Descriptions of King Lent (French)   368
Deep Song (Spanish Gypsy)   372
The Canticle for Brother Sun (Italian)   374
From *Europe a Prophecy* (English)   376

OCEANIA   377

Twelve Kura Songs from Tikopia
  (British Solomon Islands)   379
Two for the God Aia (Mekeo, New Guinea)   382
Tolai Songs (Kuanua, New Guinea)   383
Pidgin Song (Papua New Guinea)   384
The Gumagabu Song (Trobriand Islands, New Guinea)   385
Three Drum Poems (Trobriand Islands, New Guinea)   387
Songs & Spirit-Songs (Duke of York Islands,
  Melanesia)   388
The Daybreak (Mudbara, Australia)   391
Sightings: Kunapipi (Arnhem Land, Australia)   392
From *The Goulburn Island Cycle* (Arnhem Land, Australia) 395
The First Truck at Tambrey (Jindjiparndi, Australia) 403
Night Births (Hawaii, Polynesia)   407
The Woman Who Married a Caterpillar
  (Hawaii, Polynesia)   411
The Body-Song of Kio (Tuamotua, Polynesia)   412
Funeral Eva (Mangaian, Polynesia)   413
Toto Vaca (Maori, Polynesia)   414
The Lovers I (Kapingamarangi, Polynesia)   417
The Lovers II (Kapingamarangi, Polynesia)   418
Flight of the Chiefs: Song V (Fiji, Melanesia)   420
Animal Story X (Fiji, Melanesia)   423

THE STATEMENTS   425

THE COMMENTARIES   439

POST ~ FACE   627

THE PRE-FACES

P R E - F A C E (1 9 8 4)

When I first entered on the present work, sometime in the middle 1960s, it was my hope to make a fresh start, to begin at the beginning—as if, in the words of Descartes once quoted by the Dada fathers, "there were no other men before us." That meant not so much a simple rubbing-out of history as its possible expansion; & it meant, against our inherited notions of the past, a questioning of such notions at their roots. The area I set out to explore was poetry: an idea of poetry—of *language* & *reality* both—that had haunted me since my own first beginnings as a poet. The inherited view—no longer bearable—was that one such idea of poetry, as developed in the West, was sufficient for the total telling. Against this—as the facts, the poems them-selves, revealed—was the realization that poetry, like language itself, existed everywhere: as powerful, even complex, in its presumed beginnings as in many of its later works. In the light of that approach, poetry appeared not as a luxury but as a true necessity: not a small corner of the world for those who lived it but equal to the world itself. (For this the works presented herein would be a confirmation.)

Late into the assembling of *Technicians of the Sacred*, I became aware that the work coincided with a series of openings that were newly reappearing in the culture as a whole. My own sources & predecessors—as far as I knew them then—went back 150, maybe 200 years into the Western past, but the personal awakenings for me & others of my generation came in the decade immediately after the second world war. That much at least was clear to me in the several years I was working on the gathering, but what came as a surprise was that by 1966 or 1967 the desire for a new beginning had spread in a way that we wouldn't earlier have believed possible. Several correspondents, later friends, out on the West Coast first got the word to me that there was in evidence there, as Michael McClure put it, "a *massive* return to 'instinct and intuition' ": terms that I felt then & now as only a part of the human picture, but a part whose reemergence was long due. The equation I saw—& so stated in the Pre-Face to *Technicians of the Sacred*—was of "imagination" as a process of both "energy" & "intelligence"; or, put another way, that the return of what Blake had called "our antediluvian energies" would lead to a transformation of intelligence rather than its virtual obliteration. It was to this "new imagination" that the work was dedicated—as a resource book of possibilities that were often new for us but that had already been realized somewhere in the world.

All of that entered, as McClure knew it would, into the sixties maelstrom. That meant that the book confronted an audience that was already waiting for it, often with more preconceptions about the "tribal" or the "oral"—& so on—than I myself was willing to take on. But it also coincided with a series of experiments & projects, some highly visible & publicized, others carried on outside the media & the art-world nexus, but all related to what Gary Snyder elsewhere names "the real work." In the post-script to the book's original Pre-Face, I wrote: "This post-script is an incitement to those who would join in the enterprise; it is in no sense a final word." By saying that, I was calling for new work by poets & others, & in the years since, I was able to encourage some of that work & to present it in further anthologies such as *Shaking the Pumpkin, A Big Jewish Book,* & *Symposium of the Whole.** Even more so, in 1970 I joined Dennis Tedlock in founding the magazine *Alcheringa*, precisely to carry on the work of *Technicians of the Sacred* in uncovering new & old poetries & developing new means for their translation & presentation. (I later pursued this on my own in *New Wilderness Letter*.) At the same time others were documenting & displaying related works: in specialized books & wide-ranging anthologies, in little & large magazines, in film & video, & in offerings at festivals & conferences on ritual poetry & performance.

The point—again—is that the work was now emerging on its own momentum: a condition of our time that carries over to the present. And similar interests—sometimes in fruitful confrontation with our own—were part of those ethnic movements that have marked an ongoing reorganization of values & powers both in the West & in those multiple cultures of the "third world" undergoing rapid transformations. Our ideas of poetry—including, significantly, our idea of the poet—began to look back *consciously* to the early & late shamans of those other worlds: not as a title to be seized but as a model for the shaping of meanings & intensities through language. As the reflection of our yearning to create a meaningful ritual life—a life lived at the level of poetry—that looking-back related to the emergence of a new poetry & art

**Symposium of the Whole*, edited with Diane Rothenberg, now exists as a companion to the present volume, tracing the enterprise back two centuries & more, & providing detailed descriptions of matters that can only be hinted at here. I have accordingly attempted, where possible, to cross-reference to it through the pages that follow.

rooted in performance & in the oldest, most universal of human traditions.

All of that is by now so much a part of the consciousness of late twentieth-century poets & artists that the "news" of the original book is probably no longer news. But the work, by the same token, has hardly begun, & the changed paradigm of where we see ourselves in time & space has received little recognition from the literary brokers. In that sense it remains (like much that is good among us) partly, maybe largely, subterranean.

While *Technicians* has remained the pivotal work for me, I was aware then & now that in first assembling it I had to work within the limits of what was available in the middle 1960s: a tremendous amount of raw material collected by anthropologists & linguists earlier in the century, very few solid or poetically viable translations, & a big gap between the poets & the scholars concerned with this kind of project. Since its publication in 1968, the work on all sides has increased tremendously, part of it, I would like to believe, as a direct or indirect result of what that first gathering had set in motion.

My intention from the start was to be able to return at some point to *Technicians* & to revise it in the light of later work. The strategy for that revision, as I've now come to it, has been to keep the structure & approach of the book intact, while adding new material to all the sections & eliminating weaker or more dubious pieces, where that didn't interfere with the ongoing "arguments" in the commentaries. By the time of *Shaking the Pumpkin*, such new works had clearly begun to appear, & by now (along with older works previously overlooked) they form a constantly expanding source from which to build the present gathering. (That what has opened to us is only a small percentage of the world's primal poetries is something we would do well to keep in mind.)

The difference from 1968, then, works out largely in favor of the present. As such, it reflects a renewed interest in the collection of traditional poetries & an unprecedented number of translation projects whose main aim has been the re-creation of oral performances in both written & sounded versions. With this has also come a change in quality, a new degree of freedom related to the freedoms won in our own poetry—by which I don't mean a free & easy approach to the work at hand but translations & descriptions *freed from* conventional models of poetry & language that allowed us to see only a small part of what was really there. The scholars who have come into it—largely ethnographers & linguists—have developed a closer, more accurate approach to sources, while the poets have shown how translated works can be created that carry the excitement of charged language (poetry) straight over into English. But the two approaches have never been exclusive, & the crossovers between the poets & the scholars (sometimes their active collaboration) have by now blurred what once seemed to be an ironclad distinction.

This revised edition is in some sense a reflection of those fifteen years of renewal & owes more to the new translators than I can ever properly express. On their more technical side, the experiments in translation have involved such scholars as Dennis Tedlock, Dell Hymes, David McAllester, Allan Burns, & Peter Seitel, while the poets have included Nathaniel Tarn, Armand Schwerner, W. S. Merwin, James Koller, Anselm Hollo, Edward Field, & Barbara Einzig, among many others. The projects have often been extensive in scope & based on firsthand explorations ("seeing for oneself"—C. Olson): the Cree Indian tellings gathered & closely re-created by Howard Norman (a Cree speaker from childhood); the precise translations of Dennis Tedlock from Zuni & Mayan that developed a new model for transcribing oral performances in writing; the works of A. K. Ramanujan bringing us the visionary poetry of Tamil (*bhakti*) saints & madmen; Kofi Awoonor's first-hand translations of still contemporary Ewe *heno* poets; Judith Gleason's unravelings of epic Ifa divination poems; Donald Philippi's translations of the oldest Japanese writings & the story-poems, from almost the present, of Ainu shamans & singers; David Guss's recent efforts to bring the Makiritare imaginal world into English; Henry Munn's translations from the extended shamanistic sessions of María Sabina & other Mazatec healers; my own experiments, circa 1970, with "total translations" from Seneca & Navajo; & the continuing work of David McAllester, R. M. Berndt, Miguel Léon-Portilla, & Ulli Beier. Beyond the rightness of this or that translation, the versions & workings—still from a variety of approaches—are examples in themselves of that continuation or diffusion of ideas & images that has been—always—a fundamental marker of the human condition.

An assemblage like this one is by its nature an anthology of *versions*.

Among the sources absent from *Technicians*, the most conspicuous were those from Europe. Not that I had planned it that way, but I found as I got into it that I was uncertain how to distinguish a non-"literary" tradition in European poetry & was overwhelmed by the task of selection & retranslation. The materials felt too close for me to get a clear image of how they fitted with the others or to separate the European "primitive" from its development by later poets. Beyond that I was aware—& that awareness has continued to the present—of how the old poetries (the mythologies in particular) had been corrupted to serve the ends of European nationalism: that Western mythology & folklore in their nineteenth- & early twentieth-century forms were shot through with racist distortions, teutonic fakeries, & so on. The political intention of *Technicians* was in fact to call such European hegemonies into question.

The exclusion of Europe resulted, probably, in the exaggeration of the European difference: not a contrast between "primitive" & "civilized" modes of thought but a European/non-European split that leaves Europe as an entity almost entirely apart. (It also masks the fact that European cultural imperialism began against populations themselves a part of Europe & has continued there up to the present.) In the intervening years I kept going back to Europe & to the necessary sourceworks, devoting the fifth issue of *Alcheringa* to them & first conceiving *A Big Jewish Book* as a roundabout attempt to deal with the European experience through the focus of a Jewish diaspora that merged with multiple European cultures. In the meantime new translations became available from various sources that revealed more clearly than before those instances where mind—& its coming-forth through language—was at its most intense in Europe: where the poetics of the shamans (even where we saw the shamans hunted down as heretics & witches) was still in evidence for all to see & hear.

It now seems clear to me that such a European section—& the interspersing of European materials elsewhere in this book—is not only useful in itself but can have an illuminating effect on the other areas covered. My procedure here is to follow a line that runs from a conjectural tribal/oral past & has been carried forward through a series of subterranean & folk traditions, often magical or mystical in nature. In concrete terms, the work begins with a reconstructed paleolithic calendar count & with some of those Mesopotamian sources (Sumerian, Ugaritic, Hittite) that were geographically Asian but in constant interplay with ancient Europe. From there it moves to early Greek & Roman models that are themselves on the border between an oral & a written poetry, before drawing (nonchronologically) from a range of sources that include pre-Christian (pagan & shamanistic) mythologies & poetries recovered over the last 200 years from Celtic, Icelandic, Finnish, Anglo-Saxon, Serbian, & so on; works like the Syriac "round dance of Jesus" as an example of a (heretical) gnosticism that reveals a virtual process of open *poesis*; magical texts & soundtexts using—like their counterparts elsewhere— a specialized language of changes & what Malinowski called "the coefficient of weirdness"; & outcroppings of all of these in latterday folk traditions & lores, particularly as they touch the work of romantic & modern poets or affirm a counterpoetics rooted in practices resembling or related to others in these pages. (That even this much of the older work has survived I would take as the sign of a resistance—deeply, even darkly, political—to the conformities demanded by the ruling nation-states.)

Finally, it has been my decision to include a few works from the established (literary) tradition that are connected as well to the old lore in so far as it remained a living presence in the air of Europe. The persistence of such connections explains the appearance here of Rabelais, Saint Francis, Blake, & even Shakespeare—as, less surprisingly, that of Homer & Hesiod— along with my sense that the equals of the old "technicians of the sacred" aren't only to be found at the margins but at the center of our poetries as generally understood. (It is at this point that the distinction between the margins & the center begins to drop away.) That such ways-of-mind may be more intact in the oral/written work of a Shakespeare than in the more dispersed/fragmented work (however marvelous) of this or that "folk" poet is not a retreat from the proposals of *Technicians of the Sacred* but the strongest affirmation I can give them. The attempt to show this greater "great tradi- tion" is—like much else in this book—only a beginning, & its expansion would take me into a work like what George Quasha & I attempted in *America a Prophecy*: a merging of the literary & the nonliterary toward the presentation of a visionary poetics in *all* its phases.

The intention of the book—its presentation of the world's "tribal & oral poetries" / of "savage mind" wherever found—is otherwise explained in the original Pre-Face. I have reprinted it here with only some minor modifica- tions, but the event has also opened me to a review of many of the proposi- tions—my own & others'—that remain largely unresolved. It is late in the game by now, but it seems to me (given whatever experience I've had with it) that we're still overwhelmed by preconceptions as we go on with the work at hand. I have tried, myself, to deal with certain of these which I find question- able or disproven by the actual investigation. And again & again I find that part of my work the hardest to get across. A few explicit warnings, therefore:

   —that we must, above all, avoid clichés about the poetics/ethnopoetics
   of technologically *simpler* cultures—which led me to begin *Technicians*
   with an emphasis on the *complexity* of tribal/oral language & (ritual)
   art;

—that we must question—by investigation—the idea that traditional art & poetry are collective rather than individual—reflective in fact, as Paul Radin wrote, of "an individualism run riot";

—that we must not assume that it is our culture alone (or those cultures most like our own) that has introduced reflexivity/self-reflection into the creative process, when scholars like Victor Turner have taken such pains to demonstrate the reflexive nature of ritual & art throughout the full range of human cultures;

—that we can no longer assume that the poetry & ritual of traditional cultures aims at stasis rather than at change/transformation not only in a mystical sense but in a social sense as well—for, in Olson's paraphrasing of Heraclitus: "what does not change / is the will to change";

& we must be careful not to assume

—that orality totally defines "them" or that writing totally defines "us" (a major attempt of this revision is to explore—even more than in 1968—the universality of writing/drawing as a primal form of language);

nor should we overlook

—that people have thought long & hard—everywhere—about language & its accomplishment through performance;

—that a poetics—a generalized "idea of poetry"—has arisen again & again in the total human story, no more nor less "universal" than the Athenian poetics which gave a start to one such line of thinking in the West;

—that much of what we think of (too easily) as primitive or traditional is the work of our contemporaries & a response—as in many of the poems gathered herein—to a world that they & we share;

& we must remember to our own good

—that a poetry of the spirit—a visionary poetry—is not only to be found apart from us; that while it pervades many old cultures, it has, since the nineteenth century at least, been a prominent mode among our own poets (& in some sense has likely always been that, as a kind of crypto [hidden] vision).

And knowing that, we have the advantage of observing in the traditional cultures how such modes have permeated whole populations & how they've been carried forward over millennia.

By doing all this, we can also discover forms that we've barely dreamed of, or we can ignore them to our loss & hardly (as far as I can see) to *their* advantage. One result will be that our poetry will cease to be "modern" (as Tristan Tzara, a major forerunner of the present work, long ago predicted) & will emerge, with the dissolution of modernism, as what it was all along: "a state of mind (*esprit*)" . . . not an investment in a "new technique" but "in the spirit."

Jerome Rothenberg

Encinitas, California
February 10, 1984

PRIMITIVE MEANS COMPLEX

That there are no primitive languages is an axiom of contemporary linguistics where it turns its attention to the remote languages of the world. There are no half-formed languages, no underdeveloped or inferior languages. Everywhere a development has taken place into structures of great complexity. People who have failed to achieve the wheel will not have failed to invent & develop a highly wrought grammar. Hunters & gatherers innocent of all agriculture will have vocabularies that distinguish the things of their world down to the finest details. The language of snow among the Eskimos is awesome. The aspect system of Hopi verbs can, by a flick of the tongue, make the most subtle kinds of distinction between different types of motion.

What is true of language in general is equally true of poetry & of the ritual-systems of which so much poetry is a part. It is a question of energy & intelligence as universal constants &, in any specific case, the direction that energy & intelligence (= imagination) have been given. No people today is newly born. No people has sat in sloth for the thousands of years of its history. Measure everything by the Titan rocket & the transistor radio, & the world is full of primitive peoples. But once change the unit of value to the poem or the dance-event or the dream (all clearly artifactual situations) & it becomes apparent what all those people have been doing all those years with all that time on their hands.

Poetry, wherever you find it among the "primitives"* (literally *every-*

---

*The word "primitive" is used with misgivings & put in quotes, but no way around it seems workable. "Non-technological" & "non-literate," which have often been suggested as alternatives, are too emphatic in pointing to supposed "lacks" &, though they feel precise to start with, are themselves open to question. Are the Eskimo snow-workers, e.g., really "non"- or "pre-technological"? And how does the widespread use of pictographs & pictosymbols, which can be "read" by later generations, affect their users' non-literate status? A major point throughout this book is that these peoples (& they're likely too diverse to be covered by a single name) are precisely "technicians" where it most concerns them—specifically in their relation to the "sacred" as something they can actively create or capture. That's the only way in fact that I'd hope to define "primitive": as a situation in which such conditions flourish & in which the "poets" are (in a variant of Eliade's phrase) the principle "technicians of the sacred."

where), involves an extremely complicated sense of materials & structures. Everywhere it involves the manipulation (fine or gross) of multiple elements. If this isn't always apparent, it's because the carry-over (by translation or interpretation) necessarily distorts where it chooses some part of the whole that it can meaningfully deal with. The work is foreign & its complexity is often elusive, a question of gestalt or configuration, of the angle from which the work is seen. If you expect a primitive work to be simple or naïve, you will probably end up seeing a simple or naïve work; & this will be abetted by the fact that translation can, in general, only present as a single work, a part of what is actually there. The problem is fundamental for as long as we approach these works from the outside—& we're likely fated to be doing that forever.

It's very hard in fact to decide what precisely are the boundaries of "primitive" poetry or of a "primitive" poem, since there's often no activity differentiated as such, but the words or vocables are part of a larger total "work" that may go on for hours, even days, at a stretch. What we would separate as music & dance & myth & painting is also part of that work, & the need for separation is a question of "our" interest & preconceptions, not of "theirs." Thus the picture is immediately complicated by the nature of the work & the media that comprise it. And it becomes clear that the "collective" nature of primitive poetry (upon which so much stress has been placed despite the existence of individualized poems & clearly identified poets) is to a great degree inseparable from the amount of materials a single work may handle.

Now all of this is, if so stated, a question of technology as well as inspiration; & we may as well take it as axiomatic for what follows that where poetry is concerned, "primitive" means complex.

WHAT IS A "PRIMITIVE" POEM?

Poems are carried by the voice & are sung or chanted or spoken in specific situations. Under such circumstances, runs the easy answer, the "poem" would simply be the words-of-the-song. But a little later on the question arises: what *are* the words & where do they begin & end? The translation, as printed, may show the "meaningful" element only, often no more than a single, isolated "line"; thus

A splinter of stone which is white (Bushman)
Semen white like the mist (Australian)
My-shining-horns (Chippewa: single word)
etc.

but in practice the one "line" will likely be repeated until its burden has been exhausted. (Is it "single" then?) It may be altered phonetically & the words distorted from their "normal" forms. Vocables with no fixed meanings may be intercalated. All of these devices will be creating a greater & greater gap between the "meaningful" residue in the translation & what-was-actually-there. We will have a different "poem" depending where we catch the movement, & we may start to ask: Is something within this work the "poem," or is everything?

Again, the work will probably not end with the "single" line & its various configurations—will more likely be preceded & followed by other lines. Are all of these "lines" (each of considerable duration) separate poems, or are they the component parts of a single, larger poem moving toward some specific (ceremonial) end? Is it enough, then, if the lines happen in succession & aren't otherwise tied? Will some further connection be needed? Is the group of lines a poem if "we" can make the connection? Is it a poem where no connection is apparent to "us"? If the lines come in sequence on a single occasion does the unity of the occasion connect them into a single poem? Can many poems be a single poem as well? (They often are.)

What's a sequence anyway?

What's unity?

THE UNITY OF "PRIMITIVE" THOUGHT & ITS SHATTERING

The anthology shows some ways in which the unity is achieved—in general by the imposition of some constant or "key" against which all disparate materials can be measured. A sound, a rhythm, a name, an image, a dream, a gesture, a picture, an action, a silence: any or all of these can function as "keys." Beyond that there's no need for consistency, for fixed or discrete meanings. An object is whatever it becomes under the impulse of the situation at hand. Forms are often open. Causality is often set aside. The poet (who may also be dancer, singer, magician, whatever the event demands of him) masters a series of techniques that can fuse the most seemingly contradictory propositions.

But above all there's a sense-of-unity that surrounds the poem, a reality concept that acts as a cement, a unification of perspective linking

> poet & man
> man & world
> world & image
> image & word
> word & music
> music & dance
> dance & dancer
> dancer & man
> man & world
> etc.

all of which has been put in many different ways—by Cassirer notably as a feeling for "the solidarity of all life" leading toward a "law of metamorphosis" in thought & word.

Within this undifferentiated & unified frame with its open images & mixed media, there are rarely "poems" as we know them—but we come in with our analytical minds & shatter the unity. It has in fact been shattered already by workers before us.

PRIMITIVE & MODERN: INTERSECTIONS & ANALOGIES

Like any collector, my approach to delimiting & recognizing what's a poem has been by analogy: in this case (beyond the obvious definition of poems as words-of-songs) to the work of modern poets. Since much of this work has been revolutionary & limit-smashing, the analogy in turn expands the range of what "we" can see as primitive poetry. It also shows some of the ways in which primitive poetry & thought are close to an impulse toward unity in our own time, of which the poets are forerunners. The important intersections (analogies) are:

(1) the poem carried by the voice: a "pre"-literate situation of poetry composed to be spoken, chanted or, more accurately, sung; compare this to the "post-literate" situation, in McLuhan's good phrase, or where-we-are-today;

written poem as score
public readings
performance poetry

poets' theaters
jazz poetry
rock poetry etc

(2) a highly developed process of image-thinking: concrete or non-causal thought in contrast to the simplifications of Aristotelian logic, etc., with its "objective categories" & rules of non-contradiction; a "logic" of polarities; creation thru dream, etc.; modern poetry (having had & outlived the experience of rationalism) enters a post-logical phase;

Blake's multi-images
symbolisme
surrealism

deep-image

random poetry
composition by field etc

(3) a "minimal" art of maximal involvement; compound elements, each clearly articulated, & with plenty of room for fill-in (gaps in sequence, etc.): the "spectator" as (ritual) participant who pulls it all together;

concrete poetry

(4) an "intermedia" situation, as further denial of the categories: the poet's techniques aren't limited to verbal maneuvers but operate also through song, non-verbal sound, visual signs, & the varied activities of the ritual event: here the "poem" = the work of the "poet" in whatever medium, or (where we're able to grasp it) the totality of the work;

picture poems
prose poems

happenings
total theater

poets as film & video makers

poésie sonore

(5) the animal-body-rootedness of "primitive" poetry: recognition of a "physical" basis for the poem within a man's body—or as an act of body & mind together, breath &/or spirit;

dada
lautgedichte (sound poems)
beast language

line & breath
projective verse etc

in many cases too the direct & open handling of sexual imagery & (in the "events") of sexual activities as key factors in creation of the sacred;

     sexual revolution etc

     (6) the poet as shaman, or primitive shaman as poet & seer thru control of the means just stated: an open "visionary" situation prior to all system-making ("priesthood") in which the man creates thru dream (image) & word (song), "that Reason may have ideas to build on" (W. Blake).

     Rimbaud's voyant
     Rilke's angel
     Lorca's duende

     beat poetry
     psychedelic see-in's, be-in's, etc

individual neo-shamanisms, etc, works directly influenced by the "other" poetry or by analogies to "primitive art": ideas of negritude, tribalism, wilderness, etc.

What's more, the translations themselves may create new forms & shapes-of-poems with their own energies & interest—another intersection that can't be overlooked.

     In all this the ties feel very close—not that "we" & "they" are identical, but that the systems of thought & the poetry they've achieved are, like what we're after, distinct from something in the official "west," & we can now see & value them because of it. What's missing are the in-context factors that define them more closely group-by-group: the sense of the poems as part of an integrated social & religious complex; the presence in each instance of specific myths & locales; the fullness of the living culture. Here the going is rougher with no easy shortcuts through translation: no simple carry-overs. If our world is open to multiple influences & data, theirs seems largely self-contained. If we're committed to a search for the "new," most of them are tradition-bound. (The degree to which "they" are can be greatly exaggerated.) If the poet's purpose among us is "to spread doubt [& create illusion]" (N. Calas), among them it's to overcome it.

     That they've done so *without denying the reality* is also worth remembering.

THE BACKGROUND & STRUCTURE
OF THIS BOOK

The present collection grew directly out of a pair of 1964 readings of "primitive & archaic* poetry" at The Poet's Hardware Theater & The Cafe Metro in New York. Working with me on those were the poets David Antin, Jackson Mac Low, & Rochelle Owens. The material, which I'd been assembling or translating over the previous several years, was arranged topically rather than geographically—an order preserved here in the first three sections of texts. The idea for a "book of events" came from a discussion with Dick Higgins about what he was calling "near-poetry" & from my own sense of the closeness of primitive rituals (when stripped-down to the bare line of the activities) to the "happenings" & "events" he was presenting as publisher of *Something Else Press*. The last four [now five] sections roughly correspond to some kind of geographical reality—not that there aren't problems of overlap, etc., in a grouping by continents but simply that it provides an alternate way of bringing the materials together. (The reader may think of some others as well.)

While the final gathering is several times its 1964 size, I don't see it in any sense as more than a beginning. My intention from the start was to find translations that would "translate," i.e., bring-the-work-across or be a living work in English, & that's a very different thing from (in the first place) looking for representative "masterpieces" & including them whatever the nature of the translations. I also have (no question about it) my own sense of what's worth it in poetry, & I've tried to work from that rather than against it. I haven't gone for "pretty" or "innocent" or "noble" poems so much as strong ones. Throughout I've kept the possibilities wide open: looking for new forms & media; hoping that what I finally assembled could

*Throughout the book I use "archaic" [or "traditional" as its virtual, less loaded synonym] to mean (1) the early phases of the so-called "higher" civilizations, where poetry & voice still hadn't separated or where the new writing was used for setting down what the voice had already made; (2) contemporary "remnant" cultures in which acculturation has significantly disrupted the "primitive modes"; & (3) a cover-all term for "primitive," "early high," & "remnant." The word is useful because of the generalization it permits (the variety of cultures is actually immense) & because it encompasses certain "mixed" cultural situations. My interest is in whether the poetry works, not in the "purity" of the culture from which it comes. I doubt, in fact, if there can be "pure" cultures.

be read as "contemporary," since so much of it is that in fact, still being created & used in a world we share. Where there was a choice of showing poems separately or in series (as described above), I've leaned toward the in-series presentation. Since I feel that the complexity & tough-mindedness of primitive poetry have never really been shown (& since I happen to like such qualities in poems), I've decided to stress them. I've kept in general within the domain of the book's title, though sometimes I did include poems for no other reason than that they sounded good to me or moved me.

The poems are first given without any comments or footnotes, & the readers who like it like that don't have to go any further. (*They* won't, no matter what I say.) Taking poems straight in that sense is like the Australian aborigines who (wrote W. E. Roth) would borrow whole poems *verbatim* "in a language absolutely remote from [their] own, & not one word of which the audience or performers can understand the meaning of ": an extreme case of out-of-context reading but (where the culture's alive to its own needs) completely legitimate. Even so I've provided a section of "commentaries," which try in each instance to fill in the scene or to indicate a little of what the original poets would have expected their hearers to know—in other words, to sketch some of the elements for an in-context reading. These "commentaries," which the reader can approach from any direction he or she chooses, also show what the poems mean to me or to other poets in this century who have approached them out-of-context. In that sense they can be read (particularly those for the first three sections) as a running series of essays dealing with the questions about primitive poetry lightly touched-on in this introduction, or even as an approach to poetry in general. Where it seemed worthwhile I've also printed contemporary American & European poems as analogues to the "primitive" work, sometimes without further comment. As with modern & primitive art, these either show the direct influence of the other poetry or, much more frequently, a coincidence of forms arising from an analogous impulse.

I've tried to make the book usable for anyone who wants it. Likely there are places where I've explained too much (here the reader whose special knowledge exceeds my own will simply have to forgive me), & I've sometimes included materials more from the point of descriptive interest (i.e., for the story) than of "scientific" accuracy. For the reader who wants to follow up on what's given here, I've been as straightforward as possible about the sources, providing a running bibliography & cross-referencing where I could. Translations range from the very literal to the very free (there's no one method that insures a decent result in English), & the commentaries often point out how far (or not) the translator has gone. But the limits of any translation, in terms of the "information" it carries, are also obvious. Such "information" concerns the language itself as a medium, & the language of the translator can hardly be a guide, since it should (where he's giving a poem for a poem) also be working from its own imperatives. Enough to say that the original poetries presented here range from those that lean heavily on an archaic or specialized vocabulary & syntax to those that turn the common language toward the purposes of song—& that the same is true of the verse, which includes everything from the very open to the very closed.

Finally, an appendix to the book presents a series of statements about poetics from a number of poets & song-men, & other such statements are scattered throughout the commentaries. I've hoped by doing this to get across the sense of these poets as individualized & functioning human beings. To this end also I've tried where possible to name the original poets—either those who delivered the poems or the ancient figures to whom the poems were attributed.

Beyond that, it's up to the individual reader who may, like his "primitive" counterpart, enjoy finishing the work on-his-own, i.e., by filling in what's missing.

THANKS & ACKNOWLEDGMENTS, ETC.

The problem is to remember all who were helpful, & even so there's not enough space to state the ways they were. Here are the names, anyway, with thanks & in the hope they'll understand: Jerry Bloedow, David Antin, Jackson Mac Low, Rochelle Owens, Harry Smith, James Laughlin, Sara Blackburn, Anne Freedgood, Dick Higgins, Emmett Williams, Gary Snyder, Jonathan Greene, David Wang, Stanley Diamond, Flicker Hammond, Michael McClure, Marcia Goodman, Martha Rossler, David P. McAllester, & various friends at the Coldspring Longhouse (Steamburg, N.Y.) who showed me what the sacred was.

Behind the book also are a woman & a child, & I'm reminded again how central the-woman & the-child are to the "oldest" cultures that we know. The dedication of this book is therefore rightly theirs—in whose presence I've sometimes touched that oldest & darkest love.

Jerome Rothenberg

New York City
March 15, 1967

Once having gotten here the question was WHERE NOW? I've been lucky since then to have been able to work with some of the materials at closer range, moving toward a collaboration with song-men & others who could open the languages to me—& the closer one gets the more pressing becomes the problem of how to understand & to translate the *sound* of the originals. It now seems possible to do it, to get at those "meanings" which are more than the meaning-of-the-words; possible & desirable too, for the greatest secret these poems still hold is in the actual relation between the words, the music, the dance, & the event, a relation which many among us have been trying to get at in our own work. Every new translation is the uncovering of a hidden form in the language of the translator, but at the same time the rediscovery of universal patterns that can be realized by anyone still willing to explore them. In some future edition I hope to include the results of experimental work (by myself & others) in the *total translation* of these poetries. Because we have so much already, it is at last possible to have it all. *This post-script is an incitement to those who would join in the enterprise; it is in no sense a final word.*

J. R.

Allegany Reservation (Seneca)
Steamburg, N.Y.
September 1, 1968

THE TEXTS

Come, ascend the ladder: all come in: all sit down.
We were poor, poor, poor, poor, poor,
When we came to this world through the poor place,
Where the body of water dried for our passing.
Banked up clouds cover the earth.
All come four times with your showers:
Descend to the base of the ladder & stand still:
Bring your showers & great rains.
All, all come, all ascend, all come in, all sit down.

(Zuni Indian)

ORIGINS & NAMINGS

GENESIS I

Water went they say. Land was not they say. Water only then, mountains were not, they say. Stones were not they say. Fish were not they say. Deer were not they say. Grizzlies were not they say. Panthers were not they say. Wolves were not they say. People were washed away they say. Grizzlies were washed away they say. Panthers were washed away they say. Deer were washed away they say. Coyotes were not then they say. Ravens were not they say. Herons were not they say. Woodpeckers were not they say. Then wrens were not they say. Then hummingbirds were not they say. Then otters were not they say. Then jack-rabbits, grey squirrels were not they say. Then long-eared mice were not they say. Then wind was not they say. Then snow was not they say. Then rain was not they say. Then it didn't thunder they say. Then trees were not when it didn't thunder they say. It didn't lighten they say. Then clouds were not they say. Fog was not they say. It didn't appear they say. Stars were not they say. It was very dark.

(Kato Indian)

SOUNDS

1

Dad a da da
Dad a da da
Dad a da da
Da kata kai

Ded o ded o
Ded o ded o
Ded o ded o
Da kata kai

(Australia)

2

heya heya heya·a yo·ho· yo·ho· yaha hahe·ya·an
ha·yahe· ha·wena
·ho· yo·ho· yaha hahe·ya·an
ha·yahe· ha·wena
he·yo· wena hahe·yahan
ha·yahe· ha·wena
he·yo· wena hahe·yahan
he he he he·yo
he·yo· wena hahe·yahan
he he he he·yo
he·yo·   howo·   heyo
wana heya heya

(Navajo)

3

Ah pe-an t-as ke t-an te loo
O ne vas ke than sa-na was-ke
   lon ah ve shan too
Te wan-se ar ke ta-ne voo te
   lan se o-ne voo
Te on-e-wan tase va ne woo te wan-se o-ne van
Me-le wan se oo ar ke-le van te
   shom-ber on vas sa la too lar var sa
   re voo an don der on v-tar loo-cum an la voo
O be me-sum ton ton ton tol a wac—er tol-a wac-er
   ton ton te s-er pane love ten poo

By "Jack." Holy Ground. Oct. 6th 1847.

(American Shaker)

GENESIS II

[Song 159]
  Go, take that hot stone, and heat it near her clitoris:
  For the severed part is a sacred *djuda rangga*. Covering up the clitoris
    within the mat, within its transverse fibre, within its mouth, its
    inner peak . . .
  Go, the people are dancing there, like *djuda* roots, like spray, moving
    their bodies, shaking their hair!
  Carefully they beat their clapping sticks on the *mauwulan* point . . .
  Go, stand up! See the clansfolk beyond the transverse fibre of the mat!
  They come from the Sister's womb, lifting aside the clitoris, coming
    out like *djuda* roots . . .

Into the sacred shade, the *rangga* folk come dancing from the inner
    peak of the mat . . .
Only a few people will be left here: some we shall put into the coarse
    grass.
We are putting the *rangga* clansfolk . . .

[Song 160]
    Go, put out the *rangga*, making it big: open your legs, for you look
        nice!
    Yes, take Miralaidj, my Sister. Yes, the mouth of the mat is closed.
    Yes, go, rest there quietly, for the vagina is sacred, and the *rangga* are
        hidden there, like younger siblings, covered up so no one may see.
    Thus, climb up, put it into the mouth of the mat!
    What is this, blocking my penis? I rest above here, chest on her breasts!
    Do not push hard! The sound of her cry echoes.
    Covered up, so no one may see, like a younger sibling . . .
    Do not move what is within, for it is sacred!
    For it rests there within, like the transverse fibre of the mat.
    Blood running, sacredly running!
    Yes, they, the *rangga* clansfolk, are coming out like *djuda* roots, like
        spray . . .
    Go, digging within, causing the blood to flow, sacred blood from the
        red vagina, that no one may see!
    Very sacred stands the *rangga* penis!

(Arnhem Land, Australia)

EGYPTIAN GOD NAMES

I

"It is Re who created his names out of his members"

—Chapter 17, *Book of the Dead*

2

These gods are like this in their caverns, which are in the Netherworld. Their bodies are in darkness.

The Upreared One.
Cat.
Terrible One.
Fat Face.
Turned Face.
The One belonging to the Cobra.

3

They are like this in their coffins. They are the rays of the Disk, their souls go in the following of the Great God.

The One of the Netherworld.
The Mysterious One.
The One of the Cavern.
The One of the Coffin.
She who combs.
The One of the Water.
The Weaver.

4

These gods are like this: they receive the rays of the Disk when it lights up the bodies of those of the Netherworld. When he passes by, they enter into darkness.

The Adorer.
Receiving Arm.
Arm of Light.
Brilliant One.
The One of the Rays.
Arm of Dawn.

5

Salutations to Osiris.

Osiris, the Gold of Millions.
Osiris, the Great Saw.
Osiris the Begetter.
Osiris the Scepter.
Osiris the King.
Osiris on the Sand.
Osiris in all the Lands.
Osiris at the head of the Booth of the distant Marshlands.
Osiris in his places which are in the South.
Osiris at the head of his town.

6

The Cat.

Head of Horus.
Face of Horus.
Neck of Horus.
Throat of Horus.
Iii.
The Gory One.

7

The Swallower of Millions.

GENESIS III

1

From the conception the increase.
From the increase the swelling.
From the swelling the thought.
From the thought the remembrance.
From the remembrance the desire.

2

The word became fruitful:
It dwelt with the feeble glimmering:
It brought forth night:
The great night, the long night,
The lowest night, the highest night,
The thick night to be felt,
The night to be touched, the night unseen.
The night following on,
The night ending in death.

3

From the nothing the begetting:
From the nothing the increase:
From the nothing the abundance:
The power of increasing, the living breath
It dwelt with the empty space,
It produced the firmament which is above us.

4

The atmosphere which floats above the earth.
The great firmament above us, the spread-out space dwelt with the
early dawn.

Then the moon sprang forth.
The atmosphere above dwelt with the glowing sky.
Then the sun sprang forth.
They were thrown up above as the chief eyes of heaven.
Then the sky became light.
The early dawn, the early day.
The midday. The blaze of day from the sky.

(Maori, New Zealand)

IMAGES

An Eskimo Poem for the Sun
The sun up there, up there.

A Dama Poem for the Ha-Tree
O the ha-tree, O the hard tree!

A Bushman Poem for the Jackal
Canter for me, little jackal, O little jackal, little jackal.

An Eskimo Poem Against Death
I watched the white dogs of the dawn.

A Chippewa Song of the Deer
My shining horns.

A Bushman Poem for the Blue Crane
A splinter of stone which is white.

A Seneca Poem for the Crows
The crows came in.
(Variation: The crows sat down.)

BANTU COMBINATIONS

1.

> I am still carving an ironwood stick.
> I am still thinking about it.

2.

> The lake dries up at the edges.
> The elephant is killed by a small arrow.

3.

> The little hut falls down.
> Tomorrow, debts.

4.

> The sound of a cracked elephant tusk.
> The anger of a hungry man.

5.

> Is there someone on the shore?
> The crab has caught me by one finger.

6.

> We are the fire that burns the country.
> The Calf of the Elephant is exposed on the plain.

(Africa)

CORRESPONDENCES

from *The Book of Changes*

The Creative is heaven. It is round, it is the prince, the father, jade, metal, cold, ice; it is deep red, a good horse, an old horse, a lean horse, a wild horse, tree fruit.

The Receptive is the earth, the mother. It is cloth, a kettle, frugality, it is level, it is a cow with a calf, a large wagon, form, the multitude, a shaft. Among the various kinds of soil, it is the black.

The Arousing is thunder, the dragon. It is dark yellow, it is a spreading out, a great road, the eldest son. It is decisive & vehement; it is bamboo that is green & young, it is reed & rush.

    Among horses it signifies those which can neigh well, those with white hind legs, those which gallop, those with a star on the forehead.

    Among useful plants it is the pod-bearing ones. Finally, it is the strong, that which grows luxuriantly.

The Gentle is wood, wind, the eldest daughter, the guideline, work; it is the white, the long, the high; it is advance & retreat, the undecided, odor.

    Among men it means the gray-haired; it means those with broad foreheads; it means those with much white in their eyes; it means those close to gain, so that in the market they get threefold value. Finally, it is the sign of vehemence.

The Abysmal is water, ditches, ambush, bending & straightening out, bow & wheel.

    Among men it means the melancholy, those with sick hearts, with earache.

    It is the blood sign; it is red.

    Among horses it means those with beautiful backs, those with wild courage, those which let their heads hang, those with thin hoofs, those which stumble.

Among chariots it means those with many defects.

It is penetration, the moon.

It means thieves.

Among varieties of wood it means those which are firm & have much pith.

The Clinging is fire, the sun, lightning, the middle daughter.

It means coats of mail & helmets; it means lances & weapons. Among men it means the big-bellied.

It is the sign of dryness. It means the tortoise, the crab, the snail, the mussel, the hawkbill tortoise.

Among trees it means those which dry out in the upper part of the trunk.

Keeping Still is the mountain; it is a bypath; it means little stones, doors & openings, fruits & seeds, eunuchs & watchmen, the fingers; it is the dog, the rat, & the various kinds of black-billed birds.

Among trees it signifies the firm & gnarled.

The Joyous is the lake, the youngest daughter; it is a sorceress; it is mouth & tongue. It means smashing & breaking apart; it means dropping off & bursting open. Among the kinds of soil it is the hard & salty. It is the concubine. It is the sheep.

(Chinese)

GENESIS IV

And I commanded in the very lowest parts that visible things should come from invisible, & Adoil came down very great, & I beheld, & look! it was a belly of great light.

And I said: 'Spread apart, & let the visible come out of thee.'

And it spread apart, & a great light came out. And I was in the center of the light, & as light is born from light, an age came out, a great age, & it showed me all the creation I had thought to make.

And I saw that it was good.

And I set a throne up for myself, & took my seat on it, & I said to the light: 'Go up higher & fix yourself high above the throne, & be a foundation for the highest things.'

And above the light there is nothing else, & then I leaned back & I looked up from my throne.

And I commanded the lowest a second time, & I said: 'Let Archas come forth hard,' & it came forth hard from the invisible.

And it came forth hard, heavy & very red.

And I said: 'Be opened, Archas, & let there be born from thee,' & it became open, an age came out, a very great, a very dark age, bearing the creation of all lower things, & I saw that it was good & said:

'Go down below, & make yourself firm & be a foundation for the lower things,' & it happened, & it went down & fixed itself, & became the foundation for the lower things, & below the darkness there is nothing else.

(Hebrew)

AZTEC DEFINITIONS

Ruby-Throated Hummingbird

It is ashen, ash colored. At the top of its head and the throat, its feathers are flaming, like fire. They glisten, they glow.

Amoyotl (a water-strider)

It is like a fly, small and round. It has legs, it has wings; it is dry. It goes on the surface of the water; it is a flyer. It buzzes, it sings.

Bitumen (a shellfish)

It falls out on the ocean shore; it falls out like mud.

Little Blue Heron

It resembles the brown crane in color; it is ashen, grey. It smells like fish, rotten fish, stinking fish. It smells of fish, rotten fish.

Seashell

It is white. One is large, one is small. It is spiraled, marvelous. It is that which can be blown, which resounds. I blow the seashell. I improve, I polish the seashell.

A Mushroom

It is round, large, like a severed head.

A Mountain

High, pointed; pointed on top, pointed at the summit, towering; wide, cylindrical, round; a round mountain, low, low-ridged; rocky, with many rocks; craggy with many crags; rough with rocks; of earth, with trees; grassy; with herbs; with shrubs; with water; dry; white; jagged; with a sloping plain, with gorges, with caves; precipitous, having gorges; canyon land, precipitous land with boulders.

I climb the mountain; I scale the mountain. I live on the mountain. I am born on the mountain. No one becomes a mountain—no one turns himself into a mountain. The mountain crumbles.

Another Mountain

It is wooded; it spreads green.

Forest

It is a place of verdure, of fresh green; of wind—windy places, in wind, windy; a place of cold: it becomes cold; there is much frost; it is a place which freezes. It is a place from which misery comes, where it exists; a place where there is affliction—a place of affliction, of lamentation, a place of affliction, of weeping; a place where there is sadness, a place of compassion, of sighing; a place which arouses sorrow, which spreads misery.

It is a place of gorges, gorge places; a place of crags, craggy places; a place of stony soil, stony-soiled places; in hard soil, in clayey soil, in moist and fertile soil. It is a place among moist and fertile lands, a place of moist and fertile soil, in yellow soil.

It is a place with cuestas, cuesta places; a place with peaks, peaked places; a place which is grassy, with grassy places; a place of forests, forested places; a place of thin forest, thinly forested places; a place of thick forest, thickly forested places; a place of jungle, of dry tree stumps, of underbrush, of dense forest.

It is a place of stony soil, stony-soiled places; a place of round stones, round-stoned places; a place of sharp stones, of rough stones; a place of crags, craggy places; a place of *tepetate*; a place with clearings, cleared places; a place of valleys, of coves, of places with coves, of cove places; a place of boulders, bouldered places; a place of hollows.

It is a disturbing place, fearful, frightful; home of the savage beast, dwelling-place of the serpent, the rabbit, the deer; a place from which nothing departs, nothing leaves, nothing emerges. It is a place of dry rocks, of boulders; bouldered places; boulder land, a land of bouldered places. It is a place of caves, cave places, having caves—a place having caves.

It is a place of wild beasts; a place of wild beasts—of the ocelot, the *cuitlachtli*, the bobcat, the serpent, the spider, the rabbit, the deer; of stalks, grass, prickly shrubs: of the mesquite, of the pine. It is a place where wood is owned. Trees are felled. It is a place where trees are cut, where wood is gathered, where there is chopping, where there is logging: a place of beams.

It becomes verdant, a fresh green. It becomes cold, icy. Ice forms and spreads; ice lies forming a surface. There is wind, a crashing wind; the wind crashes, spreads whistling, forms whirlwinds. Ice is blown by the wind; the wind glides.

There is no one; there are no people. It is desolate; it lies desolate. There is nothing edible. Misery abounds, misery emerges, misery spreads. There is no joy, no pleasure. It lies sprouting; herbs lie sprouting; nothing lies emerging; the earth is pressed down. All die of thirst. The grasses lie sprouting. Nothing lies cast about. There is hunger; all hunger. It is the home of hunger; there is death from hunger. All die of cold; there is freezing; there is trembling; there is the clattering, the chattering of teeth. There are cramps, the stiffening of the body, the constant stiffening, the stretching out prone.

There is fright, there is constant fright. One is devoured; one is slain by stealth; one is abused; one is brutally put to death; one is tormented. Misery abounds. There is calm, constant calm, continuing calm.

Mirror Stone

Its name comes from nowhere. This can be excavated in mines; it can be broken off. Of these mirror stones, one is white, one black. The white one—this is a good one to look into: the mirror, the clear, transparent one. They named it mirror of the noblemen, the mirror of the ruler.

The black one—this one is not good. It is not to look into; it does not make one appear good. It is one (so they say) which contends with one's face. When someone uses such a mirror, from it is to be seen a distorted mouth, swollen eyelids, thick lips, a large mouth. They say it is an ugly mirror, a mirror which contends with one's face.

Of these mirrors, one is round; one is long: they call it *acaltezcatl*. These mirror stones can be excavated in mines, can be polished, can be worked.

I make a mirror. I work it. I shatter it. I form it. I grind it. I polish it with sand. I work it with fine abrasive sand. I apply to it a glue of bat shit. I prepare it. I polish it with a fine cane. I make it shiny. I regard myself in the mirror. I appear from there in my looking-mirror; from it I admire myself.

Secret Road

Its name is secret road, the one which few people know, which not all people are aware of, which few people go along. It is good, fine; a good place, a fine place. It is where one is harmed, a place of harm. It is known as a safe place; it is a difficult place, a dangerous place. One is frightened. It is a place of fear.

There are trees, crags, gorges, rivers, precipitous places, places of precipitous land, various places of precipitous land, various precipitous places, gorges, various gorges. It is a place of wild animals, a place of wild beasts, full of wild beasts. It is a place where one is put to death by stealth; a place where one is put to death in the jaws of the wild beasts of the land of the dead.

I take the secret road. I follow along, I encounter the secret road. He goes following along, he goes joining that which is bad, the corner, the darkness, the secret road. He goes to seek, to find, that which is bad.

The Cave

It becomes long, deep; it widens, extends, narrows. It is a constricted place, a narrowed place, one of the hollowed-out places. It forms hollowed-out places. There are roughened places; there are asperous places. It is frightening, a fearful place, a place of death. It is called a place of death because there is dying. It is a place of darkness; it darkens; it stands ever dark. It stands wide-mouthed, it is wide-mouthed. It is wide-mouthed; it is narrow-mouthed. It has mouths which pass through.

I place myself in the cave. I enter the cave.

The Precipice

It is deep—a difficult, a dangerous place, a deathly place. It is dark, it is light. It is an abyss.

GENESIS V

1

In the beginning the word gave origin to the father.

2

A phantasm, nothing else existed in the beginning: the Father touched an illusion, he grasped something mysterious. Nothing existed. Through the agency of a dream our Father Nai-mu-ena kept the mirage to his body, and he pondered long and thought deeply.

Nothing existed, not even a stick to support the vision: our Father attached the illusion to the thread of a dream and kept it by the aid of his breath. He sounded to reach the bottom of the appearance, but there was nothing. Nothing existed.

Then the Father again investigated the bottom of the mystery. He tied the empty illusion to the dream thread and pressed the magical substance upon it. Then by the aid of his dream he held it like a wisp of raw cotton.

Then he seized the mirage bottom and stamped upon it repeatedly, sitting down at last on his dreamed earth.

The earth-phantasm was his now, and he spat out saliva repeatedly so that the forests might grow. Then he lay down on his earth and covered it with the roof of heaven. As he was the owner of the earth he placed above it the blue and the white sky.

Thereupon Rafu-ema, the-man-who-has-the-narratives, sitting at the base of the sky, pondered, and he created this story so that we might listen to it here upon earth.

(Uitoto Indian, Colombia)

THE PICTURES

I.

(Passamaquoddy Indian)

2.

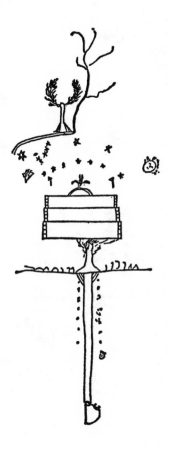

—Red Corn (Osage)

3.

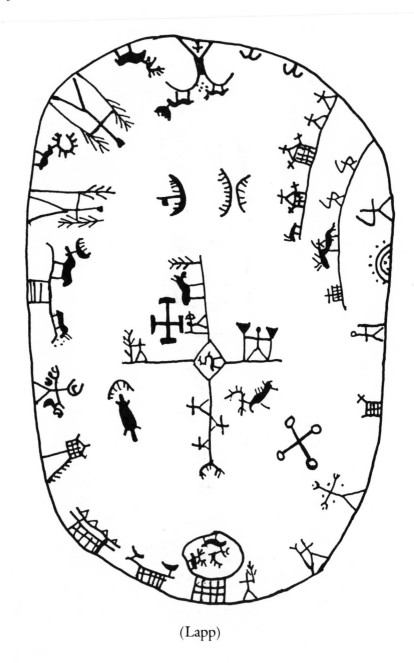

(Lapp)

4. *The Supplication*

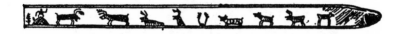

(Alaskan)

5.

(Minoan)

6.

(Easter Island)

THE GIRL OF THE EARLY RACE
WHO MADE THE STARS
(by ‖kábbo)

My mother was the one who told me that the girl arose; she put her hands into the wood ashes; she threw up the wood ashes into the sky. She said to the wood ashes: "The wood ashes which are here, they must altogether become the Milky Way. They must white lie along in the sky, that the Stars may stand outside of the Milky Way, while the Milky Way is the Milky Way, while it used to be wood ashes." They the ashes altogether become the Milky Way. The Milky Way must go round with the stars; while the Milky Way feels that, the Milky Way lies going around; while the stars sail along; therefore, the Milky Way, lying, goes along with the Stars. The Milky Way, when the Milky Way stands upon the earth, the Milky Way turns across in front, while the Milky Way means to wait, while the Milky Way feels that the Stars are turning back; while the Stars feel that the Sun is the one who has turned back; he is upon his path; the Stars turn back; while they go to fetch the daybreak; that they may lie nicely, while the Milky Way lies nicely. The Stars shall also stand nicely around. They shall sail along upon their footprints, which they, always sailing along, are following. While they feel that, they are the Stars which descend.

The Milky Way lying comes to its place, to which the girl threw up the wood ashes, that it may descend nicely; it had lying gone along, while it felt that it lay upon the sky. It had lying gone round, while it felt that the Stars also turned round. They turning round passed over the sky. The sky lies still; the Stars are those which go along; while they feel that they sail. They had been setting; they had, again, been coming out; they had, sailing along, been following their footprints. They become white, when the Sun comes out. The Sun sets, they stand around above; while they feel that they did turning follow the Sun.

The darkness comes out; they the Stars wax red, while they had at first been white. They feel that they stand brightly around; that they may sail along; while they feel that it is night. Then, the people go by night; while they feel that the ground is made light. While they feel that the Stars shine a little. Darkness is upon the ground. The Milky Way gently glows; while it feels that it is wood ashes. Therefore, it gently glows. While it feels that the girl was the one who said that the Milky Way should give a little light for the people, that they might return home by night, in the middle of the night. For, the earth would not have been a little light, had not the Milky Way been there. It and the Stars.

(Bushman, Africa)

THE FRAGMENTS

1

. . . .
command . . . .
. . . .
. . . . of the boat of the evening . . .
. . . .
. . . .
Thy face is like . . . .
. . . .
. . . .
. . . .
. . . .

2

To say: . . . . for me three meals
one in heaven, two on earth.
A lion-helmet . . . . green . . . .

3

. . . . .four . . . .
. . . . .a point . . . .
. . . . .darkness . . . .
. . . . .be not . . . .
come . . . .

4

In my wearied . . . . . ., me . . . . .
In my inflamed nostril, me . . . .
Punishment, sickness, trouble . . . me
A flail which wickedly affics, ... me

A lacerating rod .... me

A ..... hand ..... me
A terrifying message ..... me
A stinging whip .... me

. . . .
. . . . in pain I *faint* (?)

. . . .

ALL LIVES, ALL DANCES,
& ALL IS LOUD

The fish does . . . HIP
The bird does . . . VISS
The marmot does . . . GNAN

I throw myself to the left,
I turn myself to the right,
I act the fish,
Which darts in the water, which darts
Which twists about, which leaps—
All lives, all dances, and all is loud.

The fish does . . . HIP
The bird does . . . VISS
The marmot does . . . GNAN

The bird flies away,
It flies, flies, flies,
Goes, returns, passes,
Climbs, soars and drops.
I act the bird—
All lives, all dances, and all is loud.

The fish does . . . HIP
The bird does . . . VISS
The marmot does . . . GNAN

The monkey from branch to branch,
Runs, bounds and leaps,
With his wife, with his brat,
His mouth full, his tail in the air,
There goes the monkey! There goes the Monkey!
All lives, all dances, and all is loud.

(Gabon Pygmy, Africa)

YORUBA PRAISES

1

Shango is the death who kills money with a big stick
The man who lies will die in his home
Shango strikes the one who is stupid
He wrinkles his nose and the liar runs off
Even when he does not fight, we fear him
But when war shines in his eye
His enemies and worshippers run all the same
Fire in the eye, fire in the mouth, fire on the roof
The leopard who killed the sheep and bathed in its blood
The man who died in the market and woke up in the house

2

Shango is an animal like the gorilla
A rare animal in the forest
As rare as the monkey who is a medicine man
Shango, do not give me a little of your medicine
Give me all! So that I can spread it over my face and mouth
Anybody who waits for the elephant, waits for death
Anybody who waits for the buffalo, waits for death
Anybody who waits for the railway, waits for trouble
He says we must avoid the thing that will kill us
He says we must avoid trouble
He is the one who waited for the things we are running away from

(Africa)

A POEM FOR THE WIND
(by Taliesin)

Guess who it is.
Created before the Flood.
A creature strong,
without flesh, without bone,
without veins, without blood,
without head and without feet.
It will not be older, it will not be younger,
than it was in the beginning.
There will not come from his design
fear or death.
He has no wants
from creatures.
Great God! the sea whitens
when it comes from the beginning.
Great his beauties,
the one that made him.
He in the field, he in the wood,
without hand and without foot.
Without old age, without age.
Without the most jealous destiny
and he is coeval
with the five periods of the five ages.
And also is older,
though there be five hundred thousand years.
And he is as wide
as the face of the earth,
and he was not born,
and he has not been seen.
He on sea, he on land,

he sees not, he is not seen.
He is not sincere,
he will not come when it is wished.
He on land, he on sea,
he is indispensable,
he is unconfined,
he is unequal.
He from four regions,
he will not be according to counsel.
He commences his journey
from above the stone of marble.
He is loud-voiced, he is mute.
He is uncourteous.
He is vehement, he is bold,
when he glances over the land.
He is mute, he is loud-voiced.
He is blustering.
Greatest his banner
on the face of the earth.
He is good, he is bad,
he is not bright,
he is not manifest,
for the sight does not see him.
He is bad, he is good.
He is yonder, he is here,
he will disorder.
He will not repair what he does
and be sinless.
He is wet, he is dry,
he comes frequently
from the heat of the sun and the coldness of the moon.

(Welsh)

WAR GOD'S HORSE SONG I
(Words by Tall Kia ahni. Interpreted by Louis Watchman)

I am the Turquoise Woman's son.
On top of Belted Mountain
beautiful horses—slim like a weasel!
My horse with a hoof like a striped agate,
with his fetlock like a fine eagle plume:
my horse whose legs are like quick lightning
whose body is an eagle-plumed arrow:
my horse whose tail is like a trailing black cloud.
The Little Holy Wind blows thru his hair.
My horse with a mane made of short rainbows.
My horse with ears made of round corn.
My horse with eyes made of big stars.
My horse with a head made of mixed waters.
My horse with teeth made of white shell.
The long rainbow is in his mouth for a bridle
       & with it I guide him.
When my horse neighs, different-colored horses follow.
When my horse neighs, different-colored sheep follow.
       I am wealthy because of him.

       Before me peaceful
       Behind me peaceful
       Under me peaceful
       Over me peaceful—
       Peaceful voice when he neighs.
I am everlasting & peaceful.
I stand for my horse.

             (Navajo Indian)

WAR GOD'S HORSE SONG II
(by Frank Mitchell)

With their voices they are calling me,
With their voices they are calling me!

I am the child of White Shell Woman,
    With their voices they are calling me,
I am the son of the Sun,
    With their voices they are calling me,
I am Turquoise Boy,
    With their voices they are calling me!

From the arching rainbow, turquoise on its outer edge,
    from this side of where it touches the earth,
    With their voices they are calling me,
Now the horses of the Sun-descended-boy,
    With their voices they are calling me!

The turquoise horses are my horses,
    With their voices they are calling me,
Dark stone water jars their hooves,
    With their voices they are calling me,
Arrowheads the frogs of their hooves,
    With their voices they are calling me,
Mirage-stone their striped hooves,
    With their voices they are calling me,
Dark wind their legs,
    With their voices they are calling me,
Cloud shadow their tails,
    With their voices they are calling me,
All precious fabrics their bodies,
    With their voices they are calling me,
Dark cloud their skins,

With their voices they are calling me,
Scattered rainbow their hair,
 With their voices they are calling me,
Now the Sun rises before them to shine on them,
 With their voices they are calling me!

New moons their cantles,
 With their voices they are calling me,
Sunrays their backstraps,
 With their voices they are calling me,
Rainbows their girths,
 With their voices they are calling me,
They are standing, waiting, on rainbows,
 With their voices they are calling me,
The dark-rain-four-footed-ones, their neck hair falling in a wave,
 With their voices they are calling me!

Sprouting plants their ears,
 With their voices they are calling me,
Great dark stars their eyes,
 With their voices they are calling me,
All kinds of spring waters their faces,
 With their voices they are calling me,
Great shell their lips,
 With their voices they are calling me,
White shell their teeth,
 With their voices they are calling me,
There is flash-lightning in their mouths,
 With their voices they are calling me,
Dark-music sounds from their mouths,
 With their voices they are calling me,
They call out into the dawn,
 With their voices they are calling me,
Their voices reach all the way out to me,
 With their voices they are calling me,

Dawn-pollen is in their mouths,
    With their voices they are calling me,
Flowers and plant-dew are in their mouths,
    With their voices they are calling me!

Sunray their bridles,
    With their voices they are calling me,
To my right arm, beautifully to my hand they come,
    With their voices they are calling me,
This day they become my own horses,
    With their voices they are calling me,
Ever increasing, never diminishing,
    With their voices they are calling me,
My horses of long life and happiness,
    With their voices they are calling me,
I, myself, am the boy of long life and happiness,
    With their voices they are calling me!

With their voices they are calling me,
With their voices they are calling me!

(Navajo Indian)

TO THE GOD OF FIRE AS A HORSE

Your eyes do not make mistakes.
Your eyes have the sun's seeing.
Your thought marches terribly in the night
blazing with light & the fire
breaks from your throat as you whinny in battle.

This fire was born in a pleasant forest
This fire lives in ecstasy somewhere in the night.

His march is a dagger of fire
His body is enormous
His mouth opens & closes as he champs on the world
He swings the axe-edge of his tongue
        smelting & refining the raw wood he chops down.

He gets ready to shoot & fits arrow to bowstring
He hones his light to a fine edge on the steel
He travels through night with rapid & various movements
His thighs are rich with movement.
    He is a bird that settles on a tree.

(India)

THE STARS

For we are the stars. For we sing.
For we sing with our light.
For we are birds made of fire.
For we spread our wings over the sky.
Our light is a voice.
We cut a road for the soul
for its journey through death.
For three of our number are hunters.
For these three hunt a bear.
For there never yet was a time
when these three didn't hunt.
For we face the hills with disdain.
This is the song of the stars.

(Passamaquoddy Indian)

VISIONS & SPELS

THE ANNUNCIATION
(by Marpa)

*

a man born from a flower in space a man
riding a colt foaled from a sterile mare
his reins are formed from the hair of a tortoise

    a rabbit's horn for a dagger he
    strikes down his enemies

a man without lips who is speaking who
sees without eyes a man without ears
who listens who runs without legs

the sun & the moon dance
& blow trumpets

a young child touches
the wheel-of-the-law

    which turns over

*

  : secret of the body
     : of the word
       : of the heart of the gods

the inner breath is the horse of the bodhisattvas

whipped by compassion it
rears it drives the old yak
from the path of madness

       (Tibetan)

HOW ISAAC TENS BECAME A SHAMAN

Thirty years after my birth was the time.

*

I went up into the hills to get firewood. While I was cutting up the wood into lengths, it grew dark towards the evening. Before I had finished my last stack of wood, a loud noise broke out over me, chu----------, & a large owl appeared to me. The owl took hold of me, caught my face, & tried to lift me up. I lost consciousness. As soon as I came back to my senses I realized that I had fallen into the snow. My head was coated with ice, & some blood was running out of my mouth.

*

I stood up & went down the trail, walking very fast, with some wood packed on my back. On my way, the trees seemed to shake & to lean over me; tall trees were crawling after me, as if they had been snakes. I could see them.

*

At my father's home . . . I fell into a sort of trance. It seems that two shamans were working over me to bring me back to health. . . . When I woke up & opened my eyes, I thought that flies covered my face completely. I looked down, & instead of being on firm ground, I felt that I was drifting in a huge whirlpool. My heart was thumping fast.

*

Another time, I went to my hunting grounds on the other side of the river. . . . I caught two fishers in my traps, took their pelts, & threw the flesh & bones away. Farther along I looked for a bear's den amid the tall trees. As I glanced upwards, I saw an owl, at the top of a high cedar. I shot it, & it fell down in the bushes close to me. When I went to pick it up, it had disappeared. Not a feather was left; this seemed very strange. I walked down to the river, crossed over the ice, & returned to the village at Gitenmaks. Upon arriving at my fishing station on the point, I heard the noise of a crowd of people around the smoke-house, as if I were being chased away, pursued. I dared not look behind to find out what all this was about, but I hurried straight ahead. The voices followed in my tracks & came very close behind me. Then I wheeled around & looked back. There was no one in sight, only trees. A trance came over me once more, & I fell down, unconscious. When I came to, my head was buried in a snowbank.

*

I got up & walked on the ice up the river to the village. There I met my father who had just come out to look for me, for he had missed me. We went back together to my house. Then my heart started to beat fast, & I began to tremble, just as had happened before, when the shamans were trying to fix me up. My flesh seemed to be boiling, & I could hear su----------. My body was quivering. *While I remained in this state, I began to sing. A chant was coming out of me without my being able to do anything to stop it. Many things appeared to me presently: huge birds & other animals. . . . These were visible only to me, not to the others in my house. Such visions happen when a man is about to become a shaman; they occur of their own accord. The songs force themselves out complete without any attempt to compose them. But I learned & memorized those songs by repeating them.*

First Song

Death of the salmon,
my death

but the city
finds life in it

the salmon floats
in the canyon

ghosts in the city
below me

this robin, the
woman I fly with

Second Song

in mud to my knees,
a lake

where the shellfish
holds me, is

cutting my ankles,
in sleep

Third Song

a boat, a stranger's
boat, a canoe

& myself inside it, a
stranger inside it

it floats past trees,
past water

runs among
whirlpools

Fourth Song

& vision: beehives
were stinging my body

or the ghosts of bees,
giants

& the old woman
working me

until I grew   hurt me
in dreams, in my head

(Gitksan Indian)

A SHAMAN CLIMBS UP THE SKY

o

The Shaman mounts a scarecrow in the shape of a goose

above the white sky
beyond the white clouds
above the blue sky
beyond the blue clouds

this bird climbs the sky

oo

The Shaman offers horse meat to the chief drummer

the master of the six-knob
drum he takes a small piece
then he draws closer he
brings it to me in his hand

when I say "go" he bends
first at the knees when I
say "scat" he takes it all

whatever I give him

ooo

The Shaman fumigates nine robes

gifts no horse can carry
that no man can lift &
robes with triple necks
to look at & to touch
three times: to use this
as a horse blanket

sweet

prince ulgan

you are my prince
my treasure

you are my joy

oooo

Invocation to Markut, the bird of heaven

this bird of heaven who keeps
    five shapes & powerful
    brass claws (the moon

has copper claws the moon's
beak is made of ice) whose

    wings are powerful &
    strike the air whose tail

is power & a heavy wind

markut whose left wing
    hides the moon whose
        right wing hides the sun

        who never gets lost who flies
    past that-place nothing tires her
who comes toward this-place

in my house I listen
for her singing I wait
the game begins

falling past my right eye landing
here
on my right shoulder

markut is the mother of five eagles

○
_____

The Shaman reaches the 1st sky

my shadow on the landing
I have climbed to (have reached
this place called sky
& struggled with its summit)
I who stand here
higher than the moon

full moon my shadow

○
_____

The Shaman pierces the 2d sky

to reach the second landing
this further level

look!

the floor below us
lies in ruins

○○
_____

At the End of the Climb: Praise to Prince Ulgan

three stairways lead
to him three flocks
sustain him PRINCE ULGAN!

blue hill where no hill
was before: blue sky
everywhere: a blue cloud
turning swiftly

that no one can reach:
a blue sky that no one
can reach (to reach it
to journey a year by water

then to bow before him
three times to exalt him)
for whom the moon's edge
shines forever PRINCE ULGAN!

you have found use for the hoofs
of our horses you who give us
flocks who keep pain from us

sweet

prince ulgan

for whom the stars & the sky
are turning a thousand times
turning a thousand times over

(Altaic)

THE DOG VISION
(by Hehaka Sapa [Black Elk])

Standing in the center of the sacred place and facing the sunset, I began to cry, and while crying I had to say: "O Great Spirit, accept my offerings! O make me understand!"

As I was crying and saying this, there soared a spotted eagle from the west and whistled shrill and sat upon a pine tree east of me.

I walked backwards to the center, and from there approached the north, crying and saying: "O Great Spirit, accept my offerings and make me understand!" Then a chicken hawk came hovering and stopped upon a bush towards the south.

I walked backwards to the center once again and from there approached the east, crying and asking the Great Spirit to help me understand, and there came a black swallow flying all around me, singing, and stopped upon a bush not far away.

Walking backwards to the center, I advanced upon the south. Until now I had only been trying to weep, but now I really wept, and the tears ran down my face; for as I looked yonder towards the place whence come the life of things, the nation's hoop and the flowering tree, I thought of the days when my relatives, now dead, were living and young, and of Crazy Horse who was our strength and would never come back to help us any more.

I cried very hard, and I thought it might be better if my crying would kill me; then I could be in the outer world where nothing is ever in despair.

And while I was crying, something was coming from the south. It looked like dust far off, but when it came closer, I saw it was a cloud of beautiful butterflies of all colors. They swarmed around me so thick that I could see nothing else.

I walked backwards to the flowering stick again, and the spotted eagle on the pine tree spoke and said: "Behold these! They are your people. They are in great difficulty and you shall help them." Then I could hear all the butterflies that were swarming over me, and they were all making a pitiful, whimpering noise as though they too were weeping.

Then they all arose and flew back into the south.

Now the chicken hawk spoke from its bush and said: "Behold! Your Grandfathers shall come forth and you shall hear them!"

Hearing this, I lifted up my eyes, and there was a big storm coming from the west. It was the thunder being nation, and I could hear the neighing of horses and the sending of great voices.

It was very dark now, and all the roaring west was streaked fearfully with swift fire.

And as I stood there looking, a vision broke out of the shouting blackness torn with fire, and I saw the two men who had come to me first in my great vision. They came head first like arrows slanting earthward from a long flight; and when they neared the ground, I could see a dust rising there and out of the dust the heads of dogs were peeping. Then suddenly I saw that the dust was the swarm of many-colored butterflies hovering all around and over the dogs.

By now the two men were riding sorrel horses, streaked with black lightning, and they charged with bows and arrows down upon the dogs, while the thunder beings cheered for them with roaring voices.

Then suddenly the butterflies changed, and were storm-driven swallows, swooping and whirling in a great cloud behind the charging riders.

The first of these now plunged upon a dog's head and arose with it hanging bloody on his arrow point, while the whole west roared with cheering. The second did the same; and the black west flashed and cheered again. Then as the two arose together, I saw that the dogs' heads had changed to the heads of Wasichus; and as I saw, the vision went out and the storm was close upon me, terrible to see and roaring.

I cried harder than ever now, for I was much afraid. The night was black about me and terrible with swift fire and the sending of great voices and the roaring of the hail. And as I cried, I begged the Grandfathers to pity me and spare me and told them that I knew now what they wanted me to do on earth, and I would do it if I could.

All at once I was not afraid any more, and I thought that if I was killed, probably I might be better off in the other world. So I lay down there in the center of the sacred place and offered the pipe again. Then I drew the bison robe over me and waited. All around me growled and roared the voices, and the hail was like the drums of many giants beating while the giants sang: "Hey-a-hey!"

No hail fell there in the sacred circle where I lay, nor any rain. And when the storm was passed, I raised my robe and listened; and in the stillness I could hear the rain-flood singing in the gulches all around me in the darkness, and far away to eastward there were dying voices calling: "Hey-a-hey!"

The night was old by now, and soon I fell asleep. And as I slept I saw my people sitting sad and troubled all around a sacred tepee, and there were many who were sick. And as I looked on them and wept, a strange light leaped upward from the ground close by—a light of many colors, sparkling, with rays that touched the heavens. Then it was gone, and in the place from whence it sprang a herb was growing and I saw the leaves it had. And as I was looking at the herb so that I might not forget it, there was a voice that 'woke me, and it said: "Make haste! Your people need you!"

I looked and saw the east was just beginning to turn white. Standing up, I faced the young light and began to mourn again and pray. Then the daybreak star came slowly, very beautiful and still; and all around it there were clouds of baby faces smiling at me, the faces of the people not yet born. The stars about them now were beautiful with many colors, and beneath these there were heads of men and women moving around, and birds were singing somewhere yonder and there were horses nickering and blowing as they do when they are happy, and somewhere deer were whistling and there were bison mooing too. What I could not see of this, I heard.

(Sioux Indian [Lakota])

From *THE MIDNIGHT VELADA*
(by María Sabina)

I am the woman of the great expanse of the water
I am the woman of the expanse of the divine sea
I am a river woman
the woman of the flowing water
a woman who examines and searches
a woman with hands and measure
a woman mistress of measure

o

I am a saint woman
a spirit woman
I am a woman of clarity
a woman of the day
a clean woman
a ready woman
because I am a woman who lightnings
a woman who thunders
a woman who shouts
a woman who whistles

o

Morning Star woman
Southern Cross woman
Constellation of the Sandal woman, says
Hook Constellation woman, says
that is your clock, says
that is your book, says
I am the little woman of the ancient fountain, says
I am the little woman of the sacred fountain, says

o

humming bird woman, says
woman who has sprouted wings, says

o

thus do I descend primordial
thus do I descend significant
I descend with tenderness
I descend with the dew
your book, my Father, says
your book, my Father, says
clown woman beneath the water, says
clown woman beneath the sea, says
because I am the child of Christ
the child of Mary, says

o

I am a woman of letters, says
I am a book woman, says
nobody can close my book, says
nobody can take my book away from me, says
my book encountered beneath the water, says
my book of prayers

o

I am a woman and a mother, says
a mother woman beneath the water, says
a woman of good words, says
a woman of music, says
a wise diviner woman

o

I am a lagoon woman, says
I am a ladder woman, says

I am the Morning Star woman, says
I am a woman comet, says
I am the woman who goes through the water, says
I am the woman who goes through the sea, says

(Mazatec Indian)

THE DREAM OF ENKIDU

Enkidu slept alone in his sickness and he poured out his heart to
Gilgamesh, "Last night I dreamed again, my friend. The heavens
moaned and the earth replied; I stood alone before an awful
being; his face was sombre like the black bird of the storm. He fell
upon me with the talons of an eagle and he held me fast, pinioned
with his claw, till I smothered; then he transformed me so that my
arms became wings covered with feathers. He turned his stare
towards me, and he led me away to the palace of Irkalla, the
Queen of Darkness, to the house from which none who enters
ever returns, down the road from which there is no coming back.
"There is the house whose people sit in darkness; dust is their food and
clay their meat. They are clothed like birds with wings for
covering, they see no light, they sit in darkness. I entered the
house of dust and I saw the kings of the earth, their crowns put
away forever; rulers and princes, all those who once wore kingly
crowns and ruled the world in the days of old. They who had
stood in the place of the gods, like Anu and Enlil, stood now like
servants to fetch baked meats in the house of dust, to carry cooked
meat and cold water from the waterskin.
"In the house of dust which I entered were high-priests and acolytes,
priests of the incantation and of ecstasy; there were servers of the
temple, and there was Etana, that king of Kish whom the eagle
carried to heaven in the days of old. I saw also Samuqan, god of
cattle, and there was Ereshkigal the Queen of the Underworld;
and Belit-Sheri squatted in front of her, she who is recorder of the
gods and keeps the book of death. She held a tablet from which
she read. She raised her head, she saw me and spoke: 'Who has
brought this one here?'
"Then I awoke like a man drained of blood who wanders alone in a
waste of rushes; like one whom the bailiff has seized and his heart

pounds with terror. O my brother, let some great prince, some other, come when I am dead, or let some god stand at your gate, let him obliterate my name and write his own instead."

Enkidu had peeled off his clothes and flung himself down, and Gilgamesh listened to his words and wept quick tears, Gilgamesh listened and his tears flowed. He opened his mouth and spoke to Enkidu: "Who is there in strong-walled Uruk who has wisdom like this? *Strange things have been spoken, why does your heart speak strangely? The dream was marvelous but the terror was great; we must treasure the dream whatever the terror; for the dream has shown that misery comes at last to the healthy man, the end of life is sorrow.*"

And Gilgamesh lamented, "Now I will pray to the great gods, for my friend had an ominous dream."

(Mesopotamia)

A LIST OF BAD DREAMS CHANTED AS A CAUSE & CURE FOR MISSING SOULS

To dream that one's hair is falling out.
To dream that all one's teeth are falling out.
To dream that one is being saved.
To dream that one is being nursed.
To dream that one is very dirty.
To dream that one is dissolving.
To dream that one is in mourning, as shown by the hair.
To dream that one is being beaten, beaten on the neck,
up to the ears, and all about the face.

To dream that she is saying the *ngiriyn* prayer.
To dream that she is saying the *ngirogin* prayer.
To dream that she is committing adultery.
To dream that she is being saved.
To dream that she is in the red-hat festival.
To dream that she is putting a red cloth over her shoulders.
To dream that she is wearing, as well as the red cloth,
a red hat upon her head.
To dream that she is sitting on the swinging plank.
To dream that she is nursing the young soul.
To dream that she is lying among pieces of *ranehary* wood.
To dream that she is quarreling.
To dream that she is hitting someone.
To dream that she is involved in a court case.
To dream that she is paying *kati banda* fines.
To dream that she is answering a man's proposal of marriage.
To dream that she is replying and going in among
things that had been ordered which have just arrived.

To dream that she is separated from her husband.
To dream that she is finished with her husband.
To dream that she is dividing her property.
To dream that she is packing her good belongings.
To dream that she is going away.
To dream that she is resting in the bachelors' quarters,
resting at the top of the bachelors' quarters.
To dream that she is looking at the stars.
To dream that she is looking at the moon—
looking at the first day of the new moon,
looking at the first day of the dying moon,
looking at the smoky stars,
looking at the moon being swallowed by clouds.

To dream of looking at a beehive.
To dream of being swallowed by flames of fire.
To dream of resting in the old jungle.
To dream of resting on the cemetery grounds.
To dream of being hit by *tewai* bamboo.
To dream of resting at the foot of the *parai* palm.
To dream of resting at the pool of paleness.
To dream of resting at the house of the grandmother of Bubot.
To dream of resting at the house of the grandmother of Tauh.
To dream of resting at the house of Kitapung Bannau.
To dream of resting at the large stretch of low-lying land.
To dream of resting at the grove of *bemban* palms.
To dream of resting at the noisy mountain.
To dream of resting among falling boulders.
To dream of resting among rolling logs.

To dream of resting among rolling stones.
To dream of resting while in a deep hole.
To dream of resting on the slope of a mountain.
To dream of resting in an old jungle.
To dream of resting in a very deep old jungle.

To dream of resting with a coil of young vines.
Resting while sick and suffocating.
To dream of resting in someone's blacksmith shed.
To dream of resting among beating drums,
the demon's drum which is flat.
To dream of resting in the dried leaves.
To dream of resting inside the small porcupine hole.
To dream of resting along the wild boar track.
To dream of resting in the deer's pool.
Of resting on top of an anthill,
resting on top of a hill of white ants.
To dream of resting on a rotten log.
To dream of being chased by a snake.
To dream of being bayed at by a wolf.
To dream of being barked at by the dogs of demons.
To dream of resting inside a hunting shed.
To dream of sleeping at the foot of a betel-nut tree.

(Bidayuh, Sarawak)

THE KILLER

(after A'yw'ini)

Careful: my knife drills your soul
           listen, whatever-your-name-is
           One of the wolf people
listen   I'll grind your saliva into the earth
listen   I'll cover your bones with black flint
listen   ''   ''   ''   ''   ''   '' feathers
listen   ''   ''   ''   ''   ''   '' rocks
Because you're going where it's empty
           Black coffin out on the hill
listen   the black earth will hide you, will
           find you a black hut
           Out where it's dark, in that country
listen   I'm bringing a box for your bones
           A black box
           A grave with black pebbles
listen   your soul's spilling out
listen   it's blue

(Cherokee Indian)

SPELL AGAINST JAUNDICE

Yellow cock
Beat your yellow wings three times
Over a yellow hen
A yellow hen in a yellow year
In a yellow month
In a yellow week
On a yellow day
Laid a yellow egg
In yellow hay
Let the yellow hay stay
And the yellow fever leave our Milan.

Yellow bitch
Whelp your yellow pup
On a yellow day
In a yellow week
In a yellow month
In a yellow year
In a yellow wood
Let the yellow wood stay
And the yellow fever leave our Milan.

Yellow cow calve a yellow calf
On a yellow day
In a yellow week
In a yellow month
In a yellow year
In a yellow field
Let the yellow field stay
And the yellow fever leave our Milan.
Hoooh !

Yellow candle
Of yellow wax
Burn in a yellow room
Burn out
Be as if you had never been
Together with our Milan's yellow fever.

Stop—no further!
This is not your place!
Go into the deep sea
Into the high hills . . .

Get up, get out, witches and winds, you've come to eat up Milan's heart and head, but Dora is a wise-woman and is with him, and sends you out into the forest to count the leaves, to the sea to measure the sand, into the world to count all the paths, and when you come back you won't be able to do anything to him. Dora the wise-woman has blown you away with her breath, swept you away with her hand, scattered you with herbs. Look—life and health are upon our Milan.

(Serbian)

A POISON ARROW

Enough poison to make
your head spin, & chains
to pin you down, & once
they've shot the arrow
& once it lands, well
it's just like the fly & the horse:
I mean a fly that's bitten one horse
will damn sure go after another
& I mean too that this arrow's
like a pregnant woman
   hungry for some meat
& even if it doesn't break your skin
   you die
& if it gets in & does its stuff
   you die
& if it sort of touches you & drops right out
   you die
   & as long as you stay out of my blood
   what do I care whose blood you get in
   kill him
   I won't stand in the way

This is a fire that I'm setting off
& this is a fire that I'm lifting up
& this is a shadow that's burning
& this is the sun that's burning
Because the poison I've got is stronger than bullets
   & it's louder than thunder
   & it's hotter than fire
& what do I care who it gets, kill him!
      I won't stand in the way
As long as you stay out of my blood

(Hausa, Africa)

A BREASTPLATE AGAINST DEATH

I invoke the seven Daughters of the Sea,
who fashion the threads of long life.
> May three deaths be taken from me!
> May three lives be given to me!
> May seven waves of plenty be poured for me!
Phantoms shall not harm me on my journey
in my radiant breastplate without stain.
> My fame shall not perish.
May old age come to me! Death shall not find me till I am old.

I invoke my Silver Champion who has not died, who will not die!
May a period be granted to me equal in worth to white bronze.
> May my double be destroyed!
> May my right be maintained!
> May my strength be increased!
Let my gravestone not be raised,
May death not meet me on my way,
May my journey be secured!
The headless adder shall not seize me,
nor the hard-grey worm,
nor the headless black chafer.
May no thief attack me,
nor a band of women nor a faerie band.
Let me have increase of time from the King of the Universe!

I invoke Senach of the seven lives,
whom faerie women have suckled on the breasts of plenty.
> May my seven candles not be extinguished!
> > I am an indestructible fortress,
> > I am an unshakable cliff,

I am a precious stone,
I am the symbol of seven riches.
May I live a hundred times a hundred years, each hundred of
    them apart!
I summon to me their good gifts.

                                        (Irish)

OL' HANNAH

(performance version by Doc Reese)

Why don't you
        go down Old Hannah
                well well well
                don't you rise no more
                don't you rise no more
Why don't
      you
          go down Old
                Hannaaaaaah
Don't you
      rise no-o more
If you
      rise in the morning
              well well well
              bring judgment sure
              bring judgment sure
If you
      rise
        in the
           morniiiiiing
Bring judg-
      me-ent sure
Well I
      looked at Old Hannah
              well well well
              and she was turning red
              she was turning red

Well I
     looked at
         my
            partneeeeeer
And he was
       al-
         mo-ost dead
Well you
      oughta been on this old river
                 well well well
                 19 and 4
                 19 and 4
You oughta
      been on
         this old
            riveeeeeer
19
  a-and 4
You could
      find a dead man
           well well well
           right a cross your row
           right a cross your row
You could
      find
        a-a
         dead maaaaaan
Right a-
      cross your row

Why don't you
          get up old dead man
                    well well well
                    help me carry my row
                    help me carry my row
Why don't you
          get up
              old
                  dead maaaaaan
Help me
        carry my-y-y row
Well you
        oughta been on this old river
                    well well well
                    19 and 5
                    19 and 5
You oughta
        been on
              this old
                  riveeeeeer
19
   a-and 5
You couldn't hardly find a
              a man alive
              a man alive
You couldn't hardly
          find
            aaaaaa
A man
     alive

You oughta been on this old river

            well well well

            in 1910

            19 and 10

You oughta been on

        this old

           riveeeeeer

19

  a-and 10

When they were working all the women

              well well well

              right along with the men

              right along with the men

When they was working

        all the

           womeeeeeen

Right a-

    long

      with the men

Well I been on this old river

            well well well

            so jumping long

            so jumping long

I don't know

      which side of the

          brazaaaaaas

My ma-

    ma's on

        Run and call the major

        O run and call major

        Well run and call the major

. . .

Well tell him I'm worried
O my lord god
Well tell him I'm worried

. . .

Well look-a look-a yonder
O my lord god
Well look-a look-a yonder

. . .

I b'lieve I'll find the major
O my lord god
I b'lieve I'll find the major

. . .

Well you talk about
        your troubles:
                Take a look at mine
Ohhhhhhhhh, my lord
You say you got a hundred:
                I got 99
Oh my lord
Well it don't
        make no difference:
                They both life time
Ohhhhhhhhh, my lord
I say it don't make no difference
                'cause they both life time

(Afro-American)

OFFERING FLOWERS

(The Aztecs had a feast which fell out in the ninth month
& which they called: The Flowers Are Offered)

& two days before the feast, when flowers were sought, all scattered over the mountains, that every flower might be found

& when these were gathered, when they had come to the flowers & arrived where they were, at dawn they strung them together; everyone strung them

& when the flowers had been threaded, then these were twisted & wound in garlands—long ones, very long, & thick—very thick

& when morning broke the temple guardians then ministered to Uitzilopochtli; they adorned him with garlands of flowers; they placed flowers upon his head

& before him they spread, strewed, & hung rows of all the various flowers, the most beautiful flowers, the threaded flowers

then flowers were offered to all the rest of the gods

they were adorned with flowers; they were girt with garlands of flowers

flowers were placed upon their heads, there in the temples

& when midday came, they all sang & danced

quietly, calmly, evenly they danced

they kept going as they danced

o o

o

I offer flowers. I sow flower seeds. I plant flowers. I assemble flowers. I pick flowers. I pick different flowers. I remove flowers. I seek flowers. I offer flowers. I arrange flowers. I thread a flower. I string flowers. I make flowers. I form them to be extending, uneven, rounded, round bouquets of flowers.

I make a flower necklace, a flower garland, a paper of flowers, a bouquet, a flower shield, hand flowers. I thread them. I string them. I provide them with grass. I provide them with leaves. I make a pendant of them. I smell something. I smell them. I cause one to smell something. I cause him to smell. I offer flowers to one. I offer him flowers. I provide him with flowers. I provide one with fllowers. I provide one with a flower necklace. I provide him with a flower necklace. I place a garland on one. I provide him a garland. I clothe one in flowers. I clothe him in flowers. I cover one with flowers. I cover him with flowers. I destroy one with flowers. I destroy him with flowers. I injure one with flowers. I injure him with flowers.

I destroy one with flowers; I destroy him with flowers; I injure one with flowers: with drink, with food, with flowers, with tobacco, with capes, with gold. I beguile, I incite him with flowers, with words; I beguile him, I say, "I caress him with flowers. I seduce one. I extend one a lengthy discourse. I induce him with words."

I provide one with flowers. I make flowers, or I give them to one that someone will observe a feastday. Or I merely continue to give one flowers; I continue to place them in one's hand, I continue to offer them to one's hands. Or I provide one with a necklace, or I provide one with a garland of flowers.

(Aztec)

From *THE NIGHT CHANT*
(*after Bitahatini*)

In Tsegihi
In the house made of the dawn
In the house made of evening twilight
In the house made of dark cloud
In the house made of rain & mist, of pollen, of grasshoppers
Where the dark mist curtains the doorway
The path to which is on the rainbow
Where the zigzag lightning stands high on top
Where the he-rain stands high on top

O male divinity
With your moccasins of dark cloud, come to us
With your mind enveloped in dark cloud, come to us
With the dark thunder above you, come to us soaring
With the shapen cloud at your feet, come to us soaring
With the far darkness made of the dark cloud over your head, come to
    us soaring
With the far darkness made of the rain & mist over your head, come to
    us soaring
With the zigzag lightning flung out high over your head
With the rainbow hanging high over your head, come to us soaring
With the far darkness made of the rain & the mist on the ends of your
    wings, come to us soaring
With the far darkness of the dark cloud on the ends of your wings,
    come to us soaring
With the zigzag lightning, with the rainbow high on the ends of your
    wings, come to us soaring

With the near darkness made of the dark cloud of the rain & the mist,
    come to us
With the darkness on the earth, come to us

With these I wish the foam floating on the flowing water over the
    roots of the great corn
I have made your sacrifice
I have prepared a smoke for you
My feet restore for me
My limbs restore, my body restore, my mind restore, my voice restore
    for me
Today, take out your spell for me

Today, take away your spell for me
Away from me you have taken it
Far off from me it is taken
Far off you have done it

Happily I recover
Happily I become cool

My eyes regain their power, my head cools, my limbs regain their
    strength, I hear again

Happily the spell is taken off for me
Happily I walk, impervious to pain I walk, light within I walk, joyous I
    walk

Abundant dark clouds I desire
An abundance of vegetation I desire
An abundance of pollen, abundant dew, I desire

Happily may fair white corn come with you to the ends of the earth
Happily may fair yellow corn, fair blue corn, fair corn of all kinds,
    plants of all kinds, goods of all kinds, jewels of all kinds, come
    with you to the ends of the earth

With these before you, happily may they come with you
With these behind, below, above, around you, happily may they come
    with you
Thus you accomplish your tasks

Happily the old men will regard you
Happily the old women will regard you
The young men & the young women will regard you
The children will regard you
The chiefs will regard you

Happily as they scatter in different directions they will regard you
Happily as they approach their homes they will regard you

May their roads home be on the trail of peace
Happily may they all return

In beauty I walk
With beauty before me I walk
With beauty behind me I walk
With beauty above me I walk
With beauty above & about me I walk
It is finished in beauty
It is finished in beauty

(Navajo Indian)

DEATH & DEFEAT

When Hare heard of Death, he started for his lodge & arrived there crying, shrieking, *My uncles & my aunts must not die!* And then the thought assailed him: *To all things death will come!* He cast his thoughts upon the precipices & they began to fall & crumble. Upon the rocks he cast his thoughts & they became shattered. Under the earth he cast his thoughts & all the things living there stopped moving & their limbs stiffened in death. Up above, towards the skies, he cast his thoughts & the birds flying there suddenly fell to the earth & were dead.

After he entered his lodge he took his blanket &, wrapping it around him, lay down crying. *Not the whole earth will suffice for all those who will die. Oh there will not be enough earth for them in many places!* There he lay in his corner wrapped up in his blanket, silent.

(Winnebago Indian)

A PERUVIAN DANCE SONG

Wake up, woman
Rise up, woman
In the middle of the street
A dog howls

May the death arrive
May the dance arrive

Comes the dance
You must dance
Comes the death
You can't help it!

Ah! what a chill
Ah! what a wind

(Ayacucho Indian)

DEATH SONG
by Juana Manwell (Owl Woman)

In the great night my heart will go out
Toward me the darkness comes rattling
In the great night my heart will go out

(Papago Indian)

From *THE ODYSSEY*
(by Homer)
"The Journey to the Dead"

And then went down to the ship,
Set keel to breakers, forth on the godly sea, and
We set up mast and sail on that swart ship,
Bore sheep aboard her, and our bodies also
Heavy with weeping, and winds from sternward
Bore us out onward with bellying canvas,
Circe's this craft, the trim-coifed goddess.
Then sat we amidships, wind jamming the tiller,
Thus with stretched sail, we went over sea till day's end.
Sun to his slumber, shadows o'er all the ocean,
Came we then to the bounds of deepest water,
To the Kimmerian lands, and peopled cities
Covered with close-webbed mist, unpierced ever
With glitter of sun-rays
Nor with stars stretched, nor looking back from heaven
Swartest night stretched over wretched men there.
The ocean flowing backward, came we then to the place
Aforesaid by Circe.
Here did they rites, Perimedes and Eurylochus,
And drawing sword from my hip
I dug the ell-square pitkin;
Poured we libations unto each the dead,
First mead and then sweet wine, water mixed with white flour.
Then prayed I many a prayer to the sickly death's-heads;
As set in Ithaca, sterile bulls of the best
For sacrifice, heaping the pyre with goods,
A sheep to Tiresias only, black and a bell-sheep.

Dark blood flowed in the fosse,
Souls out of Erebus, cadaverous dead, of brides
Of youths and of the old who had borne much;
Souls stained with recent tears, girls tender,
Men many, mauled with bronze lance heads,
Battle spoil, bearing yet dreory arms,
These many crowded about me; with shouting,
Pallor upon me, cried to my men for more beasts;
Slaughtered the herds, sheep slain of bronze;
Poured ointment, cried to the gods,
To Pluto the strong, and praised Proserpine;
Unsheathed the narrow sword,
I sat to keep off the impetuous impotent dead,
Till I should hear Tiresias.
But first Elpenor came, our friend Elpenor,
Unburied, cast on the wide earth,
Limbs that we left in the house of Circe,
Unwept, unwrapped in sepulchre, since toils urged other.
Pitiful spirit. And I cried in hurried speech:
"Elpenor, how art thou come to this dark coast?
"Cam'st thou afoot, outstripping seamen?"
        And he in heavy speech:
"Ill fate and abundant wine. I slept in Circe's ingle.
"Going down the long ladder unguarded,
"I fell against the buttress,
"Shattered the nape-nerve, the soul sought Avernus.
"But thou, O King, I bid remember me, unwept, unburied,
"Heap up mine arms, be tomb by sea-bord, and inscribed:
"*A man of no fortune, and with a name to come.*
"And set my oar up, that I swung mid fellows."

And Anticlea came, whom I beat off, and then Tiresias Theban,
Holding his golden wand, knew me, and spoke first:
"A second time? why? man of ill star,

"Facing the sunless dead and this joyless region?
"Stand from the fosse, leave me my bloody bever
"For soothsay."
  And I stepped back,
And he strong with the blood, said then: "Odysseus
"Shalt return through spiteful Neptune, over dark seas,
"Lose all companions." Then Anticlea came.
To whom I answered:
"Fate drives me on through these deeps; I sought Tiresias."
I told her news of Troy, and thrice her shadow
  Faded in my embrace.
Then had I news of many faded women—
Tyro, Alcmena, Chloris—
Heard out their tales by that dark fosse, and sailed
By sirens and thence outward and away,
And unto Circe buried Elpenor's corpse.

                                   (Greek)

THE MOURNING SONG OF SMALL-LAKE-UNDERNEATH
(by Hayi-a'k!ᵘ)

I always compare you to a drifting log with iron nails in it.
Let my brother float in, in that way.
Let him float ashore on a good sandy beach.
I always compare you, my mother, to the sun passing behind the
    clouds.
That is what makes the world dark.

(Tlingit Indian)

THE STORY OF THE
LEOPARD TORTOISE
(by !kwéiten ta ||ken, after ‡kamme-an)

The people had gone hunting: she was ill; and she perceived a man who came up to her hut; he had been hunting around.

She asked the man to rub her neck a little with fat for her; for, it ached. The man rubbed it with fat for her. And she altogether held the man firmly with it. The man's hands altogether decayed away in it.

Again, she espied another man, who came hunting. And she also spoke, she said: "Rub me with fat a little."

And the man whose hands had decayed away in her neck, he was hiding his hands, so that the other man should not perceive them, namely, that they had decayed away in it. And he said: "Yes, O my mate! rub our elder sister a little with fat; for, the moon has been cut, while our elder sister lies ill. Thou shalt also rub our elder sister with fat." He was hiding his hands, so that the other one should not perceive them.

The Leopard Tortoise said: "Rubbing with fat, put thy hands into my neck." And he, rubbing with fat, put in his hands upon the Leopard Tortoise's neck; and the Leopard Tortoise drew in her head upon her neck; while his hands were altogether in her neck; and he dashed the Leopard Tortoise upon the ground, on account of it; while he desired, he thought, that he should, by dashing it upon the ground, break the Leopard Tortoise. And the Leopard Tortoise held him fast.

The other one had taken out his hands from behind his back; and he exclaimed: "Feel thou that which I did also feel!" and he showed the other one his hands; and the other one's hands were altogether inside the Leopard Tortoise's neck. And he arose, he returned home. And the other one was dashing the Leopard Tortoise upon the ground; while he returning went; and he said that the other one also felt what he had

95

felt. A pleasant thing it was not, in which he had been! He yonder returning went; he arrived at home.

The people exclaimed: "Where hast thou been?" And he, answering, said that the Leopard Tortoise had been the one in whose neck his hands had been; that was why he had not returned home. The people said: "Art thou a fool? Did not thy parents instruct thee? The Leopard Tortoise always seems as if she would die; while she is deceiving us."

(Bushman, Africa)

NOTTAMUN TOWN

In fair Nottamun Town, not a soul would look up,
Not a soul would look up,—not a soul would look down,
Not a soul would look up,—not a soul would look down,
To show me the way to fair Nottamun Town.

I rode a grey horse, a mule-roany mare,
Grey mane and a grey tail, a green stripe down her back,
Grey mane and a grey tail, a green stripe down her back,
There wa'nt a hair on'er be-what was coal-black.

She stood so still, she threw me to the dirt,
She tore-a my hide and she bruis-ed my shirt.
From saddle to stirrup I mounted again,
And on my ten toes I rode over the plain.

Met the King and Queen, and a company more,
A-riding behind, and a-marching before.
Come a stark-naked drummer, a-beating a drum,
With his heels in his bosom come marching along.

They laughed and they smiled, not a soul did look gay,
They talked all the while, not a word did they say;
I bought me a quart to drive gladness away,
And to stifle the dust, for it rained the whole day.

Sat down on a hard, hot, cold-frozen stone,
Ten thousand stood round me, and yet I'uz alone;
Took my hat in my hand for to keep my head warm;
Ten thousand got drown-ded that never was born.

(Appalachia, United States)

THE FLIGHT OF QUETZALCOATL

*

Then the time came for Quetzalcoatl too, when he felt the darkness
   twist in him like a river, as though it meant to weigh him down, &
   he thought to go then, to leave the city as he had found it & to go,
   forgetting there ever was a Tula

Which was what he later did, as people tell it who still speak about the
   Fire: how he first ignited the gold & silver houses, their walls
   speckled with red shells, & the other Toltec arts, the creations of
   man's hands & the imagination of his heart

& hid the best of them in secret places, deep in the earth, in mountains
   or down gullies, buried them, took the cacao trees & changed
   them into thorned acacias

& the birds he'd brought there years before, that had the richly colored
   feathers & whose breasts were like a living fire, he sent ahead of
   him to trace the highway he would follow towards the seacoast

When that was over he started down the road

*

A whole day's journey, reached
THE JUNCTURE OF THE TREE
(so-called)

        fat prominence of bark
        sky branches

I sat beneath it
saw my face/cracked
mirror

An old man

        & named it

TREE OF OLD AGE

thus to name
it to raise stones
to wound the bark
with stones

to batter it with
stones the stones to
cut the bark to fester
in the bark

TREE OF OLD AGE

stone patterns: starting
from the roots they
reach the highest leaves

*

The next day gone with walking
Flutes were sounding in his ears

Companions' voices

He squatted on a rock to rest
he leaned his hands against the rock

Tula shining in the distance

: which he saw he
saw it & began to cry
he cried the cold sobs cut his throat

A double thread of tears, a hailstorm
beating down his face, the drops
burn through the rock
The drops of sorrow fall against the stone
& pierce its heart

& where his hands had rested

shadows lingered on the rock: as if
his hands had pressed soft clay
As if the rock were clay

The mark too of his buttocks in the rock,
embedded there forever

The hollow of his hands preserved forever

A place named TEMACPALCO

*

To Stone Bridge next

water swirling in the riverbed
a spreading turbulence of water

: where he dug a stone up
made a bridge across
        & crossed it

*

: who kept moving until he reached the Lake of Serpents, the elders
waiting for him there, to tell him he would have to turn around,
he would have to leave their country & go home

: who heard them ask where he was bound for, cut off from all a man
remembers, his city's rites long fallen into disregard

: who said it was too late to turn around, his need still driving him, &
when they asked again where he was bound, spoke about a
country of red daylight & finding wisdom, who had been called
there, whom the sun was calling

: who waited then until they told him he could go; could leave his
Toltec things & go (& so he left those arts behind, the creations of
man's hands & the imagination of his heart; the crafts of gold &
silver, of working precious stones, of carpentry & sculpture &
mural painting & book illumination & featherweaving)

: who, delivering that knowledge, threw his jewelled necklace in the
    lake, which vanished in those depths, & from then on that place
    was called The Lake of Jewels

*

Another stop along the line
        This time
        THE CITY OF THE SLEEPERS

And runs into a shaman

Says, you bound for somewhere honey

Says, the country of Red Daylight know it? expect to land there probe
    a little wisdom maybe

Says, no fooling try a bit of pulque brewed it just for you

Says, most kind but awfully sorry scarcely touch a drop you know

Says, perhaps you've got no choice perhaps I might not let you go now
    you didn't drink perhaps I'm forcing you against your will might
    even get you drunk come on honey drink it up

Drinks it with a straw
        So drunk he falls down fainting
        on the road & dreams &
        snores his snoring echoes very far

& when he wakes finds silence
& an empty town, his face
reflected & the hair shaved off
        Then calls it
        CITY OF THE SLEEPERS

*

There is a peak between Old Smokey
& The White Woman

Snow is falling
& fell upon him in those days

        & on his companions
        who were with him, on
        his dwarfs, his clowns
        his gimps

                It fell

till they were frozen
lost among the dead

The weight oppressed him
& he wept for them

He sang

        The tears are endless
        & the long sighs
        issue from my chest

Further out
THE HILL OF MANY COLORS

which he sought

Portents everywhere, those
dark reminders
of the road he walks

   *

It ended on the beach
It ended with a hulk of serpents formed into a boat
& when he'd made it, sat in it & sailed away
A boat that glided on those burning waters, no one knowing when he
     reached the country of Red Daylight
It ended on the rim of some great sea
It ended with his face reflected in the mirror of its waves

The beauty of his face returned to him
& he was dressed in garments like the sun
It ended with a bonfire on the beach where he would hurl himself
& burn, his ashes rising & the cries of birds
It ended with the linnet, with the birds of turquoise color, birds the
      color of wild sunflowers, red & blue birds
It ended with the birds of yellow feathers in a riot of bright gold
Circling till the fire had died out
Circling while his heart rose through the sky
It ended with his heart transformed into a star
It ended with the morning star with dawn & evening
It ended with his journey to Death's Kingdom with seven days of
      darkness
With his body changed to light
A star that burns forever in that sky

                                   (Aztec)

THE STRING GAME

(by Día!kwain, after Xaa-ttin)

These were people
Who broke the string for me.
  Therefore
This place became like this for me,
On account of it.
Because the string broke for me,
  Therefore
The place does not feel to me
As the place used to feel to me,
  On account of it.
The place feels as if it stood open before me,
Because the string has broken for me.
  Therefore
The place does not feel pleasant to me
  Because of it.

(Bushman, Africa)

THE ABORTION

1

 East, west, north, south
 Tell me in which river
 We shall put away the child
 With rotting thatch below it
 And jungly silk above
 We will have it put away
 You at the lower steps
 I at the upper
 We will wash & go to our homes
 You by the lower path
 I by the upper
 We will go to our homes

2

 O my love
 My mind has broken
 For the spring has ceased its flow
 In the gully by the plantain
 Drink cups of medicine
 Swallow down some pills
 Like a black cow
 That has never had a calf
 You will again be neat & trim

3

 Like a bone
 Was the first child born
 And the white ants have eaten it
 O my love, do not weep
 Do not mourn

We two are here
And the white ants have eaten it

4

The field has not been ploughed
The field is full of sand
Little grandson
Why do you linger?
From a still unmarried girl
A two-months child has slipped
And that is why they stare

5

You by the village street
I by the track in the garden
We will take the child away
To the right is a bent tree
To the left is a stump
O my love
We will bury it between them

6

In the unploughed rice field, elder brother
What birds are hovering?
At midnight, the headman's middle daughter
Has taken it away
They are tearing the after-birth to pieces

(Santal, India)

IMPROVISED SONG AGAINST
A WHITE MAN
(by Zarabe)

I will tell you a terrible truth, aaa!
I've seen a girl at Tamatava,
She had her mouth eaten:
It had been devoured by a vasaha,
Her white lover.
I've seen another girl at Fenerive,
With a big wound instead of a breast:
Her white lover had devoured her breast, aaa . . .

The vasaha does not love like other men, aaa!
When he makes love,
He slavers and bites like a dog.
Go to him, Benachehina,
And return without a mouth!
Go to him, Rasoa,
And return without a breast!
D'you know why the vasaha has a golden tooth?
The dog barks before he bites,
The vasaha bites with his golden tooth
Before he makes love . . .
A calf sucks the milk of a cow,
The vasaha sucks blood from a girl's mouth!
Do you believe me, aaa?

(Malagasy, Madagascar)

PSALM 137

How can we sing King Alpha song
In a strange land?

We sat & cried along Babylon rivers
remembering Zion.

We hung up our harps on Babylon trees
when our captors asked us for songs
when they mocked us calling for a happy tune:

"Sing us one of those Zion songs!"

If I forgot you Jerusalem
my right hand would wither
my tongue would stick to the roof of my mouth
if I didn't remember you
if I couldn't start up a tune with:
"Jerusalem . . ."

YaHVeH recall the Edomites
Jerusalem's day   when they said:
"Strip her   Strip her bottom bare!"

Now   thief Babylon   (a song for you):

"Happy He'll be to pay you
the reward you've rewarded us
Happy He'll be to snatch your babies
and smash them against a rock!"

(Hebrew)

A SEQUENCE OF SONGS
OF THE GHOST DANCE RELIGION

1

My children,
When at first I liked the whites,
I gave them fruits,
I gave them fruits.

—Nawat, "Left Hand"
(Southern Arapaho)

2

Father have pity on me,
I am crying for thirst,
All is gone,
I have nothing to eat.

—Anon.
(Arapaho)

3

The father will descend
The earth will tremble
Everybody will arise,
Stretch out your hands.

—Anon.
(Kiowa)

4

The Crow—*Ehe'eye!*
I saw him when he flew down,

To the earth, to the earth.
He has renewed our life,
He has taken pity on us.

—Moki, "Little Woman"
(Cheyenne)

5

I circle around
The boundaries of the earth,
Wearing the long wing feathers
As I fly.

—Anon.
(Arapaho)

6

I'yehe! my children—
My children,
We have rendered them desolate.
The whites are crazy—Ahe'yuhe'yu!

—"Sitting Bull" (Arapaho
"Apostle of the Dance")

7

We shall live again.
We shall live again.

—Anon.
(Comanche)

THE BOOK OF EVENTS (I)

LILY EVENTS

(1) A man and woman looking for lilies.

(2) All the people going down to look for lilies.

(3) Mud taken up looking for lilies.

(4) Washing the lilies in the water to remove the mud.

(5) Washing themselves off after the mud has got on them.

(6) Lilies in a basket.

(7) Walking from the lily place "to go look for a dry place to sit down."

(Arnhem Land, Australia)

GARBAGE EVENT

1. Pigs and chickens feed on the grass in an inhabited area until it is bare of grass.

2. Garbage is added to the area.

3. The participants defend the "abandoned beauty" and "town-quality" of the environment against all critics.

> *Sample defense:*
>
> *Critic.* This place is dirty.
> *Answer.* It is filthy.
>
> *Critic.* Why don't you clean it up?
> *Answer.* We like it the way it is.
>
> *Critic.* Garbage is unhealthy.
> *Answer.* The pigs feed better in it.
>
> *Critic.* It breeds mosquitoes.
> *Answer.* There are more mosquitoes in a jungle.

(Dayak, Borneo)

BEARD EVENT

The men shave and fashion "Van Dyke" beards. The women paint.

(Arnhem Land, Australia)

STONE FIRE EVENT

The old men build a stone fire and the men inhale the smoke and squat over the fire in order to allow the smoke to enter their anuses.

Realization. All the men divide into groups around the various stone fires the old men have made. The women dance around them. All the men hold their heads over the fires and inhale the smoke and heat. They also squat over the fire to allow the smoke to enter the anal opening. Men, women and young boys then paint themselves with red ocher and kangaroo grease.

(Arnhem Land, Australia)

CLIMBING EVENT

A great jar is set up with two small ladders leaning against its sides. The performers climb up one of the ladders & down the other throughout a whole night.

(Sarawak)

FOREST EVENT

Go into a forest & hang articles of clothing from the trees.

(Hungary)

GIFT EVENT

Start by giving away different colored glass bowls.
Have everyone give everyone else a glass bowl.
Give away handkerchiefs and soap and things like that.
Give away a sack of clams and a roll of toilet paper.
Give away teddybear candies, apples, suckers and oranges.
Give away pigs and geese and chickens, or pretend to do so.
Pretend to be different things.
Have the women pretend to be crows, have the men pretend to be
something else.
Talk Chinese or something.
Make a narrow place at the entrance of a house and put a line at
the end of it that you have to stoop under to get in.
Hang the line with all sorts of pots and pans to make a big noise.
Give away frying pans while saying things like "Here is this frying
pan worth $100 and this one worth $200."
Give everyone a new name.
Give a name to a grandchild or think of something and go and get
everything.

(Kwakiutl Indian)

MARRIAGE EVENT
for Carolee Schneemann

(1) Large quantities of food & cloth are piled in a heap.

(2) The Bridegroom appears outside his own house, where a continuous stream of human bodies leads from his doorway to that of his Father-in-Law.

(3) As many people as there are permit him to walk over their backs as they lie prostrate on the ground.*

(4) When the Bridegroom reaches the Father-in-Law's house, three old women prostrate themselves so as to form a living chair for him.

(5) A fish is brought forward &, with the aid of a sharp stick, is cut up & diced on a human body. It is presented to the Bridegroom who eats it raw.

(6) The piles of food & cloth are distributed to as many people as there are, & the food is eaten. Afterwards the street of human bodies is again formed for the return.

(7) The Bridegroom's family perform the same event for the bride.

(Hervey Islands, Polynesia)

*Should the numbers be insufficient to reach the Father-in-Law's house, those first walked-on rise up quickly & run through the crowd, again to take their places in front.

THREE MAGIC EVENTS

Number 1 (to make a couple into enemies)

Take an egg and boil it hard and write the couple's names on it. Then cut the egg in two pieces and give one of the halves to a dog and the other half to a cat.

Number 2 (against rats in the barn)

When the first load of grain is carted in, those who are standing in the barn ask:

—What are you bringing here?

—We are bringing here a load of cats!

Now they ask what the rats shall have to eat.

—Stone and bone and henbane-root.

Then the first load is brought in during a dead silence.

During the following loads one talks about cats all the time.

Number 3 (for white washes)

At the washing a person who comes in shall say:

—I saw a swan.

Then the clothes will be clean and white. On the other hand the whole wash will be spoiled if he says:

—I saw a raven.

(Sweden)

GOING-AROUND EVENT

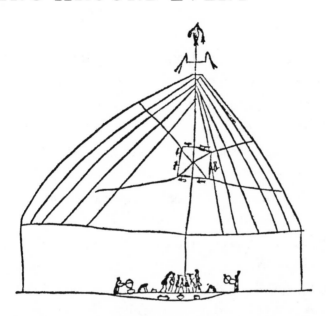

1. A long pole is fixed in the middle of a house, the upper end of which protrudes from the vent-hole. On it are two double tassels & a seal-skin float, to the flippers of which are fastened the pelt of a fox & an iron kettle. A square frame made of paddles surmounted by several wooden images of manned boats & whales is suspended halfway up the pole, by means of which people may turn the pole with the frame. Several walrus-heads form the central object of the event.

2. The wheel is turned around as quickly as possible, & in the direction of the sun's course, by people of both sexes, while several other persons beat the drum. All sing various tunes of their own choice. At last those turning the wheel stop; & the men, still running in the same direction, begin to seize women from all over the house. Every man has the right to sleep that night with the woman he has caught.

(Asiatic Eskimo)

LANGUAGE EVENT

All parts of a hut are named, and the names have references to the sexual relations between man and woman.

    Question. What is the doorstep?
    Answer. The doorstep is a woman.

    Q. And the crossbar over the door, what is that?
    A. The crossbar is a man.

    Q. When the door is being put in, what is that?
    A. That is when the man comes.

    Q. And the hingepin on the door?
    A. His penis.

    Q. What is the ceiling of the hut and the floor beneath?
    A. A boy and a girl who are mating.

    Q. And the grass bundles hanging down above them?
    A. The python.

    Q. Then what is the beaten floor?
    A. That is my aunt.

    Q. Who has been beating the floor then?
    A. A hand.

    Q. But what is the door?
    A. The door is the crocodile.

    Q. And if the door is closed, what is that?
    A. The crocodile stretching out.

    Q. What is the door from the outside?
    A. The crocodile's back.

    Q. And if that one is closed?
    A. A pregnant woman.

Q. Then what is a door that is open?
A. The woman after delivery.

Q. What are the two sides of the river?
A. A boy and a girl when they meet.

Q. But which one is the crocodile that bites?
A. That is the top one, the one below has no sense.

Q. What is the wall in front of you?
A. A man that is virile.

Q. And the wall behind you?
A. A man who is impotent.

Q. Then what is this housepost?
A. A man who rips a girl apart.

Q. And that one?
A. The striker of the thighs, the crusher of the little ribs.

(Venda, Africa)

BURIAL EVENTS

Bury the skull of a yak.

Bury the skull of a black bitch.

Hide the skulls of a dog & a pig under a child's bed, or bury a weasel's skull there, or a puppy's, or a piglet's.

Set out or bury the skulls of a fox, a badger, & a marmot in a cemetery.

Bury the heads of a fish & of an otter.

Bury the head of a wolf, a horse, or a yak at the border of an enemy's house.

Hide the skulls of a man, a dog, & a pig underneath a stupa.

Place the skull of a goat or a sheep halfway up a mountain.

Bury the skull of a monkey, a parrot or a bat where people come to hold a meeting.

Bury the skulls of a hybrid yak & of a mule somewhere in the country.

Bury the skulls of a lynx & a wolf in a pit someone has dug in the center of a city.

(Tibet)

FRIENDSHIP DANCE

Preparation

Men participants form a single file and are joined by women who dance in front of them as partners. During the song they dance counterclockwise with a shuffling trot, and in the intervals walk in a circle. At the song, when the leader begins to insert words suggestive of intimacy (see translations below), the humorous gestures and acts of the pantomime begin.

Song & Pantomime

A free rendering of the song is as follows: "Ha!-Ha! I am called an old man [poor and ugly] but I am not this. I am going to take this woman home with me, as I did not know that there was such a good shell-shaker, none like her. I'll take her home to my town."

During the song the leader may raise his hands, palms in, to shoulder height, at times turning halfway to the left and moving sideways. Throughout he is imitated by the men. Toward the end, the leader reaches the climax of his humor in the following phrase, "Ha!-Ha! We are going to touch each other's privates"; the men, holding their partners' hands, suit actions to words.

Movements (Sequence of Intimacy)

1. Greeting, holding hands facing.
2. Side by side, holding hands crossed.
3. Facing, putting palms upon partners' palms.
4. Placing hands on partners' shoulders while facing.
5. Placing arms over partners' shoulders while side by side.
6. Placing hats on women partners' heads while facing.
7. Stroking partners under chin while facing.
8. Putting hands on female partners' breasts while side by side.
9. Touching the clothing over the partners' genitals while side by side.

(Cherokee Indian)

GREASE FEAST EVENT

A great fire is lighted in the center of the host's house. The flames leap up to the roof and the guests are almost scorched by the heat, but they do not stir, else the host's fire has conquered them. Even when the roof begins to burn and the fire attacks the rafters, they must appear unconcerned. The host alone has the right to send a man up to the roof to put out the fire. While the feast is in progress the host sings a scathing song ridiculing his rival and praising himself. Then the grease is filled in large spoons and passed to the guests first. If a person thinks he has given a greater grease feast than that offered by the host, he refuses the spoon. Then he runs out of the house to fetch a copper plate "to squelch with it the fire." The host proceeds at once to tie a copper plate to each of his houseposts. If he should not do so, the person who refused the spoon would on returning strike the posts with the copper plate, which is considered equal to striking the host's face. Then the man who went to fetch his plate breaks it and gives it to the host. This is called "squelching the host's fire."

Squelching Song

1. I thought another one was causing the smoky weather. I am the only one on earth—the only one in the world who makes thick smoke rise from the beginning of the year to the end.

2. What will my rival say now—that "spider woman"; what will he pretend to do next? The words of that "spider woman" do not go a straight way. Will he not brag that he is going to give away canoes, that he is going to break coppers, that he is going to give a grease feast? Such will be the words of the "spider woman," and therefore your face is dry and mouldy, you who are standing in front of the stomachs of your guests.

3. Nothing will satisfy you; but sometimes I treated you so roughly that you begged for mercy. Do you know what you will be like? You will be like an old dog, and you will spread your legs before me when I get excited. This I throw into your face, you whom I always tried to vanquish; whom I have mistreated; who does not dare to stand erect when I am eating.

(Kwakiutl Indian)

PEACEMAKING EVENT

Preparations

An open area of ground is set aside, and across it is erected what is called a *koro-cop*. Posts are put up in a line, to the tops of these is attached a length of strong cane, and from the cane are suspended bundles of shredded palm leaf (*koro*). The "visitors" are the forgiving party, while the home party are those who have committed the last act of hostility.

Movements

The visitors enter dancing, the step being that of the ordinary dance. The women of the home party mark the time by clapping their hands on their thighs. The visitors dance forward in front of the men standing at the *koro-cop*, and then, still dancing all the time, pass backwards and forwards between the standing men, bending their heads as they pass beneath the suspended cane. The visitors may make threatening gestures at the men standing at the *koro-cop*, and every now and then break into a shrill shout. The men at the *koro* stand silent and motionless.

After dancing thus for a little time, the leader of the visitors approaches the man at one end of the *koro* and, taking him by the shoulders from the front, leaps vigorously up and down to the time of the dance, thus giving the man he holds a good shaking. The leader then passes on to the next man in the row while another of the visitors goes through the same performance with the first man. This is continued until each of the dancers has "shaken" each of the standing men. The dancers then pass under the *koro* and shake their enemies in the same manner from the back. After a little more shaking the dancers retire, and the women of the visiting group come forward and dance in much the same way, each woman giving each man of the other group a good shaking.

When the women have been through their dance the two parties of men and women sit down and weep together.

(Andaman Islands)

WILD MAN EVENTS

1. A man dressed up as a Wild Man is chased through several streets until he comes to a narrow lane across which a cord is stretched. He stumbles over the cord &, falling to the ground, is overtaken & caught by his pursuers. The executioner runs up & stabs with his sword a bladder filled with blood which the Wild Man wears around his body; a stream of blood reddens the groups. Next day a straw-man, made up to look like the Wild Man, is placed on a litter &, accompanied by a large crowd, is taken to a pool into which it is thrown by the "executioner." This is called "burying the carnival."

2. A wild man called The King is dressed in bark, ornamented with flowers & ribbons. He wears a crown of gilt paper & rides a horse, which is also decked with flowers. Attended by a judge, an executioner, & other characters, & followed by a train of soldiers, all mounted, he rides to the village square, where a hut or arbor of green boughs has been erected under the May-trees, which are firs, freshly cut, peeled to the top, & dressed with flowers & ribbons. Here the girls of the village are criticized, a frog is beheaded, & the procession rides to a place previously determined upon, in a straight, broad street. The participants then draw up in two lines & the King takes to flight. He is given a short start & rides off at full speed, pursued by the whole troop. If they fail to catch him he remains King until the next performance. But if they overtake & catch him he is scourged with hazel rods or beaten with wooden swords & compelled to dismount. Then the executioner asks, "Shall I behead this King?" The answer is given, "Behead him." The executioner brandishes his axe, & with the words, "One, two, three, let the King headless be!" he strikes off the King's crown. Amid the loud cries of the bystanders the King sinks to the ground; then he is laid on a bier & carried to the nearest farmhouse.

(Bohemia)

BOOGER EVENT

Participants

A company of four to ten or more masked men (called "boogers"), occasionally a couple of women companions. Each dancer is given a personal name, usually obscene; for example:

White Man
Black Ass
Frenchie
Big Balls
Asshole
Rusty Asshole
Burster (penis)
Swollen Pussy
Long Prick
Sweet Prick
Piercer
Fat Ass
Long Haired Pussy
Etcetera.

Prelude

The dancers enter. The audience and the dancers break wind.

First Action

The masked men are systematically malignant. They act mad, fall on the floor, hit at the spectators, push the men spectators as though to get at their wives and daughters, etc.

Second Action

The boogers demand "girls." They may also try to fight and dance. If they do, the audience tries to divert them.

Third Action

Booger Dance Song. The name given to the booger should be taken as the first word of the song. This is repeated any number of times, while the owner of the name dances a solo, performing as awkward and grotesque steps as he possibly can. The audience applauds each mention of the name, while the other dancers indulge in exhibitionism, e.g., thrusting their buttocks out and occasionally displaying toward the women in the audience large phalli concealed under their clothing. These phalli may contain water, which is then released as a spray.

Interlude

Everyone smokes.

Fourth Action

A number of women dancers, equaling the number of boogers, enter the line as partners. As soon as they do, the boogers begin their sexual exhibitions. They may close upon the women from the rear, performing body motions in pseudo-intercourse; as before, some may protrude their large phalli and thrust these toward their partners with appropriate gestures and body motions.

Postlude

The rest of the performance consists of miscellaneous events chosen by the audience.

(Cherokee Indian)

SEA WATER EVENT

The tides of the ocean and the floods are danced; certain birds and animals are included.

(Arnhem Land, Australia)

NOISE EVENT

1. Make a joyful noise unto the Lord, all the earth: make a loud noise, and rejoice, and sing praise.

2. Sing unto the Lord with the harp; with the harp, and the voice of a psalm.

3. With trumpets and sound of cornet make a joyful noise before the Lord.

4. Let the sea roar, and the fullness thereof; the world, and they that dwell therein.

5. Let the floods clap their hands: let the hills be joyful together.

(Hebrew)

THE BOOK OF EVENTS (II)

TAMING THE STORM
A Two-Shaman Vision & Event

I

[On the third evening of the storm we were solemnly invited to attend a shaman seance in one of the snow houses. The man who invited us was a pronouncedly blond Eskimo, bald and with a reddish beard, as well as a slight tinge of blue in his eyes. His name was Kigiuna, "Sharp Tooth."]

The hall consisted of two snow huts built together, the entrance leading on to the middle of the floor, and the two snowbuilt platforms on which one slept were opposite one another. One of the hosts, Tamuánuaq, "The Little Mouthful," received me cordially and conducted me to a seat. The house, which was four meters wide and six meters long, had such a high roof that the builder had had to stay it with two pieces of driftwood, which looked like magnificent pillars in the white hall of snow. And there was so much room on the floor that all the neighbors' little children were able to play "catch" round the pillars during the opening part of the festival.

The preparations consisted of a feast of dried salmon, blubber and frozen, unflensed seal carcasses. They hacked away at the frozen dinner with big axes and avidly swallowed the lumps of meat after having breathed upon them so that they should not freeze the skin off lips and tongue.

"Fond of food, hardy and always ready to feast," whispered "Eider Duck" to me, his mouth full of frozen blood.

2

The shaman of the evening was Horqarnaq, "Baleen," a young man with intelligent eyes and swift movements. There was no deceit in his face, and perhaps for that reason it was long before he fell into a trance. He explained before commencing that he had few helpers. There was his dead father's spirit and its helping spirit, a giant with claws so long that they could cut a man right through simply by scratching him; and then there was a figure that he had created himself of soft snow, shaped like a man—a spirit who came when he called. A fourth and mysterious helping spirit was Aupilalánguaq, a remarkable stone he had once found when hunting caribou; it had a lifelike resemblance to a head and neck, and when he shot a caribou near to it he gave it a head-band of the long hairs from the neck of the animal.

He was now about to summon these helpers, and all the women of the village stood around in a circle and encouraged him.

"You can and you do it so easily because you are so strong," they said flatteringly, and incessantly he repeated:

"It is a hard thing to speak the truth. It is difficult to make hidden forces appear."

But the women around him continued to excite him, and at last he slowly became seized with frenzy. Then the men joined in, the circle around him became more and more dense, and all shouted inciting things about his powers and his strength.

Baleen's eyes become wild. He distends them and seems to be looking out over immeasurable distance; now and then he spins round on his heel, his breathing becomes agitated, and he no longer recognizes the people around him: *"Who are you?"* he cries.

"Your own people!" they answer.

"Are you all here?"

"Yes, except those two who went east on a visit."

Again Baleen goes round the circle, looks into the eyes of all, gazes ever more wildly about him, and at last repeats like a tired man who has walked far and at last gives up:

"I cannot. I cannot."

At that moment there is a gurgling sound, and a helping spirit enters his body. A force has taken possession of him and he is no longer master of himself or his words. He dances, jumps, throws himself over among the clusters of the audience and cries to his dead father, who has become an evil spirit. It is only a year since his father died, and his mother, the widow, still sorrowing over the loss of her provider, groans deeply, breathes heavily and tries to calm her wild son; but all the others cry in a confusion of voices, urging him to go on, and to let the spirit speak.

3

The seance has lasted an hour, an hour of howling and invoking of unknown forces, when something happens that terrifies us, who have never before seen the storm-god tamed. Baleen leaps forward and seizes good-natured old Kigiuna, who is just singing a pious song to the Mother of the Sea Beasts, grips him swiftly by the throat and brutally flings him backwards and forwards in the midst of the crowd. At first both utter wailing, throaty screams, but little by little Kigiuna is choked and can no longer utter a sound; but suddenly there is a hiss from his lips, and he too has been seized with ecstasy. He no longer resists, but follows Baleen, who still has him by the throat, and they tumble about, quite out of their minds. The men of the house have to stand in front of the big blubber lamps to prevent their being broken or upset; the women have to help the children up on to the platform to save them from being knocked down in the scrimmage; and so it goes on for a little while, until Baleen has squeezed all the life out of his opponent, who is now being dragged after him like a lifeless bundle. Only then does he release his hold, and Kigiuna falls heavily to the floor.

There is a deathly silence in the house. Baleen is the only one who continues his wild dance, until in some way or other his eyes become calm and he kneels in front of Kigiuna and starts to rub and stroke his body to revive him. Slowly Kigiuna is brought back to life, very shakily he is put back on his feet, but scarcely has he come to his senses again when the same thing is repeated. Three times he is killed in this manner! But when Kigiuna comes to life for the third time, it is he who falls into a trance and Baleen who collapses. The old seer rises up in his curious, much too obese might, yet rules us by the wildness in his eyes and the horrible, reddish-blue sheen that has come over his face through all the ill-usage he has been subjected to. All feel that this is a man whom death has just touched, and they involuntarily step back when, with his foot on Baleen's chest, he turns to the audience and announces the vision he sees. With a voice that trembles with emotion he cries out over the hall:

"The sky is full of naked beings rushing through the air. Naked people, naked men, naked women, rushing along and raising gales and blizzards.

"Don't you hear the noise? It swishes like the beating of the wings of great birds in the air. It is the fear of naked people, it is the flight of naked people!

"The weather spirit is blowing the storm out, the weather spirit is driving the weeping snow away over the earth, and the helpless storm-child Narsuk shakes the lungs of the air with his weeping.

"Don't you hear the weeping of the child in the howling of the wind?

"And look! Among all those naked crowds, there is one, one single man, whom the wind has made full of holes. His body is like a sieve and the wind whistles through the holes: Tju, Tju-u, Tju-u-u! Do you hear him? He is the mightiest of all the wind-travelers.

"But my helping spirit will stop him, will stop them all. I see him coming calmly towards me. He will conquer, will conquer! Tju, tju-u! Do you hear the wind? Sst, sst, ssst! Do you see the spirits, the weather, the storm, sweeping over us with the swish of the beating of great birds' wings?"

At these words Baleen rises from the floor, and the two shamans, whose faces are now transfigured after this tremendous storm sermon, sing with simple, hoarse voices a song to the Mother of the Sea Beasts:

> *Woman, great woman down there*
> *Send it back, send it away from us, that evil!*
> *Come, come, spirit of the deep!*
> *One of your earth-dwellers*
> *Calls to you,*

Asks you to bite his enemies to death!
Come, come, spirit of the deep!

When the two had sung the hymn through, all the other voices joined in, a calling, wailing chorus of distressed people. No one knew for what he was calling, no one worshipped anything; but the ancient song of their forefathers put might into their minds.

And suddenly it seemed as if nature around us became alive. We saw the storm riding across the sky in the speed and thronging of naked spirits. We saw the crowd of fleeing dead men come sweeping through the billows of the blizzard, and all visions and sounds centered in the wing-beats of the great birds for which Kigiuna had made us strain our ears.

(Copper Eskimo)

CORONATION EVENT & DRAMA

CAST

Horus	The new king
Corpse of Osiris	Mummy representing the old king
Thoth	The chief officiant
Isis & Nephthys	Two wailing women
Followers of Horus	Princes; staff of embalmers, morticians, etc.
Set & henchmen	Temple & sacral personnel

SCENE I

(ACTION): THE CEREMONIAL BARGE IS EQUIPPED.

Horus requests his Followers to equip him with the Eye of power.

(ACTION): THE LAUNCHING OF THE BARGE MARKS THE OPENING UP OF THE NILE & INAUGURATES THE CEREMONY OF INSTALLING OR RECONFIRMING THE KING.

Horus (to his Followers):
> Bring me the EYE
> whose spel
> opens this river.

Horus also instructs his Followers to bring upon the scene the god Thoth, who is to act as master of ceremonies, & the corpse of his father, Osiris.

(ACTION): BEER IS PROFFERED.

SCENE II

(ACTION): THE ROYAL PRINCES LOAD EIGHT mnsh JARS INTO THE BOW OF THE BARGE.

Thoth loads the corpse of Osiris upon the back of Set, so that it may be carried up to heaven.

Thoth (to Set):
> See, you cannot

match this
god, the stronger.
    (to Osiris):
As your Heart masters his Cold.
(ACTION): THE ELDERS OF THE COURT ARE MUSTERED.

SCENE III

(ACTION): A RAM IS SENT RUSHING FROM THE PEN, TO SERVE
AS A SACRIFICE IN BEHALF OF THE KING. MEANWHILE—AS AT
ALL SUCH SACRIFICES—THE EYE OF HORUS IS DISPLAYED TO
THE ASSEMBLY.

Isis appears on the scene.

Isis (to Thoth):

That your
lips
may open
that the Word may
come
may give the EYE
to Horus.

(ACTION): THE ANIMAL IS SLAUGHTERED. ITS MOUTH FALLS
OPEN UNDER THE KNIFE.

Isis (to Thoth):

Open thy mouth—
the Word!

SCENE IV

(ACTION): PRIESTS SLAUGHTER THE RAM. THE CHIEF OFFI-
CIANT HANDS A PORTION TO THE KING & FORMALLY PRO-
CLAIMS HIS ACCESSION.

Thoth conveys the Eye to Horus.

Thoth (to Horus):

Son takes his
father's

place: the Prince
is Lord.
(ACTION): THE KING IS ACCLAIMED BY THE ASSEMBLY.

SCENE V

(ACTION): GRAIN IS STREWN ON THE THRESHING FLOOR.
Horus requests his followers to convey to him the Eye which survived the combat with Set.
Horus (to his Followers):
> Bringing your wheat
> to the barn
> or bringing me
> THE EYE
> wrenched from Set's
> clutches.

SCENE VI

(ACTION): THE CHIEF OFFICIANT HANDS TWO LOAVES TO THE KING.
The two loaves symbolize the two eyes of Horus: the one retained by Set, & the one restored to Horus by Thoth.
Thoth (to Horus):
> See, this is THE EYE
> I bring you:
> EYE-YOU-WILL-NEVER-LOSE.

(ACTION): DANCERS ARE INTRODUCED.
Horus (to Thoth):
> My EYE that dances for joy before you.

SCENE VII

(ACTION): A FRAGRANT BOUGH IS HOISTED ABOARD THE BARGE.
The corpse of Osiris is hoisted onto the back of Set, his vanquished assailant.

The Gods (to Set):

 O Set! who never will escape

 The-one-who-masters-masters-thee.

Horus (gazing on the corpse of Osiris):

 O this noble

 body, this

 lovely beautiful

 body.

 (ACTION): THE WORKMEN STAGGER UNDER THE WEIGHT OF
THE BOUGH.

Horus (to Set):

 You bend under him, you plot no more against him!

         (Egyptian)

FOR THE RAIN GOD TLALOC: A DIALOGUE FOR GOD & CHANTERS

Choir:

In Mexico we beg a loan from the god.
There are the banners of paper
and at the four corners
men are standing.

[*The verse is repeated, probably by the people, and then the priest himself addresses the divinity, imploring rain. The priest of Tlaloc mentions the victims to be offered in the festival. They are small children whose weeping, when they are sacrificed, will be an omen of heavy rain. These children, whose crying is awaited, are symbolically referred to as bundles of blood-stained ears of corn.*]

Priest of Tlaloc:

Now it is time for you to weep!
Alas, I was created
and for my god
now carry festal bundles of blood-stained
ears of corn
to the divine hearth.

You are my Chief, Prince and Magician,
and though in truth
it is you who produce our sustenance,
although you are the first,
we cause you only shame.

[*Again the choir of students or perhaps another group of priests replies in the name of Tlaloc. The god exhorts the people and the priesthood to venerate him and recognize his power:*]

Tlaloc:

If anyone

has caused me shame,
it is because he did not know me well;
you are my fathers, my priesthood,
Serpents and Tigers.

[*Then the priest of the Rain God begins to chant another song, mentioning the mansion of Tlalocan and asking the god to spread out over all parts to make the beneficent rain fall.*]

Priest of Tlaloc:
In Tlalocan, in the turquoise vessel,
it was used to coming forth, but now
Acatonal's unseen.
Spread out in Poyauhtlan,
in the region of mist!
With timbrels of mist
our word is carried to Tlalocan. . . .

[*The choir, now speaking in the name of the victim, the little girl dressed in blue who will be sacrificed to the Rain God, chants several verses of deep religious significance. The victim will go away forever. She will be sent to the Place of Mystery. Now is the time for her crying. But perhaps in four year's time there will be a transformation, a rebirth, there in the region-of-the-fleshless. He who propagates men may send once more to this earth some of the children who were sacrificed. In veiled form this hints at a kind of reincarnation, which is very seldom mentioned in the ancient texts. Now the choir speaks once more for the child:*]

Choir [speaking in the name of the victim]:
I will go away forever,
it is time for crying.
Send me to the Place of Mystery,
under your command.
I have already told
the Price of the Sad Omen,
I will go away forever,

it is time for crying.
In four years
comes the arising among us,
many people
without knowing it;
in the place of the fleshless,
the house of quetzal feathers,
is the transformation.
It is the act of the Propagator of Men.

[*The priest of Tlaloc repeats the invocation to the God of Rain. He begs him once more to be present in all parts, to make fertile the land sown with seed, to spread out and make the rain fall.*]

Priest of Tlaloc:
Go to all parts,
spread out
in Poyauhtlan,
in the region of mist.
With timbrels of mist
our word is carried to Tlalocan.

(Aztec)

AFRICA

GHOSTS & SHADOWS

The soul is a dark forest.
—D. H. Lawrence

Ghosts in this forest, shadows
thrown back by the night
Or in daylight
    like bats that drink from our veins
    & hang from moist walls, in deep caves
Behind this green moss, these awful white stones
We pray to know who has seen them
    Shadows thrown back by the night
We pray to know who has seen them

(Gabon Pygmy)

THE CHAPTER OF CHANGING INTO PTAH

I

I eat bread.
I drink ale.
I hoist up my garments.
I cackle like the Smen goose.
I land on that place hard by the Sepulchre for the festival of the Great God.
All that is abominable, all that is abominable I will not eat.
Shit is abominable, I will not eat it.
All that is abominable to my Ka will not enter my body.
I will live on what the gods live.
I will live & I will be master of their cakes.
And I will eat them under the trees of the dweller in the house of Hathor My Lady.
I will make an offering.
My cakes are in Busiris, my offerings are in Heliopolis.
I wrap a robe around me woven by the goddess Tait.
I will stand up & sit down wherever it pleases me.
My head is like the head of Ra.
I am complete like Tem.

2

I will come forth.
My tongue is like the tongue of Ptah
& my throat like that of Hathor.
With my mouth I remember the words of Tem my father.
Tem forced the woman, the wife of Keb
& broke the heads of those around him
so that people were afraid of him

& proclaimed him
& made me his heir on Keb's earth.
Then I mastered their women.
Keb refreshed me.
Keb lifted me up to his throne.
Those in Heliopolis bowed their heads to me.
I am their bull.
I am stronger than the Lord-of-the-Hour.
I have fucked all their women.
I am Master for millions of years.

(Egyptian)

THE CANNIBAL HYMN

The sky is heavy, it is raining stars.
The arches of the sky are cracking; the bones of the earthgod tremble;
The Pleiads are struck dumb by the sight of Unas
Who rises towards the sky, transfigured like a god,
Who lives off his father and eats his mother.
He is the bull of the sky; his heart lives off the divine beings;
He devours their intestines, when their bodies are charged with magic.
It is he who passes judgment, when the elders are slaughtered.
He is Lord over all meals.
He ties the sling with which he catches his prey,
He prepares the meal himself.
It is he who eats men and lives off the gods.
He has servants who execute his orders.
Skullgrabber catches them for him, like bulls with a lasso.
Headerect watches them for him and brings them to him;
Willow-croucher binds them
And tears their intestines from their bodies,
Winepresser slaughters them
And cooks a meal for him in his evening pots.
Unas swallows their magic powers
He relishes their glory.
The large ones among them are his morning meal,
the medium sized are his lunch,
The small ones among them he eats for supper.
Their senile men and women he burns as incense.
The great ones in the North sky lay the fire for him
With the bones of the elders,
Who simmer in the cauldrons themselves;
Look, those in the sky work and labor for Unas.
They polish the cookingpots for him with thighs of their wives.

O Unas has reappeared in the sky,
He is crowned as Lord of the Horizon,
Those he meets in his path he swallows raw.
He has broken the joints of the gods,
Their spines and their vertebrae.
He has taken away their hearts,
He has swallowed the red crown
He has eaten the green crown,
He feeds on the lungs of the Wise,
He feasts, as he now lives on hearts,
And on the power they contain.
He thrives luxuriously, for all their power is in his belly,
His nobility can no longer be taken away.
He has consumed the brain of every god,
His life time is eternity,
His limit is infinity.

(Egyptian)

CONVERSATIONS IN COURTSHIP

. . . .

He says:

I adore the gold-gleaming Goddess,
              Hathor the dominant,
                        and I praise her.
I exalt the Lady of Heaven,
      I give thanks to the Patron.
She hears my invocation
   and has fated me to my lady,
Who has come here, herself, to find me.
   What felicity came in with her!
I rise exultant
   in hilarity
              and triumph when I have said:
                        Now,
And behold her.
   Look at it!
                   The young fellows fall at her feet.
Love is breathed into them.

I make vows to my Goddess,
   because she has given me this girl for my own.
I have been praying three days,
   calling her name.
For five days she has abandoned me.

She says:

I went to his house, and the door was open.
   My beloved was at his ma's side
      with brothers and sisters about him.

Everybody who passes has sympathy for him,
   an excellent boy, none like him,
    a friend of rare quality.
He looked at me when I passed
   and my heart was in jubilee.
If my mother knew what I am thinking
   she would go to him at once.

O Goddess of Golden Light,
    put that thought into her,
       Then I could visit him
And put my arms round him while people were looking
And not weep because of the crowd,
    But would be glad that they knew it
       and that you know me.
What a feast I would make to my Goddess,
    My heart revolts at the thought of exit,
If I could see my darling tonight,
    Dreaming is loveliness.

He says:

Yesterday, Seven days and I have not seen her.
    My malady increases;
        limbs heavy!
           I know not myself any more.
High priest is no medicine, exorcism is useless:
   a disease beyond recognition.

I said: She will make me live,
   her name will rouse me,
Her messages are the life of my heart
   coming and going.
My beloved is the best of medicine,

more than all pharmacopoeia.
My health is in her coming,
   I shall be cured at the sight of her.
Let her open my eyes
   and my limbs are alive again;
Let her speak and my strength returns.
Embracing her will drive out my malady.
    Seven days and
               she has abandoned me.

        (Egyptian)

THE COMET

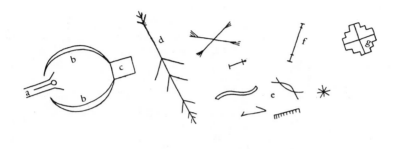

(a) A stranger enters a town. He walks up the main street between two rows of houses (b b) till he comes to the Egbo House (c).

(d) Is a comet which has lately been seen by the townspeople.

(e) Property is strewn about in disorder—denoting confusion.

(f) A seat before the Chief's house.

(g) The arm-chair in which the body of the Head Chief has been set. His death was foretold by the comet.

(hh) Two claimants to the office of Head Chief now vacant. The townsfolk have collected in the Egbo House to decide between the rivals.

(Ekoi)

THE LOVERS

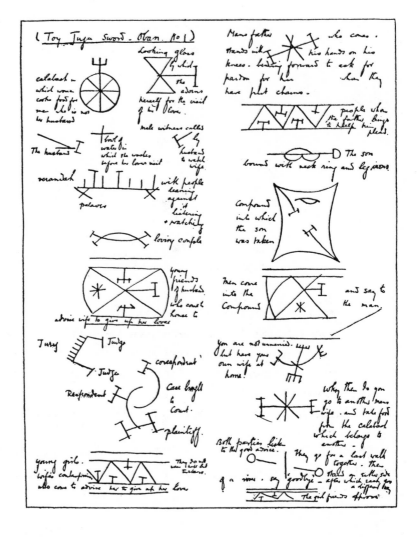

(Ekoi)

DRUM POEM #7

M–M–M–FF M–M F M–F,
MF M M–F,
M–F–F–F–F F–M–F M,
M–M–F M–M–F M,
M F FM M M–M–M,
F–F F–F F–F,
M–M–M–FF M–FM M–M–M–F–F,
M–M–M–FF M–FM M–M–M–F–F,
M–F–F–F–F F–M–F M,
M–M–F M–M–F M,
M F FM M M–M–M,
F–F F–F F–F,
M M M–F F,
F–F F F F.

Oh Witch, don't kill me, Witch
Please spare me, Witch
This Holy Drummer swears to you that
When he rises up some morning
He will sound his drums for you some morning
Very early
Very early
Very early
Very early
Oh Witch that kills our children very early
Oh Witch that kills our children very early
This Holy Drummer swears to you that
When he rises up some morning
He will sound his drums for you some morning

Very early
Very early
Very early
Very early
Hear me talking to you
Try and understand

(Ashanti)

PRAISES OF OGUN

. . . who smashes someone into pieces that are more or less big
his town's got stuff in it most people couldn't guess at
Ogun is called a thief by definition
Ogun is master of the crown Big-Ogun props up on his head
Ogun is orisha number three
he's master of his town no he won't leave anyone alone who
badmouths Ogun like a thief
he's very high & mighty
he hires an elephant to say prayers to his head
he kills the husband in a fire
he kills the wife in her foyer
he kills the babies when they try to run outside
he takes somebody's head off if he feels like
he covets his neighbor's prick
even if there's water in his house Ogun washes up with blood
Ogun makes the child kill himself with the sword he plays around
with
a man starts trembling like someone opening a door
he kills on the right & destroys on the right
he kills on the left & destroys on the left
the day Ogun got the husband & wife was the day I was afraid
he'd touch me that day we drank the palmwine of terror
quicker than lightning he scares off the loafer
the sword doesn't know the neck of the swordsmith
the place Ogun lives in town is blacker than nightfall
the day they laid his cornerstone he told his children he'd stay
homeless
master of iron, man & warrior
big old mountain on the outskirts of town
a pillar of earth falls & starts it trembling
someone who looks at him stumbles he knocks into a baobab tree

he throws his iron tools down under a coco tree
    he shoves it deep in he touches base of cock with his hand maybe
he's gone soft
    he makes sure his cock is in no it isn't soft except his balls
except his balls are drained
never clumsy on the battlefield
the yam neglected by the sick man sends shoots into the bushes
he plows the field its owner doesn't plow
he tells the sick man if he dies people will take his field away
death rattles keep the sick man from sleeping
a large-headed leaf
big swampy water seeps into the river
    a dead man balances his head on shoulder of someone who
supports him
    Ogun kills the long tits' owner on the water
battle of the crab & fish
    he finds water in his house & on the road but washes up with
blood
    Ogun sticks a bloodcovered hat on his head
& the bushes & the forest crying "sizzle sizzle"
    if someone says Ogun won't fight a minute later you see him like a
dice-cup under an elephant's foot
    Ogun makes a baby's skull hum like a pumpkin he makes a grown
man's clink like a plate
    Ogun I don't want my balls cut off for no one's ceremonies
Big-Ogun battles in blood
Big-Ogun who eats of the ram
who hangs a snake around his neck & struts up & down with it
Ogun-of-the-barbers eats other men's beards
Ogun-of-the-tattoo-artists sucks up their blood
    Ogun has four hundred wives & one thousand four hundred
children
    Ogun won't help anyone that doesn't bring him offerings of kola

Big-Ogun my husband my big boss of iron
Ogun sweet river grass abundant Ogun good to eat good to sell
good to go around with
If someone says "I'm going to die on the road" bad luck dogs him
he dies like a wild deer he drops dead like an ekiri he goes to his death
like a dying deer
he has arrows over his body as bad as any wild deer
(unless it wasn't Akisale that gave birth to an oka snake)
(unless it wasn't Akisale that gave birth to a boa)
Ogun killed Big-Ogun he captured his town & set up shop there
boss of the world who walks ahead of the orishas
big man who captures the boss of all the other big men
who eats the head of the man who was headstrong
a blacksmith does better in the market than someone working in
the fields
Ogun kills Big-Ogun he kills him completely he makes his house
into a residence
Ogun seven parts of the houses for Ogun
he is very high & very mighty
he smashes someone into pieces that are more or less big

(Yoruba)

ABUSE POEM: FOR KODZO
& OTHERS
(by Komi Ekpe)

1

Poverty moved into my homestead
Can I be this way and earn the name of a great singer?
Shall I fear death by song
and refuse to sing?

2

Hm hm hm. Beware,
I will place a load on Kodzo's head.
Nugbleza informed me that
it is the women of Tsiame
who goaded Kodzo into my song.
Questioners, this became the evil firewood
he'd gathered; his hands decayed
his feet decayed.
I am the poet; I am not afraid of you.
Kodzo, winding in the air, his asshole agape
his face long and curved
like the lagoon egret's beak.
Call him here, I say call him
and let me see his face.
He is the man from whom the wind runs,
the man who eats off the farm he hasn't planted
his face bent like the evil hoe
on its handle. Behold, ei ei ei
Kodzo did something. I forgive him his debt.
I will insult him since he poked
a stick into the flying ant's grove.

Amegavi said he has some wealth
And he took Kodzo's part.
The back of his head tapers off
as if they'd built a fetish hut on his breathing spot.
His face wags, a fool with a white ass.
The monkey opened his asshole
in display to the owner of the farm.
The lion caught a game, alas,
his children took it away from him.
Kodzo's homestead shall fall, shall surely fall.
Questioners, let evil men die
let death knock down the evil doer.
If I were the fetish in the creator's house
that will be your redemption.
Kodzo, this imbecile, evil animal
who fucks others' wives fatteningly
his buttocks run off, his teeth yellow
his penis has wound a rope around his waist
pulling him around and away,
his backside runs into a slope
his eye twisted like the sun-inspector,
he has many supporters in Tsiame
his mouth as long as the pig
blowing the twin whistle.
Something indeed has happened.

(Ewe)

WHAT FELL DOWN? PENIS!
(Vocalist: Awawo, wife of John)

Hai Hai Hai Hai Hai-i-i-i	HOE! HOE!
What fell down?	PENIS!
How did it fall?	IT FELL WITH A BANG!
The oracle	LET IT SPEAK!
Pot with noise inside	LET IT SPEAK!
Iroko tree in the compound	LET IT SPEAK!

Those who pull honey from the ground say a woman's body is sweeter
    than honey

WE DO NOT EVEN BELIEVE THEY HAVE TASTED OUR BODY

SPIRIT, EGUWA ETUMABE	LET THEM SEE!
Ridiculous men whose pubic hair	
is straight	LET THEM SEE!
Foolish men whose arms are bent	
like a monkey's	LET THEM SEE!

Elo who is supreme   *Elo*

The one with cudgel is not a woman

Elo

The supreme one has never fetched water from the river

Elo

The supreme one has never fetched firewood

Elo

He asks me to "shake my waist" a little bit *Elo*

BUT I CAN'T SHAKE MY WAIST A LITTLE BIT BECAUSE IT'S TOO
    DIFFICULT *Elo*

He asks me to lie on my back

BUT I CAN'T LIE ON MY BACK AND SPREAD MY LEGS BECAUSE IT'S

TOO DIFFICULT *Elo*
So he asks me to lie on my side a little
BUT I CAN'T LIE ON MY SIDE JUST A LITTLE BECAUSE IT'S TOO
   DIFFICULT   ELO
E-elo who is supreme

Elo
The one with cudgel is not a woman
Elo
The one with sticks on his body
is not a woman
Elo
The one with okra is not a woman
Elo
The one with an "extra body" is
not a woman
Elo

E-elo who is supreme   ELO-O-O-O

(Ekperi)

WHAT FELL DOWN? VULVA!
(Vocalist: Ogiepo, son of Aimiebo)

Hai-ai-ai-ai   HOE! HOE!
What fell down?
    Vulva!
How did it fall?   *It fell with a bang!*
The oracle   *Let it speak!*
Pot with noise inside   *Let it speak!*
Iroko tree in the compound   *Let it speak!*
Those who pull HONEY FROM THE GROUND SAY THAT A MAN'S
BODY IS SWEETER THAN HONEY
WE DO NOT EVEN BELIEVE THEY HAVE TASTED OUR BODY
THE ONE WHOSE CLITORIS IS TOO LONG
SLAP HER, THE ONE WHOSE PUBIC HAIR IS STRAIGHT
SLAP HER, THE FOOLISH ONE WHOSE ARMS ARE BENT LIKE A
MONKEY'S
SLAP HER!

Let us sing songs-of-the-mouth
    together   *Songs-of-the-mouth*
Let us sing songs-of-the-mouth
    together   *Songs-of-the-mouth*
The bottom calabash in the net   SONGS-OF-THE-MOUTH
Four-score cowries inside–o   SONGS-OF-THE-MOUTH–o
Oho koko ho–o–o   SONGS-OF-THE-MOUTH–O–O–O

No one should ask why I dance Agiela-dance
No one should ask WHY I DANCE AGIELA-DANCE
I DANCE AGIELA FOR the oracle
I DANCE AGIELA FOR Okhailopokhai
No one should ask why I dance Agiela-dance *E-e-e-e-e-e*

(Ekperi)

THE TRAIN

Iron thing coming from Pompi, from the round-house
Where Englishmen smashed their hands on it,
It has no front it has no back.
Rhino Tshukudu going that way.
Rhino Tshukudu no, coming this way.
I'm no greenhorn, I'm a strong, skillful man.
Animal coming from Pompi, from Moretele.
It comes spinning out a spider's web under a cloud of gnats
Moved by the pulling of a teat, animal coming from Kgobola-diatla
Comes out of the big hole in the mountain, mother of the great
    woman,
Coming on iron cords.
I met this woman of the tracks curving her way along the river bank
    and over the river.
I thought I'd snatch her
So I said
"Out of the way, son of Mokwatsi, who stands there at the teat."
The stream of little red and white birds gathered up all of its track
Clean as a whistle.
Tshutshu over the dry plains
Rhino Tshukudu out of the high country
Animal from the south, steaming along
It comes from Pompi, the round-house, from Kgobola-diatla.

(Hurutshe)

SPEAKING THE WORLD: SEVEN
PRAISE-MOTTOES

1

Arm and Hand

Arm, shoulder is big
Arm, separates at the elbow
Fist is small
Fingers lengthy
Palm is striated
Fingers, each with three phalanges

2

Hoe

Iron hoe says *hu*
All day; iron palm
Finger tip
Hole in the handle fits
Iron in: hafted like man and woman
Bent neck
Slenders to the grip
Poor man works with it
Rich man works with it
Who has a hoe hangs on
Even an orphan grows
By dint of:
Sun, fatigue, content.

3

Woman

Worn stirring stick.

4

Young Girl

Young girl sways
Eye of the dawn star
Gleaming neck
Breasts no bigger than
Ewe's udder
Firm as a cake of indigo
Belly flatter than
Fulani's sandal
Hips a hand could
Span the meaure of.

5

To Gazelle Mask

Greetings, goat of the bush,
Full of the beans you have eaten,
An able man shoots—
Blood flows on the ground.
All eyes are upon you—
Hare stares
Turtledove watches.
Good bush, shake your legs
Good bush, shake your body.

6

Blindness

Morning darkness, evening darkness
Always, always.

7

Ogotemmeli

Flicks away rooted obstacles.

(Dogon)

DEATH RITES I

Leader:	The gates of Dan are shut.
Company:	Shut are the gates of Dan.
Leader:	The spirits of the dead flit hurrying there.
	Their crowd is like the flight of mosquitoes.
	The flight of mosquitoes which dance in the evening.
Company:	Which dance in the evening.
Leader:	The flight of mosquitoes which dance in the evening.
	When the night has turned completely black.
	When the sun has vanished.
	When the sun has turned completely black.
	The dance of the mosquitoes.
	The whirlwind of dead leaves.
	When the storm has growled.
Company:	When the storm has growled.
Leader:	They await him who will come.
Company:	Him who will come.
Leader:	Him who will say: You, come, you, go away!
Company:	Him who will say: Come, go!
Leader:	And Khvum will be with his children.
Company:	With his children.
All:	And this is the end.

DEATH RITES II

The animal runs, it passes, it dies. And it is the great cold.
It is the great cold of the night, it is the dark.
The bird flies, it passes, it dies. And it is the great cold.
It is the great cold of the night, it is the dark.
The fish flees, it passes, it dies. And it is the great cold.
It is the great cold of the night, it is the dark.
Man eats and sleeps. He dies. And it is the great cold.
It is the great cold of the night, it is the dark.
There is light in the sky, the eyes are extinguished, the star shines.
The cold is below, the light is on high.
The man has passed, the shade has vanished, the prisoner is free!

    Khvum, Khvum, come in answer to our call!

(Gabon Pygmy)

THE PRAISES OF THE FALLS

A bo phela a morapeli, Malaola
tse phelang le tse shoeleng.

He will live who knows how to
pray. Divining the things alive
& dead.

The Fall of the Little Creeper

(1)   is one called "rascal of the circle"

(2)   is a calf that doesn't frolic, doesn't come out of the village

(3)   then it frolics & goes back to its post

The Swimming of the Sunbird

(1)   Sunbird
        secret & daring

(2)   when you take up a piece of straw

(3)   & say you imitate the hammerhead

(4)   though nobody can imitate the hammerhead

(5)   bird
        of those who take new clothes
        into deep waters

(6)   you are taking up pieces of straw
        one by one

(7)   you build above pools

(8)   the little sunbird
        mustn't fall

(9)   that falls & goes *phususu*
        in the pool

(10)   the patient man
        is sitting on the drift

(11)   watching his sins pass by

(12)   & sees the river reed
mocking
the reed of the plain

(13)   it says:
when the grass is burning

(14)   the other one laughing also
saying:
when the river fills up

The Fall or Swimming of the Molele

(1)   of
mothers
of "give me some fat
to smear myself"

(2)   & fat to smear it on the road

(3)   to wait
a long time, not to
smear
if going to your husband

(4)   the smooth face of some monkey

(5)   & the space in front of him

(6)   those shining stones

The Swimming of the Red Sparrow

(1)   Red sparrow
never be a stranger

(2)   Stranger with stunted horns

(3)   & open guilt

(4)   This big turd was the stranger's

(5)   Our headsman's
turd
is such a
paltry thing

The Fall of Shaping the Hammer

(1)   some irons eating
                 some others
                 in the pincers

(2)   the positions of the bushmen's huts

(3)   the bushman's son
                 throwing
                 his arrow
                 is turning his back

(4)   & hits the eland in the udder

(5)   & these attract crowds
                 & are facing each other

(6)   one died at the drift

(7)   & one in the public places

(8)   take their hoes
                 & spades

(9)   let's bury the witchdoctors

Of the Witchdoctor Who Stopped the Pig by His Cleverness

(1)   The sky is eating
                 is whispering

(2)   & eating
                 it roots in the straw

(3)   that the asparagus may stay with its garbage

(4)   sky
                 of distant lands
                 & of the hearth

(5)   now that the sky has stopped
                 raining
                 joy, joy
                 cries the pig

(6)   & is an animal

that grows fat
in fair weather

The Masibo Plant of the Power

(1)   Who doesn't belong to the powerful
       doesn't grow from the power

(2)   This is the eland
       & the small antelope

(3)   & the beast with a mane

(4)   This eland has bewitched
       the eland of the shepherds

(5)   has arisen
       has taken a new skin

(6)   Does the cow suck power from her calf?

(7)   The woman sucks power from her child

The Famous Masibo of the Swimming

(1)   Swim on the deep waters
       lie upon them

(2)   who have no hippos & no little things

(3)   no beast of prey
       biting
       while it moves

(4)   & coiling itself in a corner

(5)   only the little hippos were swimming

(6)   the big ones
       never swim here anymore

(7)   Why are the crocodiles
       fighting in the water?

(8)   They are fighting for an old
       crocodile

(9)   for many talks in the water

(10)   which says: I do not

bite, I only
play
(11)   will bite some other year
(12)   when the mimosa
& the willow tree
are growing

The Fame of the Lamp
(1)   O mother elephant
(2)   O mother elephant, I'm going blind
(3)   O mother elephant, I came here in secret
(4)   O mother elephant, their road was red
(5)   O mother elephant, there was blood & disorder
(6)   O mother elephant, who shakes her ear
O running elephant

The Fame of the Creepers
(1)   This is the big creeper
(2)   whose leaves have fallen
(3)   We warm ourselves
at its embers
We use it again
(4)   You are light
the lamp
(5)   which says:
make light for us

poor people

The Appearance of the Orchis of the Basutos
(1)   of the children of one clan
(2)   & of one who distributes
posterity

(3)   & of the white calabash
for remembrance

(4)   & the distribution of meat

(5)   of sheep & of kids

(6)   of the springboks
bringing hunger
to our bellies

The Lamp of the Seers

(1)   The angry man
fights with his mother-in-law

(2)   What was the good of those lamps?

(3)   Seeing wonders
every morning

(4)   your sins passed by
& you saw them

(5)   & saw the child of a cow
& of a human being

(6)   saw them, could tell them
apart

from the entrails

The Rise of the Cobra

(1)   He fell on the rock
& lay down

(2)   but he got up with his luggage

(3)   got up & shook off
the dust

(4)   White head?
Wear ornaments

(5)   White hair is a sign

(6)   something

        the ancestors long for

(7)   fur from the head

        of a hare

        would make it

(8)   This is the last time

(Basuto)

IKA MEJI

Greetings for the sacrifice!
Now let us praise Ika Meji—
Can you see how Ifa came to this designation?
Up against the wall's no place
    to extend "long life!" to your elders;
Coming straight on,
    gazing vaguely away
    signifies a voracious visitor;
Might look as though I were up to no good,
    followed by all of you; stay home,
    said the snake to his hungry children

Made Ifa for Slim-pickings,
    stubby little fellow who will survive
    twenty thousand years in this world
    if he sacrifice
    ten pigeons, a scroungy cock, and ten bags of cowries.
He sacrificed, they made Ifa leaves for him,
    and he did not die—
    unlike the broom swept into a wisp,
    he stayed together
We have sacrificed efficaciously.

Now let's get on to row two:
King of the counting house

don't count me
Turn around, misery,
count me out;
Snake-eyes,
if we're being counted,
why'd ya call me?
Accountable for no-account?
No one's seen me sin;
no wickedness on me.
Mother counts the baskets
Father counts the bins
One by one they counted us down,
but we fixed them.
Ifa, hearing this:
How is it all of you who live
in this rickety town
have icky names?
'Cause hicks are what we called ourselves
till you hit the scene.
So that's the reason, Ifa said,
All your lives you've been higgledy-piggledy, sick, sick, sick,
like housewives rushing before the storm
picking laundry off limbs.
Now go distribute money to snails,
for it's their shells that spiral in—
like Mother Yemoja making medicine
with viper's head. You dig?
She covered herself with prickly cloth;
and when this hedgehog edged over to sit
beside her victim, they said:
Go feed grass to *that* horse
standing by the corn bin.
When hedgehog hit

it was beancake-vendor
fell down dead.
Now snail turned gravedigger;
viper mourned the death
of beancake-vendor.

Creeping snail upon snail
adds insult to injury;
If witch's snare can't smell the entrance,
snail within will survive forever.
Will dog bite the heel of bush cow?
Never! We sneaked out of the way
to our rickety town
early in the morning.

Trading for years and nothing to show for it
    called on
Axe strikes tree, definitively,
    diviner of the house of Orunmila.
Secret arrived on foot,
    blessed the rackety-packety inhabitants of Ika;
and when he had done,
we praised the diviner, saying:
Secret said I will have money,
    and here is money.
Axe strikes tree, definitively,
    as blade's edge
    is the tongue of secrets.
Diviner says I will have a wife—
    Here she is.
Axe strikes tree
    Power sits
    in the mouth
    of Ifa

Diviner says I will have offspring—
    Here are children.
    His tongue speaks
    with authority:
Diviner says I will build me a house—
    See, over there—
    Secret's spit is commanding.
Diviner says I will see good things—
    There they are, everywhere, everything—
    Energy fills the speech of diviner.
Then he started singing:

Spiky fingers	*grip iniquity*
Aka leaves	*bind hands of mine enemy*

Reverse wickedness!

Close their hands	*globe, peel, pound, knead*
Till there's no remainder!	
May they die young!	
Spiny cloth	*slim leaves*
bend and twist	*till there be*
no vise in	*hostility*

So be it!

Greetings! May our sacrifice see us through this thicket.

(Yoruba)

LITTLE LEPER OF MUNJOLÓBO
(as told by Mā Kelezensia Kahamba)

I give you a story.
AUDIENCE: I give you another.
I came and I saw.
AUDIENCE: See so that we may see.

oo

N-o-w
    there was a girl.
THE GIRL WAS B-E-A-U-T-I-F-U-L.
SHE WAS BEAUTIFUL.
Now men continually come to court her, but
    she refuses . . .
                They come to court.
She refuses . . .
                They come to court. She refuses . . .
Eh-Eh! The chief s-a-y-s,
              "I'll go and court her myself."

o

The chief chooses and chooses men
                and sends them.

o

They go, but she says, "No."
EH! HE PICKS OUT ONE HANDSOME MAN, HAS HIM RUBBED WITH
    BUTTERFAT, DRESSES HIM IN BEAUTIFUL CLOTHES OF GOLD.
    NO!
He goes to arrange a marriage and she refuses.

o

Then there volunteered a short man who was LEPROUS.
He had contracted leprosy.
THE LITTLE ONE HAD BECOME ALL DRY AND HARD.
He says, "I'm going to search for her."
They say, "You, Little Leper, you?
You go and bring the girl?"
He says, "I'll bring her."

o

Mh! He takes out a leather cape. He takes out butterfat and he
     annoints himself. He dresses.
Just like that.
                    He goes.

o

He goes and finds the g-i-r-l.
She's there in the entrance to her h-o-u-s-e.
She's weaving a basket.

o

He says to her,
"The chief has sent me to you."
                              She says, "You?
To you, to you I say never."

o

As she's weaving the basket,
                         he jumps up and snatches her
     empindwi.
She's using it to weave the basket.

o

He runs and reaches the courtyard.
"Little Leper, Little Leper of Munjolóbo,
give me my *empindwi*."
He says,
(sings)   "Beautiful soft grass of the palace,
                 Here, take your *empindwi*.
                 Beautiful young calf of the palace,
                 Here, take your *empindwi*."

o

(Narrator's aside: Look at the cooking pot, Benja.)
                 "Beautiful young calf of the palace,
                 Here take your *empindwi*."
(sings)   "Little Leper, Little Leper of Munjoló—"
That's the girl.
(sings)   "Little Leper, Little Leper of Munjolóbo,
                 You don't give me my *empindwi*."
                 "Mother, fertile piece of land,
                 Here, take your *empindwi*.
                 Beautiful soft grass of the palace,
                 Here, take your *empindwi*."
                 "Little Leper, Little Leper of Munjolóbo,
                 You don't give me—"
NOW, THEN
        THEY LEAVE THERE
and go for about two hours.

o

THE GIRL . . .
        followed the Little Leper.
                        HE TOOK

HER *EMPINDWI*
AND IS RUNNING
to take her to the chief.

o

EH-Eh!
They're moving along.
They go for about six hours.
THEN THE GIRL . . . .
     doesn't know the way back.
NOW THAT LITTLE LEPER . . .
is running on the way to the palace
to take her to the chief.
     AND THE *EMPINDWI,*
he's taken it.
Eh-Eh! They move along. They go and stop, stop and go,
  bit by bit.
THEN THE GIRL . . .
has begun to cry.
She tries again:
    "Little Leper, Little Leper of Munjolóbo,
    You don't give me my *empindwi.*"
    "Beautiful farmland of the palace,
    Here, take your *empindwi.*
    Beautiful young calf of the palace,
    Here, take your *empindwi.*"
EH-EH!
THEY MOVE ALONG. They go on for about nine hours.

o

THEN THE GIRL . . .
     has begun to cry.
All that's left is a j-o-u-r-n-e-y . . .
       of about half an hour

to reach the palace.
Then the palace residents . . .

> go outside.

> > They say, "Chief,"

> > > they

s-a-y,
"The Little Leper has brought the woman."

> > > Eh-Eh!

The one who said this first,
the chief cuts him down.
He takes out a machete
AND CUTS HIM DOWN.
EH-EH!
THE SECOND ONE SAYS,
"MY LORD,

> DON'T KILL PEOPLE.

THE LITTLE LEPER HAS BROUGHT THE WOMAN."

o

EH-EH! HE SAYS, "KILL HIM ALSO."
THEY CUT HIM DOWN TOO,
WITH A MACHETE.
MH-MH!

o

THEN THE TWO OF THEM

> > go and stop, stop and go, bit

> by bit. There's only a half hour to go.
WHEN THEY APPROACHED CLOSE BY THE PALACE,
THEN THE GIRL BEGAN TO CRY . . .
THAT LITTLE LEPER

> > was running ahead with her *empindwi*,
JUMPING UP AND RUNNING AHEAD,
JUMPING UP

AND RUNNING AHEAD.
EH-EH!
> *The one who raced out of the palace this time was a royal*
> *adviser, a favorite of the chief.*

He says, "I'll go and tell the chief."
He says, "My Lord,
stop killing people."
He says, "THE LITTLE LEPER HAS BROUGHT
THE WOMAN."
Eh-Eh! They leave the house.
They take our beautiful clothes of GOLD . . .
THEY GO AND DRESS HER . . .
THEY PICK HER UP . . .
THEY PUT HER ON THEIR SHOULDERS . . .
AUTOMOBILES . . .
BUSES . . .
THE KING'S DRUMS SOUND . . .
CANNON . . .
They bring her into the house.
As for the Little Leper . . .
the chief gives him cattle.
He presents him with a maidservant.
He presents him with a manservant.
When I saw them giving him a manservant,

giving him

a maidservant,

and he himself eating plantains,

o

I left there . . .

o

I said, "Let me go and report."

o

It's done.

(Haya)

THE VOICE OF THE KARAW

(1)

Bursts of twilight's frantic wing-beats, submit to me, I am Yori
I am as the arching sky, as encounter of crossroads in space
Green savanna, entirely fresh, green savanna entirely outstretched
    where no dog may scavenge
Hornbill of deaf-mute village I am deaf-mute chief.
What sort of a thing is this? *Come, old tearers-to-shreds, submit to me, I*
    am Yori.
Astonishing! What we are learning now existed already, arriving from
    beforehand: rhythm
I entered the flow and found it was transformation—
Rhythm, beginning of all beginning speech, was the crowned crane's:
    I speak, said the crowned crane,
    meaning I know I speak.
Oh, if I here misspeak, may heat of error be sufficient
    to pardon my mistakes;
If I omit, may omission be forgiven that anticipates!
Old knives, having been sheathed, cannot transpierce the mystery—
    come, old tearers-to-shreds, submit to me,
    I am Yori
I am as the arching sky, as encounter of crossroads in space,
I am as the unique sun!
Cock's head of night's transformation, Father of my instruction,
    see, my arm is bent behind my back as you wish;
Memory itself is to blame for all mistakes,
    memory which makes me stumble, if I do
As for oblivion—blame inattention of spirit;
Perhaps a running knot will form along the cord of my speech;
    but all cords are corridors leading to embrace
And all antechambers lead to our common origin: Mande
All having derives from another's possession

To have you come, you arrive by means of instruction;
Transformation, where true possession takes place,
    even moderate insight
    anticipates penetration.
His word has been translated exactly!
Transformation, all transformation, man's furnace,
    crucible of patience,
    I say all waiting is pure patience
If these words be spoken at the crossroads of space!

(2)

Be at peace, old tearers-to-shreds, here am I, Yori,
As handle of spear I am, as the arching sky
I am as the unique sun,
You there, slapping the face of twilight,
    calm yourselves; here am I, Yori,
I as the arching sky, I as the unique sun
Deaf-mute hornbill, fire which spared the bone,
    chief of deaf-mute village,
I say mumble mumble, I say caw-caw the cacophonous,
Sheathed, sheathed are the old knives. Yori, my father,
    Yori, my mother, Yori, my ancestor,
    I have gone to question our founder.
The old man as if seized by uncontrollable itching
    scratches his head; thoughtfully rotates his jaw
    as if pestered by a piece of gristle;
    then hastens to Ségou to consult the sages;
For some things may be found in the enemy's house
    that the friend's house lacks;
    and that which is lacking makes enemies friends;
Founder, my father, my friend, exacerbation of questing

is calmed within; there the true task begins;
    but transformation is arduous, arduous.
Come, what we are learning now existed already;
    let us accomplish the rhythm;
All cords are corridors leading to embrace of origin.

                                        (Bamana)

GASSIRE'S LUTE

Four times Wagadu stood there in all her splendor. Four times Wagadu disappeared and was lost to human sight: once through vanity, once through falsehood, once through greed, and once through dissension. Four times Wagadu changed her name. First she was called Dierra, then Agada, then Ganna, then Silla. Four times she turned her face. Once to the north, once to the west, once to the east, and once to the south. For Wagadu, whenever men have seen her, has always had four gates: one to the north, one to the west, one to the east, and one to the south. Those are the directions whence the strength of Wagadu comes, the strength in which she endures no matter whether she be built of stone, wood, and earth or lives but as a shadow in the mind and longing of her children. For really, Wagadu is not of stone, not of wood, not of earth. Wagadu is the strength that lives in the hearts of men and is sometimes visible because eyes see her and ears hear the clash of swords and ring of shields, and is sometimes invisible because the indomitability of men has overtired her, so that she sleeps. Sleep came to Wagadu for the first time through vanity, for the second time through falsehood, for the third time through greed, and for the fourth time through dissension. Should Wagadu ever be found for the fourth time, then she will live so forcefully in the minds of men that she will never be lost again, so forcefully that vanity, falsehood, greed, and dissension will never be able to harm her.

Hoooh! Dierra, Agada, Ganna, Silla! Hoooh! Fasa!

Every time that the guilt of man caused Wagadu to disappear she won a new beauty which made the splendor of her next appearance still more glorious. Vanity brought the song of the bards which all peoples (of the Sudan) imitate and value today. Falsehood brought a rain of gold and pearls. Greed brought writing as the Burdama still practice it today and which in Wagadu was the business of the women.

Dissension will enable the fifth Wagadu to be as enduring as the rain of the south and as the rocks of the Sahara, for every man will then have Wagadu in his heart and every woman a Wagadu in her womb.

Hoooh! Dierra, Agada, Ganna, Silla! Hoooh! Fasa!

Wagadu was lost for the first time through vanity. At that time Wagadu faced north and was called Dierra. Her last king was called Nganamba Fasa. The Fasa were strong. But the Fasa were growing old. Daily they fought against the Burdama and the Boroma. They fought every day and every month. Never was there an end to the fighting. And out of the fighting the strength of the Fasa grew. All Nganamba's men were heroes, all the women were lovely and proud of the strength and the heroism of the men of Wagadu.

All the Fasa who had not fallen in single combat with the Burdama were growing old. Nganamba was very old. Nganamba had a son, Gassire, and he was old enough, for he already had eight grown sons with children of their own. They were all living and Nganamba ruled in his family and reigned as a king over the Fasa and the doglike Boroma. Nganamba grew so old that Wagadu was lost because of him and the Boroma became slaves again to the Burdama who seized power with the sword. Had Nganamba died earlier would Wagadu then have disappeared for the first time?

Hoooh! Dierra, Agada, Ganna, Silla! Hoooh! Fasa!

Nganamba did not die. A jackal gnawed at Gassire's heart. Daily Gassire asked his heart: "When will Nganamba die? When will Gassire be king?" Every day Gassire watched for the death of his father as a lover watches for the evening star to rise. By day, when Gassire fought as a hero against the Burdama and drove the false Boroma before him with a leather girth, he thought only of the fighting, of his sword, of his shield, of his horse. By night, when he rode with the evening into the city and sat in the circle of men and his sons, Gassire heard how the heroes praised his deeds. But his heart was not in the talking; his heart listened for the strains of Nganamba's breathing; his heart was full of misery and longing.

Gassire's heart was full of longing for the shield of his father, the shield which he could carry only when his father was dead, and also for the sword which he might draw only when he was king. Day by day Gassire's rage and longing grew. Sleep passed him by. Gassire lay, and a jackal gnawed at his heart. Gassire felt the misery climbing into his throat. One night Gassire sprang out of bed, left the house and went to an old wise man, a man who knew more than other people. He entered the wise man's house and asked: "Kiekorro! When will my father, Nganamba, die and leave me his sword and shield?" The old man said: "Ah, Gassire, Nganamba will die; but he will not leave you his sword and shield! You will carry a lute. Shield and sword shall others inherit. But your lute shall cause the loss of Wagadu! Ah, Gassire!" Gassire said: "Kiekorro, you lie! I see that you are not wise. How can Wagadu be lost when her heroes triumph daily? Kiekorro, you are a fool!" The old wise man said: "Ah, Gassire, you cannot believe me. But your path will lead you to the partridges in the fields and you will understand what they say and that will be your way and the way of Wagadu."
Hoooh! Dierra, Agada, Ganna, Silla! Hoooh! Fasa!

The next morning Gassire went with the heroes again to do battle against the Burdama. Gassire was angry. Gassire called to the heroes: "Stay here behind. Today I will battle with the Burdama alone." The heroes stayed behind and Gassire went on alone to do battle with the Burdama. Gassire hurled his spear. Gassire charged the Burdama. Gassire swung his sword. He struck home to the right, he struck home to the left. Gassire's sword was as a sickle in the wheat. The Burdama were afraid. Shocked, they cried: "That is no Fasa, that is no hero, that is a Damo [a being unknown to the singer himself]." The Burdama turned their horses. The Burdama threw away their spears, each man his two spears, and fled. Gassire called the knights. Gassire said: "Gather the spears." The knights gathered the spears. The knights sang: "The Fasa are heroes. Gassire has always been the Fasa's greatest hero. Gassire has always done great deeds. But today Gassire was greater than Gassire!" Gassire rode into the city and the heroes rode behind him. The heroes sang: "Never before has Wagadu won so many spears as today."

Gassire let the women bathe him. The men gathered. But Gassire did not seat himself in their circle. Gassire went into the fields. Gassire heard the partridges. Gassire went close to them. A partridge sat under a bush and sang: "Hear the *Dausi!* Hear my deeds!" The partridge sang of its battle with the snake. The partridge sang: "All creatures must die, be buried and rot. Kings and heroes die, are buried and rot. I, too, shall die, shall be buried and rot. But the *Dausi*, the song of my battles, shall not die. It shall be sung again and again and shall outlive all kings and heroes. Hoooh, that I might do such deeds! Hoooh, that I may sing the *Dausi!* Wagadu will be lost. But the *Dausi* shall endure and shall live!"

Hoooh! Dierra, Agada, Ganna, Silla! Hoooh! Fasa!

Gassire went to the old wise man. Gassire said: "Kiekorro! I was in the fields. I understood the partridges. The partridge boasted that the song of its deeds would live longer than Wagadu. The partridge sang the *Dausi*. Tell me whether men also know the *Dausi* and whether the *Dausi* can outlive life and death?" The old wise man said: "Gassire, you are hastening to your end. No one can stop you. And since you cannot be a king you shall be a bard. Ah! Gassire. When the kings of the Fasa lived by the sea they were also great heroes and they fought with men who had lutes and sang the *Dausi*. Oft struck the enemy *Dausi* fear into the hearts of the Fasa, who were themselves heroes. But they never sang the *Dausi* because they were of the first rank, of the Horro, and because the *Dausi* was only sung by those of the second rank, of the Diare. The Diare fought not so much as heroes for the sport of the day but as drinkers for the fame of the evening. But you, Gassire, now that you can no longer be the second of the first [i.e., King], shall be the first of the second. And Wagadu will be lost because of it." Gassire said: "Wagadu can go to blazes!"

Hoooh! Dierra, Agada, Ganna, Silla! Hoooh! Fasa!

Gassire went to a smith. Gassire said: "Make me a lute." The smith said: "I will, but the lute will not sing." Gassire said: "Smith, do your work. The rest is my affair." The smith made the lute. The smith brought the lute to Gassire. Gassire struck on the lute. The lute did not sing. Gassire said: "Look here, the lute does not sing." The smith said: "That's what I told you in the first place." Gassire said: "Well, make it sing." The smith said: "I cannot do anything more about it. The rest is your affair." Gassire said: "What can I do, then?" The smith said: "This is a piece of wood. It cannot sing if it has no heart. You must give it a heart. Carry this piece of wood on your back when you go into battle. The wood must ring with the stroke of your sword. The wood must absorb down-dripping blood, blood of your blood, breath of your breath. Your pain must be its pain, your fame its fame. The wood may no longer be like the wood of a tree, but must be penetrated by and be a part of your people. Therefore it must live not only with you but with your sons. Then will the tone that comes from your heart echo in the ear of your son and live on in the people, and your son's life's blood, oozing out of his heart, will run down your body and live on in this piece of wood. But Wagadu will be lost because of it." Gassire said: "Wagadu can go to blazes!"

Hoooh! Dierra, Agada, Ganna, Silla! Hoooh! Fasa!

Gassire called his eight sons. Gassire said: "My sons, today we go to battle. But the strokes of our swords shall echo no longer in the Sahel alone, but shall retain their ring for the ages. You and I, my sons, will that we live on and endure before all other heroes in the *Dausi*. My oldest son, today we two, thou and I, will be the first in battle!"

Gassire and his eldest son went into the battle ahead of the heroes. Gassire had thrown the lute over his shoulder. The Burdama came closer. Gassire and his eldest son charged. Gassire and his eldest son fought as the first. Gassire and his eldest son left the other heroes far behind them. Gassire fought not like a human being, but rather like a Damo. His eldest son fought not like a human being, but like a Damo. Gassire came into a tussle with eight Burdama. The eight Burdama pressed him hard. His son came to help him and struck four of them down. But one of the Burdama thrust a spear through his heart. Gassire's eldest son fell dead from his horse. Gassire was angry. And shouted. The Burdama fled. Gassire dismounted and took the body of his eldest son upon his back. Then he mounted and rode slowly back to the other heroes. The eldest son's heart's blood dropped on the lute which was also hanging on Gassire's back. And so Gassire, at the head of his heroes, rode into Dierra.

Hoooh! Dierra, Agada, Ganna, Silla! Hoooh! Fasa!

Gassire's eldest son was buried. Dierra mourned. The urn in which the body crouched was red with blood. That night Gassire took his lute and struck against the wood. The lute did not sing. Gassire was angry. He called his sons. Gassire said to his sons: "Tomorrow we ride against the Burdama."

For seven days Gassire rode with the heroes to battle. Every day one of his sons accompanied him to be the first in the fighting. And on every one of these days Gassire carried the body of one of his sons, over his shoulder and over the lute, back into the city. And thus, on every evening, the blood of one of his sons dripped on to the lute. After the seven days of fighting there was a great mourning in Dierra. All the heroes and all the women wore red and white clothes. The blood of the Boroma (in sacrifice) flowed everywhere. All the women wailed. All the men were angry. Before the eighth day of the fighting all the heroes and the men of Dierra gathered and spoke to Gassire: "Gassire, this shall have an end. We are willing to fight when it is necessary. But you, in your rage, go on fighting without sense or limit. Now go forth from Dierra! A few will join you and accompany you. Take your Boroma and your cattle. The rest of us incline more to life than fame. And while we do not wish to die fameless we have no wish to die for fame alone."

The old wise man said: "Ah, Gassire! Thus will Wagadu be lost today for the first time."

Hoooh! Dierra, Agada, Ganna, Silla! Hoooh! Fasa!

Gassire and his last, his youngest, son, his wives, his friends and his Boroma rode out into the desert. They rode through the Sahel. Many heroes rode with Gassire through the gates of the city. Many turned. A few accompanied Gassire and his youngest son into the Sahara.

They rode far: day and night. They came into the wilderness and in the loneliness they rested. All the heroes and all the women and all the Boroma slept. Gassire's youngest son slept. Gassire was restive. He sat by the fire. He sat there long. Presently he slept. Suddenly he jumped up. Gassire listened. Close beside him Gassire heard a voice. It rang as though it came from himself. Gassire began to tremble. He heard the lute singing. The lute sang the *Dausi*.

When the lute had sung the *Dausi* for the first time, King Nganamba died in the city Dierra; when the lute had sung the *Dausi* for the first time, Gassire's rage melted; Gassire wept. When the lute had sung the *Dausi* for the first time, Wagadu disappeared—for the first time.

Hoooh! Dierra, Agada, Ganna, Silla! Hoooh! Fasa!

Four times Wagadu stood there in all her splendor. Four times Wagadu disappeared and was lost to human sight: once through vanity, once through falsehood, once through greed, and once through dissension. Four times Wagadu changed her name. First she was called Dierra, then Agada, then Ganna, then Silla. Four times she turned her face. Once to the north, once to the west, once to the east, and once to the south. For Wagadu, whenever men have seen her, has always had four gates: one to the north, one to the west, one to the east, and one to the south. Those are the directions whence the strength of Wagadu comes, the strength in which she endures no matter whether she be built of stone, wood, or earth or lives but as a shadow in the mind and longing of her children. For, really, Wagadu is not of stone, not of wood, not of earth. Wagadu is the strength which lives in the hearts of men and is sometimes visible because eyes see her and ears hear the clash of swords and ring of shields, and is sometimes invisible because the indomitability of men has overtired her, so that she sleeps. Sleep came to Wagadu for the first time through vanity, for the second time through falsehood, for the third time through greed, and for the fourth time through dissension. Should Wagadu ever be found for the fourth time, then she will live so forcefully in the minds of men that she will never be lost again, so forcefully that vanity, falsehood, greed, and dissension will never be able to harm her.

Hoooh! Dierra, Agada, Ganna, Silla! Hoooh! Fasa!

Every time that the guilt of man caused Wagadu to disappear she won a new beauty which made the splendor of her next appearance still more glorious. Vanity brought the song of the bards which all peoples imitate and value today. Falsehood brought a rain of gold and pearls. Greed brought writing as the Burdama still practice it today and which in Wagadu was the business of the women. Dissension will enable the fifth Wagadu to be as enduring as the rain of the south and as the rocks of the Sahara, for every man will then have Wagadu in his heart and every woman a Wagadu in her womb.

Hoooh! Dierra, Agada, Ganna, Silla! Hoooh! Fasa!

(Soninke)

AMERICA

MIDĒ SONGS & PICTURE-SONGS

An Imploration for Clear Weather

I swing the spirit like a child

The sky is what I was telling you about

We have lost the sky

I am helping you

Have I made an error?

(Silence)

I am using my heart

What are you saying to me & am I in-my-senses?

The spirit wolf

I didn't know where I was going

I depend on the clear sky

I give you the-other-village, spirit that you are

The thunder is heavy

We are talking to each other

(Ojibwa)

SEVEN CHIPPEWA (OJIBWA) SONGS

I

a loon
I thought it was
but it was
my love's
splashing oar

—by *Mary English*

2

(a death song)

large bear
deceives me

—by *Gawitayac*

3

the odor of death
I discern the odor of death
in front of my body

—by *Namebines*

4

(a war song)

in the coming heat
of the day
I stood there

—by *Memengwa*

5

as my eyes
search
the prairie
I feel the summer in the spring

—by *Ajidegijig*

6

(a death song)

whenever I pause
the noise
of the village

—by *Kimiwun*

7

(song of the game of silence)

it is hanging
in the edge of sunshine
it is a pig I see
with its double hoofs
it is a very fat pig
the people who live in a hollow tree
are fighting
they are fighting bloodily
he is rich
he will carry a pack toward the great
    water

—by *John W. Carl (Mejakigijig)*

From *THE WISHING BONE CYCLE*

(by Jacob Nibenegenesabe)

1

I try to make wishes right
but sometimes it doesn't work.
Once, I wished a tree upside down
and its branches
were where the roots should have been!
The squirrels had to ask the moles
"How do we get down there
to get home?"
One time it happened that way.
Then there was the time, I remember now,
I wished a man upside down
and his feet were where his hands
should have been!
In the morning his shoes
had to ask the birds
"How do we fly up there
to get home?"
One time it happened that way.

2

There was an old woman I wished up.
She was the wife
of an old pond.
You could watch her swim in her husband
if you were
in the hiding bushes.
She spoke to him by the way she swam
gently.

One time in their lives there was no rain
and the sun began making the pond smaller.
Soon the sun took the whole pond!
For many nights the old woman slept
near the hole where her husband once lived.
Then, one night, a storm came
but in the morning there still was no water
in her husband's old house.
So she set out on a journey to find her husband
and followed the puddles on the ground
which were the storm's footprints.
She followed them for many miles.
Finally she came upon her husband
sitting in a hole. But he was in the wrong hole!
So the old woman brought her husband home
little by little in her hands.
You could have seen him come home
if you were
in the hiding bushes.

3

Once I wished up a coat
wearing a man inside.
The man was sleeping
and when he woke
the coat was on him!
This was in summer, so many asked him
"Why do you have that coat on?"
"It has me in it!"
he would answer.
He tried to take it off
but I wished his memory shivering with cold
so it wouldn't want to remember

how to take a coat off.
That way it would stay warm.
I congratulated myself on thinking of that.
Then his friends came,
put coats on,
and slowly showed him how they took coats off.
Even that didn't work.
Things were getting interesting.
Then his friends
tried to confuse the coat
into thinking it was a man.
"Good morning," they said to it,
"Did you get
your share of fish?"
and other things too.
Some even invited the coat to gossip.
It got to be late summer
and someone said to the coat
"It is getting colder.
You better go out
and find a coat to wear."
The coat agreed!

Ha! I was too busy laughing
to stop that dumb coat
from leaving the man it wore
inside.
I didn't care.
I went following the coat.
Things were getting interesting.

(Swampy Cree)

THREE TETON SIOUX SONGS

1

owls
(were) hooting
in the passing of the night
owls
(were) hooting

—by *Brave Buffalo*

2

from everywhere
they come
flying
(from) the north
the wind is blowing
to earth
rattling
flying
they come
they come
from everywhere
they come

—by *Bear Necklace*

3

today
is mine (I claimed)
(to) a man
a voice
I sent

you grant me
this day
is mine (I claimed)
(to) a man
a voice
I sent
now
here
(he) is

—by *Shell Necklace*

From
BATTISTE GOOD'S WINTER COUNT

1794–'95 Killed-the-little-faced-Pawnee winter

1795–'96 The-Rees-stood-the-frozen-man-up-with-the-buffalo-stomach-in-his-hand winter

1796–'97 Wears-the-War-Bonnet-died winter

1797–'98 Took-the-God-Woman-captive winter

 1798–'99 Many-women-died-in-childbirth winter

 1799–1800 Don't-Eat-Buffalo-Heart-made-a-
commemoration-of-the-dead
winter

 1800–'01 The-Good-White-Man-came winter

 1801–'02 Smallpox-used-them-up-again winter

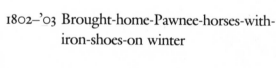 1802–'03 Brought-home-Pawnee-horses-with-
iron-shoes-on winter

1803–'04 Brought-home-Pawnee-horses-with-
them winter

1804–'05 Sung-over-each-other-while-on-the-
warpath winter

(Dakota)

PEYOTE SONGS

1 It has a red flower, it has power.
2 Daylight. Red flower.
3 It moves along.
4 Yellow.
5 Dawn rays are standing.
6 Power is flying.
7 Bird.

1 Horse is coming down.
2 Move into line, it's daylight.
3 Male antelopes, breeding.
4 Bird is circling, crying out.
5 Hell-diver's circling, crying out.
6 Bird getting ready to fly.
7 Beaver, it's dawn.

(Comanche)

SONG OF THE HUMPBACKED FLUTE PLAYER

Kitana-po, ki-tana-po, ki-tana-po,
 ki-tana-PO!
Ai-na, ki-na-weh, ki-na-weh
Chi-li li-cha, chi-li li-cha
Don-ka-va-ki, mas-i-ki-va-ki
Ki-ve, ki-ve-na-meh
HOPET!

(Hopi)

COYOTE & JUNCO
(by Andrew Peynetsa)

SON'AHCHI.
  SONTI^{LO}———NG A$_{GO}$

AT STANDING ARROWS
OLD LADY JUNCO HAD HER HOME
and COYOTE
Coyote was there at Sitting Rock with his children.
He was with his children
and Old Lady Junco
was winnowing.
Pigweed
and tumbleweed, she was winnowing these.
With her basket
she winnowed these by tossing them in the air.
She was tossing them in the air
    while Coyote
Coyote
was going around hunting, going around hunting for his children
    there
when he came to where Junco was winnowing.
"What are you DOING?" that's what he asked her. "Well, I'm winnow-
    ing," she said.
"What are you winnowing?" he said. "Well

pigweed and tumbleweed"
    that's what she told him.
    "Indeed.

What's that you're saying?" "Well, this is
    my winnowing song," she said.
"NOW SING IT FOR ME
so that I
may sing it for my children," he said.
Old Lady Junco
sang for Coyote:

    YUUWA HINA YUUWA HINA
    YUUWA HINA YUUWA HINA
      YU HINA YU HINA

    (*blowing*) PFFF PFFF
      YU HINA YU HINA

    (*blowing*) PFFF PFFF

That's what she said.
"YES, NOW I
can go, I'll sing it to my children."
Coyote went on to Oak Arroyo, and when he got there MOURNING
    DOVES FLEW UP
and he lost his song.
He went back:
(*muttering*) "Quick! sing for me, some mourning doves made me
lose my song," he said.
Again she sang for him.
He learned the song and went on.
He went through a field there
and broke through a gopher hole.
Again he lost his song.
Again, he came for the third time
to ask for it.
Again she sang for him.
He went on for the third time, and when he came to Oak Arroyo
BLACKBIRDS FLEW UP and again he lost his song.
He was coming for the fourth time

when Old Lady Junco said to herself, (*tight*) "Oh here you come

but I won't sing," that's what she said.

She looked for a round rock.

When she found a round rock, she

dressed it with her Junco shirt, she put her basket of seeds with the
 Junco rock.

(*tight*) "As for you, go right ahead and ask."

Junco went inside her house.

Coyote was coming for the fourth time.

When he came:

"Quick! sing it for me, I lost the song again, come on," that's what he
 told her.

Junco said nothing.

"Quick!" that's what he told her, but she didn't speak.

"ONE," he said.

"The fourth time I

speak, if you haven't sung, I'll bite you," that's what he told her.

o

"Second time, TWO," he said.

"Quick sing for me," he said.

She didn't sing. "THREE. I'll count ONCE MORE," he said.

o

Coyote said, "QUICK SING," that's what he told her.

She didn't sing.

Junco had left her shirt for Coyote.

He bit the Junco, CRUNCH, he bit the round rock.

Right here (*points to molars*) he knocked out the teeth, the rows of
 teeth in back.

(*tight*) "So now I've really done it to you." "AY! AY!"

that's what he said.

THE PRAIRIE WOLF WENT BACK TO HIS CHILDREN,

and by the time he got back there his children were dead.
Because this was lived long ago, Coyote has no teeth here
(*points to molars*). LEE————SEMKONIKYA. (*laughs*)

(Zuni)

THE TENTH HORSE SONG OF FRANK MITCHELL

Key: wnn Ngahn n NNN

Go to her my son N wnn & go to her my son N wnn N wnnn N nnnn
    N gahn
Go to her my son N wnn & go to her my son N wnn N wnnn N nnnn
    N gahn

Because I was thnboyngnng raised ing the dawn NwnnN go to her my
    son N wnn N wnn N nnnn N gahn
& leafing from thuhuhuh house the bluestone home N gahn N wnn N
    go to her my son N wnn N wnn N nnnn N gahn
& leafing from the (rurur) house the shining home NwnnnN go to her
    my son N wnn N wnn N nnnn N gahn
& leafing from thm(mm) (mm) swollen house my breath has blown
    NwnnN go to her my son N wnn N wnn N nnnn N gahn
& leafing from thnn house the holy home NwnnN go to her my son N
    wnnn N wnn () nnnn N gahn
& from the house hfff precious cloth we walk upon N wnn N nnnn N
    go to her my son N wnn N wnn N nnnn N gahn
with (p)(p)rayersticks that are blue NwnnN go to her my son N wnn
    N wnn N nnnn N gahn
with my feathers that're blue NwnnN go to her my son N wnn N wnn
    N nnnn N gahn
with my spirit horses that're blue NwnnN go to her my son N wnn N
    wnn () nnnn N gahn
with my spirit horses that're blue & dawn & wnnN go to her my son N
    wnn N wnn N nnnn N gahn
with my spirit horses that rrr bluestone & Rwnn N wnn N go to her
    my son N wnn N wnn N nnnn N gahn
with my horses that hrrr bluestone & rrwnn N wnn N go to her my

son N wnn N wnn N nnnn N gahn
with cloth of evree(ee)ee kind to draw (nn nn) them on & on N wnn N
    go to her my son N wnn N wnn N nnnn N gahn
with jewels of evree(ee)ee kind to draw (nn nn) them on & wnn N go
    to her my son N wnn N wnn N nnnn N gahn
with horses of evree(ee)ee kind to draw (nn nn) them on N wnn N go
    to her my son N wnn N wnn N nnnn N gahn
with sheep of ever(ee)ee kind to draw (nn nn) them on N wnn N go to
    her my son N wnn N wnn N nnnn N gahn
with cattle of evree(ee)ee kind to draw (nn nn) them on N wnn N go
    to her my son N wnn N wnn N nnnn N gahn
with men of ever(ee)ee kind to lead & draw (nn nn) them on N wnn
    N go to her my son N wnn N wnn N nnnn N gahn
from my house of precious cloth to her backackeroom N gahn N wnn
    N go to her my son N wnn N wnn N nnnn N gahn
in her house of precious cloth we walk (p)pon N wnn N gahn N go
    to her my son N wnn N wnn N nnnn N gahn
vvvveverything that's gone befffore & more we walk upon N wnn N
    go to her my son N wnn N wnn N nnnn N gahn
& everything thadz more & won't be(be)be poor N gahn N go to her
    my son N wnn N wnn N nnnn N gahn
& everything thadz living to be old & blesst N wnn then go to her my
    son N wnn N wnn N nnnn N gahn
(a)cause I am thm boy who blisses/blesses to be old N gahn N nnnn
    N go to her my son N wnn N wnn N nnnn N gahn

Go to her my son N wnnn N go to her my son N wnn N wnnn N nnnn
    N gahn
Go to her my son N wnnn N go to her my son N wnn N wnnn N nnnn
    N gahn

(Navajo)

A SONG OF THE WINDS

(by Santo Blanco)

Below the sea there is the mouth of a cave
In which all the winds are born.
He comes below the sea and mounts up
To where there is no sun.
But the cave is light, like the sun.

Another mouth is smooth and slippery
and hard, like ice.
He stands erect with his arms outstretched
and from each finger there comes a wind.

First he blows the White Wind
then he blows the Red Wind
then he blows the Blue Wind.
And from his little finger
he blows the Black Wind,
which is stronger than them all.

The White Wind comes from the north
and is very hot.
Blue comes from the south.
The Red Wind comes from the west
In the middle of the day, and is soft.
The Black Wind comes from beyond the mountains
and is strongest of them all.
The whirlwind comes from the east.

(Seri)

SIX SERI WHALE SONGS
(by Santo Blanco)

I

The sea is calm
there is no wind.
In the warm sun
I play on the surface
with many companions.
In the air spout
many clouds of smoke
and all of them are happy.

2

The mother whale is happy.
She swims on the surface, very fast.
No shark is near
but she swims over many leagues
back and forth, very fast.
Then she sinks to the bottom
and four baby whales are born.

3

First one comes up to the surface
in front of her nose.
He jumps on the surface.
Then each of the other baby whales
jumps on the surface.
Then they go down
into the deep water to their mother
and stay there eight days
before they come up again.

4

The old, old whale has no children.
She does not swim far.
She floats near the shore and is sad.
She is so old and weak
she cannot feed like other whales.
With her mouth on the surface
she draws in her breath—hrrr—
and the smallest fish and the sea birds are swallowed up.

5

The whale coming to shore is sick
the sharks have eaten her bowels
and the meat of her body.
She travels slowly—her bowels are gone.
She is dead on the shore
and can travel no longer.

6

Fifty sharks surrounded her.
They came under her belly
and bit off her flesh and her bowels
and so she died. Because she had no teeth
to fight the sharks.

(Seri)

FLOWER WORLD: THREE POEMS FROM THE YAQUI DEER DANCE

I

o flower fawn
             about to come out, playing
                      in this flower water
out there
             in the flower world
                      the patio of flowers
in the flower water
             playing
                      flower fawn
about to come out, playing
             in this flower water

2

(where is the rotted stick that screeches lying?)
the screeching rotted stick is lying over there
(where is the rotted stick that screeches lying?)
the screeching rotted stick is lying over there
there in the flower world
             beyond us
                      in the tree world
the screeching rotted stick
             is lying
                      over there the screeching
rotted stock is lying
             over there

3

flower
                              with the body of a fawn
                                        under a cholla flower
          standing there
                              to rub your antlers
                                        bending
          turning where you stand to rub
                              your antlers
                                        in the flower world
          the dawn
                              there in its light
                                        under a cholla flower
          standing there
                              to rub your antlers
                                        bending turning where you stand
          to rub your antlers
                              flower
                                        with the body of a fawn
          under a cholla flower
                              standing there
                                        to rub your antlers
          bending
                              turning where you stand to rub
                                        your antlers

                              (Yaqui)

TO FIND OUR LIFE
(after Ramón Medina Silva)

A few hundred yards down the trail the peyote pilgrims halted once more. Facing the mountains and the sun, they shouted their pleasure at having found their life and their pain at having to depart so soon. "Do not leave," they implored the supernaturals, "do not abandon your places, for we will come again another year." And they sang, song after song—their parting gift to the *kakauyarixi*:

> What pretty hills, what pretty hills,
> So very green where we are.
> Now I don't even feel,
> Now I don't even feel,
> Now I don't even feel like going to my rancho.
> For there at my rancho it is so ugly,
> So terribly ugly there at my rancho,
> And here in Wirikuta so green, so green.
> And eating in comfort as one likes,
> Amid the flowers, so pretty.
> Nothing but flowers here,
> Pretty flowers, with brilliant colors,
> So pretty, so pretty.
> And eating one's fill of everything,
> Everyone so full here, so full with food.
> The hills very pretty for walking,
> For shouting and laughing,
> So comfortable, as one desires,
> And being together with all one's companions.
> Do not weep, brothers, do not weep.
> For we came to enjoy it,

We came on this trek,
To find our life.

For we are all,
We are all,
We are all the children of,
We are all the sons of,
A brilliantly colored flower,
A flaming flower.
And there is no one,
There is no one,
Who regrets what we are.

(Huichol)

THE PAINTED BOOK
(after Nezahualcoyotl)

I

In the house of paintings
the singing begins,
song is intoned,
flowers are spread,
the song rejoices.

Above the flowers is singing
the radiant pheasant:
his song expands
into the interior of the waters.
To him reply
all manner of red birds:
the dazzling red bird
sings a beautiful chant.

Your heart is a book of paintings,
You have come to sing,
to make Your drums resound.
You are the singer.
Within the house of springtime,
You make the people happy.

You alone bestow
intoxicating flowers,
precious flowers.
You are the singer.
Within the house of springtime,
You make the people happy.

2

With flowers You write,
O Giver of Life:
with songs You give color,
with songs You shade
those who must live on the earth.

Later You will destroy eagles and ocelots:
we live only in Your book of paintings,
here, on the earth.

With black ink You will blot out
all that was friendship,
brotherhood, nobility.

You give shading
to those who must live on the earth.
We live only in Your book of paintings,
here on the earth.

3

I comprehend the secret, the hidden:
O my lords!
Thus we are,
we are mortal,
men through and through,
we all will have to go away,
we all will have to die on earth.
Like a painting,
we will be erased.
Like a flower,
we will dry up
here on earth.

Like plumed vestments of the precious bird,
that precious bird with the agile neck,
we will come to an end.
Think on this, my lords,
eagles and ocelots,
though you be of jade,
though you be of gold
you also will go there,
to the place of the fleshless.
We will have to disappear,
no one can remain.

(Nahuatl, Texcoco)

From *CODEX BOTURINI*
"The Origin of the Mexica Aztecs"

The six
patriarchal clans
lived in barrios
around their temple
on Aacatl Island,
Water-&-Reed Island,
later called Aztlan.
They were ruled
by a priest
who took his name
from the place,
and by a priestess
named Chimalma,
Shield Hand Lady.

In the year
5-Flint
[648 A.D.?]
they went to find
the sanctuary
of their chief god,
Huitzilopochtli,
the Blue
Hummingbird
of the Left.

They found it
at Colhuacan,
Bent Mountain:
the god's face
came from the mouth
of a hummingbird
inside his grass temple.
Words rose
from the god's mouth:
he told them
they must wander.

8 clans asked to join them:

The Matlatzincas,
The Hip-Net People;

The Tepanecs,
Those Who Live on Rocks;

The Tlahuicas,
The Hunting People;

The Malinalcas,
The Twisted Grass People;

The Colhuas,
The Turning Water People;

The Xochimilcas,
The Patrons of Flowers;

The Chalcas,
The Precious Stone People;

The Huexotzincas,
The Bowlegged People.

They began their journey,
led by 3 priests & a priestess:

Chimalma:
Shield Hand
Lady.

Cuauhcoatl:
Eagle Snake.

Apanecatl:
He who
Passes Rivers.

Tezcacoatl:
Serpent Mirror—
this priest
carried the
god's bundle
on his back.

237

They came to
Tamoanchan,
The Place of Origins,
& built a temple.
As they were feasting
at the end
of 5 counts of time,
the sacred tree
broke open—
this was the omen
that told them
to leave that place.

Aacatl told a representative of the 8 tribes
that they would have to continue their journey
along separate paths;
in sorrow the representative agreed.

Before leaving,
the Mexica
did penance
before Huitzilopochtli,
& prayed
for guidance.

(the path
of the alienated tribes
goes off the page)

Huitzilopochtli, as Eagle-Sun,
gave them bows & arrows,
& taught them their use.

The 4 holy ones lead the Mexica
on their way.

Aacatl, the high priest,
sacrificed 3 sorcerers
in thanks
for the gift of archery:
it was a powerful omen
& a mandate—
it guided them
toward their destiny.

(Aztec)

From *THE POPOL VUH:*
BLOOD-GIRL & THE CHIEFS
OF HELL

[After the Twin Gods, 1 and 7 Hunter, had been murdered by the Chiefs of Hell, their skulls were hung like fruit from a tree at Dusty Court. Blood-Girl found them there, and, while they spoke to her, spittle from the skulls dripped in her womb and filled her. Six months pregnant when her father, Blood Chief, discovered it and cursed her for her fornication; sent four owls to kill her and bring her heart back in a jar. To whom she pleaded, and they, having decided they would spare her, asked what they could bring back as her heart.]

"Take the fruit of this tree,"
    Said the maiden then.
For red was the sap of the tree
    That she went and gathered in the jar,
And then it swelled up
    And became round
And so then it became an imitation heart,
    The sap of the red tree.
Just like blood the sap of the tree became
    An imitation of blood.
Then she gathered up there in it
    What was red tree sap
And the bark became just like blood,
    Completely red when placed inside the jar.
When the tree was cut by the maiden
    Cochineal Red Tree it was called,
And so she called it blood

Because it was said to be the blood of the croton.
"So there you will be loved then;
        On earth there will come to be something of yours,"
She said then
        To the Owls.
"Very well,
        Oh maiden,
We must go back
        And appear directly;
We shall go right back.
        We feel it must be delivered,
This seeming imitation of your heart,
        Before the lords,"
Then said
        The messengers.
So then they came before the lords,
        Who were all waiting expectantly.
"Didn't it get done?"
        Then asked 1 Death.
"It is already done,
        Oh Lords,
And here in fact is her heart.
        It is down in the jar."
"All right,
        Then I'll look,"
Said 1 Death then.
        And when he poured it right out,
The bark was soggy with fluid,
        The bark was bright crimson with sap.
"Stir the surface on the fire well
        And put it over the fire," said 1 Death then.
So then they dried it over the fire
        And those of Hell then smelled the fragrance.

They all wound up standing there,
     Bending over it.
It really smelled delicious to them,
     The aroma of the sap.
Thus it was that they were still crouching there
     When the Owls came who were guiding the maiden,
Letting her climb up through a hole to the earth.
     Then the guides turned around and went back down.
And thus were the lords of Hell defeated.
     It was by a maiden that they were all blinded.

(Maya)

MAYAN DEFINITIONS
(by Alonzo Gonzales Mó)

THINGS

When they say, "There is a thing."
It is a thing lying on the ground.
Or a thing comes down the road,
noise.
One might say it is a snake
or a beast
or a thing someone will show you.
You feel like this,
"What will he show me?"
Well, who knows what he will show me?
Perhaps what he will show me,
perhaps palm
or gold.
Perhaps he will show me
things of the house.
Perhaps a thing, too.
Perhaps a cunt.
Perhaps a cockroach, too.
Or a small cockroach,
or an iguana,
or a scorpion,
or a tarantula,
or a centipede,
or a small iguana,
or a large iguana,
or a large centipede,
or a woman
embracing.

She is kissing a man.
Lonely street,
fence near the road.
Or a thing one will ask of you.
The thing he asks of you,
a person asks of you,
a thing to buy.
You answer,
"There is that thing
I will sell, also."
We are waiting for a thing
to carry us.
As we leave it appears.
A bus.
Let's get on.

SHADE

Where does a horse shade itself?
Under the shade of a tree.
Shade.
Where do cattle shade themselves?
Under the shade of a tree.
Shade.
Where do chickens, turkeys, ducks shade themselves?
Under the shade of a tree.
Shade.
Where do deer shade themselves?
By a fence,
under the shade of a tree.
Shade.
Where do wild boars shade themselves?
Under the shade of a tree.
Shade.

Where do birds shade themselves?
Under the shade of a tree.
That is the reason for shade.
For all animals, even for people.
Shade.

PERHAPS

Perhaps, maybe, we'll see how the world ends.
Perhaps the day will come of hunger.
There are those who will see what will come to pass on the
     earth.
Perhaps we'll die too. We don't know what day.
Perhaps we'll go to Mérida or another town.
Perhaps I'll come to visit your house or home too.
Perhaps I'll buy what I need.
Perhaps soon I'll have money too
with the little that I'll sell.
Perhaps soon I'll have a woman too,
to marry.
Perhaps soon I'll have land to work,
to build a house to live in.
Perhaps I'll go far away too,
to know places.
Perhaps soon I'll have a cow, a horse, a milpa.

From *INATOIPIPPILER*
(by Akkantilele)

[*The Living Beings*]

Down below a way is being opened for them
Under the great waves the boys come to life again
In front of them a world of living beings is moving, living beings are
    swimming
In front of them living beings are wavering, living beings are making a
    noise
All like golden bells the living beings sound down below
All like golden guitars the living beings sound down below
All like golden watches the living beings sound down below
The living beings make a noise like panpipes and flutes
The living beings make a noise down below like the *kokke*-flute
The living beings are making a noise down below
The living beings make a noise like that of many different instruments
In front of them the living beings are making a noise like the *suppe*-flute
The living beings are making a noise down below
The living beings make a noise like the *tolo*-flute
The living beings are making a noise down below
The living beings make a noise like the *tae*-flute
The living beings are making a noise down below
The living beings make a noise like many different instruments

o o o o o o o

The boys have come to life again: in front of them a world of living
    beings is teeming
In front of them the world is making a noise, living beings are
    fluttering

Uncle Oloyailer's river opens up
Uncle Oloyailer's river lies flaming
The boys stand regarding the place
The boys go forward into the empty space
The boys descend along the middle of the river
Uncle Oloyailer's river opens up
The river lies with bays and inlets as from big rocks
The river lies with bays and inlets as from seaweed
The wind of Uncle Oloyailer's river is blowing
The wind of the river is rippling the ground

[*The Boy Inatoipippiler*]

The boy Inatoipippiler stands looking around
The river of Kalututuli is rising, the river of Kalututuli is illuminating
    the place
Beside Kalututuli, beside the river bank, Uncle Nia's women are
    expecting them
The boy Inatoipippiler stands arranging his hair, he stands letting
    down his hair
The boy Inatoipippiler stands taking off his shirt and pants
He stands taking off his white shirt
He descends into the middle of the river, he is bathing in the river
He is combing his noble hair, he is letting down his hair, his hair is
    reaching far down
Among the tufts of his hair the fish of the sea, the sardines are
    swimming
The boy Inatoipippiler climbs up on the river bank
He stands arranging his hair, he stands combing his hair
With the comb he stands loosening his hair
He stands spreading out his hair, he stands twisting his hair
He stands putting the comb into his hair
The boy Inatoipippiler stands putting on his shirt and pants

He stands putting on his white shirt
He stands tying his golden necktie for the sake of the feast
He stands putting on his golden coat, he stands putting on his golden
    chain
His golden chain hangs down eightfold as he stands
The golden chain glistens as he stands, the golden chain shines
    reaching down to his waist
The boy Inatoipippiler stands putting on his golden socks, he stands
    putting on his golden shoes
He stands putting on his golden hat, he stands with his golden hat
    shining
He stands with his golden hat glistening like the sun
He stands with his golden hat shining, he stands with his golden shoes
    creaking

                                                          (Cuna)

From *THE ELEGY FOR THE GREAT INCA ATAWALLPA*

... You all by yourself fulfilled
    Their malignant demands,
But your life was snuffed out
    In Cajamarca.

Already the blood has curdled
    In your veins,
And under your eyelids your sight
    Has withered.
Your glance is hiding in the brilliance
    Of some star.

Only your dove suffers and moans
    And drifts here and there.
Lost in sorrow, she weeps, who had her nest
    In your heart.

The heart, with the pain of this catastrophe,
    Shatters.
They have robbed you of your golden litter
    And your palace.
All of your treasures which they have found
    They have divided among them.

Condemned to perpetual suffering,
    And brought to ruin,
Muttering, with thoughts that are elusive
    And far away from this world,
Finding ourselves without refuge or help,
    We are weeping,
And not knowing to whom we can turn our eyes,
    We are lost.

Oh sovereign king,
    Will your heart permit us
To live scattered, far from each other,
    Drifting here and there,
Subject to an alien power,
    Trodden upon?

Discover to us your eyes which can wound
    Like a noble arrow;
Extend to us your hand which grants
    More than we ask,
And when we are comforted with this blessing
    Tell us to depart.

(Quechua)

THREE QUECHUA POEMS

1

Where are you where are you going
they say
and we still have to go on

sun and moon go past
    and go past
        six months to get from Cuzco to Quito

at the foot of Tayo we'll rest

fear nothing
lord Inca fear nothing
we're going with you we'll get there together

2

I'm bringing up a fly
    with golden wings
    bringing up a fly
    with eyes burning

it carries death
    in its eyes of fire
carries death
    in its golden hair
    in its gorgeous wings

in a green bottle
    I'm bringing it up

    nobody knows
    if it drinks

    nobody knows
    if it eats

at night it goes wandering
    like a star

    wounding to death
    with red rays
    from its eyes of fire
it carries love
    in its eyes of fire
    flashes in the night
    its blood
    the love it bears in its breast

insect of night
fly bearing death

in a green bottle
I'm bringing it up
    I love it
    that much

but nobody
    no
nobody knows

if I give it to drink
nobody knows if I feed it

3

It's today I'm supposed
    to go away
I won't
    I'll go
    tomorrow

you'll see me go
    playing a flute
made from a bone of a fly

carrying a flag
made from a spider's web

beating an ant's egg
drum

with a humming-bird's nest for a hat
with my head
in a humming-bird's nest

POEMS FOR A CARNIVAL

1

That's the big
boss's house
shining with the money
studded in it
rolls of bank notes
papered on it
his cows even
shit gold

2

The carnival was
a sad old man it was
under the bridge
sniffing around he was
I saw him with his
such'i fish moustache
in his bag
two eggs there were
I tried to grab them
but hollow they were

3

The politicians from the valley
have no mouths
being without mouths
they peck with their nails

(Quechua)

RAISING THE MEDIATING CENTER & THE FIELD OF EVIL WITH THE TWENTY-FIVE THOUSAND ACCOUNTS & THE CHANT OF THE ANCIENTS

(by Eduardo Calderón)

Con Cipriano poderoso,
With powerful Saint Cyprian,

Cabalista y cirujano, viejo caminante
Cabbalist and surgeon, old traveler,

Y en los cuatro vientos y los cuatro caminos,
And with the four winds and the four roads,

Y en las veinticinco mil cuentas,
And with the twenty-five thousand accounts,

Justicieras, curanderas, y ganaderas,
Good, curing, and evil,

Ajustando con mis buenos rambeadores, mis sorbedores.
Adjusting with my good assistants, my absorbers.

Con buenas cuentas.
With good accounts,

Así vengo parando,
Thus I come raising,

En todo su encanto y su poder:
With all his enchantment and his power:

Cerro Blanco, Cerro Colorado,
White Mountain, Red Mountain,

Cerro Chaparri, Cerro Yanahuanga,
Mount Chaparri, Mount Yanahuanga,

Cerro Chalpón, poderoso y bendito,
Mount Chalpón, powerful and blessed,

Con tu volcanazo de fuego ardiendo,
With your great volcano of burning fire,

Donde cuenta el encanto del Padre Guatemala.
Where the enchantment of Father Guatemala is accounted,

Y en sus grandes poderes,
And with your great powers,

Todos sus encantos voy llamando,
All his enchantments I go calling,

Voy contando.
I go accounting.

Cerro Pelagato, Cerro Huascarán,
Pelagato Mountain, Mount Huascarán,

Cerro del Ahorcado, Cerro Campanario,
Hanged Man's Mountain, Belfry Mountain,

Cerro Cuculicote y su gran poder,
Cuculicote Mountain and its great power,

Donde vengo ajustando,
Where I come adjusting,

Y a mi banco,
And at my bench,

En todos sus encantos y poderes,
With all its enchantments and powers,

Voy contando.
I go accounting.

Y en mi buena laguna encantada,
And with my good enchanted lagoon,

Mi Huaringana,
My Huaringana,

Donde voy llamando.
Where I go calling,

Mi buena Laguna Shimbe,
My good Shimbe Lagoon,

Siempre linda y poderosa,
Always beautiful and powerful,

Donde juega mi maestro Florentino García,
Where my master Florentino Garcia plays,

En su gran poder del chamán,
With his great power as a shaman.

Y así vengo contando,
And thus I come accounting,

Con todos mis encantos,
With all my enchantments.

Vara por vara,
Staff by staff,

Cerro por cerro,
Mountain by mountain,

Laguna por laguna,
Lagoon by lagoon,

Y en el chorro de Santo Crisanto,
And in the Stream of Santo Crisanto,

Voy llamando.
I go calling.

En mis hermosos jardines bien floridos,
With my beautiful flowery gardens,

Con todas sus hierbas y sus encantos,
With all their herbs and their enchantments,

Voy llamando.
I go calling.

Cuenta por cuenta, voy jugando,
Account by account, I go playing,

Y en mi Huaca poderosa de los Gentiles,
And with my powerful Temple of the Ancients.

Donde voy contando, jugando, floreciendo.
Where I go accounting, playing, flowering.

Huaca Prieta, Huaca del Sol, y Huaca de la Luna,
Huaca Prieta, Temple of the Sun, and Temple of the Moon,

Juega a mi ciento.
Play at my game.

Con la hierba del hombre,
With the herb of man,

Con la hierba del león,
With the herb of the lion,

Con la hierba de la coqueta,
With the herb of the coquette,

Voy cantando.
I go singing.

Con mis buenos hierbateros voy llamando,
With my good herbalists I go calling,

Todos los poderes y los encantos,
All the powers and the enchantments,

Que mi buen remedio viene ya,
So that my good remedy comes now,

Buscando, justificando, levantando, parando,
Looking, justifying, raising, standing up.

Con sus buenos encantos.
With their good enchantments,

Todos los grandes maestros,
All the great masters,

Van contando donde cuento.
Go accounting where I account.

A las doce de la noche entera,
At twelve midnight,

Y a la madrugada,
And at dawn,

Seis de la mañana al ojo del sol,
Six in the morning under the eye of the sun,

Voy llamando,
I go calling,

Estoy contando y refrescando,
I am accounting and refreshing.

Buena hora, buenos vientos,
Good time, good winds,

Voy llamando y contando,
I go calling and accounting,

De mis buenas maravillas,
With my good marvels,

Vengo levantando todo mi banco.
I come raising all of my bench,

Donde cuentan todos los grandes poderosos.
Where all the great powers are accounted,

Voy dominando todo golpe,
I go dominating all spiritual shocks,

Floreciendo en buena hora.
Flowering in good time.

(Spanish, Peru)

THE MACHI EXORCISES THE SPIRIT HUECUVE

get out right now Huecuve get
out
—they got after me
with 4 firebrands, a swarm
of young men running me out—:
That's what you'll tell them
when you get back home.
Get out; go; quick; now.
—this *machi* shoved me—: that's
what you'll say later.
Look this is a poor man why
do you enter him?
Go take over a rich one
so get out Huecuve;
                            the master of men
that's who sent me.
In the midpoint of the sky
I see a bull
lizard-color.
—that foul *machi* forced me out—:
say that to your mother and father

(Araucanian)

WORDS FROM SEVEN
MAGIC SONGS
(by Tatilgäk)

inop   ihumanut   erinaliot
For a man's mind   a magic song
      Big man,

      Big man!

      aglgagjuarit
      Your big hands

      Your big feet,

      make them smooth
      And look far ahead!

      Big man,

      Big man!

Your thoughts   smooth out

      and look far ahead!

      Big man,
      Big man!
Your weapons   let them fall!

(Copper Eskimo)

MY BREATH

(by Orpingalik)

This is what I call my song, because it is as important for me to sing it
as it is to draw breath.

This is my song: a powerful song.
Unaija-unaija.
Since autumn I have lain here,
helpless and ill,
as if I were my own child.

Sorrowfully, I wish my woman
to another hut,
another man for refuge,
firm and safe as the winter-ice.
Unaija-unaija.

And I wish my woman
a more fortunate protector,
now I lack the strength
to raise myself from bed.
Unaija-unaija.

Do you know yourself?
How little of yourself you understand!
Stretched out feebly on my bench,
my only strength is in my memories.
Unaija-unaija.

Game! Big game,
chasing ahead of me!
Allow me to re-live that!
Let me forget my frailty,

by calling up the past!
Unaija-unaija.

I bring to mind that great white one,
the polar bear,
approaching with raised hind-quarters,
his nose in the snow—
convinced, as he rushed at me,
that of the two of us,
he was the only male!
Unaija-unaija.
Again and again he threw me down:
but spent at last,
he settled by a hump of ice,
and rested there,
ignorant that I was going to finish him.
He thought he was the only male around!
But I too was a man!
Unaija-unaija.

Nor will I forget that great blubbery one,
the fjord-seal that I slaughtered
from an ice-floe before dawn,
while friends at home
were laid out like the dead,
feeble with hunger,
famished with bad luck.
I hurried home,
laden with meat and blubber,
as though I were just running across the ice
to view a breathing-hole.
Yet this had been an old and cunning bull,
who'd scented me at once—
but before he had drawn breath,

my spear was sinking
through his neck.

This is how it was.
Now I lie on my bench,
too sick to even fetch
a little seal oil for my woman's lamp.
Time, time scarcely seems to pass,
though dawn follows dawn,
and spring approaches the village.
Unaija-unaija.

How much longer must I lie here?
How long? How long must she go begging
oil for the lamp,
reindeer-skins for her clothes,
and meat for her meal?
I, a feeble wretch:
she, a defenseless woman.
Unaija-unaija.

Do you know yourself?
How little of yourself you understand!
Dawn follows dawn,
and spring is approaching the village.
    Unaija-unaija.

(Netsilik Eskimo)

ESKIMO PROSE POEMS

A Mother & Child

A pregnant woman brought forth a child. The child was hardly born before it flung itself upon its mother & killed her, & began eating her.

Suddenly the infant cried:

My mother's little first finger stuck crosswise in my mouth, & I could hardly manage to get it out again.

And with these words, the infant killed itself, after first having murdered & eaten its mother.

(Told by Inugpasugjuk)

The Woman Who Took In a Larva to Nurse

There was once a barren woman, who could never have any children. At last she took in a larva & nursed it in her armpits, & it was not long before the larva began to grow up. But the more it grew the less blood the woman had for it to suck. Therefore she often went visiting the homes near by, to set the blood in motion, but she never stayed long away from home, for she was always thinking of her dear larva, & hurried back to it. So greatly did she long for it, so fond of it had she grown, that whenever she came to the entrance of her house, she would call out to it:

Oh, little one that can hiss, say "te-e-e-e-E·r."

And when she said that, the larva would say in answer: Te-e-e-e-E·r.

The woman then hurried into the house, took the larva on her lap & sang to it:

Little one that will bring me snow

when you grow up
Little one that will find meat for me
when you grow up!

And then she would bite it out of pure love.

The larva grew up & became a big thing. At last it began to move about the village among the houses, & the people were afraid of it & wanted to kill it, partly because they were afraid & partly because they thought it was a pity to let the woman go on growing paler & paler from loss of blood.

So one day when the woman was out visiting, they went into her house & threw the larva out into the passage. Then the dogs flung themselves on it & bit it to death. It was completely filled with blood, & the blood poured out of it.

The woman who had been out visiting came home all unsuspecting, & when she got to the entrance of her house, called out to the larva as she was wont to do. But no one answered, & the woman exclaimed:

Oh, they have thrown my dear child out of the house.

And she burst into tears & went into the house weeping.

(Told by Ivaluardjuk)

When Houses Were Alive

One night a house suddenly rose up from the ground and went floating through the air. It was dark, & it is said that a swishing, rushing noise was heard as it flew through the air. The house had not yet reached the end of its road when the people inside begged it to stop. So the house stopped.

They had no blubber when they stopped. So they took soft, freshly drifted snow & put it in their lamps, & it burned.

They had come down at a village. A man came to their house & said:

Look, they are burning snow in their lamps. Snow can burn.

But the moment these words were uttered, the lamp went out.

(Told by Inugpasugjuk)

ASIA

THE QUEST OF MILAREPA

1

When named I am the man apart;
I am the sage of Tibet;
I am Milarepa.
I hear little but counsel much;
I reflect little but persevere much;
I sleep little but endure in meditation much.
My narrow bed gives me ease to stretch and bend;
my thin clothing makes my body warm;
my scanty fare satisfies my belly.
Knowing one thing I have experience of all things;
knowing all things I comprehend them to be one.
I am the goal of every great meditator;
I am the meeting place of the faithful;
I am the coil of birth and death and decay.
I have no preference for any country;
I have no home in any place;
I have no store of provisions for my livelihood.
I have no fondness for material things;
I make no distinction between clean and unclean in food;
I have little torment of suffering.
I have little desire for self-esteem;
I have little attachment or bias;
I have found the freedom of Nirvana.
I am the comforter of the aged;
I am the madman who counts death happiness;
I am the playmate of children.

2

When the tiger-year was ending
and the hare-year beginning
on the sixth day of the month of the barking of the fox,
I grew weary of the things of this world;

and in my yearning for solitude
I came to the sanctuary wilderness, Mount Everest.
Then heaven & earth took counsel together
and sent forth the whirlwind as messenger.
The elements of wind & water seethed
and the dark clouds of the south rolled up in concert;
the sun and the moon were made prisoner
and the twenty-eight constellations of the moon were fastened
    together;
the eight planets in their courses were cast into chains
and the faint milky way was delivered into bondage;
the little stars were altogether shrouded in mist
and when all things were covered in the complexion of mist
for nine days & nine nights the snow fell,
steadily throughout the eighteen times of day and night it fell.
When it fell heavily the flakes were as big as the flock of wool,
and fell floating like feathered birds.
When the snow fell lightly the flakes were small as spindles,
and fell circling like bees.
Again, they were as small as peas or mustard-seed,
and fell turning like distaffs.
Moreover the snow surpassed measure in depth,
the peak of white snow above reached to the heavens
and the trees of the forest below were bowed down.
The dark hills were clad in white,
ice formed upon the billowing lakes
and the blue Tsangpo was constrained in its depths.
The earth became like a plain without hill or valley,
and in natural consequence of such a great fall
the lay folk were mewed up;
famine overtook the four-footed cattle,
and the small deer especially found no food;
the feathered birds above lacked nourishment,
and the marmots and field-mice below hid in their burrows;
the jaws of beasts of prey were stiffened together.

In such fearsome circumstances
this strange fate befell me, Milarepa.
There were these three: the snowstorm driving down from on high,
the icy blast of mid-winter,
and the cotton cloth which I, the sage Mila, wore;
and between them rose a contest on that white snow peak.
The falling snow melted into goodly water;
the wind, though rushing mightily, abated of itself,
and the cotton cloth blazed like fire.
Life and death wrestled there after the fashion of champions,
and swords crossed victorious blades.
That I won there the heroic fight
will be an example to all the faithful
and a true example to all great contemplatives;
more especially will it prove the greater excellence
of the single cotton cloth & the inner heat.

3

That the white ice-peak of Tisé, great in fame,
is just a mountain covered with snow,
proves the whiteness of Buddha's teaching.
That the turquoise lake of Mapang, great in fame,
is water through which water flows,
proves the dissolution of all created things.
That I, Milarepa, great in fame,
am an old and naked man,
proves that I have forsaken & set at nought self-interest.
That I am a singer of little songs,
proves that I have learned to read the world as a book.

(Tibetan)

KEEPING STILL / THE MOUNTAIN

The Judgment

KEEPING STILL. Keeping his back still
So that he no longer feels his body.
He goes into his courtyard
And does not see his people.
No blame.

1

Mountains standing close together:
The image of KEEPING STILL.

2

Keeping his toes still.
No blame.
Continued perseverance furthers.

3

Keeping his calves still.
He cannot rescue him whom he follows.
His heart is not glad.

4

Keeping his hips still.
Making his sacrum stiff.
Dangerous. The heart suffocates.

5

Keeping his trunk still.
No blame.

6

    Keeping his jaws still.
    The words have order.
    Remorse disappears.

7

    Noblehearted keeping still.
    Good fortune.

               (Chinese)

THE MARRYING MAIDEN

The Judgment

THE MARRYING MAIDEN
Undertakings bring misfortune.
Nothing that would further.

1

Thunder over the lake:
The image of THE MARRYING MAIDEN.

2

The marrying maiden as a concubine.
A lame man who is able to tread.
Undertakings bring good fortune.

3

A one-eyed man who is able to see.
The perseverance of a solitary man furthers.

4

The marrying maiden as a slave.
She marries as a concubine.

5

The marrying maiden draws out the allotted time.
A late marriage comes in due course.

6

The sovereign *I* gave his daughter in marriage.
The embroidered garments of the princess
Were not as gorgeous

As those of the servingmaid.
The moon that is nearly full
Brings good fortune.

7

The woman holds the basket, but there are no fruits in it.
The man stabs the sheep, but no blood flows.
Nothing that acts to further.

(Chinese)

From *THE NINE SONGS*

Song V

The Big Lord of Lives

The gates of Heaven are open wide;
Off I ride, borne on a dark cloud!
May the gusty winds be my vanguard,
May sharp showers sprinkle the dust!
The Lord wheels in his flight, he is coming down;
I will cross K'ung-sang and attend upon you.
But all over the Nine Provinces there are people in throngs;
Why think that his task is among *us?*
High he flies, peacefully winging;
On pure air borne aloft he handles Yin and Yang.
I and the Lord, solemn and reverent,
On our way to God cross over the Nine Hills.
He trails his spirit-garment,
Dangles his girdle-gems.
One Yin for every Yang;
The crowd does not understand what we are doing.
I pluck the sparse-hemp's lovely flower,
Meaning to send it to him from whom I am separated.
Age creeps on apace, all will soon be over;
Not to draw nearer is to drift further apart.
He has driven his dragon chariot, loudly rumbling;
High up he gallops into Heaven.
Binding cassia-branches a long while I stay;
Ch'iang! The more I think of him, the sadder I grow,
The sadder I grow; but what does sadness help?
If only it could be forever as this time it was!

But man's fate is fixed;
From meetings and partings none can ever escape.

Song VI

The Little Lord of Lives

The autumn orchid and the deer-fodder
Grow thick under the hall,
From green leaves and white branches
Great gusts of scent assail me.
Among such people there are sure to be lovely young ones;
You have no need to be downcast and sad.
The autumn orchid is in its splendour;
Green its leaves, purple its stem.
The hall is full of lovely girls;
But suddenly it is me he eyes and me alone.

When he came in he said nothing, when he went out he said no word;
Riding on the whirlwind he carried a banner of cloud.
There is no sadness greater than that of a life-parting;
No joy greater than that of making new friends.
In coat of lotus-leaf, belt of basil
Suddenly he came, and as swiftly went.
At nightfall he is to lodge in the precincts of God.
Lord, for whom are you waiting, on the fringe of the clouds?
I bathed with you in the Pool of Heaven,
I dried your hair for you in a sunny fold of the hill.
I look towards my fair one; but he does not come.
With the wind on my face despairing I chant aloud.
Chariot-awning of peacock feathers, halcyon flags—
He mounts to the Nine Heavens, wields the Broom-star.
Lifts his long sword to succour young and old;
Yes, you alone are fit to deal out justice to the people.

Song VIII

The River God (Ho-po)

With you I wandered down the Nine Rivers;
A whirlwind rose and the waters barred us with their waves.
We rode in a water-chariot with awning of lotus-leaf
Drawn by two dragons, with griffins to pull at the sides.
I climb K'un-lun and look in all directions;
My heart rises all a-flutter, I am agitated and distraught.
Dusk is coming, but I am too sad to think of return.
Of the far shore only are my thoughts; I lie awake and yearn.

In his fish-scale house, dragon-scale hall,
Portico of purple-shell, in his red palace,
What is the Spirit doing, down in the water?
Riding a white turtle, followed by stripy fish
With you I wandered in the islands of the River.
The ice is on the move; soon the floods will be down.
You salute me with raised hands, then go towards the East.
I go with my lovely one as far as the southern shore.
The waves surge on surge come to meet him,
Fishes shoal after shoal escort me on my homeward way.

(Chinese)

SONG OF THE DEAD, RELATING THE ORIGIN OF BITTERNESS	

(Set One)

To learn to do things here is bitterness	Ssu-ssa-zo of Shu-lo	when he was old but didn't know it
made a yellow wooden bowl	went to wash gold in it	Ssu-ssa-zo's shadow was projected on the water
he saw his shadow reflected on the water	his own shadow	that he saw reflected
he was old then & he knew it	on the horizon where the clouds touch heaven the old crane still didn't know that he was old	

(Set Two)		
How he was shaking his own body	his own white feathers dropping down before him	now that he knew that he was old
old tiger of the place called Such-&-Such	still didn't know that he was old	his long white fangs were falling down before him
& now he knew that he was old	At Such-&-Such-Another-Place	the white stag didn't know that he was old
now he was shaking his own body	his white antlers were falling down before him	then he knew that he was old

(Set Three)		
Now we will go with the dead & will suffer the bitterness of the dead	we will dance again & vanquish demons again	but if no one had told us where the dance began
we would never dare to speak about the dance	for unless one knows the origin of the dance	one cannot dance it

On top of Such-&-Such-a-Mountain	the yak said he would like to dance	but for the yak	there was no custom of the dance

no custom for the goat that followed	The sons of bitterness are here— they wear their hats

(Set Four)		
The yak will dance there, as the custom is	on top of Such-&-Such-a-Mountain	the stag said he would like to dance there
but for the stag	there was no custom of the dance	Shoes of elfskin & white toes
the sons of bitterness will wear them	the stag will dance there, as the custom is	& where the pinetrees grow the young deer try to dance
they beat their cloven hoofs in rhythm	swaying, dancing, as the custom is	& all the people of the village

(Set Five)	
& all the sons of bitterness	who have slim hips & sway in rhythm
who sway & dance again, as is the custom	*we will follow the crane to his clouds*
will go with the tiger to his high mountain	*& with our ancestor into the sky*
the crane wants to fly to the shining white gate in the clouds	all those born with wings
have followed the crane to his clouds	*but his ability we do not allow to pass*

(Na-Khi, China)

A SHAMAN VISION POEM

(Shao Yeh's birthplace was situated over ten miles from Wen Yuan. After his death the people of this district while observing a religious ceremony asked a shamanka to put a mourning cap on & do a dance. Suddenly the shamanka muttered: "Old Mr Shao has come to me in a vision." The people thought he was uttering nonsense & to frustrate him challenged him at once: "Old Shao was a notable poet. Can you get him to compose some poetry for us?" But before anyone could think, he'd made a poem, of melancholic phrase. No other poet could have done it. Shao's townspeople who understood poetic composition were deeply moved & sighed.)

From graygreen mists
                    at the foot of a mountain
I see a youth appear,
                    frustrated, once,
to the point
            of forsaking
his native town:
                unbearable sorrow
if he looked back
                would see
—distantly, across the river,—
                        into the hut
where he'd been born & raised.

(Chinese)

AL QUE QUIERE!
11 Pai-hua

18 year-old girl;
3 year-old boy:
he pees & shits
in his pajamas,
has to be carried off
& tucked into bed.
sleeps until midnight,
then it's milk he wants.
whippity-whap!
(2 little slaps),—
"I'm your *wife*,
not your *mother*!"

(Northern China)

if you have a daughter
don't marry her to a scholar
knowing how to close a door
& how to sleep alone.

if you have a daughter,
don't marry her to a farmer
with cowshit on his feet
& dirt all in his hair.

if you have a daughter,
marry her, quickly,
to a U.S.-bound traveler:

once on board the oceanliner
he'll be rich just like Rockefeller.

> (Toishan district of Kwangtun
> province)

like planting a rose on a heap of cow turds,
like marrying a crow (that s.o.b.) to the queen of birds,
golden rings & silver hairpins—what's the use?
gold nor silver can never take the place
of my dream lover.

> (Hunan province)

it's bitter to be poor.
really, it's no joke!
not even a rag
to patch a hole.
a girl grows into teens,
her butt exposed
herding waterbuffaloes.

> (Kweichow province)

shrill cries of crickets:
it's time to harvest.
my crop's withered already—
I'll have to go & pawn my old lady.
my old lady, those tears,
my old lady, I beg you, stop.
'cos I'll come back for you
after selling next year's crop!

> (Anhwei province)

I want to cry, yet dare not cry out—
precisely as a knife blade against my throat—
my heart's not hard, heartless,
but to abandon a child—, such anguish!
O! waters of the Yangtze!
please flow gently, ever gently!
don't dash against your rocks
my little girl!

(Szechuan province)

young girl by the river
washing her brassiere
tracing the flowing waters
with her ten fingers
he who drinks there
inspired by an endless fire

(Shantung province)

Oo La LA!
I take off my pants:
shiny white thighs!
Oo La LA!
I take off my blouse:
what a pair of boobs!
Oo La LA!
I'm going to marry
whoever's loaded with cash!

(Toishan district of Kwangtung
province)

money-grubbing slave,
stingy skinflint,

no food for the hungry,
no cash for the poor,
says,
money's my very life—
flay me,
torture me,
you'll never touch my silver!

             (Kiangsu province)

horses to graze,
waterbuffaloes to graze,
graze 'em where?
graze 'em up on Phoenix Hill.
back home, I'm hungry,
& sneak a peek inside the pot.
inside the pot, local mud soup.
boiling mad, I break down
in a long, loud wail.

             (Kiangsu province)

heaven's old grandfather,
old beyond years,
your ears can't hear
& your eyes see only stars:
you can't see people,
you can't hear their cries.
vegetarian monks
starve themselves to death.
murderers & arsonists
lead lives of wealth & ease.
heaven's old grandfather,
you don't know how
to rule up there—
why don't you just jump?

             (Peking)

From *THE KOJIKI: HOW OPO-KUNI-NUSI BIDS FAREWELL TO HIS JEALOUS WIFE, SUSERI-BIME, IN SONG*

[Again the deity's chief queen, SUSERI-BIME-NÖ-MIKÖTÖ, was extremely jealous. Her husband, highly distressed on this account, was about to leave IDUMO and go up to the land of YAMATÖ.

When he had completed dressing and was about to depart, he put one hand on the saddle of his horse and one foot in the stirrup, singing:]

All dressed up
    In my jet-black clothes,
When I look down at my breast,
    Like a bird of the sea,
Flapping its wings,
    This garment will not do;
I throw it off
    By the wave-swept beach.

All dressed up
    In my blue clothes,
Blue like the kingfisher,
    When I look down at my breast,
Like a bird of the sea,
    Flapping its wings,
This garment will not do;
I throw it off
    By the wave-swept beach.

All dressed up
  In my clothes dyed
With the juice
  Of pounded ATANE plants
  Grown in the mountain fields,
Now when I look down at my breast,
  Like a bird of the sea,
Flapping its wings,
  This garment will do.

Beloved wife of mine,
When I go off
With my men
Flocking like flocking birds;
When I go off
With my men
Accompanied like birds of a company;
Although you may say
That you will not weep—
Your head drooping,
Like the lone reed of SUSUKI grass
On the mountain side,
You will weep;
And your weeping will rise
Just as the morning rain
Rises into a mist.
O my young wife
Like the young grass!
These are
The words,
The words handed down.

(Japanese)

A SONG OF THE SPIDER GODDESS
(by Hiraga Etenoa)

Doing nothing but needlework,
I remained with my eyes
focused on a single spot,
and this is the way
I continued to live
on and on until

One day
from far out at sea
a god was heard coming this way
with a loud roaring
and rumbling.
After a while
he stopped his chariot
over
my house.

All around
it grew silent.
Then after a while,
the voice of a god
came ringing out.
This is what he said:

"Greetings,
o goddess dwelling
in this place.
Listen to

what I have
to say.

"Behind
the Cloud Horizon
there dwells
Big Demon,
and he has fallen in love
with you
and you alone.
Because of this,
he is now
getting ready
to come here.
I have come [to warn you]
because I was
worried about you
in case Big Demon
should arrive
unexpectedly."

The voice of the god
rang out with these words.
Nevertheless.
I thought to myself:

"Am I
a deity with weak powers?"

Thinking this,
I paid no attention.

After that,
doing nothing but needlework,

I remained with my eyes
focused on a single spot,
and this is the way
I continued to live
on and on
uneventfully until

One day
a god was heard moving
shoreward
with an even louder
roaring
and rumbling.
After a while
he stopped his chariot
over
my house.
The voice of a god
came ringing out.

"It was not
a lie
that I told you, but
you, weighty goddess,
seem to have
doubted me,
for you do
nothing about it
even while Big Demon
is on his way here.
This is why
I have come here
to give you
a warning."

At these words,
I turned and looked,
and true enough,
Big Demon
was on his way.
Thus,
at my sitting place
I set in waiting
Thin Needle Boy.
In the middle of the fireplace
I set in waiting
Chestnut Boy.
At the window
I set in waiting
Hornet Boy.
In the water barrel
I set in waiting
Viper Boy.
Above the doorway
I set in waiting
Pestle Boy.
Above the outer doorway
I set in waiting
Mortar Boy.
After that
I transformed myself
into a reed stalk
and waited.

Just then,
outside the house
there was the sound of a voice.
Without hesitation
some sort of being

came in,
wiggling its way through
the narrow doorway.
The one who came in
was surely
the so-called
Big Demon,
he who dwells
behind
the Cloud Horizon.
He stepped along
the right-hand side of the fireplace
and sat down
at my sitting place
on the right-hand side of the fireplace.
He started to dig up
the hidden embers in the fireplace,
uttering these words
while he did so:

> "I thought that
> the goddess dwelling
> in this place
> was here
> just a moment ago,
> but now she is gone.
> Where could she
> have gone?"

Saying these words,
he dug up the embers.
When he did that,
there was a loud snap
in the middle of the fireplace.

Chestnut Boy
popped into
one of the eyes
of Big Demon.
When that happened,

    "*Hai*, my eye!"

he cried, and
fell over backward.

When he did that,
Needle Boy
jabbed him
in the flesh on his rump.
When that happened,

    "*Hai*, my eye!
    Hai, my rump!"

he cried, and
stood up and
went
toward the window.

Then Hornet Boy
stung him
in one of his eyes.
After that,

    "*Hai*, my eyes!
    Hai, my rump!"

he cried, and
went
toward the water barrel.

Then Viper Boy
bit
Big Demon
on one of his hands.

When that happened,
Big Demon cried:

"*Hai*, my hand!
Hai, my eyes!
Hai, my rump!"

Crying this,
he went out.
Then Pestle Boy
tumbled down
on top of the head
of Big Demon.

Then Big Demon
moaned in pain,
crying:

"*Hai*, my eyes!
Hai, my hand!
Hai, my rump!
Hai, my head!"

Crying this,
he went outside,
Then when he went out
through the outer doorway,
Mortar Boy
tumbled down
on top of his head.
Right away
Big Demon
was heard moving off dying
with a loud rumbling
and roaring.

When it was all over,
everything grew quiet all around.

After that,
I came out
by the fireside
and did nothing but needlework,
remaining with my eyes
focused on a single spot,
and this is the way
I live on and on
uneventfully.

This tale was told by Spider Goddess.

(Ainu)

THINGS SEEN BY THE SHAMAN KARAWE

I slept and my souls went away.

They set out for way up there to look at, to visit, Sun, Dawn, and Creator.

On the road they said to me: "What's this slow movement of yours? Take our harnesses!"

Dawn and Sun spoke in that way. Dawn said: "I'll go with you. It's good for me to go with the drum. When I'm in between both of you, keeping up with the drum."

These souls went under the earth and no longer came back, even though I called them back. When they started walking they were walking on the earth and under the earth, they were seeing everything above the earth and in the high places, they didn't want to come back, no matter how much I called them back from there.

But in the summer I was with the herd and fell asleep in front of the herd. Two came on reindeer, the bedding of their sledges worn from traveling so long. The hooves of the deer were ground down from galloping. I looked at them and my mind got confused, my body weakened and became like water. I was turned from a strong one into a weak one, fond of sleep, hardly walking in daylight.

To my herd were born such reindeer, as in the harness of those people. A wild buck came to the herd, turned tame and quiet and sired children of his same color. These reindeer of my neighbors—my own.

On the river's steep bank lives a person, a voice there exists and speaks. I saw the master of this voice and spoke with him. He submitted to my power, bent down and sacrificed to me. He arrived yesterday.

Small grey bird with the blue breast, who shamanizes sitting in the hollow of the tree and calls the spirits, arrives and answers my questions. Woodpecker strikes his drum in the tree with his drumming bill. Under the blows of the axe the tree trembles and wails, like a drum under the drumstick . . . it was my helping spirit; it arrives and I hold it in my hands.

My souls are flying like birds in all directions, observing everything there is at once and bringing news to my breast, like food to the nest. It's good for me to fly with my souls in the round canoe.

My friend! Not far away from here I saw that from the river Oloi a great storm's advancing and it hits everything. Between the tents a river was flowing, full of blood. Soon we'll hear news of murder. I heard how Creator was angry that we, the inhabitants of this country, are paying tribute to the Russians—papers of mixed-up colors that we receive in exchange for different skins—are accepting foreign signs, and because of this he makes the pasture of the deer deteriorate and creates limping mothers and young calves with atrophied limbs, so that many of our people have already become poor.

Everything still lives; the lamp walks, walls of the house have their own voice, and even the piss-pot has its own country and tent, wife and children, and serves as a helping spirit. Skins, lying in bags as stock for trade, are having conversations through the night. Antlers on the graves of the dead are walking in procession around the graves, and in the morning they're coming back to their former places, and the dead themselves are getting up and coming to the living.

(Chukchee)

PRAISE SONG OF THE BUCK-HARE

I am the buck-hare, I am,
The shore is my playground
Green underwood is my feeding.

I am the buck-hare, I am,
What's that damn man got wrong with him?
Skin with no hair on, that's his trouble.

I am the buck-hare, I am,
Mountaintop is my playing field
Red heather my feeding.

I am the buck-hare, I am,
What's wrong with that fellow there with his eye
    on a girl?
I say, is his face red!

I am the buck-hare, I am,
Got my eyes out ahead
You don't lose me on a dark night, you don't.

I am the buck-hare, I am,
What's wrong with that bloke with a poor coat?
Lice, that's what he's got, fair crawlin' he is.

I am the buck-hare, I am,
I got buck teeth.
Buck-hare never gets thin.

I am the BUCK-HARE, I am,
What's that fool got the matter with him?
Can't find the road! Ain't got no road he CAN find.

I am the buck-hare, I am,
I got my wood-road,
I got my form.

I am the buck-hare, I am,
What ails that fool man anyhow?
Got a brain, won't let him set quiet.

I am the buck-hare, I am,
I live in the big plain,
There's where I got my corral.

I am the buck-hare, I said so.
What's wrong with that loafer?
He's been to sleep in a bad place, he has.

I am the buck-hare,
I live in the bush, I do,
That's my road over yonder.

I am the buck-hare, I said so,
Women that don't get up in the morning,
I know how they look by the chimney.

I am the buck-hare, I said it,
I can tell any dumb loafer
Lying along by the hedge there.

I am the buck-hare,
Women don't love their men?
I can tell by what their cows look like.

(Teleut)

SETCHIN THE SINGER

old man with visored hat
setchin old singer
for whom these words come:
in the old man's house
prince of the town they made
the clawed beast sit
ferocious claws they set up
in the old man's house
old man with visored hat
& sent a messenger
a handspan high:
he didn't come
they sent two messengers:
he didn't come
a third time sent a messenger
a handspan high
old man with visored hat
who buckles on his wife's
threadbare old coat of wolverine
he wraps his wife's dogleash around
his waist
& on his head he sets
a hat of shredded hemp
then with an icey wooden staff
starts on the road
with an icey wooden staff
knocks down
the heavy redwood door
its iron hinges
work of a master's hands he turns

to toothpicks
and he enters
on his back he wears his wife's
threadbare old coat of wolverine
his wife's dogleash
around his waist
and on his head a hat of shredded
hemp   each time
he hammers with his icey staff
against the floor
great knots swell up like teacups
with his icey wooden staff
confronts the muzzle of
the little sacred beast

*

"by your father's rotten blood"
(the bear says) "why do you sit here
"songless crouching in a corner?"
(says the man) "where did you carry off
"the dearest of my dear sons?"
(& the bear replies)
"you have your second son still left
"your youngest
"my water spirit my ambassador of waters
"I sent out through the waters
"& my forest spirit my ambassador of forests
"I sent out through the forest
"my father Numi-Torem made me
"with a corner of my belly
"furious   here below
"in a corner of my belly drunk
"with anger
"I lock up this taunt

*

Old man with visored hat comes back
into his house   he tells his wife
"go find me what in distant moscow
"as a boy I dragged out from the waters
"bring me my lovely shining robe
"& bring me my belt with cotton fringes
"& bring me my blackrimmed hat
"& bring me a fatted horse's haunch
"& bring me a fatted horse's rib
"& bring me a silver bowl three handspans wide"
she did & he put on
his lovely shining robe
hooked on his belt with cotton fringes
stuck on his blackrimmed hat
& in the silver bowl three handspans wide
he crammed
the fatted horse's haunch
then took a tree he strung with wolfgut strings
& headed out

*

"watching from this side I saw
"a woman's son appear
"from who knows where
"a son of privilege from who knows where
"I looked & saw
"under his left arm
"was a tree with five strings
"looked & on his right side
"saw
"a silver bowl three handspans wide
"& saw

"a chunk of fatted horse's haunch
"I took a harder look
"old man with visored hat: he stood
"before the muzzle of
"the little sacred beast
"set down
"a silver bowl three handspans wide
"three nights & days
"I watched
"a dish that ran with horse's fat
"& watched
"three nights & days
"a lovely play of whirling legs
"he touched the low string
"of his five-stringed tree
"the string shook with the voice of the lower sky
"he touched the high string
"the string shook with the voice of the upper sky
"a lovely play of twisting hands
"he made for me"

*

it is for good cause one says
"this is a man expert in song"
it is for good cause one says
"this is a man expert in lore"

(Vogul)

MANTRA FOR BINDING A WITCH

I

    I bind the sharp end of a knife
    I bind the glow-worm in the forehead
    I bind the magic of nine hundred gurus
    I bind the familiars of nine hundred witches
    I bind the fairies of the sky

Let the sky turn upside down, let the earth be overturned, let horns
    grow on horse and ass, let moustaches sprout on a young girl, let
    the dry cow-dung sink and the stones float, but let this charm not
    fail

2

    I bind the glow-worm of a virgin
    I bind every kind of Massan
    The nail of bone
    The lamp of flesh
    Who binds the spirits?
    The guru binds and I the guru's pupil
    May the waters of the river flow uphill
    May the dry cow-dung sink and stones float
    But let my words not fail.

          (Baiga, India)

THE PIG

1

Crushing the Pig

Ter na ni na O! Ter na ni na O!
Make a hole in the big gourd. I will go for water.
The old mother blows me out of the house.

O ter na ni na O!
The leaves of the parsa tree have long stalks.
You've been lying with your son.

I am going to cut my bewar.
You've been sleeping with your brother.
I am busy making rope.

You've been lying with your sister's son.
I am roasting gram.
I am lying with you, and your mother's watching us.

I am cutting wood for the fire.
You've been lying with a little boy.
Ter na ni na O! Ter na ni na O!

2

The Blood-Letting

Bring water, bring water! I'll wash his feet with water.
Bring oil, bring oil! I'll wash his feet with oil.
Bring milk, bring milk! I'll wash his feet with milk.

Teri na ho! Na na re na! Teri na na mor na na!
Today is Saturday, this is the night for the Laru!
We put the belwanti on the feet of the god.
I make a square of pearls.

O master, sit here on your throne.
Tare nake namare nana saheb! Tare nake namare nana!

3

The Coming of the Demon

Ter nana ke nano ho!

Where were you born? Where is your dwelling-place?
I was born down below. I live on the fence.
I am going to live with you.

Then I'll sleep with your sister.
O Phulera, dance and dance again.
Are you cooking in your kitchen?

May a cat dishonour you!
Don't have an old woman, she looks so very dirty.
By enjoying young girls, my life is satisfied.

Bring the root of adrak: may your father have you!
Where are you off to, girl?
May your brother dishonor you!

(Baiga, India)

TWO COSMOLOGIES

[1]

> The goddess Laksmi
> loves to make love to Vishnu
> from on top
> looking down she sees in his navel
> a lotus
> and on it Brahma the god
> but she can't bear to stop
> so she puts her hand
> over Vishnu's right eye
> which is the sun
> and night comes on
> and the lotus closes
> with Brahma inside

[2]

> Krishna went out to play
> Mother
> and he ate dirt
>
> Is that true Krishna
>
> No
> who said it
>
> Your brother Balarama
>
> Not true
> Look at my face
>
> Open your mouth.
>
>   he opened it

and she stood speechless

inside was
the universe

may he protect you

(Sanskrit, India)

From *THE GUIDE TO LORD MURUKAN*
(by Nakkirar)
"The Shaman & the Red God"

The possessed shaman with the spear
wears wreaths of green leaves
    with aromatic nuts between them
and beautiful long pepper,
    wild jasmine and the three-lobed
    white nightshade;

his jungle tribes
    have chests bright with sandal;
the strong-bowed warriors
    in their mountain village
drink with their kin
sweet liquor, honey brew
    aged in long bamboos,
they dance rough dances
    hand in hand
        to the beat of small
        hillside drums;

the women
wear wreaths of buds
    fingered and forced to blossom
    so they smell differently,
wear garlands
    from the pools on the hill
    all woven into chains,

cannabis leaves
    in their dense hair,

white clusters
    from a sacred *katampu* tree
    red-trunked and flowering,
arrayed between large cool leaves
    for the male beetle to suck at,

in leaf-skirts
    shaking
    on their jeweled mounds of venus,
and their gait sways with the innocence
    of peacocks;

the shaman
is the Red One himself,
is in red robes;

young leaf of the red-trunk *asoka*
flutters in his ears;

He wears a coat of mail,
    a warrior band on his ankle,
        a wreath of scarlet ixora;

has a flute,
    a horn,
    several small instruments
    of music;

for vehicles
    he has a ram,
    a peacock;

a faultless rooster
    on his banner;

the Tall One

with bracelets on his arms,
with a bevy of girls, voices
    like lutestrings,
a cloth
cool-looking above the waist-band
tied so it hangs
all the way to the ground;

his hands large
    as drumheads
    hold gently
    several soft-shouldered
        fawnlike women;

he gives them proper places
    and he dances
    on the hills:

and all such things happen
because
of His being
there.

And not only there.

(Tamil, India)

FOR THE LORD OF CAVES
(by Allama Prabhu)

I

I saw an ape tied up
at the main gate of the triple city,
taunting
every comer.

When the king came
with an army,
he broke them up at one stroke
and ate them.

He has a body, no head, this ape:
    legs without footsteps,
    hands without fingers;
    a true prodigy, really.

Before anyone calls him, he calls them.
I saw him clamber over the forehead of the wild elephant
born in his womb
and sway in play
in the dust of the winds.

I saw him juggle his body as a ball
in the depth of the sky,
play with a ten-hooded snake
in a basket; saw him blindfold
the eyes of the five virgins.
I saw him trample the forehead
of the lion that wanders in the ten streets,
I saw him raise the lion's eyebrows.
I saw him grow from amazement

to amazement, holding a diamond
in his hand.

Nothing added,
nothing taken,

the Lord's stance
is invisible
to men untouched
by the Linga of the Breath.

2

Looking for your light,
I went out:

it was like the sudden dawn
of a million million suns,

a ganglion of lightnings
for my wonder.

O lord of Caves,
if you are light,
there can be no metaphor.

(Kannada, India)

EUROPE & The Ancient Near East

THE CALENDAR

Moon of the Thaw

Moon of the Spring Salmon Run

Moon of the Calving

Moon of the Flowers

Moon of the Moulting

Moon of the Rutting Bison

Moon of the Nut

Moon of the First Frost

(Upper Paleolithic)

THE VULVA SONG OF INANA

I am lady I
who in this house
of holy lapis
praying
in my sanctuary say
my holy prayer
I who am lady
who am queen of heaven
let the chanter
chant of it
the singer sing of it
& let my bridegroom
my Dumuzi my wild bull
delight me
let their words fall
from their mouths
o singers
singing for their youth
their song that rises up
in Nippur gift to give
the son of god
I who am lady sing to
praising him
the chanter chants it
I who am Inana
give my vulva song to him
o star my vulva of the dipper
vulva slender boat of heaven
new moon crescent beauty vulva
unploughed desert vulva

fallow field for wild geese
where my mound longs
for his flooding
hill my vulva lying open
& the girl asks:
who will plough it?
vulva wet with flooding
of myself the queen
who brings this ox to stand here
"lady he will plow for you
"our king Dumuzi he will plow for you
o plow my vulva o my heart
my holy thighs are soaked with it
o holy mother.

(Sumerian)

THE BATTLE BETWEEN ANAT &
THE FORCES OF MOT

The Virgin Anat
Camouflages her divine aura
And puts on

The smell of goats and rabbits

She closes both the doors
Of the Palace of Anat

She catches up to the troops
In the mountain's slit

In the valley
Between the cities
How she slays them!

She cleaves the Shore folk
She smashes the Western man.

All around her

Heads—a swarm of locusts
Hands—like crickets, as many
Soldiers' hands as thorns on cactus

Anat bundles up her
Prize

She loads up the heads
On her back:
She ties the hands
On her belt.

And, returning from
The valley

Her knees slosh through
The soldiers' blood,
The soldiers' flesh
Up to her hips.

She prods the captives
With the back of her bow.

And Anat comes home
Unsatisfied with her slaughters
In the valley.
She fights on, indoors.

She sets up

Chairs for soldiers
Tables for soldiers
Stools to be soldiers.

How she slays them!

She smites them, then
Stands back
Her liver full of laughter
Her heart filled with joy
Overjoyed
For her knees wade in
Soldiers' blood:
Soldiers' flesh
Up to her hips.

When she has finished
Fighting in the house
Lunging between the tables

She is full

And she rubs her hands
In the soldiers' blood.

                                        She pours the rich oil
                                        Into a basin

And she washes
Her hands
Virgin Anat
Washes
Her fingers

The Sister-of-the-Peoples
Washes
Her hands in the blood
Of the soldiers
Her fingers in the gore
Of the soldiers

The chairs are only chairs again
The tables, tables
The footstools, footstools

                                        She pours out water

To wash
In the dew of the heavens
In the oil of the land
The rain from Cloudrider.

The Heavens' dew
Bathes her.

                                        The rain bathes her.

                                        (Ugaritic [Canaanite])

From *THE SONG OF ULLIKUMMI*

fucked the Mountain
fucked her but good his mind
sprang forward
and with the rock he slept
and into her let his manhood
go five times he let it go
ten times he let it go

in ikunta luli she is three
dalugasti long
she is one and a half
palhasti wide. What below she has
up on this his mind sprang upon

When Kumarbi his wisdom
he took upon
his mind
he took his istanzani
to his piran   hattatar
istanzani   piran daskizzi

Kumarbis-za   istanzani piran hattatar
daskizzi

sticks wisdom
unto his mind   like his cock

into her
iskariskizzi

the fucking
of the Mountain

      fucked the mountain   went right through it and came out
the other side

the father of all the gods
from his town Urkis
he set out
and to ikunta luli
he came

and in ikunta luli a great rock
lies
sallis perunas
kittari   he came upon
What below she has
               he sprang upon
with his mind
          he slept
with the rock   kattan sesta
with the peruni

         and into her misikan X-natur
andan his manhood
      flowed
into her

And five times he took her
nanzankan   5-anki das
and again ten times he took her
namma man zankan   10-anki das

Arunas
the Sea

             (Hittite)

From *THEOGONY*
[THE GODBIRTHS]
(by Hesiod)

children of Zeus
　　grant me song
of the gods who are forever
　　who were born out of Earth and star-lit Sky
　　　　　dark Night and Salt Sea

　　　Speak tell me
how we were born the beginning
　　　　of the ground we walk on
　　　rivers ponds lakes
　　sea without end swelling rushing
　　　　　　stars sending light
　　　　sky cupped overhead
　　　　　　gods born of them
　　　the gods givers of good things
dividing wealth among themselves
　　　honors titles a palace in the mountains
　　　　　　　　　　　　　　Olympos

Muses living in the houses of Olympos
　　　who was first?

　"Gap was first
　　　　then Earth the great chair with her immense teat

　　then Pit hard to see
　　deep in the wombs of Earth

next Love
loveliest of gods
who unstrings the body
tames the heart
breaks the mind
whether god or man
within his heart

the children of Gap were Gloom and Night
whom Love joined
their children were bright Air and Day

Earth's firstborn was star-lit Sky
a lover to cover her
equal in every particular

he made her his chair
the seat forever for the happy gods

o   o   o   o

as soon as his children were born
Sky hid them away
he deprived them of light
shoving them back deep into the wombs of Earth
he went away and laughed

Earth crowded groaned
she thought of something clever and ugly
she made gray adamant
made a sickle of it
made her children understand what she wanted done with it
sorrowing in her heart
she encouraged them

'pay him back for what he has done
he was first to hurt'
this is what she said

they were afraid
none of them answered
but great Kronos who thinks around corners was not afraid
he spoke to his wise mother
'I shall do it
I shall finish it
I do not love my father
he was first to hurt'
he spoke huge Earth shook with joy in her heart
she hid him in a place of ambush
she put the sickle with jagged teeth in his hand
she showed him her plan

great Sky came
bringing night
lying heavy on Earth in love and desire
she opened receiving him
their son stretched out his left hand from ambush
in his right he held the great sickle with jagged teeth
he chopped off his father's balls
he threw them to the wind behind him
they flew away a bloody track in the air
which Earth enfolded
in full time she gave birth to the strong Curses
and the great Titans
full-armored bursting with light shaking long spears
and the Meliads nymphs of the ash tree
all over boundless Earth
when his balls cut down by adamant

fell from boundless Earth
onto high Sea
battered they swam open currents
from that deathless flesh foam blossomed
inside the pink flower a girl was born and grew
she passed by holy Cythera
she came to Cyprus surrounded by water's flood
she stepped onto land
august lovely goddess
grass sprung up under her tapered feet
Aphrodite born of foam Cytheria the well-garlanded
because she grew inside the bloody foam
because she passed near Cythera
Cyprogene because there she was born
on Cyprus wave washed
Philomedes because she loves Love's bone
because she was born inside her father's balls
Love walks with her
Desire follows

(Greek)

SONG OF THE ARVAL BROTHERS

Then the Dancing Priests of Mars go into a room which is locked behind them. They tie up their robes and pick up the texts. They divide into (? three) groups to dance and sing:

field gods help
field gods help
field gods help

please Marmar
for most of us
no death
no disease

please Marmar
for most of us
no death
no disease

war Mars
enough no more
dance through our doorway
stop here
whip earth

war Mars
enough no more
dance through our doorway
stop here
whip earth

war Mars
enough no more
dance through our doorway

stop here
whip earth

war Mars
enough no more
dance through our doorway
stop here
whip earth

talk
to all the Seeders of the field
one by one

talk
to all the Seeders of the field
one by one

talk
to all the Seeders of the field
one by one

Marmor help
Marmor help
Marmor help

one two THREE
one two THREE
one two THREE

again
three times
again

After the Dance of the Three Steps, a signal is given. Public slaves
come in and put away the texts.

(Roman)

BIRTH OF THE FIRE GOD

heaven and earth labored
the crimson sea labored
          and in the sea
the red reed labored
from the reed's tip
          smoke rose
from the reed's tip
          flame rose
          and in the flame
a youth was running
he had hair of fire
          a beard of flame
and his eyes were suns

(Armenian)

THE ROUND DANCE OF JESUS

"A praise poem
"we sing now
"will go to meet what is to come
& had us form a circle
we stood in with folded hands
himself   was in the middle
(said)   You answer
Amen
then started singing
praises   saying
"Praises   Father
circling & we answered him
Amen   (said)
Praises   Word   (said)
Praises   Grace
Amen   (said)
Praises   Spirit   (said)
Praises   Holy Holy   (said)
O thee transfiguration   (said)
Amen   (said)
Praises   Father
Thank you   Sunshine   Light
no darkness   (said)
"I will inform you now
"the reason for this thanks
(then said)
I save
& will be saved
Amen
I free

& will be freed
Amen
I hurt
& will be hurt
Amen
Am born
& will give birth
Amen
I feed
& will be food
Amen
I hear
& will be heard
Amen
I will be known
all knowing mind
Amen
I will be washed
& I will wash
Amen
all Grace Sweet Mind the Dance is round
I blow the pipe for
all are in the Round Dance
I will pipe
all dance along
Amen
I will moan low
all beat your breasts
Amen
the One & Only Eight
plays up for us
Amen
Old Number Twelve

stomps up above
Amen
the Universe controls
the dancer
Amen
whoever isn't dancing
's in the dark
Amen
I will go
& I will stay
Amen
I will dress thee
& I will dress
Amen
I will be Oned
& I will One
Amen
I have no house
& I have houses
Amen
I have no place
& I have places
Amen
I have no temple
& I have temples
Amen
I am a lamp to thee
who see me
Amen
I am a mirror to thee
who view me
Amen
I am a door to thee

who come thru me
Amen
I am a way to thee
wayfarer
Amen (said)
"Follow
"my Round Dance
"& see yourself in me
"the Speaker
"& seeing what I speak
"keep silent on
"my mysteries
"or dancing think of what
"I do
"make yours the suffering of a man
"that I will suffer
"yet powerless to understand your suffering
"without a word
"the Father sent language thru me
"the sufferer you saw
"& saw me suffering
"you grew restless
"shaken
"you were moved toward wisdom
"lean on me
"I am a pillow
"who am I?
"you only will know me
"when I'm gone—
"but am not he for whom
"I am now taken—
"will know it when you reach it
"& knowing suffering will know

"how not to suffer
"myself will teach you what
"you do not know
"I am your god
"not the betrayer's
"will harmonize the Sweet Soul with my own
"the Word of Wisdom speaks in me
"says
"Praises   Father
& we answered him
Amen   (said)
Praises   Word   (said)
Praises   Grace
Amen   (said)
Praises   Spirit   (said)
Praises   Holy Holy   (said)
"& if thou wouldst understand that which is me
"know this   all that I have said I have uttered
"playfully   & I was by no means ashamed of it
"I danced
"& when you dance in understanding
"understand & say
"Amen

(Syriac)

A SONG OF AMERGIN

I am the wind which breathes upon the sea,
I am the wave of the ocean,
I am the murmur of the billows,
I am the bull of seven battles,
I am the vulture upon the rocks,
I am a tear shed by the sun,
I am the fairest of plants,
I am a wild boar for courage,
I am a salmon in the water,
I am a lake in the plain,
I am a word of science,
I am the point of the lance in battle,
I am the god who created fire in the head.
Who is it who throws light into the meeting on the mountain?
Who announces the ages of the moon?
Who teaches the place where the sun rests?

(Irish)

From *THE RED BOOK OF HERGEST*

(attributed to Llywarch Hen)

Let the cock's comb be red; naturally loud
Be his voice, from his triumphant bed:
Man's rejoicing, God will recommend.

Let the swineherds be merry at the sighing
Of the wind; let the silent be graceful;
Let the vicious be accustomed to misfortune.

Let the bailiff impeach; let evil be a tormentor;
Let clothes be fitting;
He that loves a bard, let him be a handsome giver.

Let a monarch be vehement, and let him be brave;
And let there be a hurdle on the gap;
He will not show his face that will not give.

Fleet let the racers be on the side
Of the mountain; let care be in the bosom;
Unfaithful let the inconstant be.

Let the knight be conspicuous; let the thief be wary;
The rich woman may be deceived;
The friend of the wolf is the lazy shepherd.

Let the knight be conspicuous: fleet be the horse;
Let the scholar be ambitious;
Let the prevaricating one be unfaithful.

Let cows be round-backed; let the wolf be gray;
Let the horse over barley be swift;
Like gossamer will he press the grain at the roots.

Let the deaf be bent; let the captive be heavy;
Nimble the horse in battles;

Like gossamer will he press the grain the ground.

Let the deaf be dubious; let the rash be inconstant;
Let the mischievous wrangle;
The prudent need but be seen to be loved.

Let the lake be deep; let the spears be sharp;
Let the brow of the sick be bold at the shout of war;
Let the wise be happy—God commends him.

Let the exile wander; let the brave be impulsive;
Let the fool be fond of laughter.

Let the furrows be wet; let bail be frequent;
Let the sick be complaining, and the one in health merry;
Let the lapdog snarl; let the hag be peevish.

Let him that is in pain cry out; let an army be moving;
Let the well-fed be wanton;
Let the strong be bold; let the hill be icy.

Let the gull be white; let the wave be loud;
Let the gore be apt to clot on the ashen spear;
Let the ice be gray; let the heart be bold.

Let the camp be green; let the suitor be reproachless;
Let there be pushing of spears in the defile;
Let the bad woman be with frequent reproaches.

Let the hen be clawed; let the lion roar;
Let the foolish be pugnacious;
Let the heart be broken with grief.

Let the tower be white; let the harness glitter;
Let there be beauty—many will desire it;
Let the glutton hanker; let the old man mediate.

(Welsh)

TWO POEMS FOR
ALL-HALLOWS' EVE

1

Winter's Eve,
baiting of apples,
who is coming out to play?

A White Lady
on the top of the tree,
whittling an umbrella stick.

It's one o'clock,
it's two o'clock,
it's time for the pigs to have dinner.

2

A tailless Black Sow
& a headless White Lady:

may the tailless Black Sow
snatch the hindmost.

A tailless Black Sow
on Winter's Eve:

thieves coming along,
knitting stockings.

(Welsh)

THE FAIRY WOMAN'S LULLABY

My little dun buck thou,

Offspring of the lowing cow,
For whom the Mull cow lows,
My darling and my fair one,
My soul and my delight!
Thou art not of the race of Clan Donald,
But of a race dearer to us—
The race of Leod of the galleys,
The race of the weighty saplings,
The race of the breastplates,
    Norway was thy patrimony!

    Faire fire
Thou art not the calf of
    Faire fire
The old shriveled cow,
    Faire fire
Thou art not the little kid
    Faire fire
Whom the she-goat brought forth,
    Faire fire
Thou art not the lamb
    Faire fire
Whom the sheep brought forth,
    Faire fire
Thou art not the foal
    Faire fire
Of a lean old mare,
    Faire fire
Though thou art not,

Faire fire
Thou art my calf!

Fairim firim obh obh!
May I not hear of thy wounding,
May I not see thy tears,
Until thy shoes are holed,
Until thy nose grows sharp,
Until thou duly becomest grey
As hoar as the clouds,
Until thy day becomes dark
        Within the precincts of Dunvegan!

(Scottish Gaelic)

THE NINE HERBS CHARM

remember mugwort what you did reveal
what you did at Regenmeld
you have strength against three and against thirty
you have strength against poison and against infection
you have strength against the foe who fares through the land

and you plaintain mother of herbs
open to the east   mighty within
chariots have creaked over you   queens have ridden over you
brides have moaned over you   over you bulls gnashed their teeth
all these you did withstand and resist
so may you withstand poison and infection
and the foe who fares through the land

this herb is called stime   it grew on a stone
it resists poison   it fights pain
it is called harsh   it fights against poison
this is the herb that strove with the snake
it has strength against poison   it has strength against infection
it has strength against the foe who fares through the land

now cock's-spur grass conquer the greater poisons   though you
      are the lesser
you the mightier vanquish the lesser until he is cured of both

remember mayweed what you did reveal
what you brought to pass at Alorford
where he did not lose his life because of infection
because mayweed was placed on his food

this is the herb called wergulu
it crossed the ocean on the back of a seal
it came to heal the hurt of other poison
these nine herbs against nine poisons

a snake came crawling   it bit a man
Woden took nine glorious herbs
struck the serpent into nine parts
the apple brought this to pass against poison
no more to enter her house

thyme and fennel   a pair of great power
put in the world to help all   the poor and the rich
to stand against pain   to resist venom
they have power against three and against thirty
against the fiend's hand and the sudden trick
against witchcraft of evil creatures

now these nine herbs have power against nine evil spirits
against nine poisons and against nine infectious diseases
against the red poison   against the running poison
against the white poison   against the blue poison
against the yellow poison   against the green poison
against the black poison   against the blue poison
against the brown poison   against the crimson poison
against snake blister   against water blister
against horn blister   against thistle blister
against ice blister   against poison blister
if any poison comes flying from the east or if any poison comes flying
      from the north
or if any poison comes flying from the west upon the people

i alone know running water   let the nine serpents heed it
may all pastures now spring with herbs
the seas   all salt water   be destroyed
when I blow this poison from you

mugwort, plaintain, open to the east, lamb's cress, cockspur grass, mayweed, nettle, crabapple, thyme and fennel, old soap; crush the herbs to dust, mix with the soap and the apple's juice. make a paste of water and ashes; take fennel, boil it in the paste and bathe with egg moisture, either before or after he puts on the salve. sing this charm on each of the herbs, three times before he works them together and on the apple also; and sing the same charm into the man's mouth and into both his ears and into the wound before he puts on the salve.

(Anglo-Saxon)

From *SHAKESPEARE'S* LEAR

[*Enter* EDGAR *disguised as a madman.*]

EDG. Away! the foul fiend follows me!

Through the sharp hawthorn blows the cold wind.

Humh! go to thy cold bed, and warm thee.

LEAR. Hast thou given all to thy two daughters? And art thou come to this?

EDG. Who gives any thing to poor Tom? whom the foul fiend hath led through fire and through flame, through ford and whirlpool, o'er bog and quagmire; that hath laid knives under his pillow and halters in his pew; set ratsbane by his porridge; made him proud of heart, to ride on a bay trotting-horse over four-inched bridges, to course his own shadow for a traitor. Bless thy five wits! Tom's a-cold,—O, do, de, do de, do de. Bless thee from whirlwinds, star-blasting, and taking! Do poor Tom some charity, whom the foul fiend vexes: there could I have him now,—and there,—and there again, and there.

[*Storm still.*]

LEAR. What, has his daughters brought him to this pass?

Could'st thou save nothing? Didst thou give them all?

FOOL. Nay, he reserved a blanket, else we had been all shamed.

LEAR. Now, all the plagues that in the pendulous air

Hang fated o'er men's faults light on thy daughters!

KENT. He hath no daughters, sir.

LEAR. Death, traitor! nothing could have subdued nature

To such a lowness but his unkind daughters.

Is it the fashion that discarded fathers

Should have thus little mercy on their flesh?

Judicious punishment! 't was this flesh begot

Those pelican daughters.

EDG. Pillicock sat on Pillicock-hill.

Halloo, halloo, loo, loo!

FOOL. This cold night will turn us all to fools and madmen.

EDG. Take heed o' the foul fiend; obey thy parents; keep thy word justly; swear not; commit not with man's sworn spouse; set not thy sweet heart on proud array. Tom's a-cold.

LEAR. What hast thou been?

EDG. A serving-man, proud in heart and mind; that curled my hair; wore gloves in my cap; served the lust of my mistress' heart, and did the act of darkness with her; swore as many oaths as I spake words, and broke them in the sweet face of heaven; one that slept in the contriving of lust, and waked to do it. Wine loved I deeply, dice dearly; and in woman outparamoured the Turk. False of heart, light of ear, bloody of hand; hog in sloth, fox in stealth, wolf in greediness, dog in madness, lion in prey. Let not the creaking of shoes nor the rustling of silks betray thy poor heart to woman. Keep thy foot out of brothels, thy hand out of plackets, thy pen from lenders' books, and defy the foul fiend. Still through the hawthorn blows the cold wind: Says suum, mun, ha, no, nonny. Dolphin my boy, my boy, sessa! let him trot by.

[*Storm still.*]

LEAR. Why, thou wert better in thy grave than to answer with thy uncovered body this extremity of the skies. Is man no more than this? Consider him well. Thou owest the worm no silk, the beast no hide, the sheep no wool, the cat no perfume. Ha! here's three on's are sophisticated! Thou art the thing itself; unaccommodated man is no more but such a poor, bare, forked animal as thou art. Off, off, you lendings! come, unbutton here. [*Tearing off his clothes.*]

FOOL. Prithee, nuncle, be contented; 'tis a naughty night to swim in. Now a little fire in a wild field were like an old lecher's heart; a small spark, all the rest on's body cold. Look, here comes a walking fire.

[*Enter* GLOUCESTER, *with a torch.*]

EDG. This is the foul fiend Flibbertigibbet. He begins at curfew, and walks till the first cock. He gives the web and the pin, squinies the eye, and makes the hare-lip; mildews the white wheat, and hurts the poor creature of earth.

> St. Withold footed thrice the old;
> He met the night-mare and her nine-fold;
> Bid her alight,
> And her troth plight,
> And, aroint thee, witch, aroint thee!

KENT. How fares your grace?

LEAR. What's he?

KENT. Who's there? What is't you seek?

GLOU. What are you there? Your names?

EDG. Poor Tom, that eats the swimming frog, the toad, the tadpole, the wall-newt and the water; that in the fury of his heart, when the foul fiend rages, eats cow-dung for sallets; swallows the old rat and the ditch-dog; drinks the green mantle of the standing-pool; who is whipped from tithing to tithing, and stock-punished, and imprisoned; who hath had three suits to his back, six shirts to his body, horse to ride, and weapon to wear;

> But mice and rats, and such small deer,
> Have been Tom's food for seven long year.

Beware my follower. Peace, Smulkin; peace, thou fiend!

(English)

ODIN'S SHAMAN SONG
[From *The Elder Edda*]
"The Runes"

I know I hung   on the gust-beat-gallows
    nine full nights,
gashed with a stake   and given to fire-see,
    myself to myself,
on that ash-tree   of which none know
    from where the roots rise.

They did not comfort me   with bread
    nor with a drinking horn:
    I looked down,
I took up the runes,   shrieking their names
    I fell back from there.

I got nine mighty songs   from the famous son
    of Bolthorn, Bestla's father,
and I got a drink   of precious mead
    sprinkled as from the heart.

Then I began to thrive   and bear wisdom
    I grew and prospered;
Each word drew   another word from me,
each deed drew   another deed from me.

Runes you will find,   fateful signs
    that the king of singers coloured
and the great gods have made,
good strong staves   good stout staves
carved by a god-ruling spirit.

Odin for the gods,   Dain for the elves,

and Dvalin for the dwarfs,
Asvid for giants   and humankind
   and some I wrote myself.

Know how to cut   know how
   to read them?
Know how to tint   know how
   to test them?
Know how to plead   know how
   to proffer?
Know how to send   know how
   to surrender?

Better no prayer   than too big an offering,
   By your getting measure your gift;
Better no gain   than too big a sacrifice,
as Thund wrote   before lives were laid down
where he rose up   when he came home.

                  (Icelandic)

From *KALEVALA*
"Fire"

Ilmarinen struck
fire, Väinämöinen
flashed above eight heavens, in
    the ninth sky: a spark
    dropped down through the earth
    through Manala, and
through the smoke-hole caked with soot
    the children's cradle
    it broke maidens' breasts
and burned the mother's bosom.
The mother knew more of it:
she shoved it into the sea
lest the maid go to Mana
lest the fire should burn her up
    lest the flame roast her.

That gloomy Lake Alue
three times on a summer night
foamed as high as the spruces
in the torment of the fire
the flame's overwhelmingness.

    A smooth whitefish swam
    and swallowed the spark:
torment to the swallower
came, hardship to the gulper.
    A grey pike swam up
    swallowed the whitefish
    a light lake-trout swam
    swallowed the grey pike

a red salmon swam
and swallowed the light lake-trout:
it swam, it darted about
in between the salmon-crags
in the torment of the fire.

    It said in these words
it uttered along these lines:
    "Fire once burned much land
one evil summer of fire
one year of flame without help.
A small piece was left unburned
at the turn of Ahti's fence
at the rear of Hirska's bank."
    It was hoed and dug
and Tuoni's maggot was found
and Tuoni's maggot was burned
    in a copper boat
in an iron-bottomed punt.
Its ashes were sown upon
the shore of Lake Alimo:
    flax without like grew
    peerless linen rose
in a single summer night.
It was quickly stripped
now taken to the water
now the linen put in soak.
    The sisters spun it
    the brothers wove cloth
    and fashioned a net.
Sturdy old Väinämöinen
put the young ones on the net.
They drew across the water:
    that fish did not come

for which the net was fashioned.
They drew along the water:
    that fish did not come
for which the net was fashioned.
They drew against the water:
the salmon splashed in the sea.

Sturdy old Väinämöinen
could not bear to put his hand
without mittens of iron:
took his mittens of iron
split open the red salmon—
    the light lake-trout came
from the red salmon's belly
split open the light lake-trout—
    the grey pike came out
he split open the grey pike—
    the smooth whitefish came
split open the smooth whitefish—
    and the spark came out.

There the fire was lulled
and the flame was rocked
at a misty headland's tip
    there the fire was lulled
    in a silver sling:
the golden cradle jingled
the copper mantle trembled
    as the fire was lulled.

(Finnish)

THE FOX

who runs along the wolf's way
follows
the wolf's track, he finds
much meat there
then sleeps inside the clearings
& when he falls asleep his shape
turns over   like a skin
it prowls relentlessly
after the reindeer herds
o body left to ravens
wolves & eagles
for a song   the night birds
crunch its bones
eagles & foxes shit
the flesh & bones on hillsides
then the crows take turns
to eat their shit
so hungry after meat
they are   he is himself
he eats so much
he vomits
then sucks his vomit up
o twisty are the fox's tracks
that sly beast
whom no devil can catch up with
master gonnif
precious is thy fur
thy pelt & not thy skin worth taking

(Lapp)

BLOOD RIVER SHAMAN CHANT

then grasped
my sky tree   grasped it
all my friends
would bend their backs to me
they sprang up to their feet
then stretched me on their laps
"now I must harness the sky's reindeer
"the smallest of the seven
"must hold the reindeer's reins
cloud island sledge
shot off   we found
the grass ridge
there at the ridge's foot we found
a hill with lawns
bored through by seven lizards
who bored through it
"mother lizard   grandmother
"give thou a child
"a child give to my friend
the lizard child   my friend
bored through my side
we found the ice ridge then
& at its side
found a blood river
the blood river started flowing
its currents started flowing
in the currents the blood river
tufts of hair flowed by
for me to cut   to cut the river
with bare hands

would make the blood stop
the river & the current stop
until we crossed the river
& the blood   we found
the iron tent
I went into the iron tent
the seven women sat there
I embraced them   seven women
swaddling seven boys
cloud island sledge
shot off   again it took us
to our tent
"I must unhitch
"our spirit reindeer
"the smallest of the seven
"I must head back to camp
"my friends must head back
"of the seven let a single one remain
then they took back my sky tree
left me   I have found no place
to camp but here
inside this fire I fall
to pieces

(Nenets)

BALD MOUNTAIN ZAUM-POEMS

1

Kumara
Nich, nich, pasalam, bada.
Eschochomo, lawassa, schibboda.
Kumara
A.a.o – o.o.o – i.i.i. – e.e.e. – u.u.u. – ye.ye.ye.
Aa, la ssob, li li ssob lu lu ssob.
Schunschan
Wichoda, kssara, gujatun, gujatun, etc.

2

io, ia, – o – io, ia, zok, io, ia,
pazzo! io, ia, pipazzo!
Sookatjema, soossuoma, nikam, nissam, scholda.
Paz, paz, paz, paz, paz, paz, paz, paz!
Pinzo, pinzo, pinzo, dynsa.
Schono, tschikodam, wikgasa, mejda.
Bouopo, chondyryamo, boupo, galpi.
Ruachado, rassado, ryssado, zalyemo.
io, ia, o. io, ia, zok. io nye zolk, io ia zolk.

(Russian)

A POEM FOR THE GODDESS HER CITY & THE MARRIAGE OF HER SON & DAUGHTER

she builds her city
    the white goddess
  builds it
not on the sky or earth
    but on a cloud branch
  builds
three gates to enter it
    one gate she builds
  in gold
the second pearls
    the third in scarlet
  where the gate is dry gold
there the goddess' son
    is wedded
  where the gate
is pearl
    the goddess' daughter
  is the bride
& where the gate is scarlet
    solitary
  sits the goddess
solitary glances
    everywhere
  she sees
the lightning
    playing with the thunder
  the precious sister

with two brothers
                & the bride
        plays with
the bridegroom's
           brothers
       there the goddess sees
the lightning
           win it all
      the precious sister
over her two brothers
             & the bride
      over her bridegroom's brothers
& the goddess was enchanted by it

(Serbian)

THE MESSAGE OF KING SAKIS & THE LEGEND OF THE TWELVE DREAMS HE HAD IN ONE NIGHT

1

I saw a gold pillar from earth to heaven.

2

I saw a dark towel
hanging from heaven to earth.

3

I saw three boiling kettles:
one of grease, one of butter, and one of water,
and grease boiled over into butter
and butter into water
but the water boiled all by itself.

4

I saw an old mare with a colt
and a black eagle pulling grass by its roots
and laying it down before the mare
while the colt neighs.

5

I saw a bitch lying on a dunghill
while the puppies were barking from her womb.

6

I saw many monks soaked in pitch
wailing because they can't get out.

7

I saw a beautiful horse
grazing with two heads—
one in front, one in the back.

8

I saw precious stones, pearls, and royal wreaths
scattered over the whole kingdom,
but fire came down from heaven
and burnt everything into ashes.

9

I saw the rich giving workers
gold or silver or rice,
but when they came back to ask for their rewards
found that no one was left.

10

I saw evil-faced rocks descending
from the sky
and walking all over the earth.

11

I saw three virgins in a stubble field
bearing wreaths of sunlight on their heads
and sweet-smelling flowers in their hands.

12

I saw men with narrow eyes,
with hairs standing up and cruel fingernails,
and these were the devil's own servants.

(Serbo-Croatian)

A LOVE POEM WITH WITCHES

I got up this morning
woke up early this morning
rinsed my eyes out with water
kneeled down before the saints
threw on a white gown
ran over to the church
stepped across the threshold
nobody there had seen me
nobody there had heard me
nobody but the witches
nobody but the brujas
they made a crazy racket
with their hair out in the wind
they dragged me out of town
they wrapped me in a snakeskin
smeared me with fish & tar
made me the world's great fool
then I shouted
and I bellowed
nobody there had heard me
nobody there had seen me
nobody but Saint Mary
with her golden staff came down to me
she took me by the hand
she led me down the road to Abraham's
dropped me off in the Jordan fountain
stuffed a cuckoo into my mouth
that everyone thought was a nightingale
everyone there looked out for me
dressed me up for sweet loving

I wandered down to the highway
sick people there were looking for me
young boys climbed up on the fences
old ladies ran out without shawls
old men without caps
& young boys without belts
they all asked:
who is this
beautiful woman?
this sharp lady admiral
for now & forever
may everyone cuddle & love her

(Rumanian)

THE DESCRIPTIONS OF KING LENT

(by François Rabelais)

[1]

"Lent was a little better proportioned in his external parts," Xenomanes continued, "except that he had seven ribs more than a common man."

His toes were like the keyboard of a spinet.
His nails like a gimlet.
His feet like guitars.
His heels like clubs.
His soles like hanging-lamps.
His legs like snares.
His knees like stools.
His thighs like a crank-arbalest.
His hips like borers.
His potbelly was buttoned up in the old fashion and belted high.
His navel was like a fiddle.
His pubic bone was like a cream cake.
His member like a slipper.
His ballocks like a double leather bottle.
His genitals like a carpenter's plane.
His testicle-strings like tennis rackets.
His perineum like a flageolet.
His arse-hole like a crystal mirror.
His buttocks like a harrow.
His loins like a pot of butter.
The base of his spine like a billiard table.
His back like a large cross-bow.
His vertebrae like a bagpipe.

His ribs like a spinning-wheel.

His chest like a canopy.

His shoulder-blades like mortars.

His breast like a portable organ.

His nipples like cattle-horns.

His armpits like chessboards.

His shoulders like a wheel-barrow.

His arms like round hoods.

His fingers cold as friary andirons.

His wrist bones like a pair of stilts.

His arm-bones like sickles.

His elbows like rat-traps.

His hands like curry-combs.

His neck like a beggar's bowl.

His throat like a punch-strainer.

His adam's apple like a barrel with a pair of bronze goitres hanging down from it, fine pieces which matched and were shaped like an hour-glass.

His beard was like a lantern.

His chin like a toadstool.

His ears like a pair of mittens.

His nose like a high boot, hung on like a small shield.

His nostrils like babies' caps.

His eyebrows were like dripping pans, and beneath the left one he had a mole of the size and shape of a piss-pot.

His eyelids were like fiddles.

His eyes like comb-cases.

His optic nerves like tinder-boxes.

His forehead like an earthenware bowl.

His temples like watering-cans.

His cheeks like a pair of clogs.

His jaws like a drinking-cup.

His teeth were like boar spears; and you will find specimens of his

milk-teeth at Coulonges-sur-l'Autize in Poitou, where there is
one, and at La Brosse in Saintonge, where there are two hung
above the doors of the cellar.
His tongue was like a harp.
His mouth like a horse-cloth.
His misshapen face like a mule's pack-saddle.
His head twisted to one side like a retort.
His skull like a game-bag.
The sutures of his skull like the Pope's seal.
His skin like a gabardine coat.
His epidermis like a sieve.
His hair like a scrubbing-brush.
His whiskers as already described.

[2]

If he spat, it was basketfuls of artichokes.
If he blew his nose, it was salted eels.
If he wept, it was ducks in onion sauce.
If he trembled, it was great hare-pies.
If he sweated, it was stock-fish in butter sauce.
If he belched, it was oysters in the shell.
If he sneezed, it was barrels full of mustard.
If he coughed, it was boxes of quince-jelly.
If he sobbed, it was pennyworths of water-cress.
If he yawned, it was potsful of pea-soup.
If he sighed, it was smoked ox-tongues.
If he whistled, it was hods full of fairy-tales.
If he snored, it was bucketsful of shelled beans.
If he frowned, it was pigs' trotters fried in their own fat.
If he spoke, it was far from being that crimson silk out of which
Parysatis wanted whoever spoke to her son Cyrus, King of
the Persians, to weave his words. What it was, was coarse
Auvergne frieze.

If he blew, it was boxes for indulgences.
If he blinked his eyes, it was waffles and wafers.
If he grumbled, it was March-born cats.
If he nodded his head, it was iron-bound wagons.
If he pouted, it was broken staves.
If he mumbled, it was the law clerks' pantomime.
If he stamped his foot, it was postponements and five-year
    adjournments.
If he stepped back, it was piles of cockle-shells.
If he slobbered, it was communal ovens.
If he was hoarse, it was an entry of the Morris-dancers.
If he farted, it was brown cow-hide gaiters.
If he pooped, it was Cordova-leather shoes.
If he scratched himself, it was new regulations.
If he sang, it was peas in the pod.
If he shat, it was toadstools and morels.
If he puffed, it was cabbages fried in oil, alias, in the language of
    Languedoc, *caules d'amb'olif.*
If he made a speech, it was last year's snows.
If he worried, it was for the bald and the shaven alike.
If he gave nothing to the tailor, the embroiderer did no better.
If he woolgathered, it was of members flying and creeping up walls.
If he dreamt, it was of mortgage deeds.

(French)

DEEP SONG

1

in the middle of the sea
a stone
my love was sitting on
to tell her troubles:
only to the earth, oh only
to the earth I tell
what happened to me
nowhere in the world would find
someone to tell
but every morning
would go out
& ask the rosemary:
if love's so bad
can there still be a cure
before I die from it?

2

I climbed the wall   the wind
would answer me
"why all this sighing, sighing
"& no end to it
the wind would cry to me
on seeing
these long gashes in my heart
until I loved
the wind   wind of a woman
as a woman is a wind
I stayed in
& was jealous of the wind

that brushed your face
if that wind was a man
I'd kill him
& not be afraid to row
but rowing, rowing
only the wind to frighten me
up from your harbor

(Spanish Gypsy)

THE CANTICLE FOR BROTHER SUN
(by Francesco d'Assisi)

Most high omnipotent good lord:
all praise is yours & honor glory
every blessing
yours & only yours
& no man living fit to say your name

Be praised my lord with all your creatures
but especially with Mr. Brother Sun
because you show us light & day through him
& he is lovely glowing with great shine
from you my lord: his definition

Be praised my lord for Sister Moon & for the stars
because you made them for your sky their
loveliness is white & rare

Be praised my lord for Brother Wind
& for the air & cloudy days
& bright & all days else because
through these you give your creatures
sustenance

Be praised my lord for Sister Water
because she shows great use & humble-
ness is hers & preciousness
& depth

Be praised my lord for Brother Fire
through whom you light all nights upon the earth
Because he too is lovely
full of joy & manly strength

Be praised my lord because our sister
Mother Earth sustains & rules
us & because she raises
food to feed us: colored flowers
grass

Be praised my lord for those who pardon by your love
& suffer illnesses & grief
Bless those who undergo in silence
the poor for whom you hold a crown

Be praised my lord for Sister Death-of-Body
whom no man living will escape
And pity those who die in mortal sin
& everyone she finds who minds you
bless: no second death
to bring them hurt

Oh praise my lord & bless my lord & thank
& serve my lord with humbleness
Triumphant

(Italian)

From *EUROPE A PROPHECY*
(by William Blake)

Five windows light the cavern'd Man; thro' one he breathes the air;
Thro' one, hears music of the spheres; thro' one, the eternal vine
Flourishes, that he may recieve the grapes; thro' one can look.
And see small portions of the eternal world that ever groweth;
Thro' one, himself pass out what time he please, but he will not;
For stolen joys are sweet, & bread eaten in secret pleasant.

So sang a Fairy mocking as he sat on a streak'd Tulip,
Thinking none saw him: when he ceas'd I started from the trees!
And caught him in my hat as boys knock down a butterfly
How know you this said I small Sir? where did you learn this song
Seeing himself in my possession thus he answerd me:
My master, I am yours. command me, for I must obey.

Then tell me, what is the material world, and is it dead?
He laughing answer'd: I will write a book on leaves of flowers,
If you will feed me on love-thoughts, & give me now and then
A cup of sparkling poetic fancies; so when I am tipsie,
I'll sing to you to this soft lute; and shew you all alive
The world, where every particle of dust breathes forth its joy.

I took him home in my warm bosom: as we went along
Wild flowers I gatherd; & he shew'd me each eternal flower:
He laugh'd aloud to see them whimper because they were pluck'd.
They hover'd round me like a cloud of incense: when I came
Into my parlour and sat down, and took my pen to write:
My Fairy sat upon the table, and dictated EUROPE.

(English)

OCEANIA

TWELVE KURA SONGS FROM TIKOPIA

1

o kume kume of the falling rain
kume to draw near
and to ask after kume

And One-Before-Us to draw near

to do something to enter, o
to do something to turn to us

2

stand firm, my housepost
and stand firm for me, my housepost
rata was dancing in front
he had followed me

he had followed me, o
he had followed me here like the iron tree
he had followed me, o

3

& knock away the rear of the hermit crab, o
my maleness had long been prepared
now was ready

now that you've turned on your back
& sleep snoring

4

your pit, your cherry
is concealed and must stay hidden

must not spread your legs apart
but hide what smells there

5

take it
& keep on scorching it
& turn it over nicely
with legs apart

& call the long one penis
to turn it over nicely
& desire it

6

he is like a spider, he shits
& comes on as a tree trunk

& shits, o he shits on that road
all men reach for

7

& is red as rata
& as all this land
& its mountains

8

asking my wife to come near
to hold up my penis
& say:
you are penis

like the cunt of an unmarried woman
his penis is dark

9

    the woman you found on the road
    who stayed on the road
    and brought the men to fulfillment

    whose buttocks are black as an oven

10

    leave me only
    the lips of my throat
    o my belly is hungry

    o this bright red flower
    you carried away
    & my fear you would drop it

11

    the bright red flower of that road
    adorned by woman

    you came walking down that road
    your body glowing

12

    your penis, penis of the hot cordyline root
    your fruit-dark penis

    that looks dark, looks dark to me
    in front of you
    & darker, like a cowry shell
    for darkness

               (British Solomon Islands)

TWO FOR THE GOD AIA

1

The Cycle of A'alsa

Water all over
all all over
darkness all over
all all over

Aia sitting seated
Aia living alive

Aia sitting seated
sitting forever
Aia living alive
living forever
Aia without beginning
Aia without end

Aia above the water
Aia has lived
Aia has watched
above the darkness
Aia has lived
Aia has watched

Aia creator of our earth
Aia creator of our home
Creator of earth
creator creating
creator of home
creator creating

2

Aia walks on the road
Aia all naked.
He walks on the road.

Aia my hand is faultless
Aia all naked
My hand is faultless!

Aia you shake your spear!
Aia all naked
you shake your spear!

Aia in war decoration
Aia all naked
Aia in war decoration.

(Mekeo, New Guinea)

TOLAI SONGS

1

The Chinaman rode on a bicycle,
Carrying a bunch of cabbages.
Where is your village?
The little bird flew around, around, around.

2

He is after you, ladyfriend.
A friend wrote it like this:
A yellow fish. Guard the use of your name,
A policeman is after you and you are afraid.

3

Three boys went by canoe to Gumu,
To the river at Gavi.
And what is the reason for the difference
Between the Catholic Church and the Methodists?
And what is the reason for the difference
Between the Catholic Church and the S.D.A.'s?

(Kuanua, New Guinea)

PIDGIN SONG

Time me look so very young
Allo people i wandim me
And alogeter wandim talko too much longo me
But time me ready for die
No more man i save come longo me
No more man i save wandim talko lelebiti longo me.

Mummy and my Daddy
Come sit down withim me
Sorry and karai kasim me now
Oh Mummy and my Daddy
Come say good bye longo me
Time bilongo me for die come kolosap now.

Ande alogeta leavim me
No more man i save come longo me
No good all i kasim sikinis i kasim me
Oh my angel up in heaven
Come down and pick up me
No good all i makim foolu too much longo me.

(Papua New Guinea)

THE GUMAGABU SONG
(by Tomakam)

I

The stranger of Gumagabu sits on the top of the mountain.
"Go on top of the mountain, the towering mountain . . ."
——They cry for Toraya. . . .——
The stranger of Gumagabu sits on the slope of the mountain.
——The fringe of small clouds lifts above Boyowa;
The mother cries for Toraya——
"I shall take my revenge."
The mother cries for Toraya.

II

Our mother, Dibwaruna, dreams on the mat.
She dreams about the killing.
"Revenge the wailing;
Anchor; hit the Gabu strangers!"
——The stranger comes out;
The chief gives him the *pari*;
"I shall give you the *doga*;
Bring me things from the mountain to the canoe!"

III

We exchange our *vaygu'a*;
The rumour of my arrival spreads through the Koya
We talk and talk.
He bends and is killed.
His companions run away;
His body is thrown into the sea;
The companions of the stranger run away,
We sail home.

IV

   Next day, the sea foams up,
The chief's canoe stops on the reef;
The storm approaches;
The chief is afraid of drowning.
The conch shell is blown:
It sounds in the mountain.
They all weep on the reef.

V

   They paddle in the chief's canoe;
They circle round the point of Bewara.
"I have hung my basket.
I have met him."
So cries the chief,
So cries repeatedly the chief.

VI

   Women in festive decoration
Walk on the beach.
Nawaruva puts on her turtle rings;
She puts on her *luluga'u* skirt.
In the village of my fathers, in Burakwa.
There is plenty of food;
Plenty is brought in for distribution.

(Trobriand Islands, New Guinea)

THREE DRUM POEMS

Introduction

sezètu
sezètutu
sezeżagarasèku selùtutu
sagàra sagàra sagàra sagàra sagàra zèku

Dugon Dance

sezezelùtu
sezètutu selètutu
sagarazètutu
sagarazètutu
zèku zèku zèis selùtu
zèku sagarazèis zezezelùtu

Wallaby Dance

sèzèzèzèsagarazèlu
sezezelùtu
seizelùtu sagarazètu
seizelùtu sagarazètu

(Trobriand Islands, New Guinea)

SONGS & SPIRIT-SONGS

1

Women's Song at a Wedding Feast

He takes hold of her:
"A rainbow!"
They sing out
uin ueu.
She says: "Look!
a new stripe
in the rainbow."
With their most beautiful ornaments
on their bodies
they go bathing.
She bites him.

2

Song of a Men's Secret Society

A woman sees the tumbuan-spirit's cock feathers.
She vomits,
cries: *Noi jaja*;
the spirit looks down,
moves like a snake in the water
and sings. One man beats the slit-gong,
all paint their foreheads,
all go into the bush,
all see the bush-spirit Leleo—
he comes down from a tree,
his body painted like a snake's skin;
all sound gongs,
all put on feathers,
the sound carries over the sea.

3

Men's Song

She cries out sobbing
as she sees
the shadow
with a mouth: Stay there,
stay there, you ghost!
E au!

4

Men's Song

She spins round dancing
before his eyes,
he waves to her with his hand
and turns to go away.
"You have such beautiful eyes."
io!
She goes among the seaweed
and picks it.
"There! look! what a
man! what a fine body!" She sees
the other man and
calls sadly after her
own man.
Then she goes to the beach.

5

Women's Song

Strong wind,
the storm-spirit rages and roars
auinai au
all the women see him—his

head is bristly—
are startled
—they sit down and sing.
Then they all walk about
together.
One says: Now it is over—
we will go to the beach
and go out in a boat.

(Duke of York Islands, Melanesia)

THE DAYBREAK

Day breaks: the first rays of the rising Sun, stretching
    her arms.
Daylight breaking, as the Sun rises to her feet.
Sun rising, scattering the darkness; lighting up the
    land . . .
With disc shining, bringing daylight, as the birds
    whistle and call . . .
People are moving about, talking, feeling the warmth.
Burning through the Gorge, she rises, walking
    westwards,
Wearing her waist-band of human hair.
She shines on the blossoming coolibah tree, with its
    sprawling roots,
Its shady branches spreading . . .

(Mudbara, Australia)

SIGHTINGS: KUNAPIPI

(1st Set)

1   The musk of her
        red-walled vagina
     inviting coitus

2   Her skin soft like fur

3   She is shy at first, but soon they laugh together

4   Laughing-together
    Clitoris
    Soft-inside-of-the-vagina

5   Removing her pubic cloth
     opening
        her legs
     lying between them &
    coming

6   And copulating for a child

7   Fire   Fire
    Flame   Ashes

8   fire sticks &
    flames are
    flaring
    sparks
    are flying

9   Urination
     Testes
     Urination

10   Loincloth
     (red)
     Loincloth
     (white)
     Loincloth
     (black)

(2nd Set)

1   "penis"   incisure   incisure
     penis   penis   semen

2   Semen white like the mist

3   with penis erect
     the kangaroo
     moves its buttocks

4   step by step
     (she) walks away from coitus
     her back to them

5   the catfish swimming
     & singing

6   the bullroarer's string

7   The nipples of the young girl's breasts protrude—
     & the musk of her vagina—

8   creek
       moving
       "creek"

9   mist covering
       the river

10   cypress branches
       cypress cone
       seeds of the cone

(Arnhem Land, Australia)

From *THE GOULBURN ISLAND CYCLE*

Song 11
>They saw the young girls twisting their strings, Goulburn Island men
>   and men from the Woolen River:
>Young girls of the western clans, twisting their breast girdles among
>   the cabbage palm foliage . . .
>Stealthily creeping, the men grasp the cabbage tree leaves to search for
>   their sweethearts.
>Stealthily moving, they bend down to hide with their lovers among
>   the foliage . . .
>With penis erect, those Goulburn Island men, from the young girls'
>   swaying buttocks . . .
>They are always there, at the wide expanse of water . . .
>Always there, at the billabong edged with bamboo.
>Feeling the urge for play, as they saw the young girls of the western
>   clans,
>Saw the young girls hiding themselves, twisting the strings . . .
>Girls twisting their breast girdles, making string figures: and men with
>   erect penes,
>Goulburn Island men, as the young girls sway their buttocks.

Song 12
>They seize the young girls of the western tribes, with their swaying
>   buttocks—those Goulburn Island men . . .
>Young girls squealing in pain, from the long penis . . .
>Girls of the western clans, desiring pleasure, pushed on to their backs
>   among the cabbage palm foliage . . .
>Lying down, copulating—always there, moving their buttocks . . .
>Men of Goulburn Islands, with long penes . . .
>Seizing the beautiful young girls, of the western tribes . . .

They are always there at that billabong edged with bamboo . . .
Hear the sound of their buttocks, the men from Goulburn Islands
  moving their penes . . .
For these are beautiful girls, of the western tribes . . .
And the penis becomes erect, as their buttocks move . . .
They are always there at the place of Standing Clouds, of the rising
  western clouds,
Pushed on to their backs, lying down among the cabbage palm
  foliage . . .

Song 13

Ejaculating into their vaginas—young girls of the western tribes.
Ejaculating semen, into the young Burara girls . . .
Those Goulburn Island men, with their long penes;
Semen flowing from them into the young girls . . .
For they are always there, moving their buttocks.
They are always there, at the wide expanse of water . . .
Ejaculating, among the cabbage palm foliage:
They cry out, those young girls of the Nagara tribe . . .
He ejaculates semen for her, among the cabbage palm foliage . . .
Ejaculating for the young girls of the western clans . . .
From the long penes of men from Goulburn Islands . . .
They are always there at the open expanse of water, at the sea-eagle
  nest . . .
Ejaculating semen, for the young girls . . .
Into the young girls of the western tribes . . .
For they are ours—it is for this that they make string figures . . .[the
  men say]
Thus we ejaculate for her—into the young girl's vagina.
Semen, among the cabbage palm foliage . . .
Thus we push her over, among the foliage;

We ejaculate semen into their vaginas—young girls of the western
tribes . . .
Ejaculating semen, into the young Burara girls . . .
For they move their buttocks, those people from Goulburn Islands.

Song 14

Blood is running down from the men's penes, men from Goulburn
Islands . . .
Blood running down from the young girls, like blood from a speared
kangaroo . . .
Running down among the cabbage palm foliage . . .
Blood that is sacred, running down from the young girl's uterus:
Flowing like water, from the young girls of the western tribes . . .
Blood running down, for the Goulburn Island men had seen their
swaying buttocks . . .
Sacred blood running down . . .
Like blood from a speared kangaroo; sacred blood flows from the
uterus . . .
They are always there, at the wide expanse of water, the sea-eagle
nests . . .
They are sacred, those young girls of the western tribes, with their
menstrual flow . . .
They are always there, moving their buttocks, those Goulburn Island
people . . .
Sacred, with flowing blood—young girls of the western clans . . .
They are always there, sitting within their huts like sea-eagle nests,
with blood flowing . . .
Flowing down from the sacred uterus of the young girl . . .
Sacred young girls from the western tribes, clans from the Woolen
River:
Blood, flowing like water . . .

Always there, that blood, in the cabbage palm foliage . . .
Sacred blood flowing in all directions . . .
Like blood from a speared kangaroo, from the sacred uterus . . .

Song 15

They talked together, we heard them speaking the western language:
Heard their words—men from the western clans, and from Goulburn
  Islands.
They are always there, in the huts like sea-eagle nests: young girls
  leaning against the walls . . .
We heard the speech of the western clans, clans from the Woolen
  River . . .
Heard them speaking, girls and men of the western tribes . . .
Flinging their words into the cabbage palm foliage . . .
They are always talking there, at the billabong edged with bamboo:
  their words drift over the water . . .
There at the Sea-Eagle place, we heard them speaking the western
  language . . .
Heard their words at the Sea-Eagle place—clans from the Woolen
  River . . .
Talking there, Goulburn Island men of the long penes . . .
They are always there, at the wide expanse of water . . .
We heard their words, men from the western tribes, and clans from the
  Woolen River . . .

Song 16

Get the spears, for we feel like playing!
They are always there, at the billabong edged with bamboo . . .
They fling them one by one as they play, the bamboo-shafted
  spears . . .
Twirling the shaft, pretending to throw, then flinging them back and
  forth . . .

The wind catches the spear, and blows it point upwards into the
   cabbage palm . . .
Thin shaft twisting up like a snake, as they fling it in play . . .
Spears travelling to different places, and different tribes . . .
We saw the spear-throwers' chests and buttocks swinging—those
   Goulburn Island people . . .
They are always there, at the billabong edged with bamboo . . .
They feel like playing, and flinging spears—Goulburn Island men,
   clans from the Woolen River:
Twirling the shaft, pretending to throw: the point twists up like a
   snake . . .
They feel like play, leaning back on the forked sticks within the
   huts . . .

Song 17

The pheasant cries out from the door of its nest . . .
Crying out from the door, at the sound of the coming rain . . .
Rain and wind from the west, spreading over the country . . .
It cries out, perched on the top rails of the huts.
It is always there, at the wide expanse of water, listening for the rising
   wind and rain:
Wind and rain from the west, as the pheasant cries out . . .
The pheasant, within its wet-season hut—for it has heard the coming
   rain . . .
Darkness, and heavy rain falling . . .
It is for me! [says the pheasant] My cry summons the wind and
   rain . . .
Noise of the rain, and of thunder rolling along the bottom of the
   clouds . . .
The pheasant cries out from its nest, from the door of its hut . . .
`t is always there, at the billabong edged with bamboo.

Song 18

They take the fighting clubs, standing them upright . . .
We saw their chests, men of the western clans, of the rising clouds.
Carefully they stand them up in the ground, these groups of clubs . . .
Carefully, assembling them in rows, like a line of clouds in the west.
They are always there, at the wide expanse of water . . .
We saw their chests, men of the west, invoking the rising clouds . . .
Assembling the fighting clubs, like lines of clouds . . .
At the place of Standing Clouds, of the Rising Western Clouds,
     spreading all over the country.
They drift over the huts, the sea-eagle nests, at the billabong edged
     with bamboo:
Carefully they assemble the clubs in rows, like a line of clouds in the
     west . . .
From within these rows of clubs, from the lines of clouds, comes the
     western rain . . .
Thus we assemble the fighting clubs in rows, like lines of clouds . . .

Song 19

From those fighting clubs, assembled in rows, come the western
     clouds . . .
Dark rain clouds and wind, rising up in the west . . .
They make them for us, clouds from within the rows of fighting
     clubs . . .
Clouds that spread all over the sky, drifting across . . .
Above Milingimbi, above the Island of Clouds . . .
Rising all over the country—at Goulburn Islands, and at the Sea-
     Eagle place,
Clouds building up, spreading across the country—at the place of the
     Rising Clouds, the place of Standing Clouds,
They spread all over the sky, clouds that they make in the camp at the
     billabong edged with bamboo . . .
At the open expanse of water—large rain clouds rising . . .

Dark rain clouds and wind, rising up in the west . . .
They come rising up, for thus we assemble the clubs,
Groups of fighting clubs, assembled in rows.

Song 20

Thunder rolls along the bottom of the clouds, at the wide expanse of
water . . .

Thunder shaking the clouds, and the Lightning Snake flashing through
them . . .

Large Snake, at the billabong edged with bamboo—its belly, its skin
and its back!

Thunder and lightning over the camps, at the wide expanse of
water . . .

Sound of thunder drifting to the place of the Wawalag Sisters, to the
place of the Boomerang . . .

I make the thunder and lightning, pushing the clouds, at the billabong
edged with bamboo [says the Lightning Snake] . . .

I make the crash of the thunder—I spit, and the lightning flashes!

Sound of thunder and storm—loud 'stranger' noise, coming from
somewhere . . .

Coming to Caledon Bay, the storm from the west . . .

Thunder and rain spread across to Caledon Bay . . .

I make the thunder and lightning, at the billabong edged with bam-
boo! [says the Lightning Snake]

Song 21

The tongues of the Lightning Snake flicker and twist, one to the
other . . .

They flash among the foliage of the cabbage palms . . .

Lightning flashes through the clouds, with the flickering tongues of
the Snake . . .

It is always there, at the wide expanse of water, at the place of the
Sacred Tree . . .

Flashing above those people of the western clans . . .
All over the sky their tongues flicker: above the place of the Rising
    Clouds, the place of Standing Clouds . . .
All over the sky, tongues flickering and twisting . . .
They are always there, at the camp by the wide expanse of water . . .
All over the sky their tongues flicker: at the place of the Two Sisters,
    the place of the Wawalag . . .
Lightning flashes through the clouds, flash of the Lightning Snake . . .
Its blinding flash lights up the cabbage palm foliage . . .
Gleams on the cabbage palms, and on the shining semen among the
    leaves . . .

                        (Arnhem Land, Australia)

THE FIRST TRUCK AT TAMBREY
(by Toby Wiliguru Pambardu)

The strange thing comes closer,
    coming into view for inspection.
The strange thing comes closer,
    coming into view for inspection.

The strange thing comes closer,
    coming—into view for inspection.
The strange thing comes closer,
    coming—full length into view.
Now we have seen you, stranger,
    coming—full length into view.

Now we have seen you, stranger,
    coming—full length into view.
Poor fellow you, stranger,
    —your transparent eyes reaching everywhere,
You stand there, fire spitting: eedj!
    —your transparent eyes reaching everywhere.

You stand there, fire spitting: eedj!
    —your transparent eyes reaching everywhere,
You stand there, fire spitting: eedj!
    transparent.—With its splutter
Inside below the engine
    is built—with its splutter.

Inside below the engine
    is built—with its splutter,
Inside below the engine
    is built—the starter,
Chirping "njeen njeen" in the front
    like crickets—the starter.

Chirping "njeen njeen" in the front
    like crickets—the starter,
Chirping "njeen njeen" in the front
    like crickets.—Up and down
Smell the petrol going through
    by the big end!—up and down.

Smell the petrol going through
    by the big end—up and down!
Smell the petrol going through
    by the big end!—Bubbles,
See them suddenly blown high,
    boiling   —bubbles!

See them suddenly blown high
    boiling   —bubbles
See them suddenly blown high
    boiling.—Both shaking

. . . . . . you two,
    clever men,—both shaking.

. . . . . . you two,
    clever men—both shaking
. . . . . . you two,
    clever men—in the sleek cabin
Sitting on a seat to drive,
    all gadgets!—in the sleek cabin.

Sitting on a seat to drive,
    all gadgets!—in the sleek cabin
Sitting on a seat to drive,
    all gadgets!—The noise swells,
When they accelerate along the road
    to a rumble—the noise swells.

When they accelerate along the road
   to a rumble—the noise swells
When they accelerate along the road
   to a rumble—a buzz sets in.
The wheels make miles,
   at a proper speed—a buzz sets in.

The wheels make miles
   at a proper speed—a buzz sets in.
The wheels make miles,
   at a proper speed—the tyre marks spin
Around in the dust like mad,
   like firesticks   —the tyre marks spin.

Around in the dust like mad,
   like firesticks   —the tyre marks spin
Around in the dust like mad,
   like firesticks—its sides rattle,
Jerking when a load is pulled
   by the truck—its sides rattle.

Jerking when a load is pulled
   by the truck—its sides rattle,
Jerking when a load is pulled
   by the truck.—The ground whirls past,
When you look out front it is swaying,
   running straight—the ground whirls past.

When you look out front it is swaying,
   running straight—the ground whirls past.
When you look out front it is swaying,
   running straight—   —the roar's like a meteor
Blundering from star to star,
   running through the bend—the roar's like a meteor.

Blundering from star to star,
    running through the bend—the roar's like a meteor.
Blundering from star to star,
    running through the bend—fading far away
The noise making miles
    like a firestick   —fading far away.

(Jindjiparndi, Australia)

NIGHT BIRTHS
(*from* The Kumulipo *by Keaulumoku*)

o

At the time when the earth became hot
At the time when the heavens turned about
At the time when the sun was darkened
To cause the moon to shine
The time of the rise of the Pleiades
The slime, this was the source of the earth
The source of the darkness that made darkness
The source of the night that made night
The intense darkness, the deep darkness
Darkness of the sun, darkness of the night
   Nothing but night

I

The train of walruses passing by
Milling about in the depths of the sea
The long lines of opule fish
The sea is thick with them
Crabs and hardshelled creatures
They go swallowing on the way
Rising and diving under swiftly and silently
Pimoe lurks behind the horizon
On the long waves, the crested waves
Innumerable the coral ridges
Low, heaped-up, jagged
The little ones seek the dark places
Very dark is the ocean and obscure
A sea of coral like the green heights of Paliuli
The land disappears into them

Covered by the darkness of night
    Still it is night

2

With a dancing motion they go creeping and crawling
The tail swinging its length
Sullenly, sullenly
They go poking about the dunghill
Filth is their food, they devour it
Eat and rest, eat and belch it up
Eating like common people
Distressful is their eating
They move about and become heated
Act as if exhausted
They stagger as they go
Go in the land of crawlers
The family of crawlers born in the night
    Still it is night

3

The parent rats dwell in holes
The little rats huddle together
Those who mark the seasons
Little tolls from the land
Little tolls from the water courses
Trace of the nibblings of these brown-coated ones
With whiskers upstanding
They hide here and there
A rat in the upland, a rat by the sea
A rat running beside the wave
Born to the two, child of the Night-falling-away
Born to the two, child of the Night-creeping-away

The little child creeps as it moves
The little child moves with a spring
Pilfering at the rind
Rind of the 'ohi'a fruit, not a fruit of the upland
A tiny child born as the darkness falls away
A springing child born as the darkness creeps away
Child of the dark and child in the night now here
   Still it is night

4

Fear falls upon me on the mountain top
Fear of the passing night
Fear of the night approaching
Fear of the pregnant night
Fear of the breach of the law
Dread of the place of offering and the narrow trail
Dread of the food and the waste part remaining
Dread of the receding night
Awe of the night approaching
Awe of the dog child of the Night-creeping-away
A dog child of the Night-creeping-hither
A dark red dog, a brindled dog
A hairless dog of the hairless ones
A dog as an offering for the oven
Palatable is the sacrifice for supplication
Pitiful in the cold without covering
Pitiful in the heat without a garment
He goes naked on the way to Malama
Where the night ends for the children of night
From the growth and the parching
From the cutting off and the quiet
The driving Hula wind his companion

Younger brother of the naked ones, the 'Olohe
Out from the slime come rootlets
Out from the slime comes young growth
Out from the slime come branching leaves
Out from the slime comes outgrowth
Born in the time when men came from afar
   Still it is night

(Hawaii, Polynesia)

THE WOMAN WHO MARRIED A CATERPILLAR

Kumuhea the night-caterpillar loves the woman
with his daylight man-body takes her for wife, handsome
man huge caterpillar, at night
gorges on sweet-potato leaves
Kumuhea huge night-caterpillar
bloated back home mornings
soft Kumuhea flabby Kumuhea, through
him shiftless the wife starves
Where does he go nights, her father says, Where
does he go nights, says the hemp string
his wife fastens to track him where he goes nights;
after him through brush on his crawl
the long string snarls, the night-
caterpillar is strong with anger, tears
into leaves all around
        all people cry Kane help us
        night-caterpillar kills our food, do him in
        in his hill-cave home, he
        kills our food
merciful Kane slices him to bits
we now call cut-worm cut-worm cut-worm

(Hawaii, Polynesia)

THE BODY-SONG OF KIO
(by Ruea-a-raka)

Then Kio again spoke to Oatea, saying:
Take hold of my flattened-crown
    ″   ″   ″ ″ wrinkled-brow
    ″   ″   ″ ″ observing-eye
    ″   ″   ″ ″ obstructed-nose
    ″   ″   ″ ″ conversing-mouth
    ″   ″   ″ ″ chattering-lips
    ″   ″   ″ ″ flower-decked-ears
    ″   ″   ″ ″ distorted-chin
    ″   ″   ″ ″ descending-saliva
    ″   ″   ″ ″ crooked-neck
    ″   ″   ″ ″ broad-chest
    ″   ″   ″ ″ contracted-hands
    ″   ″   ″ ″ grasping-fingers
    ″   ″   ″ ″ pinching-nails
    ″   ″   ″ ″ flexed-side
    ″   ″   ″ ″ bulging-ribs
    ″   ″   ″ ″ inset-navel
    ″   ″   ″ ″ princely-belly
    ″   ″   ″ ″ small-of-the-back
    ″   ″   ″ ″ swollen-penis
    ″   ″   ″ ″ tightly-drawn-testicles
    ″   ″   ″ ″ evacuating-rectum
    ″   ″   ″ ″ twisted-knee
    ″   ″   ″ ″ splay-foot
    ″   ″   ″ ″ given-over-body

(Tuamotua, Polynesia)

FUNERAL EVA
(by Koroneu)

(Solo)   Oh, Priest Pangeivi, you let go
my son, the canoe of his life
is dashed and sunk.

(Chorus)   O Tane, you could have saved him,
made him return, a
sapling among our aging forest.
But he died, woman-like, wet
on his pillow, far from the
crash of spears and adzes. You could have
done better than god Turanga, a bag
of lies not worth our prayers.

Your belly full, you can't be bothered.
Let shitballs be thrown at you,
Let you be smeared all over,
Let piss and shit dribble down your
fat cheeks, you bum god. Any man
can do better.

(Solo)   Fart, O Tiki, let your wind go.
Fart on this phony god not worth
our curses.

(Chorus)   Fart, fart, fart.
Swallow the wind, O Pangeivi.
Having eaten my son, you
shall eat our feces.

(Mangaian, Polynesia)

TOTO VACA

I

Ka tangi te kivi	Kiwi cries the bird
kivi	Kiwi
Ka tangi te moho	Moho cries the bird
moho	Moho
Ka tangi te tike	Tieke cries the bird
ka tangi te tike	Tieke
tike	only a belly
he poko anahe	rises into the air rises into the air
to tikoko tikoko	continue your road
haere i te hara	rises into the air
tikoko	here's the second year
ko te taoura te rangi	Kauaea
kaouaea	here is the catcher of men
me kave kivhea	Kauaea
kaouaea	make room and drag him
a-ki te take	Kauaea
take no tou	drag where
e haou	Kauaea
to ia	Ah the root
haou riri	the root of Tou
to ia	Heh the wind
to ia	drag further
to ia ake te take	raging wind
take no tou	drag further the root
	the root of the Tou

II

ko ia rimou ha ere	So push, Rimo
kaouaea	Kauaea
totara ha ere	go on Totara
kaouaea	Kauaea

poukatea ha ere	go on Pukatea
kaouaea	Kauaea
homa i te tou	give me the Tou
kaouaea	Kauaea
khia vhitikia	give me the Maro
kaouaea	Kauaea
takou takapou	stretch stretch (the hauling rope)
kaouaea	Kauaea
hihi e	my belly
haha e	Kauaea
pipi e	kihi, e
tata e	haha, e
a pitia	pipi, e
ha	tata, e
ko te here	apitia
ha	HA;
ko te timata	
e—ko te tiko pohue	together
e—ko te aitanga a mata	ha
e—te aitanga ate	me the rope
hoe-manuko	ha
	me the rope
	me the spear
	me the silex-child
	me the child of the Manuka-oar

III

ko aou ko aou	I am I am
hitaoue	a long procession
make ho te hanga	dead is the thing
hitaoue	a long procession
tourouki tourouki	goes on gliding goes on gliding

paneke paneke	to sink you to sink you
oioi te toki	brandish the axe
kaouaea	Kauaea
takitakina	
ia	
he tikaokao	only a rooster
he taraho	only a Taraho bird
he pararera	only a duck
ke ke ke ke	ke ke ke ke
he pararera	only a duck
ke ke ke ke	ke ke ke ke

(Maori, Polynesia)

THE LOVERS I
(by Tomoki)

The woman went searching inland, for what?
    May the hermit crab enter
Only this: I was up at the north here,
Spread my knees until the thing was very thick.
Floated to you at the edge of the pool, landed.
(You said) "Haul up my fat fish that I am starving for."
I then eat the part between the two ventral fins.
(You said) "Float to my mouth."
You separated, separated from me.
The hermit crab which came, cast down its eyes.

(Kapingamarangi, Polynesia)

THE LOVERS II
(by Tomoki)

Carrying his coarse mat under his arms he unrolls & spreads it
beneath his pandanus tree where a space has been cleared—then
      gropes
for his sea-urchin pencil spines, lined with ridges like the *waka*
      mara—
with these he pulls out her pubic hairs—& they pop
like the splitting of leaves *hakapaki eitu*
Only some short ones are left
                inside the vagina
                    (he asks):
Where are they?
      At the end of the space
      between the buttocks, accustomed
      place for the grinning of
      the teeth of my lover
      who rules it.
      If you were going to eat it
      the thing isn't clean

(He says)
Your eyes are red with hard crying.

(She says) I am carried up to the skies
my toes spread apart with the thrill of it   I put
my feet at their place
               around your neck.

(He says)   I land my might—
         gather to push open
         that mouth.
         Not yet soft. I

look along her belly.
She lies flat.

(She says)   Why're you
lying down
Stand
up, the rain
is coming seaward of
Hukuniu Island.
The island is buried, the rain
moves eastward
see what its nature is.

(He says)   It will pass us, it blocks
to the east of us.

(She says)   Lie
on your bed, come
back
to the swollen thing—
crawl here!

(Kapingamarangi, Polynesia)

FLIGHT OF THE CHIEFS: SONG V
(by Daubitu Velema)

I was sweating: then I hurdled the threshold.
Then I came outside; then I circled about.
I broke off the dangling uci *shrub*
And I inserted it above my ear.
When the dangling *uci* shrub is bruised,
It quivers like the tail feathers of the cock.
And now Lady Song-of-Tonga speaks:
    "Why is the dangling *uci* broken?"
And now The-Eldest answers:
    "Leaves for garlands have no worth as food;
    I am using it just as an ornament."
I descended down to the shore.
I leapt into the bow of my canoe;
Its timbers were felled at The-Task-Is-Complete;
The artist, Flaming-Moon, felled them;
Its name was The-Turmeric-of-the-Mother-and-Child.
And shells concealed the tying of its sennit.
The walls of the chief's house were hung with barkcloth.
And a large dentalium adorned the chief's house.
And there were four figureheads together.
And Lady Song-of-Tonga is weaving her fishnet.
And Fruit-of-the-Distant-Sleep crawls to her.
And she grasped the weaving hook from my hand.
I struck her with the handle of the net.
And the child is smothered black from weeping.
And now The-Eldest speaks:
    "Lady Song-of-Tonga, what evil have you done?
    You strike a helpless creature."
And I grasped the forearm of the child.

Then I slung her to my back and carried her.
And now The-Eldest speaks:
  "O my child, for what blossom are you weeping?
  Are you crying for the red *leba?*
  Look there at the ripe ones on the branch."
I grasped the handle of my ray-spined spear.
Reaching upward I tapped a fruit in the cluster.
It fell and I halved it straightway.
And the red *leba* speaks in his hand:
  "Why am I broken in half?"
And now The-Eldest answers:
  "You are halved to no purpose."
Fruit-of-the-Distant-Sleep is weeping.
She sees, and now her thoughts are soothed.
Then I threaded the leba on a girdle cord.
And dangled it there before her.
And now the child is angry and refuses to look.
And she leaps down and scratches the earth;
And she scoops up a handful and casts it on her back.
And I grasped the forearm of the child.
And I slung her to my back and carried her.
  "O my child, for what blossom are you weeping?"
And The-Eldest is looking about.
And my glance fell upon Clapping-Out-of-Time;
I saw him; then I shouted calling.
And now Clapping-Out-of-Time speaks:
  "The-Eldest, why am I called?"
And now The-Eldest speaks:
  "You are called for no purpose.
  Fruit-of-the-Distant-Sleep is weeping.
  Come dance to see if you can please her."
Leap to the mote on the landward side.
Leap to the mote on the seaward side.

And he twists bending in the dance and stands again.
Saliva drips forth from his mouth.
    "Come, watch, Fruit-of-the-Distant-Sleep."
She looks but asks no questions.
And the child is smothered black from weeping.
And I grasped the forearm of the child
And I slung her to my back and carried her.
And Sailing-the-Ocean is sorrowful.
Returning I carried Fruit-of-the-Distant-Sleep;
Went to enter The-Grass-Strewn-Floor.

(Fiji, Melanesia)

ANIMAL STORY X
(by Wiliami Naura)

Let it be told, *iya, iya, iya*
Vuai na dri, vuai na dra,
Source of the blossoms of the Malay apple.
Crane falls; Goose awakes;
Rail knocks,
Knocks at the village of The-Strong,
Cock crows, crows in the village,
Crows there in the branch of the black tree,
The rotten core of the branched taro,
And the eggs of the chicken hatch,
And the hatchlings flap their wings.
And the eggs of the rail hatch,
And the hatchlings kick their feet.
Crane flies down,
Snaps the anus of Parrot.
Defecate what? Defecate brown.
Brown woman is born therefrom.
Who is to place a name upon her?
Woman, *soqiri;* woman, *soqara.*
What ship is approaching there near Kana?
The ship of the Roko, it chugs like a steamer.
It chugs upon me, I recognize one;
It chugs upon me, I recognize two.
A Fireman is Red Rail; always knows the firewoods.
The branch of hibiscus is beating,
And there is a heap of *molau.*
One piece of *basina* is long;
It is bad, the path to River's-Mouth.
Return the song, all you young people.

One piece of *basina* is short;
It is bad, the path to Nakavakea.
Return the song, all you women.
One piece of *basina* is fine, is fine.
Mynah makes merry.
The eyes are blind, missing.
O-i! A fine village.

(Fiji, Melanesia)

The
STATEMENTS

I

This ceremony molded me. I paid the most careful attention to it. I worshiped it as best I knew how. . . . The members of the Medicine Rite told me that if, properly and reverently, I obeyed all the things the ceremony enjoined, I would return to Earthmaker. I was considerate to everyone and everyone loved me. This ritual was made with love!

(Statement by Warudjaxega, "Crashing-Thunder," Winnebago Indian)

2

The mind, *nanola,* by which term intelligence, power of discrimina-
tion, capacity for learning magical formulae, and all forms of non-
manual skill are described, as well as moral qualities, resides some-
where in the larynx. . . . The memory, however, the store of formulae
and traditions learned by heart, resides deeper, in the belly. . . . The
force of magic, crystallized in the magical formulae, is carried by men
of the present generation in their bodies. . . . The force of magic does
not reside in the things; it resides within man and can escape only
through his voice.

(Trobriands, New Guinea)

3

The chief or learned poet explains or exhibits the great extent of his knowledge . . . by composing a quatrain without thinking, that is, without studying. At this day it is by the ends of his bones he effects it, & he discovers the name by this means. The way in which it is done is this: when the poet sees the person or thing before him, he makes a verse at once with the ends of his fingers, or in his mind without studying, & he composes & repeats at the same time. . . . But . . . before Patrick's time . . . the poet placed his staff upon the person's body or upon his head, & found out his name, & the name of his father & mother, & discovered every unknown thing that was proposed to him, in a minute or two or three. . . . Patrick abolished these things [that were] among the poets when they believed, for they were profane rites . . . & could not be performed without offering to the idol gods. He did not leave them after this any rite in which offering should be made to the devil, for their profession was pure.

(From *The Ancient Laws of Ireland*)

4

Songs are thoughts, sung out with the breath when people are moved
by great forces & ordinary speech no longer suffices. Man is moved
just like the ice floe sailing here and there in the current. His thoughts
are driven by a flowing force when he feels joy, when he feels fear,
when he feels sorrow. Thoughts can wash over him like a flood,
making his breath come in gasps & his heart throb. Something like an
abatement in the weather will keep him thawed up. And then it will
happen that we, who always think we are small, will feel still smaller.
And we will fear to use words. But it will happen that the words we
need will come of themselves. When the words we want to use shoot
up of themselves—we get a new song.

(Statement by Orpingalik, Netsilik Eskimo)

5

I must first sit a little, cooling my arms; that the fatigue may go out of them; because I sit. I do merely listen, watching for a story, which I want to hear; while I sit waiting for it; that it may float into my ear. These are those to which I am listening with all my ears; while I feel that I sit silent. I must wait listening behind me, while I listen along the road; while I feel that my name floats along the road; they (my three names) float along to my place; I will go to sit at it; that I may listening turn backwards (with my ears) to my feet's heels, on which I went; while I feel that a story is the wind. It, the story, is wont to float along to another place. Then our names do pass through those people; while they do not perceive our bodies go along. For our names are those which, floating, reach a different place. The mountains lie between the two different roads. A man's name passes behind the mountains' back; those names with which returning he goes along.

(Statement by ‖kábbo, African Bushman)

6

A man who is about to transfer his membership in a certain dance calls to his house a song-maker ("man of understanding"), whose profession is musical composition and the leading of singers on ceremonial occasions, and a "word-passer," who sets words to music and on public occasions stands and chants each line in advance of the singers in order to prompt them. These two are requested to make the necessary number of songs, the number depending on the dance in question. For the Cannibal-Dancer it is sixteen. So the composers go into the woods, sometimes accompanied by another ("sitting-close-beside-the-head"), who is a novice in the art of composition. The song-maker draws inspiration chiefly from the sounds of running or dropping water, and from the notes of birds. Sitting beside a rill of falling water, he listens intently, catches the music, and hums it to himself, using not words but the vocables *hamamama*. This is his theme. Then he carries the theme further, making variations, and at last he adds a finale which he calls the "tail." After a while he goes to the word-passer, constantly humming the tune, and the word-passer, catching the air, joins in, and then sets a single word to it. This is called "tying the song," so that it may not "drift away" like an unmoored canoe. Then gradually other words are added, until the song is complete. The novice sits a little apart from the master, and if he "finds" a melody, he "carries" it at once to the song-maker, who quickly catches the theme and proceeds to develop it. Many songs are obtained from the robin, some from a waterfowl which whistles before diving, and from other birds. A witness has seen a song-maker, after employing various themes, coil a rope and then compose a song representing it. On a certain occasion when the singers were practicing new songs in the woods, the song-maker lacked one to complete the number, and he asked the others if they had a song. The other composers present said they had none. One of them looked across at a visiting woman song-maker and said to the presiding song-maker, "I will ask her." She heard the phrase, caught the inflection of the rising and falling syllables, and began to sing *hamamama*. As the sound left her lips, those on the opposite side of the circle heard it and at once began to hum, and together they composed the necessary song. This manner of catching a melody is called "scooping it up in the hands."

(Kwakiutl Indian)

7

The artist: disciple, abundant, multiple, restless.
The true artist: capable, practicing, skillful;
maintains dialogue with his heart, meets things with his mind.
The true artist: draws out all from his heart,
works with delight, makes things with calm, with sagacity,
works like a true Toltec, composes his objects, works dexterously,
    invents;
arranges materials, adorns them, makes them adjust.

The carrion artist: works at random, sneers at the people,
makes things opaque, brushes across the surface of the face of things,
works without care, defrauds people, is a thief.

(Aztec)

8

From *THE GREAT DIGEST*
[Tseng's Comment]

1

    In letters of gold on T'ang's bathtub:

        AS THE SUN MAKES IT NEW
        DAY BY DAY MAKE IT NEW
        YET AGAIN MAKE IT NEW

2

    It is said in the K'ang Proclamation:
    He is risen, renewing the people.

3

        The *Odes* say:
    Although Chou was an ancient kingdom
    The celestial destiny
    Came again down on it NEW.

        (Chinese)

9

The Book was before me. I could see it but not touch it. I tried to caress it but my hands didn't touch anything. I limited myself to contemplating it and, at that moment, I began to speak. Then I realized that I was reading the Sacred Book of Language. My Book. The Book of the Principal Ones.

I had attained perfection. I was no longer a simple apprentice. For that, as a prize, as a nomination, the Book had been granted me. When one takes the *saint children*, one can see the Principal Ones. Otherwise not. And it is the mushrooms that are saints; they give Wisdom. Wisdom is Language. Language is in the Book. The Book is granted by the Principal Ones. The Principal Ones appear with the great power of the *children*.

I learned the wisdom of the Book. Afterwards, in my later visions, the Book no longer appeared because its contents were already guarded in my memory.

(Statement by María Sabina, Mazatec Indian)

10

And I, Daniel, alone saw the vision: for the men that were with me saw not the vision; but a great quaking fell upon them, so that they fled to hide themselves.

Therefore I was left alone, & saw this great vision, & there remained no strength in me: for my comeliness was turned in me into corruption, & I retained no strength.

Yet heard I the voice of his words: & when I heard the voice of his words, then was I in a deep sleep on my face, & my face toward the ground.

(Hebrew)

The
COMMENTARIES

Page 3   COME, ASCEND THE LADDER

Source: Invocation to the *U'wannami* (rainmakers) from Matilda Coxe Stevenson, *The Zuni Indians* (Bureau of American Ethnology, Annual Report No. 23 [Washington, 1905]), pp. 175–176.

1. Sprinkling water, pollen, meal, to accompany the invocation.
2. Striking stones together, rolling them along the ground to make thunder.
3. Flute playing, shell rattling, as the rainmakers (i.e., "ghosts of dead rain priests") move up the lines of pollen & meal.

Page 7   GENESIS I

Source: Condensed from Pliny Earle Goddard, *Kato Texts* (University of California Publications in American Archaeology and Ethnology [Berkeley, 1909]), vol. 5, no. 3: 71–74.

What's of interest here isn't the matter of the myth but the power of repetition & naming (monotony, too) to establish the presence of a situation in its entirety. This involves the acceptance (by poet & hearers) of an indefinite extension of narrative time, & the belief that language (i.e., poetry) can make-things-present by naming them. The means employed include the obvious pile-up of nouns (until everything is named) & the use of "they say" repeated for each utterance. In Kato, this last is a quotative [*yaɛnɪ*], made from the root -*nɪ-n*, "to speak," & the plural prefix *yaɛ*. (Cp. use of Japanese particle -*to*; of *tzo* = "says" in Mazatec [above, p. 62].) While *yaɛnɪ* is undoubtedly less conspicuous in Kato than "they say" in English, it still gives the sense of a special (narrative or mythic) context. The editor's use of Goddard's literal over his free translation is based on such considerations; also from a feeling that "they say" plus other repetitions add something special to the English &/or American tongues. In brief: there's something going on here.

Summary & Addenda.   Repetition & monotony are powers to be reckoned with; or, as the lady said to M. Junod after having heard the tale of Nabandji, the toad-eating girl, "I should never have thought there could be so much charm in monotony."

Charm, in the old sense.

Page 8 SOUNDS

Sources: (1) "Rain-chant" quoted by Baldwin Spencer in *Native Tribes of the Northern Territory of Australia* (London, 1904). (2) A Navajo "coyote song" from Berard Haile, *Origin Legend of the Navaho Enemy Way* (Yale University Publications in Anthropology, no. 17 [1938]), p. 265. (3) Edward Deming Andrews, *The Gift to Be Simple: Songs, Dances and Rituals of the American Shakers* (Dover Publications, New York, 1962), p. 72. (See below.)

> "The words have no meaning, but the song means,
> 'Take it, I give it to you.' "
> A Navajo informant speaking to Father Berard.

Sounds only. No meaning, they say, in the words, or no meaning you can get at by translation into-other-words; & yet it functions; the meaning contained then in how it's made to function. So here the key is in the "spell" & in the belief behind the "spell"—or in a whole system of beliefs, in magic, in the power of sound & breath & ritual to move an object toward ends determined by the poet-magus.

Magic, then, is the first key & from this the idea of a special language or series of languages, extraordinary in their nature & effect, & uniting the user (through what Malinowski calls "the coefficient of weirdness") with the beings & things he's trying to influence or connect with for a sharing of power, participation in a life beyond his own, beyond the human, etc.

Such special languages—meaningless &/or mysterious—are a small but nearly universal aspect of "primitive-&-archaic" poetry. They may involve (1) purely invented, meaningless sounds, (2) distortion of ordinary words & syntax, (3) ancient words emptied of their (long since forgotten) meanings, (4) words borrowed from other languages & likewise emptied. And all these may, in addition, be explained as (1) spirit language, (2) animal language, (3) ancestral language—distinctions between them often being blurred.

C. M. Bowra, in his book on "primitive song," views sound-poems like these as truly rudimentary, a kind of rock-bottom poetics. He writes that "since such [meaningless] sounds are easier to fit to music than intelligible sounds are . . . [they] look as if they were the earliest kind of song practiced by man." And yet this mantric use of sound is as close to (say) the Hindu *om* as to "purely" emotive sounds of the ay-ay-ay & yah-yah-yah variety. One could as well argue—at least where song is magic—that the use of words-emptied-of-meaning is a *late* development, even as geometric (abstract) art follows the naturalistic cows & bulls in the caves of Europe. The reappearance of the sound-poem among some twentieth-century poets is a further reminder (along with assorted scat-songs & mouth-musics, etc.) that chronology isn't the question.

Addenda. (1) "Magic words, magic songs or magic prayers are fragments of old songs, handed down from earlier generations. . . . They may also be apparently meaningless sentences heard once in the days when the animals could talk, and remembered ever since through being handed down from one generation to another. Sometimes also a seemingly senseless jumble of words may derive force by a mystic inspiration which first gave them utterance. On the day when a man seeks aid in magic words, he must not eat of the entrails of any beast, and a man when uttering such words must have his head covered with a hood; a woman must have the whole spread of the hood behind thrown over her face." (K. Rasmussen, *Intellectual Culture of the Hudson Bay Eskimos*, p. 157)

(2) "Take the principal spell of Omarakana garden magic, which begins with the word *vatuvi* . . . (a magical form that has no grammatical setting and is a root never met with in common speech). . . . The magician, after certain preparations & under the observance of certain rules and taboos, collects herbs & makes of them a magical mixture. . . . After ritually and with an incantation offering some . . . fish to the ancestral spirits, [he] recites the main spell, *vatuvi*, over the magical mixture. [In doing this] he prepares a sort of large receptacle for his voice—a voice-trap we might call it. He lays the mixture on a mat and covers this with another mat so that his voice may be caught and imprisoned between them. During the recitation he holds his head close to the aperture and carefully sees to it that no portion of the herbs shall remain unaffected by the breath of his voice. He moves his mouth from one end of the aperture to the other, turns his head, repeating the words over and over again, rubbing them, so to speak, into the substance. When you watch the magician at work and note the meticulous care with which he applies this most effective and most important verbal action to the substance . . . then you realize how serious is the belief that the magic is in the breath and the breath is the magic." (B. Malinowski, *Coral Gardens & Their Magic*, pp. 215–216, 260)

(3) "The Moon thus says to the little Hare, that the little Hare is a little fool. Therefore his ears are red, because of the foolish things. He is not clever.

"The Moon speaks with the side of his tongue, because his tongue is upon his palate. Therefore he speaks with his tongue's tip because he feels he is the moon who tells his story, and he does so, because he feels that he is the Moon he is not a person, who will speak nicely, for he is the Moon. Therefore he tells the Moon's story, he does not tell a person's story, for he thus speaks, he thus tells the Moon's stories.

"Therefore he speaks turning up the other part of his tongue, for he feels that he is a shoe. Therefore he tells the shoe's stories, for he feels that he is not a man, but is the Moon. He is the Mantis' foot's shoe, and he feels that it was the Mantis who called his name, he will act like a shoe.

"Therefore he speaks like this, for he feels that he speaks like the Hare, he speaks in this manner, for he feels that he merely speaks with his tongue, he merely speaks like the Hare. The Hare speaks the Hare's language, he speaks like this. The Hare does like this the Hare talks. The Hare talks like his mother, he tells his mother's stories, his mother's stories as she tells them. And the little Hare listens to his mother's speech; he talks just like his mother, because he feels that his father talks like his mother, his father talks like this, for he feels that he speaks like his wife, he does like this, he speaks; they all tell one story for they feel that they talk their own language, they do not talk the people's language, for they tell their own stories, as they feel that another story is not there, that they may tell. For they tell one story, they do not tell the people's stories; for they speak like baboons, for they feel that baboons talk in this manner." (D. F. Bleek, "Speech of Animals & Moon Used by the |xam Bushmen," *Bantu Studies*, X [1936]: 187–189)

(4) "It is noteworthy and perhaps to be interpreted as a general tendency in Hindu culture to *raise certain aspects of the subliminal to consciousness*, that Hinduism in general and the Tantric sects in particular make extensive use in ritual and religious practice generally, not only of the intrinsically meaningless gestures (of the dance and iconography), but also of *intrinsically meaningless vocables*. For example, the famous *om* and *hum* and the not so famous *hrim, hrām, phat,* and many others, are meaningless, religious noises in origin, whatever symbolic meanings are given to them by the developed dogma." (M. B. Emenau in a review of La Meri's *The Gesture Language of the Hindu Dance*, in the *Journal of the American Oriental Society*, LXII [1942]: 149)

(5) The United Society of Believers in Christ's Second Appearing—called "Shakers"—originated in England in the mid-eighteenth century & soon centered around the person of Ann Lee (Mother Ann, or Mother Wisdom), who became "the reincarnation of the Christ Spirit . . . Ann the

Word . . . Bride of the Lamb." Writes Edward Deming Andrews: "The first Shaker songs were wordless tunes . . . [&] were received from Indian spirits or from the shades of Eskimos, Negroes, Abyssinians, Hottentots, Chinese and other races in search of salvation. Squaw songs, and occasionally a papoose song, were common. When Indian spirits came into the Shaker Church, the instruments would become so 'possessed' that they sang Indian songs, whooped, danced and behaved generally in the manner of 'savages' " (Andrews, p. 29). As such, they show the kind of connection between ideological & formal innovation that has characterized many movements-of-recovery, past & present.

(6) "I invented," circa 1915, "a new species of verse, 'verse without words,' or sound poems, in which the balancing of vowels is gauged & distributed only to the value of the initial line. The first of these I recited tonight. I had a special costume designed for it. My legs were covered with a cothurnus of luminous blue cardboard, which reached up to my hips so that I looked like an obelisk. Above that I wore a huge cardboard collar that was scarlet inside & gold outside. This was fastened at the throat in such a way that I was able to move it like wings by raising & dropping my elbows. In addition I wore a high top hat striped with blue & white. I recited the following:

> *gadji beri bimba*
> *glandridi lauli lonni cadori*
> *gadjama bim beri glassala*
> *glandridi glassala tuffm i zimbrabim*
> *blassa galassasa tuffm i zimbrabim*

. . . I now noticed that my voice, which seemed to have no other choice, had assumed the age-old cadence of the sacerdotal lamentation. . . . The electric light went out, as I had intended, & I was carried, moist with perspiration, like a magical bishop, into the abyss. . . ." (Hugo Ball, quoted in *The Dada Painters & Poets*, ed. Robert Motherwell [George Wittenborn Publishers, New York, 1951], p. xix; trans. Eugene Jolas)

[N.B. How different is Ball's dada-show from the Kirgiz-Tatar poet (shaman) who "runs around the tent, springing, roaring, leaping; he barks like a dog, sniffs at the audience, lows like an ox, bellows, cries, bleats like a lamb, grunts like a pig, whinnies, coos, imitating with remarkable accuracy the cries of animals, the songs of birds, the sound of their flight, and so on, all of which greatly impresses the audience" (M. Eliade, *Shamanism*, p. 97)? It is part of a world with Artaud's cries in *Pour en finir avec le jugement de Dieu* & McClure's poems, like the following, in "beast language." But there are plenty of less dramatic examples also.]

(7)   Michael McClure
                  GHOST TANTRA #1 (1964)

GOOOOOOR! GOOOOOOOOOO!
GOOOOOOOOOR!
GRAHHH! GRAHH! GRAHH!
Grah gooooor! Ghahh! Graaarr! Greeeeer! Grayowhr!
Greeeeee
GRAHHRR! RAHHR! GRAGHHRR! RAHR!
RAHR! RAHHR! GRAHHHR! GAHHR! HRAHR!
BE NOT SUGAR BUT BE LOVE
looking for sugar!
GAHHHHHHHH!
ROWRR!
GROOOOOOOOOOH!
. . . .

#51

I LOVE TO THINK OF THE RED PURPLE ROSE
IN THE DARKNESS COOLED BY THE NIGHT.
We are served by machines making satins
of sounds.
Each blot of sound is a bud or a stahr.
Body eats bouquets of the ear's vista.
Gahhhrrr boody eers noze eyes deem thou.
NOH. NAH-OHH
hrooor. VOOOR-NAH! GAHROOOOO ME.
Nah droooooh seerch. NAH THEE!
The machines are too dull when we
are lion-poems that move & breathe.
WHAN WE GROOOOOOOOOOOOOOOR
hann dree myketoth sharoo sreee thah noh deeeeeemed ez.
Whan eeeethoooze hrohh.

["These are spontaneous stanzas published in the order and with the natural sounds in which they were first written. If there is an OOOOOOOOOOOOOOOH, simply say a long loud 'oooh.' If there is a 'gahr' simply say gar and put an h in.

"Look at stanza 51. It begins in English and turns into beast language—star becomes stahr. Body becomes boody. Nose becomes noze. Everybody knows how to pronounce NOH or VOOR-NAH or GAHROOOOO ME."

—Michael McClure]

Page 9 *GENESIS II*

Source: Ronald M. Berndt, *Djanggawul: An Aboriginal Religious Cult of North-Eastern Arnhem Land* (Philosophical Library, New York, 1953), p. 256.

A heavy ripeness, the swelling & bursting of a teeming life-source, colors Australian views of the creation. The body of the sacred sister, heat around the clitoris, the budding tree roots, spray & blood, a swarming sense of life emerging—not two-by-two, in pairs, but *swarming*—was turned-from in the West, reduced to images of evil. Spenser's *Error* breeds "a thousand yong ones, which she dayly fed, / Sucking upon her poisonous dugs"; & Milton's *Sin* is the Prolific raped by her son into the production of "those yelling monsters, that with ceaseless cry / Surround me, as thou sawest, hourly conceived / And hourly born, with sorrow infinite," etc. But Blake renamed these "the Prolific" & marked a turning in man's relation to his "sensual existence."

Glossary & Synopsis. *Rangga*—sacred emblem; identified with the penis of the Djanggawul Brother. *Rangga folk*: those who initially emerged from the Djanggawul Sisters; ancestors of the present-day eastern Arnhem Landers.

Djuda—tree rangga emblem, from which trees sprang up when plunged into the ground by the Djanggawul.

Mat, or *ngainmara mat*—conically shaped; belonging to the Djanggawul Sisters; a symbol for the uterus; a whale, etc.

A major ritual work consisting of multiple songs in a narrative sequence, the *Djanggawul Cycle* is the best example the present editor knows, of the celebration of human sexuality & birth in the work of genesis. The cycle itself follows the wanderings of the Djanggawul Brother & his two Sisters, Bild-

447

jiwuraroiju & Miralaidj, who come to Arnhem Land from Bralgu (Land of the Eternal Beings), bringing with them ceremonies & sacred objects, & peopling the places through which they pass. The Brother "has an elongated penis, and each of the Two Sisters has a long clitoris . . . so long they drag upon the ground as they walk." At Marabai, "the long penis of the Brother and the clitorises of the Sisters [are shortened]. More people are born and some are circumcised." Part Nine (from which the excerpt is taken) continues this action; also "the Brother has coitus with his young sister [Miralaidj], who has an arm-band within her [i.e., something blocking the vaginal passage]; the breaking of this causes blood to flow. Dancing follows."

For more on related Australian ceremonialism, see pp. 392 & 395, with the accompanying commentaries.

Page 11   EGYPTIAN GOD NAMES

Source: Alexandre Piankoff, *The Shrines of Tut-Ankh-Amon* (Pantheon Books, New York, 1955), passim.

> Poetry is I say essentially a vocabulary just as prose is essentially not.
>
> And what is the vocabulary of which poetry absolutely is. It is a vocabulary based on the noun as prose is essentially and determinately and vigorously not based on the noun.
>
> Poetry is concerned with using with abusing, with losing with wanting, with denying with avoiding with adoring with replacing the noun. It is doing that always doing that, doing that and doing nothing but that. Poetry is doing nothing but using losing refusing and pleasing and betraying and caressing nouns.
>
> . . . So that is poetry really loving the name of anything and that is not prose.
>
> —G. Stein, *Lectures in America*, pp. 231–232

But the physicality of her description sticks: how she points to a material condition of poetry prior to verse or sequence, a way of thinking & feeling that treats words—all words—as substantive, measurable, having each a certain weight & extension, roots of words holding them firmly to earth, which the man cuts loose at will to let float up, then take root again so that their weights are again felt. And since the words are "real" (being measurable by weight & extension), they may be called forth again or withheld, & being called forth are the things called forth? This is what the man believed once who made magic—"spells" & "charms" (*carmina*) being words in search of things. Measurable words as real as measurable things where both words & things are present in the naming. And the same tangible quality of words was felt whether they were spoken (again that breath-entering-the-object Malinowski wrote of) or written or pictured or drummed. Something like that sensed then & there—rediscovered here & now.

Addenda. (1) Egyptian poetry, where it names & creates its gods, is at least as concerned with their energy as their dignity—is in fact rich in matter that Rundle Clark calls "obscene, brutal & inconsequential" & that "shows the Egyptians lived much closer to the dark powers of the unconscious than we realize." The same force turns up in other god-namings & god-poems, as when the Polynesians call Kiho:

> First-Urge
> Phallus
> Rising-Sap
> Tumidity
> The Denudation
> etc.
>
> (J. Frank Stimson, *The Cult of Kiho-Timu* [Bishop Museum, Honolulu, 1933], pp. 20–21.)

& there, too, the translation muffles the force.

(2) Among the Navajo a list of god-names became the song, called *The Twelve-Word Song of Blessing*, "a combination of names" writes Reichard "[of] tremendous power":

> TWELVE-WORD SONG
> Earth
> Sky
> Mountain Woman
> Water Woman
> Talking God
> xactceoyan

Boy-carrying-single-corn-kernel
Girl-carrying-single-turquoise
White-corn-boy
Yellow-corn-girl
Pollen Boy
Cornbeetle Girl

(G. Reichard, *Navaho Religion* [Pan-
theon, New York, 1950], Vol. One,
p. 273.)

Consider also the Polynesian genealogical poem below & African praise-
names & praise-poems (p. 477).

(3) "Victory will be above all / To see truly into the distance / To see
everything / Up close / So that everything can have a new name" (Guillaume
Apollinaire).

Page 13   GENESIS III

Source: Richard A. Taylor, *Te Ika a Maui: New Zealand and Its
Inhabitants* (William Macintosh, London, 1870), pp. 109–110.

The coming of light as pivotal moment in the world's awakening gets a
very lovely, very complex handling in Polynesian poetry. What's less appar-
ent is that these light-poems (night-poems, too) are in fact genealogical
tables tracing the rulers' descents from the gods, the gods from the cosmic
circumstances of the beginning. Night (*Te Po*) is both a name & a period of
time, a force & a god: & the language holds it in delicate balance between
concrete & abstract thought; so also for Conception, Increase, Great-
Night, Nothing, Midday, etc. A similar chant turns up in a version by J. C.
Anderson (1907), there as pure genealogy. The reciter is Mumuhu:

THE GENEALOGY OF THE GODS
FROM PRIMAL NOTHINGNESS:

1.	Te Kore	(the void)
2.	Te Kore-tua-tahi	(the first void)
3.	Te Kore-tua-rua	(the second void)
4.	Te Kore-nui	(the vast void)
5.	Te Kore-roa	(the far-extending void)
6.	Te Kore-para	(the sere void)

7.	Te Kore-whiwhia	(the unpossessing void)
8.	Te Kore-rawea	(the delightful void)
9.	Te Kore-te-tamaua	(the void fast bound)
10.	Te Po	(the Night)
11.	Te Po-teki	(the hanging Night)
12.	Te Po-terea	(the drifting Night)
13.	Te Po-wha-wha	(the moaning Night)
14.	Hine-ruaki-moe	(daughter of troubled sleep)
15.	Te Po	(the Night)
16.	Te Ata	(the Morning)
17.	Te Ao-to-roa	(the abiding Day)
18.	Te Ao-marama	(the bright Day)
19.	Whai-tua	(Space)

"[And] in *whai-tua* two existences formed without shape: *Maku* (moisture), a male, & *Mahora-nui-a-rangi* (the great expanse of heaven), a female; from whom sprang *Toko-mua*, *Toko-roto* & *Toko-pa*, parents of wind, of clouds, of mists, & fourth in birth, *Rangi-potiki*, who taking to wife *Papa*, produced the gods" (Johannes C. Anderson, *Maori Life in Ao-Tea*, p. 127).

Addenda. (1) Paul Radin's reading (*Primitive Man as Philosopher*, pp. 292 ff.) suggests a high degree of systematization: that the first section describes the development of consciousness; the second predicates a mediating principle, the *word*; the third gives a genealogical history of matter; the fourth shows the birth of light itself. Even so there are many holes, many different texts & distributions of ages. Signifying what? Either that a closed system had come apart, or that the Polynesian mind was in constant movement toward the making of a shifting series of possibilities. (See also the Hawaiian *Kumulipo*, p. 407, above, & accompanying commentary.)

(2) Greek cosmogonies like that, say, in Hesiod are the best Western tries at this sort of thing the editor knows of—at least where the translation allows the concrete force of the namings (Sky, Gap, Pit, Gloom, Night, etc.) to come through. (See p. 329—or, where available, Doria & Lenowitz's *Origins*, as a gathering of ancient Mediterranean creation texts so diverse in its concretions as to knock hell out of the notion of a single authoratative text.)

(3)   Jackson Mac Low
              1ST LIGHT POEM: FOR IRIS—10 JUNE 1962

                     The light of a student-lamp
                     sapphire light
                     shimmer
                     the light of a smoking-lamp

                     Light from the Magellanic Clouds
                     the light of a Nernst lamp
                     the light of a naphtha-lamp
                     light from meteorites

                     Evanescent light
                     ether
                     the light of an electric lamp
                     extra light

                     Citrine light
                     kineographic light
                     the light of a Kitson lamp
                     kindly light

                     Ice light
                     irradiation
                     ignition
                     altar light

                     The light of a spotlight
                     a sunbeam
                     sunrise
                     solar light

                     Mustard-oil light
                     Maroon light
                     the light of a magnesium flare
                     light from a meteor

                     Evanescent light
                     ether
                     light from an electric lamp
                     an extra light

Light from a student-lamp
sapphire light
a shimmer
smoking-lamp light

Ordinary light
orgone lumination
light from a lamp burning olive oil
opal light

Actinism
atom-bomb light
the light of an alcohol lamp
the light of a lamp burning anda-oil

Page 15 IMAGES

Sources: (1) *Report of the Canadian Arctic Expedition*, 1913–1918 (to make the sun come out by assertion of its presence); (2) H. Vedder, *Die Bergdama*, trans. into English by C. M. Bowra, *Primitive Song* (sung to a bow made of *ha*-wood); (3) Bleek & Lloyd, *Specimens of Bushman Folklore* (in the jackal's language, i.e., with a special "click" not otherwise used); (4) Knud Rasmussen, as quoted in Caillois & Lambert, *Tresor de la poésie universelle* & there titled "Contre la mort"; (5) F. Densmore, *Chippewa Music* (the song's origin was a dream in which the singer became a buffalo & was given this deer-song by other buffalos); (6) Bleek & Lloyd, *Specimens* (a hunting charm, power from description of the quarry); (7) Jerome Rothenberg & Richard Johnny John, in J. R., *Shaking the Pumpkin* (a song from the Society of the Mystic Animals).

Single-line poems, presented as such—in contrast to some of the longer works that follow & involve a linking of lines & images to make poems of greater complexity, showing development by image cluster, gaps in sequence, etc.

The poetry here is in song & image & wordplay, but only the image comes near to translating, itself enough to make a poem, or so the argument would go. What's happened, simply, is that something has been sighted & stated & set apart (by name or by description); given its own tune, too, to make it special; fixed, held fast in all this vanishing experience. It is this double sense of sighted/sited that represents the basic poetic function (a setting-apart-by-the-creation-of-special-circumstances that the editor calls "sacralism") from which the rest follows—toward the building of more complicated structures & visions. But even here there is nothing naïve or minimal about the "sightings," save their clarity & the sense that, starting now, the plot (as Cage would say) is-going-to-thicken. Thickens, in fact, while we're watching; for the "single perception" of an image like *a splinter of stone/which is white* can as easily be sensed as two perceptions, & placed against the subject (*blue crane*) as two or three. But the decision has been made to voice it as a single line or musical phrase, & that decision itself is a statement about how we know things—& a choice.

Addenda.   (1) A typical ritual song practice (but by no means the only one presented in these pages) is to repeat (often also to distort) the one line indefinitely—or as long as the dance & ritual demand—then go on to a second song in the (ritual) sequence, a third, a fourth, etc. A turn in the ritual or dance would then represent something roughly equivalent to a strophe break, where a first series of single-line poems ends & a new, but related, series begins. This is utilized by the translators of works like *Djanggawul, The Goulburn Island Cycle*, certain of the African "praise-poems," etc., who follow the "orders" of the ritual in their arrangement of single-line works into larger structures. Lines & series will often seem disconnected except when they're performed & happen together. The impact of such juxtapositions for our own time can't be ignored.

(2)   "Nothing of that, only an image—
        nothing else, utter oblivion—
        slanting through the words come vestiges of light!"

                    —Franz Kafka

(3) After Ian Hamilton Finlay

OCEAN STRIPE SERIES 2

        ---the little sail of your name---
        the little sail of your name
        --the little sail of your name--

[*Note*. Each element in Finlay's poem appeared originally on a separate page, broken lines in blue, words in red; thus color & the page boundary function with relation to his "single-image" as music does elsewhere. Thus, too, the further you get into it the less sense it makes to speak of a single-line poem—as in the "primitive" poems where any change in the music, even if the words remain unchanged, will alter the entire piece.]

Page 16 BANTU COMBINATIONS

Source: Henri A. Junod, *Life of a South African Tribe* (Macmillan & Co., 1912, 1927), passim.

Examples of plot-thickening in the area of "image": a conscious placing of image against image as though to see-what-happens. Apart from its presence in song, this juxtaposing of images turns up all over in the art, say, of the riddle—of which several of these "combinations" are, in fact, examples. Poem as opposition or balance of two or more images is also the basis of the haiku, less clearly of the sonnet. In all these the interest increases as the connection between the images becomes more & more strained, barely definable. Junod sensed this when he wrote:

> What makes a Bantu address especially interesting is . . . the *power of comparison* exhibited by Bantu speakers. . . . Sometimes the imagination is so subtle that the result is almost incoherent. They are satisfied even if the point which the two things compared have in common . . . is almost infinitesimal.

Not subtlety, though, but *energy*: the power of word & image. For it's right here that the light breaks through most clearly; not the light of logic & simile, not even the flashing of a single image or name, but what feels "deeper" because further into it by now in the process of boxing myself into some corner, & to which (for the first time) the word "vision" might be said to apply.

Addenda.

   (1)   Now I a fourfold vision see
       And a fourfold vision is given to me
       Tis fourfold in my supreme delight
       And three fold in soft Beulahs night
       And twofold Always. May God us keep
       From Single vision & Newtons sleep

                  —William Blake (1802)

(2) "The image cannot spring from any comparison but from the bringing together of two more or less remote realities. . . .

"The more distant and legitimate the relation between the two realities brought together, the stronger the image will be . . . the more emotive power and poetic reality it will possess."

—Pierre Reverdy

(3) "The African image is not an image by equation but an image by *analogy*, a surrealist image. Africans do not like straight lines and false *mots justes*. Two and two do not make four, but five, as Aimé Césaire has told us. The object does not mean what it represents but what it suggests, what it creates. . . . But as you would suppose, African surrealism is different from European surrealism. European surrealism is empirical. African surrealism is mystical and metaphysical. . . . The African surrealist analogy presupposes and manifests the hierarchized universe of life-forces." (Léopold Sédar Senghor, quoted in *Symposium of the Whole*, pp. 119–120)

(4) Contemporary Combinations

> A church leaped up
> exploding
> like a bell.

—Phillipe Soupault

> Elephants are contagious.

—Paul Eluard & Benjamin Peret

> *A White Hunter*

> A white hunter is nearly crazy.

—Gertrude Stein

> *In the Ranchhouse at Dawn*

> O corpuscle!
> O wax town!

—Kenneth Koch

Wood

I repeated it.

—Clark Coolidge

A man torments the sun.
Cows are disturbed by their calves.

—Barrett Watten

the last days like this
a red stone
all we know of fire

—Robert Kelly

[N.B. Most of these are, like their Bantu counterparts, taken from extended series of "combinations".]

Page 17 CORRESPONDENCES

Source: Selected from *The I Ching or Book of Changes*, translated from Chinese into German by Richard Wilhelm and rendered into English by Cary F. Baynes (Bollingen Series XIX, Pantheon Books, Princeton University Press, 1950), pp. 295–299.

The *I Ching*, which some have dated as far back as 2000 B.C. (& if not that old is, anyway, very ancient), is the basis in China for the kind of thought that sees life & development as a working-out or constant reshuffling of contrary forces; or, as Blake had it

without contraries is no progression;
reason & energy, love & hate, good & evil,
are all necessary to human existence.

Whereas the "practical" side of the *I Ching* deals with divination by yarrow sticks, etc., some sections, like the one given here, show a developed ability to think in images, to place name against name, quality against quality, while retaining that passion for the names of things that Gertrude Stein saw as the basis of all poetry. Partly it's a question of resemblances & analogy, but at this point in where "we" are, what's of still greater importance is the possibility of a kind of tension, energy, etc., generated by the joining of disparate, even arbitrary, images. *Observation*: Every new correspondence acts on its subject, which it changes, & on the entire field; every change a measurable burst of energy. *Questions*: Is the correspondence *there*, is it imposed, & does it finally matter? If the common term "hot" or "dry" links "fire" with "the sun, the lightning, the upper part of the trunk," what links it with "big-bellied" or "lances & weapons"? What common quality "justifies" the linking of nouns in the "keeping still" series, & if you find one (Confucius did!) are you gaining consistency through a loss of power? The editor can only witness to his sense of this series of "correspondences" being a handy ancient manual of poetic process (of *all* those levels of vision Blake spoke of)—& values it as such.

Addenda. (1) For further selections from, comments on, the *I Ching*, see above, p. 274, below, p. 567. The reader should note, too, that the *I Ching* functioned primarily as a system of divination & can compare it, e.g., to the poetics of divination in such African systems as Ifa & the Basuto "praises of the falls" (pp. 174, 181, & the accompanying commentaries).

(2)   André Breton
                  FREE UNION (1931)

My wife whose hair is a brush fire
Whose thoughts are summer lightning
Whose waist is an hourglass
Whose waist is the waist of an otter caught in the teeth of a tiger
Whose mouth is a bright cockade with the fragrance of a star of the first
     magnitude
Whose teeth leave prints like the tracks of white mice over snow
Whose tongue is made out of amber and polished glass
Whose tongue is a stabbed wafer
The tongue of a doll with eyes that open and shut
Whose tongue is incredible stone
My wife whose eyelashes are strokes in the handwriting of a child
Whose eyebrows are nests of swallows
My wife whose temples are the slate of greenhouse roofs
With steam on the windows
My wife whose shoulders are champagne
Are fountains that curl from the heads of dolphins over the ice

My wife whose wrists are matches
Whose fingers are raffles holding the ace of hearts
Whose fingers are fresh cut hay
My wife with the armpits of martens and beech fruit
And Midsummer Night
That are hedges of privet and nesting places for sea snails
Whose arms are of sea foam and a land locked sea
And a fusion of wheat and a mill
Whose legs are spindles
In the delicate movements of watches and despair
My wife whose calves are sweet with the sap of elders
Whose feet are carved initials
Keyrings and the feet of steeplejacks who drink
My wife whose neck is fine milled barley
Whose throat contains the Valley of Gold
And encounters in the bed of the maelstrom
My wife whose breasts are of the night
And are undersea molehills
And crucibles of rubies
My wife whose breasts are haunted by the ghosts of dew-moistened roses
Whose belly is a fan unfolded in the sunlight
Is a giant talon
My wife with the back of a bird in vertical flight
With a back of quicksilver
And bright lights
My wife whose nape is of smooth worn stone and wet chalk
And of a glass slipped through the fingers of someone who has just drunk
My wife with the thighs of a skiff
That are lustrous and feathered like arrows
Stemmed with the light tailbones of a white peacock
And imperceptible balance
My wife whose rump is sandstone and flax
Whose rump is the back of a swan and the spring
My wife with the sex of an iris
A mine and a platypus
With the sex of an algae and old fashioned candles
My wife with the sex of a mirror

My wife with eyes full of tears
With eyes that are purple armor and a magnetized needle
With eyes of savannahs
With eyes full of water to drink in prisons
My wife with eyes that are forests forever under the axe
My wife with eyes that are the equal of water and air and earth and fire

(Translation by David Antin)

Page 19   GENESIS IV

Source: Adapted from "The Secrets of Enoch," chapters 25 & 26, in
The Lost Books of the Bible and the Forgotten Books of Eden, reprinted by World
Publishing Co. (Cleveland [1926], 1963), p. 90.

God's sexuality—lonely, hermaphroditic—is another, very natural way
of imagining the creation. The most famous such account in the Near East
was the Egyptian masturbation genesis:

> Heaven had not been created . . .
> The earth had not been created . . .
> I formed a spell in my heart . . .
> I made forms of every kind . . .
> I thrust my cock into my closed hand . . .
> I made my seed to enter my hand . . .
> I poured it into my mouth . . .
> I broke wind under the form of SHU . . .
> I passed water under the form of TEFNUT . . .

But even the priestly Genesis (Hebrew) couldn't unhook the mind from its
old imaginings, hypotheses, etc.; *vide* the section collaged into the beginning
of the fifth chapter:

> This is the book of the generations of Adam. In the day that God
> created man, *in the likeness of God* made he him;
> *Male & female* created he them; & blessed them, & *called their
> name Adam.*

But the idea—re-explored in the medieval *Zohar*—was already very old.

Page 20 *AZTEC DEFINITIONS*

Source: Bernardino de Sahagún, *Florentine Codex: General History of the Things of New Spain*, translated by Charles E. Dibble & Arthur J. O. Anderson (University of Utah Press & the School of American Research, 1963), Vol. XII, passim.

Fray Bernardino de Sahagún, a Franciscan monk, began in 1547—only twenty-six years after the fall of Mexico-Tenochtitlan—to compile documents in Nahuatl from Indian elders who repeated what they had learned by memory in their schools, the *Calmécac* & the *Telpochcalli*. These Nahuatl texts have been preserved in three codices, two in Madrid & one in Florence. In the eleventh book of the Florentine codex—a kind of glossary of "earthly things"—the elders' minds & words are drawn toward definitions of the most ordinary debris of their lives.

Addenda. (1) "Everything goes but the words: the fragments of speech of a people who had learned that the mind's grain is our final clue to the real. He led them to a reconsideration, to an assemblage of 'the things of New Spain'—of their gods, their days, their signs & omens, their sacrifices, their songs, their defeats. . . . But . . . more astonishing than all that is how the habit of their minds begins to play among the everyday debris. . . . Here the mind finds release in a strange new encounter; free of ritual & myth [The-System]; it approaches its objects as if for the first time testing their existence. IT IS DARK, IT IS LIGHT: IT IS WIDE-MOUTHED, IT IS NARROW-MOUTHED: all of this said with no apparent sense of contradiction, as if, among these objects, the old pattern holds: of preparing chaos for the birth of something real.

"Having come to this for ourselves, we can draw close to them, can hear in these 'definitions' the sound of a poetry, a measure-by-placement-&-displacement not far from our own. . . . For surely it should be clear by now that poetry is less literature than a process of thought & feeling & the arrangement of that into affective utterances. The conditions these definitions meet are the conditions of poetry." (J. R., from "Introduction to Aztec Definitions," *some/thing* [Spring 1965], p. 2)

(2)   David Antin
                   From DEFINITIONS FOR MENDY (1965)

loss is an unintentional decline in or disappearance of
        a value arising from a contingency
a value is an efficacy a power a brightness
it is also a duration

to lose something keys hair someone
we suffer at the thought
he has become absent imaginary false
a false key will not turn a true lock
false hair will not turn grey
mendy will not come back
but longing is not imaginary
we must go down into ourselves
down to the floor   that is not imaginary
where hunger lives and thirst
hunger imagine bread   thirst imagine water
the glass of water slips to the floor
thirst is a desert
value a glass of water
loss is the glass of water slipping to the floor
loss is the unintentional decline in or disappearance of a glass of water arising
        from a contingency
the glass   pieces of glass
the floor is a contingency
the floor is a floor
is a contingency
made of wood
the fire is a contingency
the bread is burned
burning is not a contingency
the presence of the dead is imaginary
the absence is real
henceforth it will be his manner of appearing
so he appears   in an orange jacket and workpants and a blue denim shirt
his hair is black his eyes are black
and a blue crab is biting his long fingers

he is trying to hold the bread
he is trying to bring the water to his mouth
his mouth is a desert
the glass of water will not come
the glass of water keeps slipping through his fingers
the floor is made of wood it is burning
it is covered with pieces of glass
arising from a contingency
his face is the darkened face of a clock
it is marked with radium
the glass is falling from his face
the face of a clock in which there is a salamander
whose eyes are bright with radium
radium is a value that is always declining
radium is a value that is always disappearing
lead is also a value
but it is less bright than radium

loss is an unintentional decline in or disappearance of a value arising from a
  contingency
a value is an efficacy a power a brightness
it is also a duration

o o o o

[*Note.* "The initial definition of *loss* is quoted from p. 22 of *Principles of Insurance* by Mehr & Cammack, & the initial definitions of *value* are from *Webster's New International Dictionary*, 1927 edition." (D. A.) But the rhythm & interplay of concrete names & "facts"—here & elsewhere in Antin's poem—bear a direct relation to the Aztec definitions first printed by him & the present editor in their magazine, *some/thing.*]

Page 25   *GENESIS V*

Source: Translation from K. T. Preuss, *Die Religion und Mythologie der Uitoto* (1921), *in* Margot Astrov, *The Winged Serpent: An Anthology of American Indian Prose and Poetry* (The John Day Company, New York, 1946), pp. 325–326.

Creation by word & thought, but more particularly, the recognition of "dream" as model for the creative process: a "reality" of a different order, of new combinations of objects: "thought" running ahead of "thinker," toward the making of a "world."

"Word" & "origin" & "father" immediately suggest St. John (result of Preuss's German?)—though there the Word didn't *make*, rather *was-with* & *was*, the father. And Aristotle too had taught that the origin of the gods was in men's dreamings, "for when the soul is alone in sleep, then it takes its real nature." In Australia (see below), the mythic period of the creative-beings was called the Dream Time or the Dreaming, which also included such latterday phenomena as participated in the sacred. Siberian & North American shamans received word & song in dreams, as did the Jewish prophets & certain Christian saints & poets.

In the early twentieth century, dream (like drugs later) was turned to, to sanction the use of alternative, "nonlogical" thought processes in poetry, painting, etc., until some realized that no such sanction was needed. But dreaming remains everyone's chance for exposure to the possibilities of poetic process: of making the unknown "known."

Addenda. (1) **alcheringa** [Arunta of Australia, *alcheringa*], *n.* 1. The Eternal Dream Time, The Dreaming of a sacred heroic time long ago when man and nature came to be, a kind of narrative of things that once happened. 2. A kind of charter of things that still happen. 3. A kind of *logos* or principle of order transcending everything significant. *v.* 1. The act of dreaming, as reality and symbol, by which the artist is inspired to produce a new song. 2. The act by which the mind makes contact with whatever mystery it is that connects the Dreaming and the Here-and-Now. (Adapted from W. E. H. Stanner)

(2) "From the moment when it is subjected to a methodical examination, when, by means yet to be determined, we succeed in recording the contents of dreams in their entirety . . . we may hope that the mysteries which really are not will give way to the great Mystery. I believe in the future resolution of these two states, dream and reality, which are seemingly so contradictory, into a kind of absolute reality, a *surreality*, if one may so speak. It is in quest of this surreality that I am going, certain not to find it but too unmindful of my death not to calculate to some slight degree the joys of its possession." (André Breton, *The First Surrealist Manifesto*, 1924)

Page 26 THE PICTURES

Sources: (1), (2), (4), & (6) from Garrick Mallery, *Picture-Writing of the American Indians* (Bureau of American Ethnology, Annual Report No. 10

[1888–1889]), pp. 472, 167, 499, 170; (3) see Arthur Spencer, *The Lapps* (Crane, Russak & Co., New York, 1978), p. 96; (4) see Ernst Doblhofer, *Voices in Stone* (Souvenir Press, London, 1961), pp. 268–269.

Here & elsewhere in the anthology are examples of visual poetry, i.e., nonverbal &/or pictorial structures with a language function analogous to but not (necessarily) identical with that of the poem. Workings of this kind are surprisingly widespread among "nonliterate" peoples—most only a step away from writing, some having surely crossed the line. In Japanese, the verb *kaku* means both "to write" & "to draw," & in these examples too it is hard to keep the functions separate or to assert with any confidence that writing is a late development rather than indigenous, in some form, to the human situation everywhere. Arts merge, then, & boundaries shift, & what started as an aid to memory develops as a distinct (but never isolated) activity; or, where it becomes a system of writing, develops also into the art of calligraphy.

o   o   o   o

1. Depiction of "the Giant Bird Kaloo . . . most terrible of all creatures . . . who caught the [Badger-Trickster] in his claws & . . . let him drop, & he fell from dawn to sunset."

2. The chart accompanies a tradition chanted by the members of a secret society of the Osage tribe. It was drawn by an Osage, Red Corn, & images the world & early man's emergence. Tree of life & river at the top; sun, moon & stars beneath; four heavens or upper worlds at center, through which the ancestors passed before coming to this earth, etc. The pictographs are (mnemonic) clues to songs but the whole pictorial device is more-than-that (see description of the Midē songs, below, p. 542).

3. A major form of verbovisual art & divination before destruction by the missionaries, the "magic drums" of the north European Lapps served as virtual poem-maps of the shaman's world. "Some drums had well over a hundred pictures— . . . each picture (god, man, animal, building) a self-contained concept which is of value in reading the message of the drum. There is no intention of recording incidents, or of telling a story," but an approximate sectioning of the drum cuts the surface into quarters, "each representing a different part of the Lapp universe." Otherwise, an open distribution of elements by the poet-shaman—in the creation of a field. (The drum shown here dates from the seventeenth century or earlier.)

4. Pictographs in sequence (incised on an ivory bow) show hunter & shaman in postures of supplication & divination amid scenes of trees, dwell-

ings, animals, etc., & (lower left) "a demon sent out by the shaman to drive the game in the way of the hunter." Pictured to the demon's left are his assistants.

5. Using pictographic images while likely crossing-over to a sounded script, the two-sided terra-cotta disc dates back to circa 1700 B.C. "The highly pictorial signs, which show no relationship with [other] Cretan pictographs, number 241, and include forty-five symbols, such as human figures and parts of the body, animals, plants, and tools." The signs follow a set order, possibly of a ritual text associated with a shrine of the Phoenician god Baal.

6. Easter Island *rongorongo* writing: drawn on tablets called "singing wood" or "wood with hymns for recitation": thus (apparently) a system of writing for the transmission of (sacred) song. More recent workers have come up with tentative readings of the poems, though none with great assurance.

o   o   o   o

Addenda. (1) "Therefore, & in a certain measure, philosophers are painters; poets are painters & philosophers; painters are philosophers & poets. He who is not a poet & a painter is no philosopher. We say rightly that to understand is to see imaginary forms & figures; & understanding is fancy, at least it is not deprived of fancy. He is no painter who is not in some degree a poet & thinker, & there can be no poet without a measure of thought & representation." (Giordano Bruno [1591], as quoted by poet & artist Dick Higgins)

(2) "The word & the image are one. Painting & composing poetry belong together. Christ is image & word. The word & the image are crucified." (Hugo Ball [1916] quoted in *The Dada Painters & Poets*, ed. Robert Motherwell, p. 52)

(3) "Christ, these hieroglyphs. Here is the most abstract & formal deal of all the things this people dealt out—and yet, to my taste, it is precisely as intimate as verse is. Is, in fact, verse. Is their verse. And comes into existence, obeys the same laws that, the coming into existence, the persisting of verse, does." (Charles Olson, *The Mayan Letters*)

(4) Some "modern" examples, out of many, follow; other instances of picture-writings, etc., appear elsewhere (pp. 157, 205, 215, 219, 236, 281).

BEHEMOTH & LEVIATHAN (1825)
William Blake

HORSE CALLIGRAM (1918)

Guillaume Apollinaire

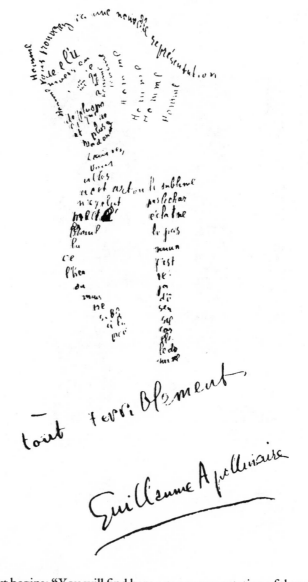

The text begins: "You will find here a new representation of the universe. The most poetic and the most modern."

ÔLHO POR ÔLHO (1964)

Augusto de Campos

"Ôlho por ôlho" (eye for eye) is a "popcrete" poem. The original, in color, collaged from magazines, is 50 cm by 70 cm.

RIVER / SANDBANK (c. 1965)

Seiichi Niikuni

川| kawa = river

州| sasu = sand-bank

"A splendid flash of concrete poetry."—E. Fenollosa.

FILMIC FRIEZE (1978)

Nina Yankowitz

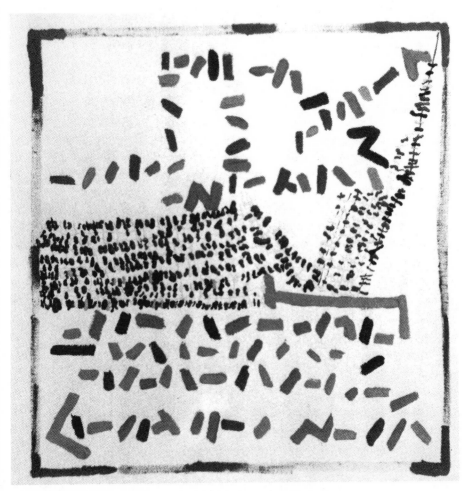

Subtitled: "A Text for Scanning for Male & Female Voice."

Page 32 THE GIRL OF THE EARLY RACE WHO MADE
THE STARS

Source: Wilhelm H. I. Bleek & Lucy C. Lloyd, *Specimens of Bushman Folklore* (George Allen & Co., London, 1911), p. 72.

The Bleek-Lloyd workings—the English was apparently Lucy Lloyd's—are the best examples the editor knows of how a "literal" translation, when handled with respect for the intelligence & sense of form of the original maker, can point to the possibility of new uses in the translator's own language. Wilhelm H. I. Bleek, German-born philologist & collector, died in 1875, so that his contributions to the *Specimens* are from before that date & those of his sister-in-law not much later. This makes their very modern sound all the more astonishing—as close to the language, say, of Gertrude Stein (see below) as the form of an African mask is to the paintings of Picasso or Modigliani.

"The Girl of the Early Race" was narrated by ||kábbo (lit. "Dream") as told him by his mother !kwi-an. He was also the maker or transmitter of the Jackal's song (p. 15) & the account of the "floating names" that appears in the STATEMENTS section of the present volume.

Addenda. (1) Another characteristic of the Bleek-Lloyd translations is that they call into question the distinction (still strong among us) between poetry & prose, thus more faithful to the primitive situation; or, as Boas noted:

> The form of [our] prose is largely determined by the fact that it is read, not spoken, while primitive prose is based on the art of oral delivery and is, therefore, more closely related to modern oratory than to the printed literary style. . . . In other cases [the prose passages] are of rhythmic form and must be considered poetry or chants rather than prose. (*Race, Language & Culture*, p. 491)

Today, too, poetry & prose are coming to a place-of-meeting in the spoken language—& the distinctions made by previous centuries have come to mean much less.

(2)   Gertrude Stein
                 From LISTEN TO ME (A Play, 1936)

                              Act III
                              Scene II
                             The moon

No dog barks at the moon.
The moon shines and no dog barks
No not anywhere on this earth.
Because everywhere anywhere there are lights many lights and so no dog
knows that the moon is there
And so no dog barks at the moon now no not
anywhere.
And the moon makes no one crazy no not now
anywhere.
Because there are so many lights anywhere.
That the light the moon makes is no matter.
And so no one is crazy now anywhere.
Because there are so many lights anywhere.
That the light the moon makes is no matter.
And no one is crazy now anywhere.
Because there are so many lights anywhere.
And so then there it does not matter
The sun yes the sun yes does matter
But the moon the moon does not matter
Because there are so many lights everywhere that any dog knows that
lights any night are anywhere.
And so no dog bays at the moon anywhere.
This is so
This we know
Because we wondered why,
Why did the dogs not bay at the
moon.
They did not but why
But of course why
Because there are lights everywhere
anywhere.
And that is what they meant by never
yesterday.

[*Note*. The editor has chosen to present the preceding as a running piece, though in the original the lines are spoken by five characters.]

Page 34 THE FRAGMENTS

Sources: (1), (2), & (3) from Samuel A. B. Mercer, *The Pyramid Texts in Translation and Commentary* (Longmans, Green & Co., New York, 1952), Utterances 561, 501, 502; (4) from S. Langdon, *Babylonian Penitential Psalms* (Librairie Orientaliste Paul Geuthner, Paris, 1927), p. 21.

Time & chance have worked on the materials, not only to corrode but to create new structures: as if "process" itself had turned poet, to leave its imprints on the work. This explains the gaps, the holes-punched-out-by-time. But the workers who pieced such scraps together have left their marks too: not only dots as here, but brackets, parentheses, numbers, & open spaces. So something else appears: a value, a new form to attract the mind: as a Greek statue that has lost its colors, tempts the sculptor into the sight of marble: something tough as rock.

The pyramid texts themselves (arranged by Sethe & others into 714 "utterances," over 2000 lines) come from eight pyramids "constructed, and apparently inscribed, between the years 2350 and 2175 B.C.," with many of the verses still older, perhaps 3000 B.C., writes Mercer, "perhaps long before."

Addenda.

(1)　　　　　　　　　Ezra Pound
　　　　　　　　　　PAPYRUS

　　　　　　　　　　Spring . . .
　　　　　　　　　　Too long . . .
　　　　　　　　　　Gongola . . .

　　　　　　　　　　(From *Lustra*, 1916)

(2)　　　　　　　　Armand Schwerner
　　　　　　　From THE TABLETS (1966)

the calyx, the calyx, someone has ripped it
it will not make loam, it will crumble
the pig (god?) has pulled life off ++++++++++++++++++++
the pig (god?) is stronger than a thoughtless child
my chest empties...my chest
I can no longer stand in the middle of the field and +++++++++++

I am missing, my chest has no food for the maggots
there is no place for the pollen, there is only a hole in the flower
the hummingbird.................pus......................nectar
the field is a hole without pattern (shoes?)
there are no eyes in back of the wisent's sockets
the urus eats her own teats and her.......................
the urus lies in milk and blood
the urus is a hole in the middle of the field
[testicles]...................................for the ground
"with grey horses" drinks urine
"having fine green oxen" looks for salt
let us hold.........................the long man upside down
let us look into his mouth.....................selfish saliva
let us pluck +++++++++++++++++++++++++++for brother tree
let us kiss the long man, let us carry the long man
let us kiss the long man, let us fondle the long man
let us carry the long man as the ground sucks his drippings
let us feel the drippings from his open groin
let us kiss the hot wound, the wet wound.................nectar
let us wait until he is white and dry..................my chest
let us look into his dry evil mouth, let us fondle the long man
let us bypass the wisent on the river-road pintrpnit
let us avoid the urus on the river-road pintrpnit
let us smell the auroch on the river-road pintrpnit
let us carry the beautiful (strange?) children to the knom
let us sing with the children by the knom
let us set the children's beautiful (strange?) skulls by the hearth
when the rain comes
let us have rain
let us have rain
+++++++++++++++++++++++++++++++
++
+++++++++++++++++..tremble

[Schwerner writes of this: "The modern, accidental form of Sumero-
Akkadian tablets provided me with a usable poetic structure. They offered,
among other things, ways out of closure—which I find increasingly oner-
ous—as well as the expansion of the constricting girdle of English syntax.
They also invited spontaneous phonetic improvisations, . . . made me feel

comfortable in re-creating the animistic . . . & (enabled me) to put in holes wherever I wanted, or wherever they needed. . . .

["What is more, the rapid shifts in tonality & texture found in some archaic & primitive materials contribute a helpful antidote to 'civilized' modes concerned with characterological & dramatic imperatives of consistency. . . . [These] tonal & textural shifts . . . help place in some perspective the contemporary mystique of line-endings & their poetic importance. The question is not, Where does the line end; the question is, When is verse not charged with the power of the varied possible? The question is, What is meaningfulness?"]

Page 36   *ALL LIVES, ALL DANCES, & ALL IS LOUD*

Source: Translated by C. M. Bowra from R. P. Trilles, *Les Pygmées de la Forêt Equatoriale* (Paris, 1931), & printed in Bowra, *Primitive Song* (World Publishing Co., Cleveland, 1962), p. 106.

UNIVERSAL PRIMITIVE & ARCHAIC VISION OF ALL LIFE IN MOTION & SHARING A SINGLE NATURE WHICH IS SACRED

20TH CENTURY AMERICAN NOSTALGIA TO ADDRESS & TO ANIMATE THE THING-WORLD

Addenda.   (1) "Primitive man by no means lacks the ability to grasp the empirical differences of things. But in his conception of nature and life these differences are obliterated by a stronger feeling: the deep conviction of a fundamental and indelible *solidarity of life* that bridges over the multiplicity and variety of its single forms. . . . Life is felt as an unbroken continuous whole. . . . The limits between (its) different spheres are not insurmountable barriers; they are fluent and fluctuating. . . . By a sudden metamorphosis everything may be turned into everything. If there is any characteristic and outstanding feature of the mythical world, any law by which it is governed— it is this law of metamorphosis." (E. Cassirer)

(2)   A SONG OF THE BEAR
                     Sung by Eagle Shield

                     my paw is sacred
                     all things are sacred

                     (F. Densmore, *Teton Sioux Music*, p. 264)

(3)   "For everything that lives is holy."
                (W. Blake, *A Song of Liberty*)

Summary. A common ideology in what Cassirer calls "the consanguinity of all forms of life"; a common method in the free interchange of terms within the poem. *Question:* Is the order you speak of "natural" or is it "imposed"? *Answer:* Please repeat the question.

Page 37 *YORUBA PRAISES*

Source: Bakare Gbadamosi & Ulli Beier, *Yoruba Poetry* (Ministry of Education, Nigeria, 1959), p. 16.

Shango—the Yoruba god of thunder; said to have been the third king of the town of Oyo.

The praise-poem (Yoruba *oriki*, Zulu *izibongo*, Basuto *lithoko*, etc.) turns up through much of Black Africa. At its simplest it's the stringing together of a series of praise-names (usually independent utterances) describing the qualities owned by a particular man, god, animal, plant, place, etc.—anything, in short, that makes a "deep impression" on the singer (see Addenda 1, below). Often, too, it's not a question of "praise" but of delineation according to a certain method. The method itself is a kind of "collaging" from a fixed set of verses, lines & tags which are at the poet-diviner's disposal & can be supplemented by new invention. Among the Yoruba, e.g., each individual has a series of praise-names in the form of "descriptive phrases . . . that may be invented by relatives or neighbors or—most frequently—by the drummers" (Gbadamosi/Beier, p. 7) or, particularly in the case of god names, handed down from the past. The actual singing (or drumming) of the praise-poem involves the arrangement of already existing materials into a new & coherent composition "having as its subject a single individual." The individual poet takes off from the work of the collectivity, to which he adds as last in a line of makers. But his "art" is one of assemblage—the weighing of line against line.

Addenda. (1) "To the imaginative mind of the Bantu everything that causes a deep impression, even material objects, affords an occasion for the utterance of lofty phrases and words of praise. Once when traveling south of Delagoa Bay through the desert, our party arrived in the neighborhood of the Umbelozi railway. The train was heard in the distance. One of my servants was busy cleaning pots; I heard him muttering the following words:

The one who roars in the distance
The one who crushes the braves in pieces & smashes them
The one who debauches our wives—
They abandon us, they go to the towns to lead bad lives—
The seducer! And we remain alone

He was extolling the huge thing and lamenting his misfortune and the curse it has brought upon the country." (Henri A. Junod, *Life of a South African Tribe* [1912], Vol. II, p. 196)

(2) Further examples of praise-poems appear throughout the AFRICA section, above. The reader may also be interested in the combination of praise-poem technique with "composition by chance" in the Basuto divining poems (see commentary, p. 536); also in the similarity of praise-poems to earlier Egyptian workings (see "The Cannibal Hymn," p. 152; "Egyptian God Names," p. 11) & to the epic genealogies of Polynesia (see commentary, p. 450). In looking for modern analogues, three areas of resemblance should be distinguished: to modern poets using techniques of assemblage or collage; to efforts, e.g., by dadaists, surrealists, & others, to write group-poems; & to poems, irrespective of method, in which a series of phrases is made to turn around a single subject-as-pivot. The first two at least witness to a modern-primitive concern with the transpersonal—but that's just part of the story. (See also *Symposium of the Whole*, pp. 125–128.)

(3) "The poet . . . ('the maker of plots or fables' as Aristotle insists) . . . is pre-eminently the maker of the plot, the framework—not necessarily of everything that takes place within that framework! The poet creates a *situation* wherein he invites other persons & the world in general to be co-creators with him! He does not wish to be a dictator but a loyal co-initiator of action within the free society of equals which he hopes his work will help to bring about." (Jackson Mac Low)

(4)   Takis Sinopoulos
                     IOANNA RAVING

Constantinos is a door.
He is a face behind the door.
He is a door that suddenly slams and crushes your fingers.
Constantinos is an empty room.
Scream of peril in an empty room.
Constantinos is a house, a gloomy house.

Within him unexplored religions of blood smolder.

Constantinos is tomorrow tomorrow tomorrow (tomorrow countlessly repeated).

He has two bodies, one red the other black.

Sometimes I deprive him of one, sometimes of the other. Together they reduce me to ashes.

Constantinos disappears if you look at him squarely.

Constantinos appears if you dream of him.

He battles night, falls on her blind with rage and thus is filled with wounds that constantly fester.

He tortures himself with the faces, the vagueness tyrannizes him, fumbling my body, the light of my face and persistent tears shatter him.

Constantinos is the sun that determines the shadow of grass with his continuous movement.

Constantinos is the design on a carpet of stifled flowers.

Constantinos is the struggle with rooms and birds.

He always speaks of a river that will cleanse his back of the soil and impurities of this earth.

He recovers from the dark motives that excite his blood and then he sleeps.

Constantinos has much filth in his imaginary life.

Constantinos is a questionable fact.

Constantinos is a half-eaten mask.

He wears this winter coat and presumes he is constantly transforming.

Constantinos is a dark oppressive day when the wind carries dust to the windows.

Behind the face of Constantinos stirs the black Constantinos.

Constantinos burns at night with a passion more terrible than his words.

I repeat Constantinos is a house.

He is a house full of contrivances whose claws slash your back.

Constantinos repents for deeds that never happened.

He confuses what he did with what he planned to do.

He constructed dreadful buildings and held them hopelessly in his hands until they tumbled and smashed us.

Constantinos is responsible for whatever happens inside us.

Constantinos is a mirror that shatters in endless paranoia and reflections of fantastic surprises.

He always calls my face dark ravine of the moon. (My face itself is light.)

Constantinos is terrifying when he flays the layers of his skin one by one.

I don't know how to calm Constantinos.
Hour after hour madness stands by him and it shines from within his bowels
  like a lighted lamp.

This is Constantinos.

(Translation from the Greek by George Economou)

Page 38 *A POEM FOR THE WIND*

Source: Translation by Robert Williams in William F. Skene, *The*
Four Ancient Books of Wales, Containing the Cymric Poems Attributed to the
Bards of the Sixth Century (Edmonston & Douglas, Edinburgh, 1868), Vol. I,
pp. 535–537.

> *I am a cell*
> *I am a cleft*
> *I am a restoration*
> *I am the depository of song*
> *I am a man of letters*

The legendary poet Taliesin goes back to (probably) the sixth cen-
tury A.D. & a post-Roman period of struggles with the invading Saxon
kingdoms. A product, at origin, of bardic & oral traditions, the work of the
Celtic seer-poets wasn't written into final form until some centuries after—in
such works as the *Llyfer* (= book of) *Taliesin*. Along with the praises of
warriors & poems composed on Christian & "prophetic" lines, Taliesin's
oeuvre includes a kind of metamorphic praise-poetry in which the poet is the
first-person speaker of his own works & transformations. Thus, in a recent
translation:

> I have been a blue salmon,
> I have been a dog, a stag, a roebuck on the mountain,
> A stock, a spade, an axe in the hand,
> A stallion, a bull, a buck,
> A grain which grew on a hill,
> I was reaped, and placed in an oven,
> I fell to the ground when I was being roasted
> And a hen swallowed me.
> For nine nights I was in her crop.

I have been dead, I have been alive,
I am Taliesin.

> (English by J. E. Caerwyn Williams in
> Sir Ifor Williams, *The Poems of
> Taliesin*, 1968)

All of which leads to a story-as-explanation—but likely developed after the (shamanic) poem itself—that traces Taliesin back to one Gwion Bach, who steals from the shamaness Cyrridwen a liquid like Odin's mead-of-poetry, taking three drops therefrom onto his finger (thumb). Pursued by Cyrridwen, he runs through the kinds of changes given in the poem—as she does, too, in pursuit—& ends as a grain of wheat that Cyrridwen qua hen swallows up, to give birth nine months later to a resurrected Gwion. Still out to get him, she sews him in a bag & drops him, as babe, into the ocean, from which Prince Elphin pulls him & "because of his lovely forehead (*tal*) renames him *Tal-iesin* (beautiful brow)"; then

> . . . [Elphin] was astounded when the beautiful browed infant began to talk with the wisdom of a patriarch, not only in prose, but in flowing rhyme as well. Poems streamed out of his mouth. Gwyddno, Elphin's father, when he came in, asked about the catch at the weir. "I got something better than fish," his son replied. "What was that?" "A poet." "Alas," said the father, "what is a thing like that worth?"—using another Welsh word, *tal*, meaning worth, value. The child immediately answered back, "He is worth more than you ever got out of the weir," punning on *Tal-iesin* again, as if it meant "fine value." "Canst thou speak, though so small?" asked the other. "I can say more," said Taliesin, "than thou canst ask." (Ibid., pp. xvii–xviii)

Of such knowledge, etc., the "riddle of the wind" is an example—& one that seems to hide an even older mystery & reality. But the boasts of Taliesin acknowledge that old lore as well, as in the addenda to the *Mabinogion*: "Samson got / within the towers of Babylon / all the magical arts / of Asia // I got / in my bardic song / all the magical arts / of Europe & Africa."

Addenda. The reiterated statements, "he is good, he is bad," etc., reflect an approach to the world-at-large which is a common feature of many primitive/archaic (= primal) thought systems, much as Gladys Reichard, say, has shown it in her studies of Navajo symbolism:

> Although Navaho dogma stresses the dichotomy of good and evil, it does not set one off against the other. It rather emphasizes one quality or element in a being which in different circumstances may be the opposite. Sun, though "great" and a "god," is not unexceptionally good. . . . Similarly, few things are wholly bad: nearly everything can be brought under control, and when it is, the evil effect is eliminated. Thus evil may be transformed into good; things predominantly evil, such as snake, lightning, thunder, coyote, may even be invoked. If they have been the cause of misfortune or illness, they alone can correct it. . . . Good then in Navaho dogma is control. Evil is that which is ritually not under control. And supernatural power is not absolute but relative, depending on the degree of control to which it is subjected. In short, definition depends upon emphasis, not upon exclusion. (G. Reichard, *Navaho Religion*, p. 5)

Page 40   WAR GOD'S HORSE SONG I
Page 41   WAR GOD'S HORSE SONG II

Sources: (I) Slightly revised from Dane & Mary Roberts Coolidge, *The Navaho Indians* (Houghton Mifflin, Boston, 1930), p. 2. (II) Collected by David P. McAllester & previously unpublished. Variations on the same matter from the blessingway of Frank Mitchell (d. 1967) of Chinle, Arizona. This is No. 13 of seventeen horse songs in Mitchell's possession—the series a major example of minimal adjustments & variations on a single theme.

Following publication of these two versions in 1968, the present editor became closely involved in an experimental translation of the Frank Mitchell horse songs (see p. 224). In the songs on which I worked, the metaphoric/metamorphic descriptions fell away, while the changes on a fixed series of utterances became overwhelming. But even more, I was led to a realization of the sound-play in the original & took it as the principal quality to be (re)created in the English. That sound & imaginal correspondences are inseparable in this poetics seems to me crucial to an understanding of the poetry enterprise anywhere—how & why it works.

The "war god" introduced into the Coolidges' title is the primal hero, Enemy Slayer or Slayer of Monsters, who went to the house of the Sun (his father) in the search for horses. For more on the (horse) body & its treatment as *imago mundi*, see the note, immediately following, on "To the God of Fire as a Horse"—& for a related metaphoric mapping, the poem by Césaire, below.

Addenda.   Aimé Césaire
          HORSE / FOR PIERRE LOEB

My horse falters against skulls hopscotched in rust
my horse rears in a storm of clouds which are putrefactions of shipwrecked
    flesh
my horse neighs in the fine rain of roses which my blood becomes in the
    carnival scenery
my horse falters against the clumps of cacti which are the viper knots of my
    torments
my horse falters neighs and falters toward the blood curtain of my blood
    pulled down on all the trash who shoot craps with my blood
my horse falters before the impossible flame of the bit howled by the vesicles
    of my blood
Great horse my blood
my blood wine of a drunkard's vomit
I give it to you great horse
I give you my ears to be made into nostrils capable of quivering
my hair to be made into a mane as wild as they come
my tongue to be made into mustang hooves
I give them to you
great horse
so that you can approach the men of elsewhere and tomorrow at the extreme
    limits of brotherhood
on your back a child with barely moving lips
who for you
will disarm
the chlorophyllous dough of the vast ravens of the future.

(Translation by Clayton Eshleman & Annette Smith)

Page 44   *TO THE GOD OF FIRE AS A HORSE*

Source: A hymn from the Rig-Veda (1500–1200 B.C.) in an English version by Robert Kelly.

Agni was the Vedic Aryan god of fire & personification of the sacrificial fire itself. The connection of sun- & fire-gods with the horse is familiar enough from (say) Greek mythology, & it's interesting too that the Navajo figure identified by the Coolidges as the war-god (see "War God's Horse Song" above) appears in McAllester's variation as "son-of-the-Sun" who (like an untragic Phaeton) receives his father's multi-colored horses, etc. A text from the very ancient *Brhad Aranyaka Upanishad* equates various parts of the sacrificial horse with elements of the cosmos, much as the Navajo does:

> Dawn . . . is the head of the sacrificial horse. The sun is his eye; the wind, his breath; the sacrificial fire his open mouth; the year is the body of the sacrificial horse. The sky is his back; the atmosphere, his belly; the earth, his underbelly; the directions, his flanks; the intermediate directions, his ribs; the seasons, his limbs; the months and half-months, his joints; days and nights, his feet; the stars, his bones; the clouds, his flesh. Sand is the food in his stomach; rivers, his entrails; mountains, his liver and lungs; plants and trees, his hair; the rising sun, his forepart; the setting sun, his hindpart. When he yawns, then it lightnings; when he shakes himself, then it thunders; when he urinates, then it rains. Speech is actually his neighing.

The reader may want to compare these compositions with the African praise-poems (see pp. 37, 161, & 170).

Page 45   THE STARS

Source: J. R.'s translation from A. E. Preyre's French version as printed in Roger Caillois & Jean-Clarence Lambert, *Trésor de la poésie universelle* (Gallimard, Paris, 1958), p. 35. An earlier English version goes back to C. G. Leland (1902).

A 1921 version by Leland's collaborator, John Dyneley Prince, has two significant changes: *our light is a voice* > *our light is a star*, & *this is the song of the stars* > *this is a song of the mountains*.

Page 49   THE ANNUNCIATION

Source: Adapted by J. R. from J. Bascot, *La vie de Marpa* (Librairie Paul Geuthner, Paris, 1937), p. 31.

Marpa (eleventh century A.D.) was third guru in the line founded by Tilo in India & successor to his own teacher, Naropa. He was the first Tibetan master of the Kargyudpa sect & the instructor of the more famous Milarepa. Theirs "was essentially a ritualist system based upon spells and diagrams (mantras & yantras), the power to use which could only be imparted directly from adept to disciple. Hence the name of [the] sect, [i.e.] the followers of the oral tradition" (Sir Humphrey Clarke, *The Message of Milarepa*, p. xii). The original religion of Tibet, called *Bon*, had been strongly shamanistic, & the powers of the Kargyudpa teachers were such that their brand of Buddhism could easily merge with & replace it.

Marpa traveled a good deal & translated half a hundred works from Sanskrit, which earned for him his nickname of *Sgrasgyur*, The Translator. Like all the gurus of his line, he was the subject of a biography, & in it much was made of his violent temper as a child, an instability he had to master & transform. His personality was, in this sense, very much like that attributed to the shamans (see below, p. 486). Like them too, he was said to have the power of ecstasy, & his soul could leave his body & enter another's. He made many songs & spells, though Milarepa seems to have surpassed him there.

See, too, the note on Milarepa, p. 565, below.

Page 50   HOW ISAAC TENS BECAME A SHAMAN

Source: Selected & adapted from Marius Barbeau, *Medicine-Men on the North Pacific Coast* (National Museum of Canada Bulletin No. 152 [Ottawa, 1958]), pp. 39ff.

A. *The Experience.* The word *shaman* (Tungus: *šaman*) comes from Siberia & "in the strict sense is pre-eminently a religious phenomenon of Siberia & Central Asia" (M. Eliade). But the parallels elsewhere (North America, Indonesia, Oceania, China, etc.) are remarkable & lead also to a consideration of coincidences between "primitive-archaic" & modern thought. Eliade treats shamanism in-the-broader-sense as a specialized technique of ecstasy & the shaman as technician-of-the-sacred. In this sense, too, the shaman can be seen as protopoet, for almost always his technique hinges on the creation of special linguistic circumstances, i.e., of song & invocation.

In 1870 Rimbaud first used the term *voyant* (seer) to identify the new breed of poet who was to be "absolutely modern," etc.:

> one must, I say, become a seer,
> make oneself into a seer

or, as Rasmussen writes of the Iglulik Eskimos:

> the young aspirant, when applying to a shaman, should always
> use the following formula
> > *takujumaqama:* I come to you
> > because I desire to see

& the Copper Eskimos called the shaman-songman "*elik*, i.e., one who has
eyes."

o   o   o   o

Isaac Tens' experience is not only extraordinary but typical of (1) the
psychology of shamanism, (2) the shaman's "initiation" through dream &
vision, (3) transformation of vision into song. The dream & vision aspect, in
fact, goes way past any limits, however loosely drawn, of shamanism, into
areas where a priesthood (as developer & transmitter of a *fixed* system)
predominates, &, on the other hand, into areas where "all men" are "sham-
ans," i.e., are "open" to the "gift" of vision & song. Thus:

> The future [Bororo] shaman walks in the forest and suddenly sees
> a bird perch within reach of his hand, then vanish. Flocks of
> parrots fly down toward him and disappear as if by magic. The
> future shaman goes home shaking and uttering unintelligible
> words. An odor of decay . . . emanates from his body. Suddenly a
> gust of wind makes him totter; he falls like a dead man. At this
> moment he has become the receptacle of a spirit that speaks
> through his mouth. From now on he is a shaman. (A. Métraux,
> "Le Shamanisme chez les Indiens de l'Amérique du Sud tropi-
> cale," 1944, in Eliade, *Shamanism*, p. 82)

> Then the bear of the lake or the inland glacier will come out, he
> will devour all your flesh and make you a skeleton, and you will
> die. But you will recover your flesh, you will awaken, & your
> clothes will come rushing to you. (Wm. Thalbitzer, "The
> Heathen Priests of East Greenland," 1910, in Eliade, *Shamanism*,
> p. 59)

> He dreams of many things, and his body is muddled and becomes
> a house of dreams. And he dreams constantly of many things, and

on awaking says to his friends: "My body is muddled today; I dreamt many men were killing me; I escaped I know not how. And on waking, one part of my body felt different from the other parts; it was no longer alike all over." (H. Callaway, *The Religious System of the Amazulu*, Natal, 1870, p. 259)

All Blackfoot songs, except those learned from other tribes, are said to have been obtained through dreams or visions. . . . A man may be walking along and hear a bird, insect, stone or something else singing; he remembers the song and claims it as especially given to him. A man may get songs from a ghost in the same way. (C. Wissler, "Ceremonial Bundles of the Blackfoot Indians," *Anthropological Papers of the American Museum of Natural History*, Vol. VII, Part 2 [1912], p. 263)

Anything, in fact, can deliver a song because anything—"night, mist, the blue sky, east, west, women, adolescent girls, men's hands & feet, the sexual organs of men & women, the bat, the land of souls, ghosts, graves, the bones, hair & teeth of the dead," etc.—is alive. Here is the central image of shamanism & of all "primitive" thought, the intuition (whether fiction or not doesn't yet matter) of a connected & fluid universe, as alive as a man is—just that much alive.

And all this seems thrust upon him—a unifying vision that brings with it the power of song & image, seen in his own terms as power to heal-the-soul & all disease viewed as disorder-of-the-soul, as disconnection & rigidity. Nor does he come to it easily—this apparent separation of himself from the normal orders of men—but often manifests what Eliade calls "a resistance to the divine election."

We're on familiar ground here, granted the very obvious differences in terminology & place, materials & techniques, etc.—recognizing in the shaman's experience that systematic derangement of the senses Rimbaud spoke of, not for its own sake but toward the possibility of sight & order. For the shaman-poet

like the sick man . . . is projected onto a vital plane that shows him the fundamental data of human existence, that is, solitude, danger, hostility of the surrounding world. But the primitive magician, the medicine man, or the shaman is not only a sick man; he is, above all, a sick man who has been cured, who has succeeded in curing himself. (Eliade, *Shamanism*, p. 27)

So, something more than literature is going on here: for ourselves, let me suggest, the question of how the concept & techniques of the "sacred" can persist in the 'secular" world, not as nostalgia for the archaic past but (as Snyder writes) "a vehicle to ease us into the future."

Addenda.

(1)

Demon or bird! (said the boy's soul,)
Is it indeed toward your mate you sing? or is it really to me?
For I, that was a child, my tongue's use sleeping, now I have heard you,
Now in a moment I know what I am for, I awake,
And already a thousand singers, a thousand songs, clearer, louder and more
    sorrowful than yours,
A thousand warbling echoes have started to life within me, never to die.

O you solitary singer, singing by yourself, projecting me,
O solitary me listening, never more shall I cease perpetuating you,
Never more shall I escape, never more the reverberations,
Never more the cries of unsatisfied love be absent from me,
Never again leave me to be the peaceful child I was before what there in the
    night,
By the sea under the yellow and sagging moon,
The messenger there arous'd, the fire, the sweet hell within,
The unknown want, the destiny of me.

                —Walt Whitman
                from *Out of the Cradle Endlessly Rocking*

(2)   Allen Ginsberg
                 PSALM IV

Now I'll record my secret vision, impossible sight of the face of God:
It was no dream, I lay broad waking on a fabulous couch in Harlem
having masturbated for no love, and read half naked an open book of Blake
    on my lap
Lo & behold! I was thoughtless and turned a page and gazed on the living
    Sun-flower
and heard a voice, it was Blake's, reciting in earthen measure:
the voice rose out of the page to my secret ear that had never heard before—
I lifted my eyes to the window, red walls of buildings flashed outside, endless
    sky sad in Eternity,

the sunlight gazing on the world, apartments of Harlem standing in the
    universe
—each brick and cornice stained with intelligence like a vast living face—
the great brain unfolding and brooding in wilderness!—Now speaking aloud
    with Blake's voice—
Love! thou patient presence & bone of the body! Father! thy careful watching
    and waiting over my soul!
My son! My son! the endless ages have remembered me! My son! My son!
    Time howled in anguish in my ear!
My son! My son! my Father wept and held me in his dead arms.

Sept. 1, 1957
Ischia

Note. The actual vision must have taken place in the summer of 1948. He
writes of it elsewhere: "That is to say, looking out at the window, through the
window at the sky, suddenly it seemed that I saw into the depths of the
universe, by looking simply into the ancient sky. The sky suddenly seemed
very *ancient*. And this was the very ancient place that [Blake] was talking
about, the sweet golden clime. I suddenly realized that *this* existence was *it!*
And, that I was born in order to experience up to this very moment that I was
having this experience, to realize what this was all about—in other words that
this was the moment I was born for. This initiation."

o   o   o   o   o   o   o

    B. *The Songs.* The songs were recorded in 1920 from Isaac Tens, an old
member of the Gitenmaks tribe of the Gitksan at Hazelton, B.C. The free
workings here are by J. R. & are based on Barbeau's literal translations plus
interpretations & descriptions of the accompanying visions, apparently from
Tens himself. His total song property consisted of three groups of songs—
twenty-three in all, or somewhat more than the average Gitksan shaman.
Some of his comments follow.
    "When I am called to treat a patient, I go into something like a trance, &
I compose a song, or I revive one for the occasion . . . [*Of the ending of the first
song*]: This cannot be explained rationally, because it is a vision, & visions are
not always intelligible. In my vision I dreamt that I was very sick, & my spirit
became sick like me; it was like a human being but had no name. In the same
dream I saw that there had been a heavy run of salmon headed by a large
Salmon. This would bring relief to the people who were starving. The huge

489

Salmon appeared to me in my vision, although he was way down deep in the canyon. The She Robin came to me, & she lifted me out of my sickness. That is how I was cured . . . [*Commenting further on the origin of one of the songs*]: When getting ready for the songs, I fell into a trance & saw a vast fine territory. In the middle of it a house stood. I stepped into it, & I beheld my uncle Tsigwee who had been a medicine-man [*halaait*]. He had died several years before. Then another uncle appeared—Gukswawtu. Both of them had been equally famous in their day. The songs above are those I heard them sing. While they were singing, the Grizzly ran through the door, & went right around. Then he rose into the air behind the clouds, describing a circle, & came back to the house. Each of my uncles took a rattle & placed it into one of my hands. That is why I always use two rattles in my performances. In my vision I beheld many fires burning under the house. As soon as I walked out of the house, my trance ended. From then on I sang those chants just as I had learned them in my vision."

Addenda.   Gary Snyder
FIRST SHAMAN SONG

In the village of the dead,
Kicked loose bones
        ate pitch of a drift log
        (whale fat)
Nettles and cottonwood. Grass smokes
                in the sun

Logs turn in the river
        sand scorches the feet.
Two days without food, trucks roll past
        in dust and light, rivers
        are rising.
Thaw in the high meadows. Move west in July.

Soft oysters rot now, between tides
        the flats stink.
I sit without thoughts by the log-road
Hatching a new myth
Watching the waterdogs
        the last truck gone.

—from *Myths & Texts*, 1960

Page 54 A SHAMAN CLIMBS UP THE SKY

Source: J. R.'s translation from Roger Caillois & Jean-Clarence Lambert, *Trésor de la poésie universelle* (Gallimard, Paris, 1958), pp. 55–57. Original texts in Wilhelm Radlov, *Aus Siberien* (Leipzig, 1884), Vol. II, pp. 20–50.

But the shaman's techniques-of-the-sacred made him, more than the modern poet, supreme physician & custodian of the soul. The belief was enough to validate the function—that he could climb to heaven or descend to the underworld or into the sea, could find a cure or an answer to misfortune, or after death guide the soul to its place-of-rest, etc.

In the rites accompanying a climb, a tree or ladder was generally used (see "Climbing Event," p. 115), but often too the shaman's drum was itself viewed as vehicle-of-motion; "the drum," said the Yakut shamans, "is our horse." The journey—to "heaven" or "hell"—took place in stages marked by "obstacles," the shaman-songs being the keys to unlock them. Thus, when the Altaic "black" shaman in his descent reaches "the Chinese desert of red sand (&) rides over a yellow steppe that a magpie could not fly across, (he) cries to the audience: 'By the power of songs we cross it!' " In singing & dancing he has the help of assistants, & sometimes the audience joins him in chorus.

In the ascent itself, the shaman climbs from notch to notch on the tree, while singing his actions & the obstacles that meet him. A horse is sacrificed, killed by breaking its backbone so that "not a drop of its blood falls to the ground or touches the sacrificers." The scarecrow-goose follows & overtakes the horse's soul, while the shaman both sings & responds by imitating the bird's cry. The climb ends with the address to Bai Ulgan, from whom he learns "if the sacrifice has been accepted & . . . what other sacrifices the divinity expects."

The subtitles only give a sketch of the actions (events) accompanying the songs; the interested reader can consult Eliade (*Shamanism*, pp. 190–197) for the fuller scenario.

Page 58 THE DOG VISION

Source: *Black Elk Speaks: Being the Life Story of a Holy Man of the Oglala Sioux*, as told through John G. Neihardt (William Morrow & Co., 1932; University of Nebraska Press, 1961), pp. 186–191.

Hehaka Sapa or Black Elk. Born "in the Moon of the Popping Trees (December) on the Little Powder River in the Winter when the Four Crows Were Killed (1863)." Died August 1950 on the Pine Ridge Reservation,

Manderson, South Dakota. Given a "great vision" in his childhood (comparable in its complexity to that of biblical Ezekiel), he was a "holy man" or "priest" (*wichasha wakon*) of the Oglala Sioux &, like his second cousin Crazy Horse, a great "visionary seer." But unable to live out his visions for the rescue of his people, he did finally deliver to strangers a record of those sightings & of the rituals entrusted to him by the former "keepers of the sacred pipe." And, more than eighty years after his great vision & initiation, was able to say of his "defeat":

> . . . Now that I can see it all as from a lonely hilltop, I know it was the story of a mighty vision given to a man too weak to use it; of a holy tree that should have flourished in a people's heart with flowers and singing birds, and now is withered; and of a people's dream that died in bloody snow.

The Dog Vision came to Black Elk at age eighteen, the culmination of that ceremony called *hanblecheyapi* or "crying for a vision," & was, like his earlier "great vision," not only a personal event but a testimony to his people's struggle with the Wasichus (= Federales). Like his "great vision" too, it awaited completion in performance—serving in this case as scenario for a heyoka ceremony peopled with sacred clowns "doing everything wrong or backwards to make the people laugh . . . so that it may be easier for the power to come to them." The connections between vision & performance, the sacred & the comic, & the private & public good, have rarely been more clearly stated.

Page 62   *FROM THE MIDNIGHT VELADA*

Source: Translation from Mazatec by Henry Munn, with Eloina de Estrada Gonzales, in *New Wilderness Letter* (New York, 1978), nos. 5–6, pp. 1–4. Munn's more detailed English translation appears in Álvaro Estrada, *María Sabina: Her Life & Chants* (Ross-Erikson Publishers, Santa Barbara, California, 1981).

A major Wise One (= shaman) among the Mazatecs of Oaxaca, Mexico, María Sabina receives her poems/songs through use of the Psilocybe mushroom at all-night curing sessions (veladas): a practice going back to pre-Conquest Mexico & witnessed by the Spanish chronicler who wrote: "They pay a sorcerer who eats them [the mushrooms] & tells what they have taught him. He does so by means of a rhythmic chant in full voice." The sacred mushrooms are considered the source of Language itself—are, in Henry Munn's good phrase, "the mushrooms of language." Thus: "If you ask a shaman where his imagery comes from, he is likely to reply: I didn't say it, the mushrooms did. No mushroom speaks, only man speaks, but he who eats these mushrooms, if he is a man of language, becomes endowed with an inspired capacity to speak. The shamans who eat them . . . are the oral poets of the people, the doctors of the word, the seers and oracles, the ones possessed by the voice. 'It is not I who speak,' said Heraclitus, 'it is the logos.' " This source of the specific poem in a hypostatized Language is emphasized by the shaman's practice of ending each chanted line with the word *tzo*, i.e., the third person singular, present tense of the verb *to say*. "The *says* at the end of each utterance," writes Munn, "is a point of emphasis, an enunciatory mark, a vocal stop that punctuates the flow of the chant. Lacan: 'In the unconscious, it speaks.' Heidegger: 'Language first of all and inherently obeys the essential nature of speaking: it says.' " (For more on María Sabina, see *Symposium of the Whole*, pp. 187–191, 475–479.)

Addenda. As an instance of direct influences across cultures, note the following in which the American poet Anne Waldman, having come across a literal & very rough translation of the María Sabina chantings, used its revealed structure to model a work called *Fast Speaking Woman*, which she performed at poetry readings & as part of Bob Dylan's shortlived *Rolling Thunder* movie.

o   o   o   o

Anne Waldman
From FAST SPEAKING WOMAN (1975)

because I don't have spit
because I don't have rubbish
because I don't have dust
because I don't have that which is in air
because I am air
let me try you with my magic power:

   I'm a shouting woman
   I'm a speech woman
   I'm an atmosphere woman
   I'm an airtight woman

I'm a flesh woman
I'm a flexible woman
I'm a high style woman

I'm an automobile woman
I'm a mobile woman
I'm an elastic woman
I'm a necklace woman
I'm a silk scarf woman
I'm a know nothing woman
I'm a know it all woman

I'm a day woman
I'm a doll woman
I'm a sun woman
I'm a late afternoon woman
I'm a clock woman
I'm a wind woman
I'm a white woman

I'M A SILVER LIGHT WOMAN
I'M AN AMBER LIGHT WOMAN
I'M AN EMERALD LIGHT WOMAN

I'm an abalone woman
I'm the abandoned woman
I'm the woman abashed, the gibberish woman
the aborigine woman, the woman absconding
the absent woman
the transparent woman
the absinthe woman

the woman absorbed, the woman under tyranny
the contemporary woman, the mocking woman
the artist dreaming inside her house

                    o   o   o   o

[N.B. The reader can compare the structure of the María Sabina chants with the Celtic incantations of Taliesin & others (pp. 341, 480), as well as the various African praise-poems throughout this volume.]

Page 65   THE DREAM OF ENKIDU

Source: *The Epic of Gilgamesh*, English version by N. K. Sandars (Penguin Books, 1960), pp. 89–90.

Gilgamesh—"The hero of the Epic; son of the goddess Ninsun & of a priest in Kullab, fifth king of Uruk (Erech) after the flood, famous as a great builder & as a judge of the dead. A cycle of epic poems has collected around his name."

Enkidu—"Moulded by Aruru, goddess of creation, out of clay in the image of Anu, the sky-god; described as 'of the essence of Anu' & of Ninurta the war-god. He is the companion of Gilgamesh, & is wild or natural man; he was later considered a patron or god of animals."

Sandars' version is a reconstruction based on previous translations from Sumerian, Akkadian, & Hittite originals. It reads very well & for many poets of the editor's generation has been a way into the material. A "collation" (we might now call it a collage), it is in that sense, as Sandars in fact points out, like "the 'Standard Text' created by the scribes of Assurbanipal in the seventh century: [also] a collation." But certainly an example of what to do with archaic material to get it back in circulation.

Page 67   A LIST OF BAD DREAMS CHANTED AS A
            CAUSE & CURE FOR MISSING SOULS

Source: Slightly abridged from translation by Carol Rubenstein, in C. Rubenstein, *Poems of Indigenous Peoples of Sarawak* (Sarawak Museum Journal Special Monograph No. 2, 1973), Part I, pp. 508–509. Reprinted in C. Rubenstein, *The Honey Tree Song: Poems and Chants of the Sarawak Dayaks* (Ohio University Press, 1984).

Part of a longer group of prayers used by the Bidayuh (Land Dayaks) of Sarawak, Malaysia, as a means for coming at the cause of illnesses brought on by soul-wandering. The chant accompanies the spirit-medium's trance journey to the Underworld (Sebayan) & unfolds a catalogue of dream-names—as if to set down *all* those possibilities so that the real work can begin. A prototype in that sense of those deliberate dream-investigations that poets have pursued throughout this century.

For more on dreams, etc., see p. 463.

Page 70   THE KILLER

Source: Translation by J. R. from Claire Goll version in Roger Caillois & Jean-Clarence Lambert, *Trésor de la Poésie Universelle* (Gallimard, Paris, 1958), p. 36, & English version in James Mooney, *Sacred Formulas of the Cherokees* (Bureau of American Ethnology, Annual Report No. 7 [Washington, 1891]), p. 391.

"This formula is from the manuscript book of A'yu^{n}ini (Swimmer) who explained the whole ceremony. . . . As the purpose of the ceremony is to bring about the death of the victim, everything spoken of is symbolically colored black. . . . The declaration [at] the end, 'It is blue,' indicates that the victim now begins to feel the effects of the incantation, and that as darkness comes on, his spirit will shrink and gradually become less until it dwindles away to nothingness." (Mooney, pp. 391–392)

As another instance of the power of obsessive, single-color imagery, Eliade (*Shamanism*, p. 201) describes an Altaic descent to the underworld in which

> as each "obstacle" is passed (the shaman) sees a new subterranean epiphany; the word *black* recurs in almost every verse. At the second "obstacle" he apparently hears metallic sounds; at the fifth, waves and the wind whistling; finally, at the seventh, where the nine subterranean rivers have their mouths, he sees Erlik Khan's palace, built of stone and black clay and defended in every direction.

Addenda.   The best-known modern example of this fairly common technique would have to be Lorca's *Somnambule Ballad* (Green, green, I want you green, etc.) but the editor has chosen the following as a more recent example & one that refers back directly to the Cherokee text.

o   o   o   o

Diane Wakoski
BLUE MONDAY

Blue of the heaps of beads poured into her breasts
and clacking together in her elbows;
blue of the silk
that covers lily-town at night;
blue of her teeth

that bite cold toast
and shatter on the streets;
blue of the dyed flower petals with gold stamens
hanging like tongues
over the fence of her dress
at the opera/opals clasped under her lips
and the moon breaking over her head a
gush of blood-red lizards.

Blue Monday. Monday at 3:00 and
Monday at 5. Monday at 7:30 and
Monday at 10:00. Monday passed under the rippling
California fountain. Monday alone
a shark in the cold blue waters.

> You are dead: wound round like a paisley shawl.
> I cannot shake you out of the sheets. Your name is
> still wedged in every corner of the sofa.
> Monday is the first of the week
> and I think of you all week.

> I beg Monday not to come
> so that I will not think of you
> all week.

You paint my body blue. On the balcony
in the soft muddy night, you paint me
with bat wings and the crystal
the crystal
the crystal
the crystal in your arm cuts away
the night, folds back ebony whale skin
and my face, the blue of new rifles,
and my neck, the blue of Egypt,
and my breasts, the blue of sand,
and my arms, bass-blue,
and my stomach, arsenic;

there is electricity dripping from me like cream;
there is love dripping from me I cannot use—like acacia or
jacaranda—fallen blue & gold flowers, crushed into the street.

Love passed me in a blue business suit
and fedora.
His glass cane, hollow and filled with
sharks and whales . . .
He wore black
patent leather shoes
and had a mustache. His hair was so black it was
almost blue.

"Love," I said.
"I beg your pardon," he said.
"Mr. Love," I said.
"I beg your pardon," he said.

So I saw there was no use bothering him on the street.

Love passed me on the street in a blue
business suit. He was a banker
I could tell.

So blue trains rush by in my sleep.
Blue herons fly overhead.
Blue paint cracks in my
arteries and sends titanium
floating into my bones.
Blue liquid pours down
my poisoned throat and blue veins
rip open my breast. Blue daggers tip
and are juggled on my palms.
Blue death lives in my fingernails.

If I could sing one last song
with water bubbling through my lips
I would sing with my throat torn open,
the blue jugular spouting that black shadow pulse
and on my lips
I would balance volcanic rock
emptied out of my veins. At last
my children strained out

of my body. At last my blood
solidified and tumbling into the ocean.
It is blue.
It is blue.
It is blue.

Page 71   *SPELL AGAINST JAUNDICE*

Source: Vasko Popa, *The Golden Apple: A Round of Stories, Songs, Spells, Proverbs and Riddles*, translated by Andrew Harvey & Anne Pennington (Anvil Press Poetry, London, 1980), pp. 68–69.

Compare the poem's obsessive color imagery to that of the Cherokee charm, preceding, as an indication of the (geographical) range of this type of language-magic.

A major poet himself, Popa in his three-volume anthology of Serbian folk-workings draws principally from the collections of Vuk Stefanović Karadžić (1787–1862), who started such gatherings of Slavic oral poetries & created a new literature on that base.

Addenda.   Jerome Rothenberg
A POEM IN YELLOW AFTER TRISTAN TZARA (1980)

> angel slide your hand
> into my basket   eat my yellow fruit
> my eye is craving it
> my yellow tires screech
> o dizzy human heart
> my yellow dingdong

Page 73   *A POISON ARROW*

Source: J. R.'s translation from Roger Rosfelder, *Chants Haoussa* (Editions Seghers, Paris, 1952).

Page 74   *A BREASTPLATE AGAINST DEATH*

Source: Eleanor Hull, *Folklore of the British Isles* (Methuen & Co., London, 1928), pp. 170–171, with emendations from prose translation in

David Greene & Frank O'Connor, *A Golden Treasury of Irish Poetry* (Macmillan, London, 1967), pp. 34–35.

"Ascribed to an Abbot Conry in Westmeath named Fer fio (d. 762) . . . the charm has a resemblance to Norse legends of the Norns, who wove the strands of the fate of men." While invoking the old gods throughout, the poem in its transcribed form ends with a Christian (Latin) benediction: "Domini est salus (3x); Christi est salus (3x); populum tuum, Domine, benedictio tua!" The term *lorica*, or breastplate, is used for a protective charm in the pre-Christian or "druidic" tradition.

For more on the Celtic faerie-world, etc., see below, p. 592.

Page 76 OL' HANNAH

Source: Transcription by Eric Sackheim, in E. Sackheim, *The Blues Line: A Collection of Blues Lyrics* (Grossman Publishers, New York, 1969), pp. 26–28.

A prison work-blues, "Ol' Hannah" leaps to an evocation of the Sun as female being, but never abandons that use of "local & historic particulars" that makes the blues such a precise instrument when delivered by its master poets. Of the range of materials in the developed form, Samuel Charters writes:

> In many of the blues which use arrangements of verses to develop emotional attitudes there is often a power of suggestion in the juxtaposition of verses that seem to have little relationship. This poetic technique has been used by several modern poets as a conscious artistic device, and it gives to the blues singers the same technical control over their material. They use it most often to compress their idiom, to imply, with the juxtaposition of verses, an association of events that would take several verses to explain and would lose the dramatic effect in the explanation. Often the blues seems to be only the lightly sketched outline of an emotional turmoil . . . sometimes so vague that it is difficult to decide on the meaning of a particular line, and the singers themselves, because the poetic language of the blues has been part of their lives, often feel that the meaning of the line is its own sense. But the imaginative power of the blues is still felt even when the meaning is obscure. (*Poetry of the Blues*, p. 40)

Eric Sackheim's transcriptions of blues verses, here & elsewhere, aim by typographical & other means to give an accurate rendering of the individual singer's style ("breath, pause, break; spacing, weight"), even when working with traditional matter; i.e., "that he *sings* it on a particular occasion, confronts his universe with a structure of sound and meaning in a way appropriate to himself and relevant to a specific point in time."

Page 81   OFFERING FLOWERS

Source: Bernardino de Sahagún, *Florentine Codex: General History of the Things of New Spain*, translated by Arthur J. O. Anderson & Charles E. Dibble (School of American Research, Santa Fe, New Mexico, & the University of Utah, 1951, 1963), Vol. III, pp. 101–103; Vol. XII, pp. 214–215.

The Aztecs (they say) rode on lakes of flowers, & decorated bodies, gods & houses with flowers, which their language made into synonyms for speech/ heart/soul & for the sun as world-heart/world-flower. Men waged a "flowering war" of the spirit in which "if spirit wins," writes Laurette Sejourné, "the body 'flowers' & a new light goes to give power to the Sun." Only later, the Aztec rulers literalized this into a series of staged battles against already conquered peoples, that the foredoomed losers paid for (literally) with their hearts. So, too, the ceremony given here (the only monthly ritual without human sacrifice) was not devoted to Xochipilli, the god of flowers & the soul, but to the war god Huitzilopochtli.

Correspondences of heart & word & flower are repeated by the Japanese Seami, who speaks of the "flower" (the "flower-thought" of the Buddhists) as the Nō actor's hidden ability, a matter of the heart & voice. In the dance & gesture language of India, Wilson D. Wallis tells us

> when the fingers are straight and are brought together so that the tips touch, the gesture means "flower bud." When conveyed to the mouth and thrust outward, it means "speech." In Hawaii this gesture means "flower"; or, if made at the mouth, it means "talk" or "song." (In Stanley Diamond, ed., *Culture in History: Essays in Honor of Paul Radin* [1960], p. 330)

But it's the same too in Francis of Assisi's "little flowers" & in the dead words of our own language that speak of eloquence as "flowery" or "florid"—terms that have lost their currency, except when Carlos Williams, say, makes them alive again in *Asphodel, that greeny flower*. And there are other instances to remind us, & a memory perhaps of that "great flower" of Dante's—"high fantasy" he called it, & "living flame."

(For continuation of the flower poetics in a contemporary Indian/ Mexican group, see p. 229 & the accompanying commentary.)

Page 83 From THE NIGHT CHANT

Source: Washington Matthews, *The Night Chant, a Navaho Ceremony* (Memoirs of the American Museum of Natural History [New York, 1902]), pp. 143–145.

Tsegehi—a dwelling of the gods.

Night Chant or Night Way is only one part of the very complex Navajo system of myths & ceremonies directed mainly toward healing. Other chants or ways include Beauty Way, Blessing Way, Mountain Way, Flint Way, Enemy Way, Prostitution Way, Life Way, Shooting Way, Red Ant Way, Monster Way, Moving Up Way, etc.—each with special functions, each consisting of many songs, events, & myths-of-origin—with endless subdivisions and reconstructions thereof. The whole chantway system is so complicated in fact that the individual priest or chanter (*hatali*, lit. a keeper-of-the-songs) can rarely keep in mind more than a single ceremony like the nine-day Night Chant, sometimes only part of one. There's also more room for variation by the individual singer than at first meets the eye—& this is itself a part of the system since, in transmitting the ceremonies, a gap is invariably left that the new singer must fill in on his own.

As with other "primitive" art of this complexity, the Night Chant is very much "intermedia," though on the ninth night (from which this excerpt is taken) the singing dominates & is "uninterrupted . . . from dark until day-light." At the start of this song

> patient and shaman (have positions) in the west, facing the east, and the priest prays a long prayer to each god, which the patient repeats after him, sentence by sentence. . . . The four prayers are alike in all respects, except in the mention of certain attributes of the gods. . . . (The one given here is addressed) to the dark bird who is the chief of (the sacred) pollen. While (it) is being said, the dancer keeps up a constant motion, bending and straightening the left knee, and swaying the head from side to side. (Matthews, p. 142)

While the complexity of Night Chant, etc., necessitates a collective effort in performance & transmission, the legend of its founding credits the inspiration to Bitahatini, literally His-Imagination, His-Visions, but freely translated as The Visionary. Carried off by the gods he brought back the rites for this chant (of sand-painting, dance & masks, etc.) along with the songs & instructions for curing. The Navajos said of him:

> Whenever he went out by himself, he heard the songs of spirits sung to him, or thought he heard them sung. . . . His three brothers had no faith in him. They said: "When you have returned from your solitary walks and tell us you have seen strange things and heard strange songs, you are mistaken, you only imagine you hear these songs and you see nothing unusual." Whenever he returned from one of these lonely rambles he tried to teach his brothers the songs he had heard; but they would not listen to him. (Matthews, p. 159)

The reader may want to compare this early experience of The Visionary's with that of Isaac Tens (see above, p. 50) & the nature of his spirit-journey & its conversion to performance with Black Elk's "Dog Vision" (p. 58). While these accounts are from three Indian groups that are supposed to be far apart in their approaches to the sacred, the experiences show a common (shamanic/ not priestly) pattern, with echoes throughout the "primitive & archaic" worlds. Neruda's vision of his dead friend Jimenez, with its presumably coincidental use of a Night Chant refrain (*vienes volando* = come flying, or come soaring), opens still further areas for speculation:

> Amid frightening feathers, nights,
> amid magnolias, amid telegrams,
> with the south and west sea winds
>   you come flying.
>
> Under tombs, under ashes,
> under frozen snails,
> under the earth's deepest waters
>   you come flying.
>
> And deeper, between drowned children,
> blind plants and rotting fish,
> out through the clouds again
>   you come flying.

More distant than blood and bone,
more distant than bread, than wine,
more distant than fire
    you come flying.

Etcetera

(From Clayton Eshleman's translation
of *Alberto Rojas Jimenez Viene Volando*)

Page 89   WHEN HARE HEARD OF DEATH

Source: Paul Radin, *The Road of Life and Death: A Ritual Drama of the American Indians* (Bollingen Series V, Pantheon Books, New York, 1945), pp. 23–24.

Hare (a trickster-figure or deific goof-up) is sent by Earthmaker to rescue the two-leggeds from the evil ones; but at the crucial moment (trying against the law of life to save his aunts & uncles from death) he looks back (like Orpheus or Lot's wife) against the instructions of his grandmother (earth), & "as he peeped, the place from which he had started, caved in completely & instantaneously." The wild scene that follows—of destructive frustration & hysteria—is surely more meaningful than Adam's "I was afraid because I was naked," etc., & leads in turn to the founding of the Winnebago Medicine Rite.

Page 90   A PERUVIAN DANCE SONG

Source: Translated by Margot Astrov, *The Winged Serpent: An Anthology of American Indian Prose and Poetry* (The John Day Company, New York, 1946), p. 344, from R. & M. D'Harcourt, *La musique des Incas et des survivances* (Paris, 1925).

Page 90   DEATH SONG

Source: Frances Densmore, *Papago Music* (Bureau of American Ethnology, Bulletin 90 [Washington, 1929]), p. 127.

The song was used for curing & was given to the poet (Owl Woman, called Juana Manwell) by a dead man named Jose Gomez. This was her ordinary way of receiving songs—from the "disturbing spirits" of dead

Papagos "who follow the old customs & go at night to the spirit-land." As Frances Densmore tells it:

> The spirits first revealed themselves to Owl Woman when she was in extreme grief over the death of her husband and other relatives. This was 30 or 40 years prior to the recording of her songs in 1920. The spirits took her to the spirit land in the evening and brought her back in the early dawn, escorting her along a road. . . . When the spirits had taken her many times . . . they decided that she should be taught certain songs for the cure of sickness caused by the spirits. It was not necessary that she should go to the spirit land to learn the songs. It was decided that a person, at his death, should go where the other spirits are and "get acquainted a little," after which he would return and teach her some songs. . . . She has now received hundreds of these songs, so many that she cannot remember them all. It is possible for her to treat the sick without singing, but she prefers to have the songs. (*Papago Music*, pp. 115–116)

o   o   o   o

"The Authors are in eternity."

—W. Blake.

Page 91   *From THE ODYSSEY*

Source: Translation from Book 11 of the Odyssey, in Ezra Pound, *The Cantos* (New Directions, New York, 1970), pp. 3–5. The last lines of the selection, given here in italics, are from Pound's earlier "Three Cantos" (1917).

Pound opens his master-poem, *The Cantos*, with this translation of Homer (the so-called *Nekuia* or descent-to-the-underworld section), giving it back to us as a poem of beginnings. But it was a poem, even then, calling up the dead in the oldest of poetic traditions, where the journey of the central figure retains a sense, nowhere more than here, of the former ritual. It has thus remained the prototype, in the "West," of the poem of oral, even shamanic, origins that comes into a fixed (written) form early in the development of writing. Pound's brilliance was to connect Homer as a first-poet with the sound of Old English (Anglo-Saxon) verse as another instance of a first-poetry, & to tie both of these to the *new* poetry he shared with other twentieth-century workers. And more than the poetry per se, it was a sense of powers & visions that was there to be renewed; or, again touching on the dead:

> The hells move in cycles,
>> No man can see his own end.
> The Gods have not returned. "They have never left us."
>> They have not returned.

(Canto 113)

Page 94 THE MOURNING SONG OF SMALL-LAKE-UNDERNEATH

Source: John R. Swanton, *Tlingit Myths & Texts* (Bureau of American Ethnology, Bulletin 39 [Washington, 1909]), p. 395.

Composed by Hayi-a'k!ᵁ (Small-Lake-Underneath) about a drifting log found full of nails, out of which a house was built. It is used when a feast is about to be given for a dead man "& they have their blankets tied up to their waists & carry canes."

The poem comes from a collection of 103 Tlingit songs gathered by Swanton. "By far the larger number were composed for feasts or in song contests between men who were at enmity with each other."

Page 95 THE STORY OF THE LEOPARD TORTOISE

Source: Wilhelm H. I. Bleek & Lucy C. Lloyd, *Specimens of Bushman Folklore* (George Allen & Co., London, 1911), pp. 37ff.

NARRATOR'S NOTES, ETC. The narrator explains that this misfortune happened to men of the Early Race.

And she altogether held the man firmly with it, i.e., by drawing in her neck.

The man's hands altogether decayed away in it, i.e., the flesh decayed away & came off, as well as the skin & nails, leaving, the narrator says, merely the bones.

Rub our elder sister a little with fat; for, the moon has been cut, while our elder sister lies ill: i.e., the moon "died" & another moon came while she still lay ill, the narrator explains.

Addenda. (1) "In Bushman astrological mythology the Moon is looked upon as a man who incurs the wrath of the Sun, and is consequently pierced by the knife (i.e., the rays) of the latter. This process is repeated until almost the whole of the Moon is cut away, and only one little piece left; which the Moon piteously implores the Sun to spare for his (the Moon's) children. . . . From this little piece, the Moon gradually grows again until it becomes a full moon, when the Sun's stabbing and cutting processes recommence." (W. H. I. Bleek, *A Brief Account of Bushman Folklore & Other Texts* [Cape Town, 1875], p. 9)

(2) For further comments on the Bleek-Lloyd translations, see p. 472.

Page 97 NOTTAMUN TOWN

Source: Traditional folk song in performance version by Jean Ritchie.

The editor has long been haunted by the present song, though to present it in this context as a vision-of-the-dead is to say more (& less) about it than is likely needed. Ritchie, who first sang it to prominence, reports that in her childhood in Viper, Kentucky, & environs, she took it for a nonsense song but felt, always, disturbed by it & only later learned it was, at origin, a kind of magic. The meaning, though, remained mysterious beyond the simple telling; i.e., "the song was magic, & once you came to understand it, the magic was lost."

Page 98 THE FLIGHT OF QUETZALCOATL

Source: Translated by J. R. from Spanish prose translation by Angel María Garibay K., *Epica Nahuatl* (Biblioteca del Estudiante Universitario, Mexico, 1945), pp. 59–63.

Archaic thought is coherent & directed, but the coherence isn't based on consistency of event so much as covering the widest range of possible situations. Like a shotgun blast, say, or a saturation bombing—effective against known targets & some unknown ones as well. So, the "greatest variation in legends & interpretations of the disappearance of Quetzalcoatl" may simply be noted & would have caused the Nahua makers no special discomfort. The important thing was for any account to hit home—to present the god's doings as image of how-it-really-is.

The present version comes from Sahagún's *Historia* (see above, p. 461), with the ending from the *Anales de Quauhtitlan*, & begins *after* whatever-had-happened to get him on the road. In Sahagún three sorcerers (one with a god name, two without) came to him, got him high on "white wine" (pulque?), while working other sorceries to destroy his city, Tollan ("Tula"). But the account is shapeless & lacks the thrust or point of myth-become-poetry.

The *Anales* in this case are more articulate. In brief, the gods Tezcatlipoca, Ihuimecatl, & Toltecatl decided to force Quetzalcoatl out of his city "where we intend to live." Tezcatlipoca thought to bring it off by "giving him his body," so showed him a "double mirror the size of a hand's span" & "Quetzalcoatl saw himself, and was filled with fear, and said: 'If my subjects see me, they will run away!' For his eyelids were badly inflamed, his eyes sunken in their sockets, and his face covered all over with wrinkles. His face was not human at all!" (I. Nicholson, *Firefly in the Night*, p. 69.)

The vision is repeated: always the terror of self-recognition, of the man in his dying body, his flesh. They get him drunk, have him sleep with his sister Quetzalpetatl, then wake up in sorrow:

> And he sang the sad song he had made that he might depart thence: "This is an evil tale of a day when I left my house. May those that are absent be softened, it was hard and perilous for me. Only let the one whose body is of earth exist and sing; I did not grow up subjected to servile labor." (L. Sejourné, *Burning Water*, p. 57)

And so on. In the *Anales* there's a period of four days (= dark phase of Venus) when he lies alone in a stone casket, then heads for the sea where the transfiguration (into Venus, the morning star) takes place. Sahagún is richer in the journey itself with its further revelations (also the many place-namings typical of primitive & archaic myth); has him form the raft of serpents & set off across the sea; ends with "no one knows how he came to arrive there at Tlapallan" (i.e., in Maya country, where the "plumed serpent" is the god Kukulcan)—but that's another story.

The force of the myth is in the image in the mirror: the journey a dark night before his re-emergence through fire & transfiguration. As plumed serpent Quetzalcoatl "belonged equally to the dark abyss & the celestial splendor" (Sejourné, p. 114):

> Quetzalcoatl taught that human greatness grows out of the awareness of a spiritual order; his image must therefore be the symbol of this truth. The serpent plumes must be speaking to us of the spirit that makes it possible for man—even while his body,

like the reptile's, is dragged in the dust—to know the superhuman joy of creation. (Sejourné, p. 84)

His identification with the planet Venus says this also.

Addenda. (1) The rotting face is what we start from in knowing where we are. The god isn't simply idealized as man-more-than-man-surviving-death but imaged also as man-fallen-with-man-into-rotting-flesh:

> . . . And it is said, he was monstrous.
>
> His face was like a huge, battered stone, a great fallen rock; it [was] not made like that of men. And his beard was very long—exceedingly long. He was heavily bearded. (Sahagún, *Florentine Codex*, IV, p. 13)

(2) Compare this with the Chinese (Na-Khi) *Song of the Dead, Relating the Origin of Bitterness* (p. 281 above; commentary, p. 571).

Page 104   THE STRING GAME

Source: Wilhelm H. I. Bleek & Lucy C. Lloyd, *Specimens of Bushman Folklore* (George Allen & Co., London, 1911), p. 237.

Dictated in July 1875 by Día!kwain, who heard it from his father, χaa-ttin. The song is a lament, sung by χaa-ttin after the death of his friend, the magician & rainmaker, !nuin | kui-ten, "who died from the effects of a shot he had received when going about, by night, in the form of a lion." There is also the following comment:

> Now that "the string is broken," the former "ringing sound in the sky" is no longer heard by the singer, as it had been in the magician's lifetime.

But the sense of a suspended string game ("cat's cradle") seems also implicit—a universal game of changes not far from the activity of magicians & poets.

Page 105   THE ABORTION

Source: W. G. Archer, "The Illegitimate Child in Santal Society," *Man in India*, XXIV (1944): 156–158.

The "true-poem" ("primitive" or not) doesn't repress but confronts what's most difficult to face—not only the great-existential-life-crises, etc., issues-of-reality, etc., but personal events outside all ritual pattern. Attempts to hold poetry to the (abstractly) Good & Beautiful, i.e., to "hymns to the gods & praises of famous men" (Plato), work against the poet's impulse & function, thus opening the door for platitude & art-as-propaganda. Plato who attacked poets as liars-by-nature is himself revealed as the first great liar-by-reason-of-state.

Page 107   *IMPROVISED SONG AGAINST A WHITE MAN*

Source: Arkady Fiedler, *The Madagascar I Love* (Orbis Ltd., London, 1946), p. 140.

The white man (*vasaha*) in question was himself the collector of the poem & the author of the book in which it appeared. The theme of sexual imperialism is dominant throughout.

Page 108   *PSALM 137*

Source: Harris Lenowitz's translation *in* J. Rothenberg, *A Big Jewish Book: Poems & Other Visions of the Jews from Tribal Times to Present* (Anchor Press/Doubleday, New York, 1978), p. 489.

The Hebrew text is from circa 586 B.C.: a virtual song-of-protest made *in situ* at the time of the Babylonian "captivity." Lenowitz's epigraph comes from a Jamaican reggae (Rastafarian) version by B. Dowe & F. Mc-Naughton, reflecting "another movement-in-exile in which the leaders are singers" (H. L.). The reader can compare the refusal to sing with, e.g., "what the [Acoma Indian] informant told Franz Boas in 1920":

> long ago her mother
> had to sing this song and so
> she had to grind along with it
> the corn people have a song too
> it is very good
> I refuse to tell it

> (English version by Armand
> Schwerner)

Page 109 *A SEQUENCE OF SONGS OF THE GHOST DANCE RELIGION*

Source: James Mooney, *The Ghost-Dance Religion and the Sioux Outbreak of 1890* (Bureau of American Ethnology, Annual Report No. 14 [Washington, 1896]). The versions follow Margot Astrov's condensations.

The late nineteenth-century messianic movement called the Ghost Dance, was not simply a pathetic reaction to White rule or a confused attempt to suck up Christian wisdom. The ritual use of ecstasy & the dance is clearly more Indian than Christian; & the movement's central belief that the present world would go the way of all previous worlds through destruction & re-emergence had been (for all the Christian turns it was now given) widespread throughout North America and at the heart, say, of the highly developed religious systems of the Mexican plateau.

The "messiah" of the Ghost Dance was Wovoka ("the cutter"), also called Jack Wilson, who circa 1889 was taken up to heaven by God & there given the message of redemption, with full control over the elements, etc. His doctrine spread quickly through the Indian world, under various names but always referring to the trance-like dance at its center; thus "dance in a circle" (Paiute), "everybody dragging" (Shoshoni), "the Father's dance" (Comanche), "dance with clasped hands" & "dance craziness" (Kiowa), & "ghost dance" (Sioux & Arapaho). Wovoka's own dance was described by a northern Cheyenne follower named Porcupine in terms reminiscent of Jesus' "round dance" with his disciples in the apocryphal & equally "unchristian" Acts of St. John (above, p. 336):

> They cleared off a space in the form of a circus ring and we all gathered there. . . . The Christ [i.e., Wovoka] was with them. . . . I looked around to find him, and finally saw him sitting on one side of the ring. . . . They made a big fire to throw light on him. . . . He sat there a long time and nobody went up to speak to him. He sat with his head bowed all the time. After a while he rose and said he was very glad to see his children. . . . "My children, I want you to listen to all I have to say to you. I will teach you, too, how to dance a dance, and I want you to dance it. Get ready for your dance and then, when the dance is over, I will talk to you." He was dressed in a white coat with stripes. The rest of his dress

was a white man's except that he had on a pair of moccasins. Then he commenced our dance, everybody joining in, the Christ singing while we danced. . . . [Later] he commenced to tremble all over, violently for a while, and then sat down. We danced all that night, the Christ lying down beside us apparently dead.

Of the songs themselves Mooney writes: "All the songs are adapted to the simple measure of the dance step . . . the dancers moving from right to left, following the course of the sun . . . hardly lifting the feet from the ground. . . . Each song is started in the same manner, first in an undertone while singers stand still in their places, and then with full voice as they begin to circle around. At intervals between the songs . . . the dancers unclasp hands and sit down to smoke or talk for a few minutes. . . . There is no limit to the number of these songs, as every trance at every dance produces a new one. . . . Thus a single dance may easily result in twenty or thirty new songs."

Not surprisingly Wovoka, as an adjunct to his vision-search, was one of the first Indian "revivalists" to make use of peyote—thus a forerunner of the peyote-cult with its subsequent impact on the main U.S. culture.

Page III   THE BOOK OF EVENTS (I)

Source: Most of these originally appeared in J. R.'s *Ritual: A Book of Primitive Rites & Events* (Something Else Press, New York, 1966). The realizations throughout are by J. R., with the exception of the "Three Magic Events," which were collected & adapted by Bengt af Klintberg.

LILY EVENTS. Adapted from W. Lloyd Warner, *A Black Civilization* (Harper & Row, New York, 1937, 1958), p. 419.

GARBAGE EVENT. Adapted from W. R. Geddes, *Nine Dayak Nights* (Oxford University Press, 1957, 1961), pp. 19–20.

BEARD EVENT. Adapted from Warner, *A Black Civilization*, p. 333.

STONE FIRE EVENT. Ibid., p. 318.

CLIMBING EVENT. Adapted from Mircea Eliade, *Shamanism: Archaic Techniques of Ecstasy* (Bollingen Series LXXVI, Pantheon Books, New York, 1964), p. 127.

FOREST EVENT. Adapted from Marianna D. Birnbaum, *An Anthology of Ugric Folk Literature: Tales and Poems of the Ostyaks, Voguls and Hungarians* (University of Munich, 1977), p. 6.

GIFT EVENT. Adapted from statements by Kwakiutl Indians in "The Amiable Side of Kwakiutl Life: The Potlatch and the Play Potlatch," by

Helen Codere, *American Anthropologist*, vol. 56, no. 2 (April 1956).

MARRIAGE EVENT. Adapted from William Wyatt Gill, *Life in the Southern Isles* (Religious Tract Society, London, 1876), pp. 59–60.

THREE MAGIC EVENTS. Adapted by Bengt af Klintberg from his *Svenska trollformler* (1965), in Klintberg, *The Cursive Scandinavian Salve* (Something Else Press, New York, 1967), p. 8.

GOING-AROUND EVENT. Adapted from W. Bogoras, *The Chuckchee* (Jessup North Pacific Expedition, Memoirs of the American Museum of Natural History, 1904–1909), pp. 402–403.

LANGUAGE EVENT. Adapted from N. J. v. Warmelo, "Contribution Towards Venda History, Religion and Tribal Ritual," *Ethnological Publications* (Department of Native Affairs, Union of South Africa), III (1932): 49–51.

BURIAL EVENTS. Adapted from Rene de Nebesky-Wojkowitz, *Oracles and Demons of Tibet* (Oxford University Press and Mouton & Co., 1956), pp. 517–518.

FRIENDSHIP DANCE. Adapted from Frank G. Speck & Leonard Broom, *Cherokee Dance and Drama* (University of California Press, 1951), pp. 65–67.

GREASE FEAST EVENT. Adapted from Franz Boas, "The Social Organization and Secret Societies of the Kwakiutl Indians," in *Reports of the U.S. National Museum under the Direction of the Smithsonian Institution for the Year Ending June 30, 1895* (U.S. Government Printing Office, Washington, 1897), pp. 355–356.

PEACEMAKING EVENT. Adapted from A. R. Radcliffe-Brown, *The Andaman Islanders* (Cambridge University Press, 1922, 1933), pp. 134–135.

WILD MAN EVENTS. Adapted from Sir James George Frazer, *The New Golden Bough* (Criterion Books, New York, 1959), pp. 143–144.

BOOGER EVENT. Adapted from Speck & Broom, *Cherokee Dance and Drama*, pp. 28–36. (Boogers = ghosts, spirits, foreigners, white men.)

SEA WATER EVENT. Adapted from Warner, *A Black Civilization*, p. 337.

NOISE EVENT. Adapted from The Book of Psalms.

The editor has taken a series of rituals & other programmed activities from a wide geographical area & has, as far as possible, suppressed all reference to accompanying mythic or "symbolic" explanations. This has led to two important results: (1) the form of the activities is, for the first time, given the prominence it deserves; & (2) the resulting works bear a close resemblance to those often mythless activities of our own time called events, happenings, de-coll/age, kinetic theater, performance art, sound-text, etc. It may be further noted that most of these "events"—like the (modern) inter-media art they resemble—are parts of total situations involving poetry, music, dance, painting, myth, magic, etc., as are many of the songs & visions presented elsewhere in this anthology. Having revealed this much, the editor does not wish to obscure by a series of explanatory footnotes the forms that have been laid bare. Although absence of such notes may result in some distortion, it's precisely the kind of distortion that can have a value in itself. Like seeing Greek statues without their colors.

Addenda.   The following examples of contemporary events & happenings may be instructive to the reader who has not been aware of the resemblances alluded to above. (N.B. The word *happening* itself has counterparts in, e.g., the Navajo word for "ceremonial," which, Kluckhohn & Wyman tell us, translates almost literally as "something-is-going-on," or in the wide-spread use by the Iroquois of the English word *doings*.)

Alison Knowles
GIVEAWAY CONSTRUCTION

Find something you like in the street and give it away. Or find a variety of things, make something of them, and give it away.

La Monte Young*
COMPOSITION 1960 #15
to Richard Huelsenbeck

This piece is little whirlpools
out in the middle of the ocean.

Dick Higgins
From CLOWN'S WAY:
A Drama In Three Hundred Acts

Act Five.
Climb up a ladder. At the top, smile. Climb down again.

*© La Monte Young 1963. All other rights including rights to public or private performance of *Composition 1960 #15* are retained by La Monte Young.

Bengt af Klintberg
THREE FOREST EVENTS

Number 1 (winter)

Walk out into a forest when it is winter and decorate all the
spruces with burning candles, flags, apples, glass balls and tinsel
strings.

Number 2

Walk out into a forest and wrap some drab trees, or yourself, in
tinsel.

Number 3

Climb up to a treetop with a saw. Saw through the whole
tree-trunk from the top right down to the root.

Emmett Williams
A SELECTION FROM "5,000 NEW WAYS"

select 50 compound words.
split them, and turn the freed second halves into verbs.

select 50 projections and 50 sounds.
write them on cards, and shuffle them.

fast upon reading one of the 'new ways,'
show a projection, make a sound
picked at random from the pile of cards.

N.B. at a performance in Paris in 1963, the first three operations yielded these
combinations:

text:	the new way the maiden heads
projection:	a hundred-dollar bill
sound:	draining sink
text:	the new way the banana splits
projection:	two left shoes
sound:	firecracker

text:	the new way the belly buttons
projection:	great wall of china
sound:	rooster

Carolee Schneemann
From MEAT JOY

The Intractable Rosette. Men gather women into circular
formation. A sequence of attempts to turn women into static,
then moving shapes: linking their arms, tying their legs together.
They arrange them lying down, sitting up, on their backs, & every
attempt to move them as a solid unit fails as they fall apart, roll
over, get squashed, etc. All shouting instructions, ideas, advice,
complaints. All collapse in a heap.

Serving Maid with huge tray of raw chickens, mackerel, strings of
sausages, strews them extravagantly on the bodies. Wet fish,
heavy chickens, bouncing hot-dogs. Bodies respond sporadically:
twitching, reaching, touching. Individual instructions for
fish-meat-chickens. Instances: independent woman flips, flops,
slips on the floor like a fish, jumps up, throwing, catching, falling,
running. Lateral woman attacked by others. Central woman
sucking fish. Individual man with fish follows contours of
woman's body with it. Tenderly, then wildly. All inundated with
fish & chickens.

Alan Kaprow
RAINING

(Scheduled for performance in the spring, for any number of
persons and the weather. Times and places need not be coordi-
nated, and are left up to the participants. The action of the rain
may be watched if desired.)

(For Olga and Billy Klüver, January 1965)

Black highway painted black
Rain washes away

Paper men made in bare orchard branches
Rain washes away

Sheets of writing spread over a field
Rain washes away

Little grey boats painted along a gutter
Rain washes away

Naked bodies painted gray
Rain washes away

Bare trees painted red
Rain washes away

A Further Note. When I first assembled these events, circa 1966, I attributed the relation between "primitive" ritual & contemporary performance art & poetry to an implicit coincidence of attitudes. Today the relation seems up-front, explicit, & increasingly comparable to the Greek & Roman model in Renaissance Europe, the Chinese model in medieval Japan, the Toltec model among the Aztecs, etc.: i.e., an overt influence but alive enough to work a series of distortions conditioned by the later culture & symptomatic of the obvious differences between the two. Some areas of estrangement & return, as they've entered into current work, are: the (re)creation & (re)discovery of an earth-consciousness ("earth as a religious form"—Eliade); of our links to the animal world & to our own animal natures; of body & of sexuality; of a new—& old—idea of femaleness; of rituals & performances that grow out of a careful attention to body-mind/physical-mental processes; of dreams & visions explored in so many ways since the Surrealists first projected them as central to their program of recovery; of the myths & rituals (but especially the rituals) of everyday life.

My own preference, for all of that, is for those intersections that operate at the less explicit—& possibly "deeper"—level of human experience. What seems inescapable, one way or another, is the return of poetry & art to "performance" as a necessary mode & a means of completion.

Vito Acconci
SECURITY ZONE

Pier 18, New York; February 1971

1. A person is chosen as my guard and/or opposition party. He is specifically chosen: someone about whom my feelings are ambiguous, someone I don't fully trust.

2. We are alone together at the far end of the pier: I'm blindfolded, my ears are plugged, my hands are tied behind my back.

3. I walk around the pier—I attempt to gain assurance in walking around the pier (putting myself in the other person's control—testing whether I can trust in that control). The other person decides how he wants to use the trust I am forced to have in him.

4. The piece is designed for our particular relationship: it tests that relationship, works on it, can possibly improve it.

Judy Chicago, Suzanne Lacy, Sandra Orgel, Aviva Rahmani
ABLUTIONS 1972
A performance about rape

The performance takes place in an area strewn with egg shells, piles of rope and fresh meat. A tape of women describing their experiences of being raped plays, while a naked woman is slowly and methodically bound with white gauze from her feet upward to her head. At the same time, a clothed woman nails beef kidneys into the rear wall of the space, thus defining the perimeter of the performance area, while two nude women bathe themselves in a series of tubs containing first eggs, then blood, and finally clay. Finally, two clothed women bind the performance set and the other performers into immobility with string and rope. As they leave the space, the tape repeats: "And I felt so helpless all I could do was just lie there. . . ."

Linda Montano
MITCHELL'S DEATH (April 1978)

Participants: Linda Montano, Pauline Oliveros and Al Rossi.

Structure of the event: the piece was structured around a plus sign.

> Horizontal: 1. a TV monitor with images of my face as I applied white makeup and put in acupuncture needles.
>
> 2. Pauline, sitting, and playing a Japanese bowl gong.

3. I was standing at the lectern chanting—
whitened face, a black dress and acupunc-
ture needles in my face.

4. Al Rossi, sitting, playing a sruti box.

Vertical: 1. light was projected in back of me and
created a shadow image.

2. sound amplified and delayed three times in
front of me.

The Event. I entered the space after Al and Pauline. Al began
playing the sruti box and I turned on the monitor and then the
light on the lectern. Both Al and Pauline were instructed to chant
throughout the performance, and Pauline was to play the bowl
gong whenever she felt it was necessary. I sang on one note—the
story of Mitchell's death from the moment I heard about it to the
moment I saw him in the mortuary. When the text was
completed, I turned off the light and monitor, and left the space.

Joseph Beuys
COYOTE: I LIKE AMERICA & AMERICA LIKES ME (1974)

For three days Joseph Beuys lived with a coyote in a room of the
René Block Gallery in New York. The action as such began when
Beuys, arriving from Germany, was packed into felt at Kennedy
Airport and driven by ambulance to the gallery. In the gallery in a
room divided by a grating a coyote was waiting for him. . . .
During the action Beuys was at times entirely covered in felt. Out
of the felt only a wooden cane stuck out. Beuys talked with the
coyote, attempted to find an approach to him, to establish a
relationship. They lived peacefully with each other in the cage,
man and coyote. From time to time Beuys rang a triangle which
he carried around his neck. Sounds of a turbine from a tape
recorder disturbed the atmosphere, bringing a threatening
nuance into the play. Fifty copies of the Wall Street Journal, lying
strewn about the floor, completed the environment. The coyote
urinated on the papers.

(Description by Caroline Tisdall)

"Eventually everything will be happening at once: nothing behind a
screen unless a screen happens to be in front" (John Cage).

Page 133 **THE BOOK OF EVENTS (II)**

The texts in this section give a fuller account of three selected events, in order to show the realization of such activities in context. Since the editor could have done the same for many of the preceding events—at least where dialogue &/or songs were available—this section shouldn't be thought of as an "advance" over the first but simply another way of considering ritual-theater: by letting the words, the dramatic action & the myth take a more central position.

Page 135 **TAMING THE STORM: A TWO-SHAMAN VISION & EVENT**

Source: Abridged from Knud Rasmussen, *The Intellectual Culture of the Copper Eskimos* (Report of the Fifth Thule Expedition [Copenhagen, 1932]), pp. 56–61.

Word, vision, & event come together in the work, along with the environment itself. Shakespeare's *Lear* the classic example of the simulation of a meteorological event in a theatrical situation; Kaprow's *Raining* (p. 516) & La Monte Young's *Composition #15* (p. 514) examples of the incorporation of natural weather conditions in a non-mythic "happening."

Page 140 **CORONATION EVENT & DRAMA**

Source: Theodor H. Gaster, *Thespis: Ritual, Myth and Drama in the Ancient Near East* (Anchor Books, Doubleday & Co., New York, 1961), pp. 378–383. Reworking of dialogue by J. R.

While still in the womb Osiris & Isis, son & daughter of Earth & Sky, formed the child Horus between them. Osiris's dark counterpart was Set, his brother, who later destroyed & dismembered him, Isis & Horus becoming the means to his recovery & rebirth as judge-of-the-dead, etc. In battle Horus tore out Set's testicles, while Set ripped out Horus' black (left) eye (i.e., the moon; but some say both the white & black eyes: sun & moon) & "flung it away beyond the edge of the world, & Thoth, the moon's genius & guardian" (but also: god of words & spels) "found it lying in the outer darkness" (R. T. Rundle Clark, *Myth & Symbol in Ancient Egypt*, p. 224) & restored it to Horus in the ritual of recovery here enacted.

The text is from a papyrus of the Twelfth Dynasty (circa 1970 B.C.) but Kurt Sethe (who first recognized it as theater) dated the contents from the

First Dynasty (circa 3300 B.C.). It "gives an account of the traditional cere-
monies at the installation of the king, which was celebrated in conjunction
with the New Year ceremonies during the month of Khoiakh. . . . Each detail
of the ritual program is, however, invested at the same time with a durative
significance, and this is brought out explicitly in the form of a mythological
'key' attached to every scene." (Gaster, *Thespis*, p. 81) Forty-six scenes have
been preserved, of which seven are presented here. The "events' of the
coronation are in small caps; the mythological key in italics.

Addenda. The classic modern example of a direct use of Egyptian
funerary materials is Lawrence's *Ship of Death*. The story of Osiris & Isis has
become *the* ancient myth for many of those poets who can still form attach-
ments to the old gods *per se* (see, e.g., Ed Sanders' very free reworkings of the
laments of Isis & Nephthys [p. 525]).

Page 144 FOR THE RAIN GOD TLALOC

Source: Translation into English by Miguel Léon-Portilla, in M. Léon-Portilla, *Native Mesoamerican Spirituality* (Paulist Press, New York, 1980), pp. 193–196.

Tlalocan—the Paradise of the rain god Tlaloc & one of three Aztec places-of-the-dead. A virtual garden-of-delight, eternal springtime, etc., as in the dancing figures painted at Teotihuacan:

& in sharp contrast to the terrors/tears of those sacrificed to stimulate the god.

Tlaloques—the god's assistants.

Acatonal—alternative calendrical name for Tlaloc, meaning "reed" or "stalk."

Poyauhtlan—"region of mist," a mountain home of Tlaloc as the god of rain.

With the destruction of "primitive" alternatives & in movement toward a "higher" civilization, the (human) stakes become suddenly incredible—a system of ritual sacrifice not only underpinning the Aztecs' "mystic militarism" but what Léon-Portilla calls their "perpetual & sacred theater." Played from day to day throughout the Aztec year, the rituals were theatrically complex & drew on great numbers of participants, including numerous, often anonymous, sacrificial victims who "contributed their blood to the maintenance of the life of the Sun." Among all such ritual-events, the annual ceremony for the rain god Tlaloc—celebrated on his mountain & in front of the Templo Mayor in Tenochtitlan (Mexico City)—delivers the greatest sense of pity & horror. Writes Léon-Portilla:

> Before the ceremony they arranged an artificial woods with trees, which was a kind of stage. In the middle of some bushes and shrubs was a very tall tree surrounded by four others oriented towards the four points of the compass. Round about flew banners spattered with melted rubber, a symbolic decoration in honor of Tlaloc. When the moment for the ceremony came, as [Fray Diego de] Durán writes: "The priest and dignitaries, all very adorned, took out a little girl of seven or eight years who was in a kind of tent, completely covered over, where no one had seen her, where the lords had hidden the child. In this manner the priests took on their shoulders the child who had been put in that tent, all dressed in blue, which represented the great lake and all the fountains and small rivers, with a band of reddish leather around her head and fastened to it a tuft of blue feathers. They placed this little girl who was in that tent in the woods, under that tall tree, facing towards the idol, and then they brought a drum and all sat down without dancing, with the girl in front, and they sang many and varied songs." (M. L.-P., *Pre-Columbian Literatures of Mexico*, pp. 99–100)

The scenario presented here is Léon-Portilla's reconstruction of one such chant & dialogue, based on sixteenth-century Nahuatl accounts gathered by Bernardino de Sahagún in the Codex Matritensis.

Page 149 GHOSTS & SHADOWS

Source: J. R.'s translation from R. P. Trilles, *Les pygmées de la forêt equatoriale* (Paris, 1931), reprinted in Caillois & Lambert, *Trésor de la poésie universelle*, p. 27.

Interiorizing as a mode of translation: that the pygmy "ghosts" are as elusive as "soul" or "personality" or "unconscious"—for us the last believable remnants of the mythic underworld. But the pygmies would more likely see the forest-as-a-dark-soul than as Lawrence has it.

Page 150 THE CHAPTER OF CHANGING INTO PTAH

Source: Adapted by Ben Moses from E. A. W. Budge, *The Papyrus of Ani (Book of the Dead)* (Medici Society Ltd., London, 1913), Vol. II, pp. 546–548.

Ptah—the lord of life, who conceived the elements of the universe with his heart & brought them into being with his tongue.
Ka—the double; separable part of the personality.
Hathor—goddess of the sky; divine cow who holds the stars in her belly.
Busiris & Heliopolis—Greek names for the Lower Egyptian cities of Tetu & Anu.
Ra—the Sun.
Tem (Atum)—oldest of the gods; creator.
Keb (Geb)—god of the earth & father of the gods; "in many places he is called the 'great cackler' & he was supposed to have laid the egg from which the world sprang" (Budge).
Tait—goddess of weaving.

The Book of the Dead isn't a book but a catch-all name for the Egyptian funerary papyri, the best-known set coming from the papyrus of (the scribe) Ani written down between 1500 & 1350 B.C. As with the Egyptian "namings" (see p. 11), the concern here is not with the dignity of the god-nature so much as its energy: at once more-than-human & utterly of-this-earth. It is the same vision that makes the great fanged statue of Coatlicue or the multibreasted Diana of Ephesus more interesting & probably more truthful than the Venus de Milo or Michelangelo's Pietà.

o   o   o   o

An example, partly translative, of the recovery of old Egyptian gods, glyphs, erotic visions, death symbols, etc., is Ed Sanders's poem & assemblage, below. A seminal reading of the source & not far either from the twentieth-century scholarship of T. Rundle Clark & others.

o   o   o   o

Ed Sanders
INCANTATION BY ISIS
FOR REVIVAL OF THE DEAD OSIRIS

come to thy beloved one

BEAUTIFUL BEING) triumphant!

come to Thy sister   come to thy wife
Arise! Arise! Glorious Brother!
from thy bier that I may
hover near thy genital
forever

Beautiful Boy my brother come to my breasts
take there of that milk to thy fill
thy nuts will I guard upon
nor shall the Fiends of Darkness tear at your Eye

come to your house   come to your house

BEAUTIFUL BEING) ! Boy Body!

that your cock glide forward in radiance
to our pavilion

Osiris!   Osiris!

when the Ra- (Disc) glides onward in the Sun-boat

∫ flamespurts spew off the prow

O may I catch thy spurts o brother
as the shrieking human
catches the sun!

Page 152   THE CANNIBAL HYMN

Source: Ulli Beier, "Traditional Egyptian Poetry," *Black Orpheus*, no. 18 (Ibadan, Nigeria, 1965), p. 6.

Unas (Unis)—the dead king.

Made up of Utterances 273 & 274 of the Pyramid Texts (for which see commentary, p. 474). Mercer indicates that the hymn consists, in fact, of a series of shorter utterances; the method of bringing them together & the resultant feeling of the poem is very reminiscent of later African praise-poems (described on p. 477) & suggests a continuity that is, but shouldn't be, surprising. It would seem—from other evidence as well—that the disintegration which overtook Egypt was later in coming to Black Africa.

Addenda. The picture of the dead king "slaying & devouring the gods as food" (Mercer) isn't unlike the heaven of the Jews, where the souls of the Righteous were to spend eternity feasting on the flesh of Behemoth & Leviathan—the possibility too of that having its source among the god-eaters. To say nothing of the Eucharist, etc.

Page 154   CONVERSATIONS IN COURTSHIP

Source: Excerpts from Ezra Pound's translation in *Love Poems of Ancient Egypt*, translated by Ezra Pound & Noel Stock (New Directions, New York, 1962), pp. 4–7.

"These versions are based on literal renderings of the hieroglyphic texts into Italian by Boris de Rachewiltz, which first appeared in the volume *Liriche amorose degli antichi Egizioni*, published by Vanni Scheiwiller, Milan, in 1957. Most of the original Egyptian texts have survived only in incomplete form, but, for the purpose of modern adaptation, it has seemed desirable to present each poem as complete."

Page 157   THE COMET
Page 158   THE LOVERS

Source: P. Amaury Talbot, *In the Shadow of the Bush* (Wm. Heineman, London, 1912), pp. 455, 459.

This is a form of secret-writing & gesture-language that was widespread among groups besides the Ekoi, being there the property of an all-male society called the Ngbe (= Leopard) & devoted above all (writes Robert Farris Thompson) to "the pleasurable dancing in public of secret signs and magic powers" (*Symposium of the Whole*, p. 286). Messages in Nsibidi script were cut or painted on split palm stems; in addition, they were "chalked on walls, embroidered or appliqued on cloth, painted and resist-dyed on cloth, incised on calabashes, hammered on brass containers, cut in divinatory leaves, painted on toy swords, and tattooed on human skin" (Ibid.). As a form of writing in & on space, the signs employed show a wide range of conventionalization & abstraction, e.g.:

Moon in three phases

Husband & wife love each other ardently. They love to put their arms around one another (shown by extended hands). They are rich, have three tables & a pillow at each side.

A mirror standing on a table

People arranging their hair in the mirror

Sign denoting a talkative man

Sick man lying down in his house, with three visitors

In Nsibidi, as in other complex signing systems, a close correspondence exists between the written & mimed forms. "An incomparable art," writes Thompson, "[that] communicates a calligraphic sense of line, sensuous and superb."

For other picture-writings, see pp. 26, 205, 281.

Addenda. For a contemporary work that uses a conventional coding system, the reader might consider Hannah Weiner's *Code Poems* (Station Hill Press, 1982) "taken from the International Code of Signals for the Use of All Nations[:] . . . a visual signal system for ships at sea." E.g.:

DSJ   PERSONS INDICATED PRESENT THEIR COMPLIMENTS TO

TMQ   If you please
ZGS   Do you wish to?
FBX   As you please
ZGU   If you wish
ZGV   It is my wish

LBG   Will persons please?
QTR   I or persons indicated wish to see you
ZGW   Wish to speak to you
TMW   Will you please?
ZGX   Wish you would

USR   Request the pleasure of
OCA   With pleasure. I will accept
TMU   Shall I have the pleasure to or of?
DBX   Very acceptable
OAP   Will you give me the pleasure?
TMX   With much pleasure
ZJQ   Will you write?
ZLH   Yes, I will
WRY   Will you stay or wait?
HUG   Yes, I can
JEA   Will you accompany?
DCZ   I will accompany
JGV   Will you give me the pleasure of your company at?
JGT   Very glad of your company
JGS   The pleasure of your company
TIR   I or persons indicated gratefully accept

In addition to the flag forms of the International Signal Code, Weiner's performances utilized semaphore (light signals) & morse code. The flags could be displayed both statically &, as with the Nsibidi in its most elaborated form, could be performed as "art-in-motion."

Page 159 DRUM POEM #7

Source: Adapted by Ben Moses from R. S. Rattray, *Ashanti* (Oxford University Press, 1923), pp. 269, 280.

". . . Among the Ashanti the drum is not used . . . [to rap] out words by means of a prearranged code, but . . . to sound or speak the actual words . . . drum-talking as distinct from drum-signalling . . . an attempt to imitate by means of two drums, set in different notes, the exact sound of the human voice" (Rattray, p. 242).

Ashanti is a tonal language & "the drum gives the tones, number of syllables, & the punctuation accurately. The actual vowels & the individual consonants cannot be transmitted. It is therefore generally impossible to 'read' accurately any particular word when standing alone"—though the "words" are heard distinctly as parts of larger units, aided too by the use of standard or set phrases. Thus "missionary"—in the drum language of the Kele in the Congo Basin—is given as "white man spirit of the forest," not because the latter phrase is all that common (or poetic) but because its tones leave little doubt about the meaning.

This type of poem (or poem-realization) is widespread in Africa. Among the Yoruba, e.g., "the 'dundun' drum can play any tone & glide of the . . . language & its range is an octave. . . . Just as in Semitic languages the consonants are so important that one can write the language without vowels, so in Yoruba the tones are of such great importance that vowels as well as consonants can be dropped" (U. Beier, *Yoruba Poetry*, p. 9).

In Rattray's transcriptions, two tones are given: for the low or male drum (M) & the high or female drum (F). These may be combined almost simultaneously (MF, FM, MM, FF) or grouped in syllables as indicated by the hyphens.

For a brief take on Trobriand Island drum-language, see p. 387, & the accompanying commentary. Ruth Finnegan's fuller account of African drum poetry appears in *Symposium of the Whole*, pp. 129–139.

Addenda. (1) Other forms of (so-called) "surrogate speech" turn up as horn languages, gong languages, flute languages, xylophone languages, whistling & whistle languages, yodeling, talking elephant tusks, etc. In contemporary music & (sound) poetry—particularly those forms that involve electronic manipulation & synthesis—such moves-across-media have been given a new importance. Thus, Max Neuhaus's *Realization of Jackson Mac Low's "The Text on the Opposite Page"* involves a reading by two voices of a dual series of typewritten letters, numbers, & signs that is then recorded on tape & lowered by four octaves, etc. The resulting "distortion" creates a musical composition which both is & isn't the original reading. The sound is of a very deep, very resonant & percussive piece of electronic music: the voice an undiscernible but real presence.

(2) Although the effect of conveying meaning through tones alone can't be reproduced in English, the transmission of messages with key vowels & consonants suppressed or modified enters, as a game of language, into the following verbal plays by George Brecht & Patrick Hughes:

tophalf

per.od
com,ma
c:l:n

enɗ

ero
1ne
2wo
3hree
4our
5ive

f_oor

Page 161   PRAISES OF OGUN

Source: J. R.'s translations selected from the French of Pierre Verger, *Notes sur le Culte des Orişa et Vodun* (Mémoires de l'Institut Français d'Afrique Noire, Dakar, 1957), pp. 146–150, 175–206.

Ogun is the god of iron & is worshipped by all those who use iron. He is a semihistorical figure who has become an *orisha*, i.e., a "mediary between Olorun (the supreme god) and man. . . . The orisha personifies some aspect of the divine power," & each orisha has his own set of colors, materials, etc. Assembled from a number of local variants, these "praises" of Ogun give a compound image of his range & power.

For a description of the Yoruba *oriki* (praise-poem), see p. 477.

Page 164   ABUSE POEM : FOR KODZO & OTHERS

Source: Kofi Awoonor, "Poems & Abuse-Poems of the Ewe," *Alcheringa*, old series, no. 3 (Winter 1971): 8–9.

Typical of that range of Ewe abuse or attack poetry called *halo*. Komo Ekpe (b. 1897), as a traditional poet, or *heno*, drew power from "a personal god of songs" (= Hadzivodoo), while maintaining a great deal of personal presence, even innovation, in his work. In the present example, Ekpe's principal opponent is the poet Kodzo, but the abuse is also aimed at Kodzo's supporters: "his women admirers who goaded him on & Amegavi, a wealthy elder of Tsiame." The "questioners" of the poem are "the followers of Ekpe's drum, which he calls *Question*" & which, as with the "drums" of other Ewe poets, becomes the symbol of his art.

Centered at public events such as wakes & funerals, the halo contests remind us of traditions as diverse as Eskimo song battles (above, p. 135), the flytings, etc., of pagan Europe, & the more recent Afro-American "dozens." A reminder too that good-feeling per se has rarely been the central aim of a poetry derived from the workings of shamans & sacred clowns engaged (more often & more like ourselves than we had previously imagined) in traditional rituals of abuse & *disruption*.

Page 166   **WHAT FELL DOWN? PENIS!**
Page 168   **WHAT FELL DOWN? VULVA!**

Source: Jean Borgatti, "Songs of Ritual License from Midwestern Nigeria," *Alcheringa*, new series, vol. 2, no. 1 (1976): 63, 65.

The songs come from Okpenada, one of seventeen Ejperi villages & center of a shrine & cult dating back to the late nineteenth century. The present performance was part of a ceremony involving a custodial priest & a group of elders & cult members. Writes Borgatti re performance & her own transcriptions: "The songs were partially accompanied by rhythmic hand-clapping. A chorus, consisting of children and spectators, alternately joined and followed the lead singer. An attempt has been made to visualize the patterns of singing and accompaniment through using different type faces, symbols and spacing: Lead singer alone, SINGER WITH CHORUS, *chorus alone*, handclapping, time-keeping, and over

　　　　　　　　　　　　　　　　　　　lapping."

Addenda. "The songs themselves" (writes Borgatti) "represent an occasion of ritualized verbal license in which men and women ridicule each other's genitalia and sexual habits. Normally such ridicule would be anti-social in the extreme, an offense against the elders, the living representatives of the ancestors, and hence against the continuity of life. In the ritual context, however, the songs provide recognition, acceptance, and release of that tension which exists between the sexes in all cultures, and so neutralize this potential threat to community stability."

In the West, rituals of sexual conflict have survived most often in trivialized form & have generally been restricted to male participants. An offshoot of feminist moves in contemporary poetry & art (with their attendant concern with the readjustment of sexual roles) has been the re-emergence of the (public) female voice in the assertion of sexual prerogatives.

o   o   o   o

Leslie Silko
TWO POEMS (late fall, 1972)

Si'ahh Aash'*

I

There goes one
            that's sleeping with him.
How many does that make?
15 or 20 maybe.
            He's got more women
                        than some men got horses.

2

How easy it is for you
            Si'ahh aash'
all us pretty women
            in love with you.

Mesita Men

Mesita men
            feed you
            chili stew
Then they want
            to fuck you.

**Si'ahh aash'*—*Laguna Pueblo word for the man you are sleeping with who is not your husband.*

Page 169 THE TRAIN

Source: George Economou's working from D. F. v.d. Merwe, "Hurutshe Poems," *Bantu Studies*, XV (1941): 335.

Praise-poem form transposed to new matter. Whatever enters a man's field-of-vision is part of his real world.

Of praise-poems among the Hurutshe, v.d. Merwe writes: ". . . A man may add a few lines to a poem heard by somebody else, with the result that a given poem may be the creation of two or even more persons. But the poems as recited by different people differ [also in that] the lines or stanzas composing the poems . . . sometimes change positions."

For more on praise-poems, see especially p. 477.

Page 170 SPEAKING THE WORLD

Source: Judith Gleason, *Leaf and Bone: African Praise-Poems* (Viking Press, New York, 1980), pp. 1–5. (Mainly translated from the French of Solange de Ganay, *Les Devices des Dogons*, Institut d'Ethnologie, Paris, 1938.)

Traditional Dogon *tige*, short praise-poems that mirror "a remarkable cosmology based on 'correspondences' " (Gleason). Bits of that cosmos ("as rich as that of Hesiod"—M. Griaule) were carried over into the Western world by ethnologists like Marcel Griaule & Germaine Dieterlen, whose practice related closely to impulses in the 1920s/30s shared directly with French Surrealism, etc. One of the resultant books—called "God of Water" in French, *Conversations with Ogotemmeli* in English—became one of the touchstones for twentieth-century artists looking for poetic technologies to which to relate their own (re)explorations of the "sacred." (The last of the poems given here is in fact Ogotemmeli's own praise-name.)

The use of the tige, as Gleason reports it, remains largely functional: to increase one's strength for heavy work, to give power to the hoe or to the person hoeing, to keep off the recent dead through the gazelle mask & its attendant rituals. But the deeper key is the sense that humans speak a "language" which is at the same time the elementary substance of which the earth is made. This perception of a "universe where each blade of grass, each little fly is the carrier of a word" (thus: Mme. G. Calame-Griaule) is the expression of a genuine poetics & leads to speculation by Victor Turner on "the close resemblance between Dogon myth and cosmology and those of certain Neo-Platonist, Gnostic, and Kabbalistic sects and 'heresies' that throve in the understory of European religion and philosophy." And even further: "One wonders whether, after the Vandal and Islamic invasions of North Africa, and even before these took place, Gnostic, Manichean, and Jewish-mystical ideas and practices might have penetrated the Sahara to the Western Sudan and helped to form the Dogon *Weltbild*" (*Dramas, Fields, and Metaphors*, p. 161).

More from Ogotemmeli appears in *Symposium of the Whole*, pp. 197–200.

Page 172   DEATH RITES I & II

Source: Translated by C. M. Bowra, *Primitive Song* (World Publishing Co., Cleveland, 1962), pp. 222–223, 202–203, from R. P. Trilles, *Les pygmées de la forêt équatoriale* (Paris, 1931).

Khvum (Khmvum)—father of the forest who "at times visits the sun to keep its fires burning;" he is otherwise connected (like Osiris) with judgment in the underworld.

Dan—a cavern in the forest at whose "gates" Khvum (as father of life & death) will meet the newly-born dead.

Characteristic of Pygmy poetry & of *all* poetry where sensitivity to the shifting polarities of light & darkness, etc., becomes a matter of cognition &, perhaps, of tragedy. "It is dark, it is light," reads the Aztec "definition," & the second Isaiah writes: "I form the light, & create darkness: I make peace, & create evil: I the Lord do all these things." So too, much modern poetry (where the issue, writes David Antin, is *reality*) is witness to the recovery of darkness, i.e., of darkness & light, the relation of figure to ground, etc.

o   o   o   o

Federico García Lorca
THE SONG WANTS TO BE THE LIGHT

> The song wants to be the light.
> In the darkness the song contains
> threads of phosphorous and moon.
> The light does not know what it wants.
> On its boundaries of opal,
> it meets itself face to face,
> and returns.

(Translation by James Wright)

Page 174 THE PRAISES OF THE FALLS

Source: Adapted by J. R. from Father F. Laydevant, "The Praises of the Divining Bones among the Basotho," *Bantu Studies*, VII (1933): 341–373.

The "praises"—first gathered by the Basuto writer Joas Mapetla—accompany the casting of oracle bones. Their purpose is

(1) To create, as with music, the conditions under which the bones are to be read, i.e., to provide that "coefficient of weirdness" Malinowski spoke of (see p. 442) in which the words *are* music, act upon us before their sense is clear or against the possibility of any fixed meaning;

(2) As open-ended imagery that can then—almost "falsely"—be read as secret closed statements (the functional language of the oracle) in the participants' search for clues to the unknown: the cause of disease & misfortune, etc.

Mapetla's description of the bones & the procedures for casting is never clear. There are apparently four to twenty in a set, or *litaola*: four principal ones from the hoofs & horns of oxen, with lesser bones from ankles & hindlegs of anteaters, springbok, sheep, goats, monkeys, also occasional shells, twigs & stones. The four major bones are designated as greater & lesser male & greater & lesser female, & are read according to the sides on which they fall, direction of fall, positions relative to each other & to the minor bones, etc. The greater male & female have four sides called walking, standing, covering, & dying; the lesser male & female only walking & dying. Here is Mapetla's description of the casting & "praising":

> When they are divining, the person who comes to ask for this service sweeps the ground where he has to throw them. Then the diviner loosens them from the string and gives them to the one who comes to consult.
>
> This one tosses them and lets them fall on the ground.
>
> Then the diviner examines them carefully in order to see the position they have taken.
>
> When he sees that they have fallen in a certain position, he praises that fall for a good while.
>
> Among the praises he mixes the affairs of people, of (various) things, of animals and sicknesses.
>
> When he has finished the praises, he says to the person who came to consult him: Make me divine, my friend.
>
> This one says: With these words, when you were making the praises, you pointed exactly to my case, and to my sickness.

And the diviner says: So it is, and this special position (of the bones) says the same. Then the diviner gives a charm to the consulting person, and receives a small fee from him (in exchange).

Addenda. (1) In the typical praise-poem (see p. 477) the lines or praises are independent units that the poet brings together in a kind of collage. In the present instance, however, it is the fall of the bones that suggests what verses will be used & determines their order. Thus chance—to a greater or lesser degree—serves to program the divining praises much as dice-castings, tarot-readings, random digit tables, etc., take on a structuring & selecting function for some contemporary poets.

(2) The name of a "fall" is generally that of the plant or other remedy to be used in that instance. Most African words that remain in the translations are likewise either plants or proper names—the meaning being fairly evident from the context.

(3) The editor originally printed these with some reservations about their accuracy but in the hope that others would be encouraged to do more detailed work on a body of lore & poetry that, carefully assembled, might represent an African *I Ching* or *Book of Changes*. The work of Judith Gleason (from *A Recitation of Ifa*, following) virtually fulfills that hope.

Page 181   IKA MEJI

Source: Judith Gleason, with Awotunde Aworinde & John Olaniyi Ogundipe, *A Recitation of Ifa* (Grossman Publishers, New York, 1973), pp. 139–142.

The name of both a god & a system of divination, Ifa uses a cord of eight split seeds or sixteen randomly thrown palm-nuts to summon the poetic voice of the Yoruba oracle. In Judith Gleason's abbreviated description:

> Each oracular configuration [or casting], known as Odu, is the product of sixteen times sixteen possibilities, which means that when the diviner ("father-of-secrets" or *babalawo* in Yoruba) casts for you, any one of 256 signs may appear. Further, each of these signs has many "roads" radiating out from it. To these roads are attached verses (*ese*), which are legion. When a certain Odu shows up on the board, the diviner will begin to recite some of these verses. When what he is saying seems to apply to your case, then a correct determination has been made. (*Leaf & Bone*, p. 196)

The standard structure of the Ifa divination poems ("often highly lyrical & obscure in their references") is to start with the citation of a previous, often mythic, casting, to name the diviner or diviners involved, then the name of the fictional client, the nature of his/her problem, the prescription suggested by the Odu, & the previous outcome. But further elements can enter through the intercalation of "songs and praises expressive of the 'character' of the Odu . . . as well as symbolic digressions on the meaning of the oracular system itself." The result is an open-ended & complex series of language structures: a major example of the human capacity for intricate design & concept. It is also—as discussed in the previous commentary—a still existing form of poesis that functions on the level of such divinatory/synchronistic works as the Chinese *I Ching*. (See p. 457.)

In the Odu presented here, Orunmila is another name of Ifa as god, Yemoja that of an *orisha*, or deity. The name "ika meji" suggests "fingers" & "cruelty"—& a sense of danger & randomness ("existence as scattershot") pervades the whole poem. Gleason writes further:

> Ecologically, Ika Meji is the world of the forest floor envisaged as a thin substratum of poisonous invective and countervenom, a world of baneful creepers turned snares, of treacherous twigs and prickers, a place where everything must be constantly on its guard, for anything could suddenly reveal its treacherous nature. Hypocrisy and evil intention are revealed by the diviner's proverbial names in the first verse of this recitation. The client in the first case is a poor, small creature, barely existing; in the second sequence the client is an entire town called *Ika*, which, for years "tied" by witchcraft, had been under the spell of its own name—a miserable place whose occupants, "trading for years with nothing to show for it," have, justifiably, no sense of self-respect, no ability to get themselves together without Ifa's help.
>
> Here is the twilight world of incantation, consciousness reduced to rigid reiteration of protective formulas—brilliantly conveyed in the Yoruba by an unremitting cacophony of "k" sounds: *ka, aka, akika, akara, akeke, akaka,* and so on, with tonal shifts left to point the way to meanings that are always verging on the meaningless. . . . The scene sounds like the song of Cock Robin turned tongue twister and illuminated by Beatrix Potter's sinister wit. The avatars of this wicked odu are viper, hedgehog, and snail. (*A Recitation of Ifa*, p. 143)

For more on divinations & randomness, etc., see pp. 536, 567, & *Symposium of the Whole*, pp. 147–154.

Page 185   LITTLE LEPER OF MUNJOLÓBO

Source: Peter Seitel, *See So That We May See: Performances & Interpretations of Traditional Tales from Tanzania* (Indiana University Press, 1980), pp. 107–111.

Narrative performances among the Haya take the form of tale-swapping sessions & reflect a value from childhood placed on "the use of artistic and intentionally ambiguous speech." As in other oral cultures, the process is active & depends on a close interplay between tellers & hearers—here summed up in the idea of a mutually shared "seeing" in which the audience encourages the narrator to "see" & "to project [the] images [of his tale] on an imaginary screen seen in their collective mind's eye. The narrator projects these images by 'seeing' them himself. He describes events as though they were occurring at that very moment; he becomes one character, then another, and 'sees' the events of a tale as they do." (Seitel, p. 28) This process of vision & enactment underlies the formularized opening of many of the tellings: "See so that we may see."

In bringing across this sense of an active & often highly individualized style, Seitel uses a series of typographical conventions related to the "system of notation" pioneered by Dennis Tedlock (see p. 549): simple line-breaks for a normal breath (about one second); stepped lines for a shorter pause; a longer pause marked by one or two circles (°, °°) at the left margin; LOUD VOICES BY ALL CAPS; d-r-a-w-n o-u-t w-o-r-d-s by hyphens; singsong intonations by italics. The result, as with the performances themselves, is a heightened sense of being in-the-story.

In "Little Leper," the *empindwi* is "an iron tool five or six inches long which resembles a needle and is used in decorative basket work." The formulaic opening (lines 1–4) was not in fact used in this version but added from elsewhere in Seitel's book as an indication to the reader of how-it-goes.

Page 191   THE VOICE OF THE KARAW

Source: Judith Gleason, *Leaf & Bone: African Praise-Poems* (Viking Press, New York, 1980), pp. 159–160. Translation from Dominique Zahan, *Sociétés d'initiation Bambara*, 1960, Vol. I, pp. 257–277.

Specialists of an already intricate use of voice & symbol, "the *karaw* (singular *kara*) are initiatory masters of the Bamanas' Kore society . . . the last of a sequence of six secret societies, in which man realizes mystic participation in the divine being." (Gleason, p. 175) But the word *karaw* also refers to objects used by the masters as specific symbols of knowledge & divinity: e.g., "a spatula-shaped plank of decorated wood—an emblem both of the enlightened and of the enlightening word. During karaw recitations this standard (some eight or nine feet high) is set on the ground. At mouth level (as though it were a flat, elongated mask) the kara has an opening, through which the spokesman puts the three central fingers of his left hand—tongues of the sacred utterance." Yori, the divinity of the present discourse, speaks to his initiates through such mouthpieces:

> He characterizes his mouthpieces as last-sunset-rays-attempting-to-penetrate-the-gathering-obscurity-of-the-mystery. They rip up and tear to shreds old misconceptions and spurious hypotheses. What seems twilight to them (they are at one point pictured as impatiently slapping the face of the setting sun) is in reality dawning, a new illumination announced by cockcrow. . . . The cock announces transformation, a process compared to the transmutation of matter in a smith's furnace: . . . a womb-shaped crucible out of which the liquid ore runs through a clay pipe into a trough. This structure and its function (as well as its symbolism) are compared to a clay hut of similar shape. . . . The initiate awaiting transformation and fusion with the divine essence is like a lover waiting in the antechamber while his mistress prepares the mat inside; he is like the penis beginning to enter the corridor. (Gleason, p. 176)

Two of four karaw discourses are given here. The voice of the kara(w) is in italics, that of the initiate in regular (roman) type.

Page 194 *GASSIRE'S LUTE*

Source: Leo Frobenius & Douglas C. Fox, *African Genesis* (Stackpole Sons, New York, 1937), pp. 97–109.

(1)

The blood
streams from the bodies of his sons
to feed the voice of Gassire's lute.

The men who mean good

must rage, grieve, turn with dismay

to see how "base and unjust actions, when they are the
objects of hope, are lovely to those that vehemently
admire them"

and how far men following self-interest can betray all
good of self.

(Robert Duncan, from *Passages 24*)

(2) The Soninke are a small remnant group now mostly Moslem &
inhabiting the desert oases of Tichit & Walatu in what used to be French
West Africa; but Fox suggests that the longer epic (*Dausi*) of which this is a
preserved fragment goes back to about 500 B.C., Wagadu being the legendary
city of the Fasa (Fezzan in Herodotus), the other cities mentioned having
ancient counterparts, etc. In the form given the song comes from the fourth
to twelfth centuries A.D. & was, so he tells us, the work of "troubadours."
Whatever its history, the poem's statement about the artist remains chilling.

(3)

A closed window looks down
on a dirty courtyard, and black people
call across or scream across or walk across
defying physics in the stream of their will

Our world is full of sound
Our world is more lovely than anyone's
tho we suffer, and kill each other
and sometimes fail to walk the air

We are beautiful people
with african imaginations
full of masks and dances and swelling chants
with african eyes, and noses, and arms,
though we sprawl in gray chains in a place
full of winters, when what we want is sun.

We have been captured,
brothers. And we labor

to make our getaway, into
the ancient image, into a new

correspondence with ourselves
and our black family. We need magic
now we need the spells, to raise up
return, destroy, and create. What will be

the sacred words?

> (Amiri Baraka [LeRoi Jones], from
> *Black Magic*)

Page 205 MIDĒ SONGS & PICTURE-SONGS

Source: W. J. Hoffman, *The Midēwiwin or 'Grand Medicine Society' of the Ojibwa*, Bureau of American Ethnology, Annual Report No. 7 (Washington, 1891).

The *Midēwiwin* ("society of the Midē or Shamans") consisted of four grades or degrees & involved a gradual opening-up of sense perception, powers to heal, etc. The myth-of-origin has it that Minabozho, servant of Dzhe Manido (the Midē guardian spirit), took pity on the Ojibwa ancestors, therefore delivered to "Otter" the mysteries of the Midēwiwin (sacred drum, rattles, shells, song, dance, etc.) & instructed him to pass them to the people.

The Midē songs were re-made by successive generations & recorded in pictographs "incised upon birchbark"—no mere mnemonic devices (as Hoffman gives them) but with independent meanings that varied from recorder to recorder. As verbal structures, the songs consisted (typically) of "a number of archaic words, some of which are furthermore different from the spoken language on account of their being chanted, & meaningless syllables introduced to prolong certain accentuated notes." The songs could also be repeated for as long as the singer chose—"the greater the number of repetitions . . . the greater is felt to be the amount of inspiration and power of the performance" (Hoffman, p. 164).

For more on picture-poems, etc., see pp. 26, 157, 281, & the accompanying commentaries.

Page 208 SEVEN CHIPPEWA (OJIBWA) SONGS

Source: Frances Densmore, *Chippewa Music* (Bureau of American Ethnology, Bulletins 45, 53 [Washington, 1910–1913]), passim.

Densmore makes each word of Chippewa equal a line of English (see note on Teton Sioux, following).

Song 2: The death-song was given in dream-vision or composed like this one at the time of death. The large bear was Gawitayac's "manido animal" in whose guidance he had trusted.

Song 4: war song, used in "dog feast" after eating of dog's head shortly before conclusion.

Song 5: A dream song . . . used in war dances.

Song 6: A Midē funeral song.

Song 7: The "game of silence" consisted of keeping still as long as possible in the face of nonsequential & far-out expressions meant to cause laughter.

Addenda. (1) The concreteness of the poems is in their images, which often touch indirectly (if at all) on the song's function; i.e., they suggest a "nonreferentiality" with relation to context, which they do not explain but within which they act.

(2) Kenneth Rexroth writes, specifically of materials collected by Densmore: ". . . Songs, like other things which we call works of art, occupy in American Indian society a position somewhat like the sacraments and sacramentals of the so-called higher religions. That is, the Indian poet is not only a prophet. Poetry or song does not only play a vatic role in the society, but is itself a numinous thing. The work of art is holy, in Rudolph Otto's sense—an object of supernatural awe, & as such, an important instrument in the control of reality on the highest plane" (*Assays*, pp. 56–57).

Page 210   From *THE WISHING BONE CYCLE*

Source: Howard Norman, *The Wishing Bone Cycle: Narrative Poems from the Swampy Cree Indians* (Ross-Erikson Publishing, Santa Barbara, [1972], 1982), pp. 5, 20, 33–34.

Trickster stories go far back in Cree culture (as elsewhere), but the figure here is the invention, specifically, of Jacob Nibenegenesabe, "who lived for some ninety-four years northeast of Lake Winnipeg, Canada." Nibenegenes-abe was also a teller (= *achimoo*) of older trickster narratives, the continuity between old & new never being in question. But the move in the Wishing Bone series is toward a rapidity of plot development & changes, plus a switch into first-person narration as a form of enactment. In the frame for these stories, the trickster figure "has found the wishbone of a snow goose who has wandered into the Swampy Cree region and been killed by a lynx. This person now has a wand of metamorphosis allowing him to wish anything into existence; himself into any situation" (p. 3). Norman's method of translation, in turn, involves "first listening to the narratives over & over in the source language, then re-creating them in the same context, story, etc., if not able, ultimately, to get a translation word for word."

The poems, as delivered here, represent a major example (both contemporary *and* tribal) of the "law of metamorphosis in thought & word" spoken of by Cassirer, the Surrealists, & others. (See above, p. 476; below, p. 589.) Thus Ezra Pound, circa 1918: "Our only measure of truth is . . . our perception of truth. The undeniable tradition of metamorphosis teaches us that things do not remain always the same. They become other things by swift and unanalysable process. It was only when men began to mistrust the myths and tell nasty lies for a moral purpose that these matters became hopelessly confused."

For more on tricksters, etc., see below, p. 548, & *Symposium of the Whole*, pp. 206, 425, 434.

Addenda.   Vicente Huidobro
                     From ALTAZOR

Tell me are you the son of Fisher Martin
Or are you the grandson of a stuttering stork
Or of that giraffe I see in the middle of the desert
Selfishly grazing on moon grass
Or are you the son of the hanged man who had pyramid eyes?
One day we'll know
And you'll die without your secret
And from your tomb will spring a rainbow like a bus
From the rainbow will spring a couple making love
From the love will spring a roving forest
From the forest will spring an arrow
From the arrow will spring a hare fleeing through the fields
From the hare will spring a ribbon to go marking its way
From the ribbon will spring a river and a waterfall that will save the hare
      from its pursuers

Until the hare begins to creep through a glance
And climbs to the bottom of the eye

> (Translation from Spanish by Stephen
> Fredman)

Page 213   *THREE TETON SIOUX SONGS*

Source: Frances Densmore, *Teton Sioux Music* (Bureau of American
Ethnology, Bulletin 61 [Washington, 1918]), pp. 180, 222, 237.

The first song was given by wolves in a dream; the second was sung by
Charging Thunder (Wakingyanwatakpe) who learned it from his father, Bear
Necklace (Matonapin). Song 3 was sung by Bear Eagle (Matowangbli) who
credited its making to Shell Necklace (Pangkeskanapin).

The lines of Densmore's translation correspond to single words in the
Sioux; thus each word of Sioux equals one line of English. The result,
accidental or otherwise, is to isolate the poem's structural properties (of stops
& starts, disjunctions, etc.) as basis for a new music of utterance in the
translation, providing a notation (including the parenthetical additions) that
closely parallels—remarkably so for the third song—the sound of much
contemporary poetry in English, e.g.:

Robert Creeley
I KNOW A MAN

As I sd to my
friend, because I am
always talking,—John, I

sd, which was not his
name, the darkness sur-
rounds us, what

can we do against
it, or else, shall we &
why not, buy a goddamn big car,

drive, he sd, for
christ's sake, look
out where yr going.

Page 215   From BATTISTE GOOD'S WINTER COUNT

Source: Garrick Mallery, *Picture-Writing of the American Indians* (Bureau of American Ethnology, Annual Report No. 10, [Washington, 1888–1889]), pp. 311–314.

Winter-counts (*waniyetu wowapi* in Dakota) were a widespread visual-verbal form among nineteenth-century Plains Indians. In his basic account of Indian picture-writing, Mallery defines them as "the use of events, which were in some degree historical, to form a system of chronology," i.e., to individualize each year (or winter) by a name describing an event within that year, and to record said name by a visual symbol or ideograph. While the events so selected may not always strike *us* as the most crucial—the defeat of Custer in 1876, say, isn't mentioned in most counts for that year—a story nevertheless emerges; and in the wedding of history & naming, a form in some sense suggestive of Pound's definition of epic as "a poem including history."

The ideographs were mostly drawn on buffalo hides & were organized into patterns ranging from columns to spirals. In Battiste Good's count, the ideographs appear in an ordinary paper drawing book and are painted with five colors besides black. His narrative includes a cyclical & mythic section covering the years 901 to 1700, after which the counting by year-names begins. The work is prefaced by the account of a personal vision & by a vision-drawing (for which see the Battiste Good entry in J. R.'s *Shaking the Pumpkin*, 1972).

Other Indian calendar works (moon-namings) appear also in *Shaking the Pumpkin*, & the reader may want to compare these to Alexander Marshack's reconstruction of a paleolithic sequence from Europe (p. 321).

Page 218   PEYOTE SONGS

Source: Translations by David P. McAllester, as sung by Tewaki, in McAllester, *Peyote Music* (Viking Fund Publications in Anthropology, New York, 1949).

Peyote religion in the United States goes back to at least the 1870s & was carried on thereafter through the visions of men like John Wilson, John Rave, et al. The poetry of the songs given here is typical of one line of image-making (phanopoetic) language: precise & minimal in its namings (though the practice here, as elsewhere, would be to extend the words through many repetitions). The content of each song is then itself a kind of vision—self-contained if one takes it to be so.

The reader may want to compare these songs—as poetry—with Australian Aborigine practice of the Kunapipi type (p. 392) or with the series of "images" presented on p. 15. A poem from the older Huichol peyote religion in Mexico appears on p. 231, commentary on p. 553.

Page 219   *SONG OF THE HUMPBACKED FLUTE PLAYER*

Source: Frank Waters & Oswald White Bear Fredericks, *Book of the Hopi* (Viking Press, New York, 1963, Penguin Books, 1977, pp. 38–39.

Frank Waters writes that the "locust *máhu* [insect which has the heat power] is known as the Humpbacked Flute Player, the *kachina* [spirit of the invisible forces of life] named Kókopilau, because he looked like the wood [*koko*—wood; *pilau*—hump]. In the hump on his back he carried seeds of plants and flowers"—the kachina doll often depicted with long penis to signify the sexual root of the power—"and with the music of his flute he created warmth." During the early migrations Kókopilau "would stop and scatter seeds from the hump on his back. Then he would march on, playing his flute and singing a song. His song is still remembered, but the words are so ancient that nobody knows what they mean." The resulting text bears inevitable resemblance to many varieties of wordless poetry, such as Indian songs, magical spells & mantras, medieval tropes, & the conscious sound poetry of more recent years (see pp. 8, 361, 387, & commentaries).

Addenda.

> In Canyon de Chelly on the North Wall up by a cave
> is the hump backed flute player laying on his back,
> playing his flute. Across the flat sandy canyon wash,
> wading a stream and breaking through the ice, on the
> south wall, the pecked-out pictures of some Mountain Sheep
> with curling horns. They stood in the icy shadow of the
> south wall two hundred feet away; I sat with my
> shirt off in the sun facing south, with the hump
> backed flute player just above my head.

They whispered; I whispered; back and forth
across the canyon, clearly heard.

> (From Gary Snyder, "The Hump
> Backed Flute Player")

Page 220   *COYOTE & JUNCO*

Source: Dennis Tedlock, *Finding the Center: Narrative Poetry of the Zuni Indians* (Dial Press, New York, 1972), pp. 77–83.

Junco shirt—Old Lady Junco is an Oregon junco, & her "shirt" is the hood-like area of dark gray or black that covers the head, neck, & part of the breast of this species. (D.T.)

Prairie Wolf—Alternative term for coyote, introduced by the translator to match a similar term in the original.

Son'ahchi, Lee semkonikya—Formulaic openings & closings of Zuni narratives.

Although Trickster took many forms in the Americas (Raven, Rabbit, Mink, Flint, Spider, Bluejay, Jaguar, etc.), his manifestation as Coyote has had the greatest carryover into contemporary American culture. Writes Gary Snyder: "Of all the uses of native American lore in modern poetry, the presence of the Coyote figure, the continuing presence of Coyote, is the most striking." And Simon Ortiz, from the older perspective of Acoma Pueblo brought into "modern times":

> ". . . you know, Coyote
> is in the origin and all the way
> through . . . he's the cause
> of the trouble, the hard times
> that things have. . . ."
> "Yet, he came so close
> to having it easy.
>   But he said,
> "Things are too easy. . . ."
> Of course, he was mainly bragging,
> shooting his mouth.
> The existential Man,
> a Dostoevsky Coyote.

In the present version, as one Zuni listener told Dennis Tedlock, Coyote is "just being very foolish"—a far cry, perhaps, from his work as Creator or from the tragic, obscene, & terrifying sides of him that turn up elsewhere. (See, e.g., *Shaking the Pumpkin*, pp. 102–116, 274–275, for a string of such versions: "*with blood-stained mouth / comes mad Coyote!*")

(2) Tedlock's translation is also an example of a method of representing narrative-as-performance that he pioneered & that informs a number of the translations in the present revised volume. His position has been amply set out in his own publications but also in the present editor's *Shaking the Pumpkin* and *Symposium of the Whole*. For sounding "Coyote & Junco," the reader should observe that line changes = a pause of less than one second, double spaces between lines = a two- to three-second pause, CAPITALS = loud words & passages, smaller print = soft ones, long dashes after vowels = vowels to be held for about two seconds, a line or phrase set on different levels = line to be chanted with an interval of about three half-tones between levels. Other keys to reading aloud are given, like stage directions, in parentheses.

Page 224   *THE TENTH HORSE SONG OF FRANK MITCHELL*

Source: Jerome Rothenberg's translation from the Navajo, as originally published in J. Rothenberg, *The 17 Horse Songs of Frank Mitchell X–XIII* (Tetrad Press, London, 1970).

[A NOTE ON TRANSLATION AS "TOTAL TRANSLATION"]: "The sounding presented here is the score for my experimental translation of the tenth of seventeen Navajo 'horse songs' in the blessingway of Frank Mitchell (1881–1967) of Chinle, Arizona. Their power, as with most Navajo poetry, is directed toward blessing & curing, but in the course of it they also depict the stages by which Enemy Slayer, on instructions from his mother, Changing Woman, goes to the house of his father, The Sun, to receive & bring back horses for The People. The Tenth Song marks the point in the narrative where Enemy Slayer receives the horses & instructions to bring them to the house of Changing Woman. The dialogue therein is between Enemy Slayer (= Dawn Boy) & The Sun.

"With the help of ethnomusicologist David McAllester, I attempted a number of 'total translations' from the horse songs—total in the sense that I was accounting not only for meaning but for word distortions, meaningless syllables, music, style of performance, etc. The idea never was to set English words to Navajo music but to let a whole work—words & music—emerge newly in the process of considering what kinds of statement were there to begin with. As far as I could I also wanted to avoid 'writing' the poem in English, since this seemed irrelevant to a poetry that reached a high development outside of any written system.

"Under the best of circumstances translation-for-meaning is no more than partial translation. Even more so for the densely textured Navajo. To present what's essentially a sound-poem, a *total* translation must distort words in a manner analogous to the original; it must match 'meaningless' syllables with equivalents in our very different English soundings; it may begin to sing in a mode suitable to the words of the translation; & if the original provides for more than one voice, the translation will also. Does so, in fact, in the final recorded version as I've come to it.

"In all this what matters to me most as a poet is that the process has been a very natural one of extending the poetry into new areas of sound. Nor do I think of the result as poetry plus something else, but as *all* poetry, *all* poets' work, just as the Navajo is all poetry, where poetry & music haven't suffered separation. In that sense Frank Mitchell's gift has taken me a small way toward a new 'total poetry,' as well as an experiment in total translation. And that, after all, is where many of us had been heading in the first place." (J. R., *Poems for the Game of Silence*, p. 159)

Page 226 *A SONG OF THE WINDS*

Source: Dane & Mary Roberts Coolidge, *The Last of the Seris* (E. P. Dutton & Co., New York, 1939), p. 216.

Santo Blanco was one of the few Seris to keep the songs in anything like their old form. He had seen the god of the cave too & described him as follows:

He lives in a little cave inside the big cave. I could see through him when he walked toward us, yet I was conscious he was coming closer and closer, until he was a hand's length from my face. It was dark as night, but I could see him. His arms were stretched out and his hands were hanging down, and from their tips water dripped. It was like ice. He came to me very slowly, and held his fingers over my head. He came again and spread his hands over me, and from the finger-tips I caught water in my palms.

The water is holy of course & cures—& he renews his supply of it (of the songs also?) by returning to the cave. Then

> . . . the Spirit comes out of his inner cave and sings. The Spirit is a god, but not like the God of the Gringos. He is very much more beautiful than He Who Rules Heaven and Earth, the God in the sky. He has a white hat and a black coat, very long. To his ankles. Inside this black coat there are all kinds of bright colors. (Coolidge, pp. 94–95)

Page 227 SIX SERI WHALE SONGS

Source: Dane & Mary Roberts Coolidge, *The Last of the Seris* (E. P. Dutton & Co., New York, 1939), pp. 68–69.

> "For that strange spectacle observable in all Sperm Whales dying—the turning sunwards of the head, and so expiring—that strange spectacle, beheld of such a placid evening, somehow to Ahab conveyed a wondrousness unknown before.
> "He turns and turns him to it—how slowly, but how steadfastly, his homage-rendering and invoking brow, with his last dying motions. He too worships fire; most faithful, broad, baronial vassal of the sun!"
> —Herman Melville, *Moby Dick*

Or Paulé Bartón (1916–1974), Haitian goatherd & poet:

GOING OUT TO MEET THE MOON WHALES

It was time:
>> high in the round fruit trees
>> we saw them passing
>> under the moon.

The manta rays lining up
>> to slowly flap their wings.
Then we floated out
>> on the manta waves.
There was no time
>> we were happier.

Whales, look,
I have not died too young:

I floated out
    in the wood boat
I was born in fifty years ago,
      when the moon whales were swimming here.

(Translation from the Creole by Howard Norman)

o o o o

For more on the author of the Seri whale songs, Santo Blanco, see the preceding note.

Page 229 FLOWER WORLD: THREE POEMS FROM THE YAQUI DEER DANCE

Source: J. R.'s setting of texts from Carleton S. Wilder, *The Yaqui Deer Dance: A Study in Cultural Change* (Bureau of American Ethnology, Bulletin 186 [Washington, 1963]), pp. 176–177, 181, 187–188.

"Flower world," "enchanted world" & "wilderness world" are among the English terms used to describe the other-than-human domain surrounding the settled Yaqui villages: "a region of untamed things into which man's influence does not extend" (E. Spicer). In mythic times that world (*huya aniya*) may have been *everything*, later reduced (so Edward Spicer tells us) "to a specialized part of a larger whole, rather than the whole itself. . . . Not replaced, as the Jesuits would have wished . . . it became the other world, the wild world surrounding the towns." (*The Yaquis*, p. 65) Within the frame of a native & independent Catholicism, it persists in the present, into which it brings the mythic figures of sacred Deer Dancer & Pascola clowns. The songs accompanying the very taut, very classical Deer Dance are, in their totality, an extraordinary example of traditional poesis: the cumulative construction by word & image of that Flower World from which the dancer comes.

For more on the traditional uses of flower imagery, etc., see pp. 81, 501, above.

Addenda. (1) "Our eyes remain on the surface, like water flowers, behind which we hide, our trembling bodies floating in an unseen world" (Federico García Lorca).

(2)   George Oppen
                              PSALM

                          Veritas sequitur . . .

In the small beauty of the forest
The wild deer bedding down—
That they are there!

                              Their eyes
Effortless, the soft lips
Nuzzle and the alien small teeth
Tear at the grass

                        The roots of it
Dangle from their mouths
Scattering earth in the strange woods.
They who are there.

                              Their paths
Nibbled thru the fields, the leaves that shade them
Hang in the distances
Of sun

                        The small nouns
Crying faith
In this in which the wild deer
Startle, and stare out.

Page 231 TO FIND OUR LIFE

Source: Peter Furst, "To Find Our Life: Peyote Among the Huichol
Indians of Mexico," in P. Furst, ed., *Flesh of the Gods: The Ritual Use of
Hallucinogens* (Praeger Publishers, New York, 1972), pp. 183–184.

The Huichol "peyote hunt" is part of a ceremonial, 250-mile pilgrimage
called "finding (or seeing) our life": a virtual return-to-paradise as the
Huichol place-of-origin (Wirikuta), to become in that process the god-like
ancestors who first made the journey. Toward this end the Huichol shaman
(*mara'akame*) functions as director & creator (= poet), who uses language to
transform the immediate landscape into the mythic one of Wirikuta.

Through language, then, as much as peyote, the shaman changes the desert into a flower world, the departure from which becomes a cause for lamentation. The event throughout is both a sacred enactment & a narrative: "the story of our roots," the shaman tells us. And again: "This comes to us from ancient, ancient times. . . . This is a story from those very ancient times. . . . [It] is a beautiful thing, that which is our life. It is the *hikuri* [peyote]. . . . It is like a beautiful flower, as one says. It is like the Deer. It is our life. We must go so that it will enable us to see our life." (Furst, p. 145)

The maker here is Ramón Medina Silva, a mara'akame & artist, who is also credited by Furst as the originator, circa 1965, of contemporary large-scale Huichol yarn-painting. Of the shaman's function as proto-poet, Medina Silva himself says: "It is the mara'akame who directs everything. He is the one who listens in his dream, with his power and his knowledge. . . . Then he says to his companions, look, now we will change everything, all the meanings, because that is the way it must be. . . . As it was in Ancient Times, so that all can be united." (From B. Myerhoff, *Peyote Hunt*, p. 185)

For more on Huichol poetics, etc., see *Shaking the Pumpkin*, pp. 362–65, & *Symposium of the Whole*, pp. 116–118, 225–231.

Page 233 THE PAINTED BOOK

Source: Translations by Miguel León-Portilla, *Native Mesoamerican Spirituality* (Paulist Press, New York, 1980), pp. 251–252, 244–245, 241–242.

From Mexico & elsewhere in Mesoamerica arise generations of pre-Conquest poets & books: a written tradition that reenforces & expands the spoken one. The poets' names too (at least twenty by León-Portilla's account) are here visible—but, above all, Nezahualcoyotl (1402–1472), author of more than thirty surviving compositions & chief of Texcoco for over forty years. While the tradition would still seem to be oral, the writings/paintings enter as a real presence: on stone monuments, fired vases, & painted books or "screenfolds." The latter were "made of animal skins or of the *amate*-tree bark, duly prepared so as to be transformed into a kind of thick paper"; & the writing itself took the form of pictographs ("schematic drawings of objects" & events), ideograms ("symbolic representations of ideas"), & some limited forms of phonetic transcription. (León-Portilla, p. 32) But whatever the "limits" of the form, the idea of "book" & of the man painting ideas (or having ideas painted through him) becomes, as here, the central image of a life lived with some hope of meaning.

Of all of that, fewer than twenty painted books have survived from Mesoamerica—their precise reading a continuing puzzle. Among the poets' names mentioned by Léon-Portilla & here given for the record are: Tlaltecatzin of Cuauhchinanco, Nezahualcoyotl, Cuacuauhtzin of Tepechpan, Nezahualpilli, Cacamatzin, Tochihuitzin Coyolchiuhqui, Axayacatl, Temilotzin, Tecayehuatzin of Huexotzinco, Ayocuan Cuetzpaltzin, Xicohtencatl of Tlaxcala, Chichicuepon of Chalco, & the poetess Macuilxochitzin. The name Nezahualcoyotl means Hungry Coyote.

Page 236 *From CODEX BOTURINI: THE ORIGIN OF THE MEXICA AZTECS*

Source: Karl Young's "reading" of the first four pages of the Aztec Codex Boturini. Previously unpublished.

One of a small number of surviving native books—pre- & post-Conquest—the manuscript in question exists now only as a 22-page fragment, tracing the origins & early wanderings of the Mexicas, or Aztecs. It was produced in or around Mexico City/Tenochtitlan soon after the Conquest, but shows a developed style: a simplified depiction of figures & ideas that was *one* of a number of Mexican possibilities. "As it now remains," writes Young, "the book is a strip of amatl (fig bark) paper approximately 19 cm tall and 549 cm long, folded accordion fashion into pages averaging about 24 cm across. The figures are drawn in black ink. Except for a reddish ink connecting dates, no color is used. . . . Where composition in most indigenous books is dense and crowded, suggesting the patterns in oriental rugs to some commentators, this is not the case in Codex Boturini. The scribe, as Donald Robertson has pointed out, leaves generous areas of open space, at times suggesting a spaceless landscape, an open field in which persons, dates, and place names can interact in freedom and solitude. . . . The style of Codex Boturini is deceptively simple: . . . its artist was a master who deserves our respect."

As with much Middle American writing, the Aztec system was open: a work to be interpreted, not spelled out word for word—or, as Young suggests, "despite the strong visual character of the codices, writing was an adjunct to speech in pre-Conquest Mexico and books were essentially tools for oral performance." A poet & printer himself, Young offers a minimal reading based on the relative agreements among students of the Codex. In so doing, he writes, "I have identified the icons and indicated their functions in blocks of type. I have placed these blocks of type inside rectangles below the facsimile, the placement of each block of type corresponding to the position on the page of the figure being interpreted. The facsimile is my own redrawing of the manuscript pages, rather than a photographic reproduction."

For more on the "painted books," etc., see the preceding commentary & poems.

Page 240 *From THE POPOL VUH: BLOOD-GIRL &*
THE CHIEFS OF HELL

Source: Munro S. Edmonson, *The Book of Counsel: The Popol Vuh of the Quiché Maya of Guatemala* (Middle American Research Institute, Publication 35, Tulane University, 1971).

The Popol Vuh, literally "the book of the community" (or "commonhouse" or "council"), was preserved by Indians in Santo Tomás Chichicastenango, Guatemala, & in the eighteenth century given to Father Francisco Ximénez who transcribed & put it into Spanish; vanished again & rediscovered in the 1850s by Carl Scherzer & Abbé Charles Etienne Brasseur de Bourbourg. It existed in picture-writing before the Conquest, & the version used by Father Ximénez (& since lost) may have been the work, circa 1550, of one Diego Reynoso. The book "contains the cosmogonical concepts and ancient traditions of [the Quiché nation], the history of their origin, and the chronicles of their kings down to the year 1550."

The maiden's sons, Hunahpú & Xbalanqué, later go the same road to Hell (= Xibalba), where they beat its rulers at ball & by surviving ordeals in the houses of torture.

While the poems are rich in local details, there are many motifs & myths too that are "universal"—of twin heroes, underworld trees, forbidden fruit, impregnation by tree &/or spittle, heroic labors, etc. But above all—as Munro Edmonson writes—it is about "the goodness of Quiché: the people, the place, and the religious mysteries which were all called by that name. It is a tragic theme, but its treatment is not tragic: it is Mayan."

Edmonson's translation gets away from the prose of all earlier ones (including the written Quiché) to assert an original "entirely composed in parallelistic (i.e., semantic) couplets," much of it governed by a process he calls "keying . . . in which two successive lines may be quite diverse but must share key words which are closely linked in meaning. Many of these are traditional pairs: sun-moon, day-light, deer-bird, black-white, [but] sometimes the coupling is opaque in English, however clear it may be in Quiché, as in white-laugh," etc.

Page 243 *MAYAN DEFINITIONS*

Source: Allan F. Burns, *An Epoch of Miracles: Oral Literature of the Yucatec Maya* (University of Texas Press, 1983), pp. 240–243.

"The oral literature of the Yucatec Maya can be best understood as a poetic form of speech in which performance is a dominant characteristic. As poetry, Yucatec Mayan oral literature does not rely on long, detailed descriptions of the context of events but, rather, assumes that the context can be understood by prosodic features such as voice quality, repetition of words and phrases, and gestures. Many of the narratives are short, lasting only a few minutes. This brevity is understandable if the forms are considered as poetic performances where well-chosen words and phrases are imaginative shortcuts to mythic concepts and actions. . . .

"The 'definitions' [for which Burns also implies a performative/narrative aspect] were either written down by Alonzo Gonzales Mó or dictated to me. They are experimental forms of verbal art in that they were created in order to teach me how to speak Mayan. They can also make up parts of natural conversations where such wordplay is appreciated. The form of these definitions may well be an ancient one, however, as seen in the books of Chilam Balam and the eleventh book of the Florentine Codex of the Aztecs, which contain similar items." (Burns, pp. 15, 238)

For a comparison with the ancient "Aztec definitions," see above, p. 20.

Page 246 *From INATOIPIPPILER*

Source: Nils Holmer & S. Henry Wassén, *Inatoipippiler, or The Adventures of Three Cuna Boys* (Etnologiska Studier No. 20 [Göteborg, Sweden, 1952]).

Uncle Oloyailer—name of a sea monster (*yailler* = "an animal like a seal," but the singer explains it by *nali e tule* = "shark man").

Uncle Nia—spirit owner of a fortress reached by Inatoipippiler in his undersea journey.

Sometime around 1840, three boys from Portogandí (on the San Blas coast of Panama) went fishing & didn't return. A *nele* (wise-man with shamanic powers) was consulted, who revealed facts about the disappearance that form the basis of the poem. The boys, about ten years old, were never seen again & are said to have been drowned in an eddy.

The song/poem is attributed to Akkantilele ("the *nele* of Acandí") who composed it ten days after the disaster; the present version by Belisario Guerrero (Maninibigdinapi) apparently comes in a direct line of transmission, poet to poet. Though based on an actual event, the images are vsionary & in the universal tradition of underworld journeys.

"Songs of this kind," the translators tell us, "are usually accompanied by a monotonous chant rather than singing, every line or section beginning high and gradually falling off, amidst modulations upward and downward into a prolonged cadence. . . . Repetitions are multiplied at choice, so that the singer, when he takes his time, may not be through singing until the morning hours." The lines of the original vary greatly in length.

Addenda. Not apparent in the translation is the use of a special narrative mode that shifts the perspective from third to first person, both to make the historical time immediate & to freely interiorize some of the objective material. Thus "they are approaching the ship" is literally "you are approaching my ship," & (more surprisingly) "the southwind is making a noise" is literally "making a noise in me"; or elsewhere "they go to the loft to sleep when midnight has come" is literally "when you have come in me." The translators write: "This represents the boys' thoughts; such quasi-dialogue constructions are peculiar to Cuna poetic language."

For more on such shifts, etc., see the note on the Fijian "Flight of the Chiefs," page 623, below. The most obvious modern analogues are stream-of-consciousness writers like Joyce or Faulkner, but something of the kind informs most contemporary experiments with structuring, composition-by-field, etc.

Page 249 *From THE ELEGY FOR THE
GREAT INCA ATAWALLPA*
Page 251 *THREE QUECHUA POEMS*

Sources: Workings of Spanish translations from "Incan" sources by W. S. Merwin, *Selected Translations 1968–1978* (Atheneum, New York, 1979), pp. 72, 73–74, 76. (The "elegy" is otherwise unpublished.)

Atawallpa (d. 1533), one of the last conflicting rulers of the Inca Empire, took control by force from his half-brother, Huascar, but was himself imprisoned & executed by Pizarro.

The Elegy & the three Quechua poems represent various modes of native poesis pre- & post-Conquest.

○ ○ ○ ○ ○ ○ ○

"An Indian [Incan] poet, called a *harauec*, that is, an inventor, composed quantities of . . . verses of all kinds. . . . The verses were composed in different meters, some short & others long . . . but they were as terse & precise as mathematics. There was no assonance, each verse being free. . . . I recall a love song, composed of four lines, from which may be judged the austerity of these terse compositions I spoke of; here it is with the translation:

Caylla llapi	To this tune
Puñunqui	you will sleep
Chaupituta	At midnight
Samusac	I shall come."

(Thus: Garcilaso de la Vega, *The Royal Commentaries of the Inca*. Born 1539, died 1616, he was the son of an Incan princess & a Spanish conquistador. He & Pomo de Ayala [*Nueva crónica y buen gobierno*] are the chief early chroniclers of Incan history, etc.)

Page 254 POEMS FOR A CARNIVAL

Source: Translations by Gordon Brotherston (with Ed Dorn) from Quechua texts with Spanish translations in Jesus Lara, *Poesía popular quechua* (Editorial Canata, La Paz, 1947). The English versions appeared in *Alcheringa*, old series, no. 3 (Winter, 1971): 58–59, & the central poem appeared also in Brotherston's *Image of the New World* (Thames & Hudson, London, 1979).

Contemporary "needling" pieces—writes Brotherston—"in the mode of the satirical *wawaki* songs once sung at the old Moon festival, and sung today to elicit *chicha* (maize beer) from bystanders during Carnival in Cochabamba (Bolivia). [Such a song] intimidates obliquely, with its suggestions of a hollow laugh, like that uttered by the satirists of Inca times through their skull masks." (*Image of the New World*, p. 278)

Page 255 RAISING THE MEDIATING CENTER AND
THE FIELD OF EVIL

Source: Transcription & translation by F. Kaye Sharon in Eduardo Calderón, et al., *Eduardo el Curandero: The Words of a Peruvian Healer* (North Atlantic Books, Richmond, California, 1982), pp. 54–57.

"Eduardo Calderón Palomino"—writes David Guss in summary—"is a *curandero* from the Trujillo area of Northern Peru, a region famous for its practitioners of the healing arts. Common to the practice of *curanderismo* in this area is the use of a *mesa* [table], an altarlike assemblage of 'artifacts' arranged in various fields of power. With the aid of chants and a hallucinogen made from the San Pedro cactus, these artifacts are manipulated during the healing ceremony in order to give the *curandero* the *cuenta* or 'account' necessary to diagnose his patient. This 'account,' transpiring between the *curandero* and his *mesa*, is a psychic reading that depends on the healer's ability to locate the appropriate 'artifact' through which the spirit will speak.

"Every *curandero*'s *mesa* is unique. Eduardo's is divided into three fields: that of the right, the *Campo Justiciero*, 'the Field of the Divine Judge'; that of the middle, the *Campo Medio*, the mediating 'Field of San Cyprian'; and that of the left, the *Campo Ganadero*, 'the Field of Satan,' also known as 'the Field of the Sly Dealer.' Carefully arranged on these three fields are more than seventy artifacts that include, among other things, shells, stones, crystals, rattles, daggers, tobacco, pre-Columbian shards, post-Conquest *santos*, and bottles of herbs, perfumes, and holy water. Ringing the back of the *mesa* is a row of staffs and swords which Eduardo refers to as the antennae that help transmit the 'accounts.' The attention of the seance is on balancing the energies of these different fields. Only in this way can the patient also regain the 'balance of power' which is at the very center of Eduardo's philosophy of healing." (From "Reading the Mesa: An Interview with Eduardo Calderón by David Guss," in *New Wilderness Letter* 11 [December, 1982]: 20)

In the present segment from a longer healing session, it is the middle & the left "fields" that are being raised or activated. The ceremony as a whole—like so much numinous poetry at-its-roots—involves a juxtaposition/collage of contrary meanings toward the creation of a new—& functional—"work."

Addenda. (1) The reader can compare Eduardo's procedure with divination & healing practices from the Ifa Oracle (pp. 81, 537) & the Chinese *I Ching* (pp. 457, 567), among many others.

(2) Calderón's poetics (of which, as an artist himself, he is clearly conscious) emphasizes the role of "mind" (*mente*) in contrast to the literalisms of "witchcraft," etc. In response to the question, "Is it true that witches fly," he responds: "That witches fly, that's asinine. What flies is the astral body, the double, the result of the vibration of man. There is nothing of the other world. The mind is what makes one fly. This is what's called the sense of ubiquitousness, or of transportation across distance, across matter. For ex-

ample, I am working here at my *mesa*, but my mind is elevating itself so that I can go to the United States, or to Virú Valley. This is a person's mental force, nothing more, as well as the element of the 'herb' (the potions that I drink) working united with it, that activates the 'third eye,' the 'sixth sense.' What works is the mind. Sorcery, hexing, and curing are there. Without this, there is nothing." And again: "A ruin is never going to 'speak,' except if one's mind gives it magnetic power, gives it force. For this reason, we should not confuse ourselves that the spirit, that the evil shadows, frighten us, kill us. One frightens oneself; it is not the shadow that frightens one." (*Eduardo el Curandero*, pp. 36–38)

Page 260 THE MACHI EXORCISES THE SPIRIT HUECUVE

Source: Armand Schwerner's translation from Georgette & Jacques Soustelle, *Folklore Chilien* (Insitut International de Cooperation Intellectuelle, Paris, 1938), p. 84, but originally collected by Rodolfo Lenz, circa 1897.

Writes Schwerner, after Soustelle: "The Machi is a sorceress and healer. Men are rarely machis; when they are they let their hair grow and usually dress like women." In the exorcism the Machi works on the actual malignant spirit, whose external appearance is that of a cowhide: sometimes no more formed than that, at other times an octopus inhabiting lakes & rivers & crushing its victims in its folds. As spirit it invades the body of an animal or person, causing its victim to die of consumption. Its obvious preference is for rich people.

Page 261 WORDS FROM SEVEN MAGIC SONGS

Source: Workings by Rochelle Owens after Knud Rasmussen, *Intellectual Culture of the Copper Eskimos* (Report of the Fifth Thule Expedition [Copenhagen, 1932]), pp. 112–118.

Tatilgäk explained: "One makes magic songs when a man's thoughts begin to turn towards another or something that does not concern him; without his hearing it, one makes magic songs so that there may be calm in his mind, to make his thoughts pleasant—for a man is dangerous when he is angry."

Of the words in those songs, Knud Rasmussen wrote as translator: "Translating magic words is a most difficult matter, because they often consist of untranslatable compounds of words, or fragments that are supposed to have their strength in their mysteriousness"—*coefficient of weirdness* in Malinowski's good term for it (p. 442)—"or in the manner in which words are coupled together." Obviously comprehension by others isn't the issue here "as long as the spirits know what it is that one wants"—although the level of articulation would seem to have varied from shaman to shaman. For example, the poet Orpingalik (see the following commentary) "uttered [his magic words] in a whisper, but most distinctly & with emphasis on every word. His speech was slow, often with short pauses between the words. I have endeavored to show the pauses by means of a new line of verse"—that last a clear insight on Rasmussen's part of poetry's origins in other-than-song.

   Addenda.   Rochelle Owens's most elaborate working of Eskimo data is in her play, *The String Game*: a use of "distant" materials to trace the dimensions of the human. Also in some poems, like the following.

o o o o

Rochelle Owens
SONG OF MEAT, MADNESS & TRAVEL

I

dried meat

> O glorious is dried meat.
> my wife's breast in my hand
> we stare at dried meat
>> is it not strange?

II

I pity her

> now I pity her   the woman the woman
> who calls
> in a voice of white madness
>> Let me fetch you, let me fetch you!

III

I desired to go north

> as a great singer and dancer

>   my ears my ears
>   there is singing in them
>   The big caribou cows and the big bulls
>   and men
>
>   watch for me

Page 262 MY BREATH

Source: Tom Lowenstein, *Eskimo Poems from Canada & Greenland* (Allison & Busby, London, 1973), pp. 38–40. (Lowenstein's translations, with Ida Lowenstein, are from material originally collected & translated into Danish by Knud Rasmussen.)

Orpingalik (the name means man-with-willow-twig) was a shaman, poet, & hunter, "notably intelligent & having a fertile wit" (writes Rasmussen), who could move, like other big poets, between personal modes (as here) & "magic words" given elsewhere in these pages (for which, see the preceding commentary). Obviously into it up to his elbows, he called this song "my breath" because (he said) "it is just as necessary for me to sing as it is to breathe." (The Netsilik word *anerca* is used in fact to mean both "breath" & "poetry.") The breath, which is all the more visible where he came from (in the language of the Netsilik shamans, e.g., a living person is "someone smoke surrounds"), becomes the physical projection of the process of thought, etc., that goes on inside a man. Orpingalik's extraordinary definition of poetry—"songs are thoughts sung out with the breath" (for which see p. 430)—describes an order of composition something like "projective verse": the rediscovery, that is, of a poetics-of-the-breath that marked a major line of the "new American poetry" from the 1950s on. In Charles Olson's classic formulation, circa 1950: "If I hammer, if I recall in, and keep calling in, the breath, the breathing as distinguished from the hearing, it is for cause, it is to insist upon a part that breath plays in verse which has not . . . been sufficiently observed or practiced, but which has to be if verse is to advance to its proper force and place in the day, now, and ahead. I take it that PROJECTIVE VERSE teaches, is, this lesson, that that verse will only do in which a poet manages to register both the acquisitions of his ear *and* the pressures of his breath."

Page 265 ESKIMO PROSE POEMS

Source: Knud Rasmussen, *Intellectual Culture of the Iglulik Eskimos*, translated by William Worster (Copenhagen, 1930), pp. 268, 304, 255.

The content isn't original—only the way-of-its-going. The larva-child, e.g., turns up in variants among other Eskimo groups Rasmussen recorded, but only here touches home, as something other than fantasy. The editor recalls a similar account in Swanton's *Tlingit Myths & Texts*—that one dealing with a chief's daughter who rears a woodworm which, killed by the town, becomes a clan emblem, the girl's four songs to the worm-child repeated at feasts, etc. Ivaluardjuk uses the material much differently, not to define-the-origin-of but to let the language force the mind toward a lonely & disturbing vision-of-the-real. A master of tht mode—like Russell Edson.

o o o o o o o

Russell Edson
AN AIR BABY

A woman had an air baby, with little dust eyes that wink and blink in the sunlight.

But one day she breathed deeply and breathed her little baby into herself. So that she breathes out as hard as she can. No, that is not my baby. And she breathes out again as hard as she can. No, that is not my baby either.

Nothing is your baby, you foolish dog sitting there panting, says her husband.

No, no, I breathed it in, I sucked it out of my arms into my nose.

You foolish dog, how dare you treat my unknown heir like a smell.

I had it here: it had just wet its diapers and I was just about to throw it on the floor for wetting on me. I was just summoning my breath to jump on it for wetting on me. I was just drawing deeply on the atmosphere in preparation for the punitive feat. And I drew it into one of my nostrils, or both, breaking it between my nostrils.

You are the cruel mother that eats back her young, says her husband.

And why should I not?

Because you eat well enough without that. Why just the other day I brought you a lovely insect, remember, six legs? and how you baked it in the oven? remember how I climbed on your back and said take me to Market street, where I bought you a cookbook? and we looked through it for a recipe for baked baby, and there was none? And how you baked the cookbook and how really good it was? Don't you remember anything?

I remember something that I never had.

Page 271   THE QUEST OF MILAREPA

Source: Selected from Sir Humphrey Clarke, *The Message of Milarepa* (John Murray, London, 1958), pp. 1–2, 6–9.

Mila, his actual name; *repa*, the cotton-clad, a title of those who, like him, had learned to withstand the Himalayan cold through inner heat, etc.
Tsangpo—the Brahmaputra.
Mount Tisé & Lake Mapang at its foot—originally the holy places of the Bon Shamans whom Milarepa, having proved their master in magic, dispossessed in the name of Buddhism.

In Milarepa's *Life*, "as chronicled by his favorite disciple Rechung . . . we learn how, after his father's untimely death, he and his mother and sisters were despoiled of their patrimony; how he ran away . . . and learnt the black arts from a local sorcerer; conjured up a hailstorm which ruined their crops and caused the roof of their house to fall in and kill their guests at a harvest festival; how remorse overcame him; how he then set out to find the truth and met his teacher Marpa; how Marpa, as penance, for seven years disciplined him savagely till even his spirit was almost broken, but finally initiated him; how after long contemplation in his mountain solitudes he finally attained enlightenment and was consecrated by Marpa as his successor; and how he lived to a ripe old age, teaching the faith and working miracles . . ." (Clarke, *The Message*, xi–xii).

Addenda.   (1) For more on Marpa, Tibetan Buddhism & its relation to Bon shamanism, etc., see p. 484.

(2) The sacralization-of-the-everyday has been a rite of modern poetry since Baudelaire's perception (circa 1846) of the "heroism of everyday life." It takes many forms, but the reader at this point may especially enjoy comparing Mila's "cotton shirt" with the following.

∘ ∘ ∘ ∘

Pablo Neruda
ODE TO MY SOCKS

Maru Mori brought me
a pair
of socks
which she knitted herself
with her sheep-herder's hands,
two socks as soft
as rabbits.
I slipped my feet
into them
as though into
two
cases
knitted
with threads of
twilight
and goatskin.
Violent socks,
my feet were
two fish made
of wool,
two long sharks
seablue, shot
through
by one golden thread,
two immense blackbirds,
two cannons,
my feet
were honored
in this way
by
these
heavenly
socks.

They were
so handsome
for the first time
my feet seemed to me
unacceptable
like two decrepit
firemen, firemen
unworthy
of that woven
fire,
of those glowing
socks.

Nevertheless
I resisted
the sharp temptation
to save them somewhere
as students
keep
fireflies,
as learned men
collect
sacred texts,
I resisted
the mad impulse
to put them
in a golden
cage
and each day give them
birdseed
and pieces of pink melon.
Like explorers
in the jungle who hand

over the very rare
green deer
to the spit
and eat it
with remorse,
I stretched out
my feet
and pulled on
the
magnificent
socks
and

then my shoes.

The moral
of my ode is this:
beauty is twice
beauty
and what is good is doubly
good
when it is a matter of two socks
made of wool
in winter.

(Translated by Robert Bly)

Page 274   *KEEPING STILL | THE MOUNTAIN*
Page 276   *THE MARRYING MAIDEN*

Source: From *The I Ching or Book of Changes*, German translation by Richard Wilhelm, rendered into English by Cary F. Baynes (Bollingen Series XIX, Pantheon Books, Princeton University Press, 1950), pp. 214–217, 222–226.

"The manner in which the *I Ching* tends to look upon reality seems to disfavor our causalistic procedures. The moment under actual observation appears to the ancient Chinese view more of a chance hit than a clearly defined result of concurring causal chain processes. The matter of interest seems to be the configuration formed by chance events in the moment of observation, & not at all the hypothetical reasons that seemingly account for the coincidence." (Thus: C. G. Jung, *Foreword* to Wilhelm's *I Ching*, p. iii.)

Thought of this kind, when applied to the field-of-the-poem, defines that field both in primitive/archaic & in much modern poetry: that whatever falls within the same space determines the meaning of that space. What Jung called "synchronicity" (with the problems it raises of indeterminacy & the observer's part in structuring the real) becomes a principle of composition: common link between such otherwise different modes as chance poetry, automatic writing, "deep" image, projective verse, etc., & between those & the whole world of nonsequential & noncausal thought. That modern physics at the same time moves closer to a situation in which anything-can-happen, is of interest too in any consideration of where we presently are.

For more on the *I Ching*, composition by correspondence, juxtaposition, chance, etc., see above, p. 457.

Addenda.   The *I Ching* has been a direct influence on recent poets like Jackson Mac Low or John Cage—even an instrument for random composition. But the idea of random composition itself has other roots in the modern; thus

Tristan Tzara
From MANIFESTO ON FEEBLE LOVE & BITTER LOVE

To make a dadaist poem
Take a newspaper.
Take a pair of scissors.
Choose an article as long as you are planning to make your poem.
Cut out the article.
Then cut out each of the words that make up this article & put them in a bag.
Shake it gently.
Then take out the scraps one after the other in the order in which they left the
    bag.
Copy conscientiously.
The poem will be like you.

Page 278   *From THE NINE SONGS*

Source: Arthur Waley, *The Nine Songs: A Study in Shamanism in Ancient China* (George Allen & Unwin Ltd., London, 1955), pp. 37–38, 41–42, 47.

The Big Lord of Lives (Ta Ssu-ming)—determines human longevity; apparently also maintains the balance of the world, between Yin & Yang, etc. The shaman assists him in this. "Big" & "little" in this & the next song refer to a major & a lesser festival in which the songs were used.
Nine Provinces—China; *Nine Hills*—chief mountains of China.
Ch'iang—sound effect, without meaning.

The Little Lord of Lives—you (line 6)—the god.
life-parting—where the people concerned are still alive but can't meet.
Broom-star—i.e., a comet; used by deities to sweep away evil.

The River God (Ho-po)—"He was a greedy god, often taking a fancy to & abducting mortal men's daughters, to add to his harem, or carrying off their sons to marry his daughters. . . . Sometimes he merely took a fancy to people's clothes. . . . At Yeh, in the extreme north of Honan c. 400 B.C.," shamans would round up a pretty girl each year and set her adrift "on a thing shaped like a bridal bed," letting it finally sink. Unlike the other gods of the Nine Songs "his cult went on till modern times."

The Chinese shaman (*wu*) has a history that both predates & outlasts these songs, which Waley figures about the third or fourth centuries B.C. though "the prototypes on which they were founded go back to a much earlier period." They are part of the *Ch'u Tz'u* collection ("generally translated 'Elegies of Ch'u' ") often attributed to the poet Ch'ü Yüan, & have the feel of literary reworkings of nonliterary goods. But the shamanic remnants are still strong, the sense too of an accompanying performance making use of dance & gesture, meaningless sound ("at the cesura of each line is the exclamation *hsi* which may . . . represent the panting of the shamans in a trance"), etc.—all designed to invoke the gods & bring them into the shaman's service.

The force of the address is erotic, i.e., "the shaman's relation with the Spirit is represented as a kind of love affair," though the absence of number, gender, & tense (& of an accompanying scenario) often makes it unclear whether the god or the shaman is speaking, whether the address is male to female, female to male, male to male, etc. Eliade tells of similar love-songs & sex-play between Teleut shamans (called kams) & their celestial wives:

> My darling young kam
> we shall sit together at the blue table
> My darling husband, my young kam
> let us hide in the shadow of the curtains
> & let us make love together
> & have fun
> My husband, my young kam

& Kumandin shamans of the Tomsk region had phallic games in which "they gallop with the [wooden] phallus between their legs 'like a stallion' & touch the spectators." Not surprising since in the Western world also, sexuality

(however concealed or allegorized) provides the dominant thrust in the great
god-poems, like the *Song of Songs* or the following:

San Juan de la Cruz
A POEM FOR THE ASCENT OF MOUNT CARMEL

> On a dark night, afraid
>> to love you, burning
>> Then this joy
>> to find the door
>>> (unseen)
>> the house so quiet

> Dark & safe
>> to find
> the secret stair, disguised
> rejoicing
> Dark, not touching
> anything, the house so quiet

> On that night, rejoicing
>> secretly that no one saw
>> me, that I looked at nothing
>> Had no light to lead me
>>> only
>> what burned inside my shirt

> that led me
>> like the light one afternoon
>> A place where someone
>> waited whom I knew
>> And no one came on us

> Oh night that led me, that
>> I loved beyond the dawn
>> Oh night that held
>> us close, changed
>> me through what I loved
>>> receiving

till the breasts were full
 I'd hidden for him, waiting
 for his head to sleep there
 Then I brought him gifts
 this fan of cedars with its night-air

Air of armies
 stirring through his hair
 That soft hand
 hurts my neck, suspending
 all my senses

I stayed with him, forgetting
 pressed my face against him
 Everything has left me
  gone
 My pain is fading
 vanishes among the lilies

     (Translation by J.R.)

For further examples of erotically propelled god-poems, see pp. 322, 379, 525.

Page 281 *SONG OF THE DEAD, RELATING THE*
    ORIGIN OF BITTERNESS

Source: Joseph F. Rock, *The Zhi mä Funeral Ceremony of the Na-Khi of Southwest China* (Studia Instituti Anthropos, Posieux [Fribourg], Switzerland, 1955), pp. 55, 58, 87, 90, 92. Adapted & arranged by J. R.

The Na-Khi tribe (a branch of the Ch'iang) settled in the Lichiang district probably during the Han Dynasty. Their main funeral ceremony, the Zhi mä, involves the chanting of various "books" & songs, preserved until recently in mnemonic picture-writing. While much of this writing is based on the rebus principle (of the ⬬ = I variety), there are places too where the pictograph seems to comment on matter in the spoken text; e.g., the first symbol in the song's title represents a large horsefly, such as occur on the high meadows in the summer, they emerge only when the sun shines and hide when overcast, they are blood suckers and a plague to both man and beast; the Na-Khi call them mun, here the symbol stands for *mun* = dead, it has also the meaning of old.

But the picture itself (of a horsefly) is a presence also & adds to the meaning—whether by chance or intention is outside the present editor's concern. There are also purely literal pictographs of the

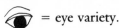 = eye variety.

The song per se is "one of several types of funeral songs, sung at the death of an old man while the body is still in the house." The manuscript consists of eighteen pages from which the present editor has excerpted & slightly adapted pages 2, 3, 13, 14, 15, juxtaposing pictures & words, etc. The song (to sum it up) proposes to relate "the origin of bitterness" & follows the dead man (possibly identified with the "first father") as he sees his image reflected, learns he's growing old, wanders to distant towns to buy long life, sees men selling silver & gold "but years he saw no one sell," then in an empty marketplace watches leaves of the bamboo turn yellow, thinks

so trees must also die, it is the custom
there is death after all

laughs & turns back.

The song now moves to a consideration of all who have died, including apparently "the father of heaven" & "the mother of the earth," so that "even in heaven there is bitterness." Then come the dance sections given here as sets 3, 4, & 5—*ritual description: "they form themselves into a circle, but not a closed one, and holding hands much like children do when at play, begin a dance"*—followed by further accounts of the dead man's ascent & the accomplishments & powers to be inherited by his son, his village, & his neighbors.

Addenda. Compare the face-in-the-mirror/flight-&-wandering themes with the Quetzalcoatl poem (p. 98; commentary, p. 507) & the flight-&-wandering with the life-quest of the dying hero in *The Epic of Gilgamesh*. The old shamans, by the way, had the power to see their own skeletons & to undertake ritual journeys to reclaim the dead. But the editor doesn't want to suggest that seeing an old face in the mirror is straight ritual symbolism; Ginsberg's poem, *Mescaline*, e.g., gets the whole thing down in more personal terms.

Page 286 *A SHAMAN VISION POEM*

Source: Translation from Chinese by C. H. Kwock & Gary Gach. Previously unpublished.

From a virtual subcategory of Chinese poetry—consisting of poems attributed to ghosts, with or without shamanic intervention. This one, identified elsewhere as "Poem Written by a Ghost Descending on a Sorcerer," is from the T'ang Dynasty (seventh to tenth centuries A.D.), but the reader can find examples of still older shamanism in, e.g., the selections from "The Nine Songs" reprinted above.

Page 287 *AL QUE QUIERE!*

Source: Poems circulated during the past few centuries & made new by C. H. Kwock & G. G. Gach.

[Translators' notes]:

"*U.S.* or *America* is in Chinese literally *Gold Mountain*.

"A Chinese colloquial for *wife* is literally *old lady*.

"Unwanted babies abandoned like Moses to rivers were not an unfamiliar practice in China, even until recently, tho' for girl babies more often than for boy babies.

"Cakes & soups made out of mud have not been uncommon in poorer parts of China.

"*Heaven's old grandfather* is the Chinese equivalent to the Christian *heavenly father*, sometimes abbreviated as *heaven*."

∘ ∘ ∘ ∘

Like its "western" counterpart, the Chinese literary tradition makes sharp distinction between "high" & "low" modes in poetry. In so doing, classicists have set aside the latter—as folklore, folk poetry, etc.—to be treated as both vital source & lesser instance. The recognition of a "folk," even "primitive," tradition in China goes back to at least *The Book of Songs* (500 B.C. or earlier), largely a gathering (& reworking) of folk materials from (probably) a range of regions & sources. An extension of this concern led to formation in the Han Dynasty (3rd century B.C. to 3rd century A.D.) of the *Yüeh-fu* or Music Bureau, which continued the collection & transcription while unable to check the class-based attitudes of the entrenched academics. A twentieth-century resurgence of such concerns (*pai hua* = "plain speech" movement, etc.) has probably been impeded as much as propelled by political/social struggles in & around China.

Page 291 From *THE KOJIKI*

Source: Donald L. Philippi, *Kojiki* (Princeton University Press, University of Tokyo Press, 1969), pp. 108–110.

Opo-kuni-nusi—creator god & culture hero of pre-Yamatö Japanese religion.

Idumo & Yamatö—earlier & later Japanese political & religious centers.

As the oldest surviving Japanese book, the *Kojiki*, or "Record of Ancient Things," completed on "the twenty-eighth day of the first month of the fifth year of Wadō" (A.D. 712), is an attempt to keep a grip on matters already at some distance from the compilers & to establish the "origins" of the Japanese court & nation on (roughly) native grounds. It is, at the same time, "a compilation of myths, historical and pseudo-historical narratives and legends, songs, anecdotes, folk etymologies, and genealogies." Like other such works (see p. 450), it begins with the generations of the gods & follows their creation of—& descent into—this-place-here.

The section on the jealousy of Suseri-bime is from the myth-centered opening book & includes one of the *Kojiki*'s 111 songs ("among the oldest recorded in the Japanese language"). Of their possible ritual origins & functions, Philippi writes: "As the texts of the songs do not always seem appropriate to the narrative in which they are incorporated, they may have an independent origin. Also, we should not forget the magico-religious role of song in the ceremonial life of the early court." In the present instance, "the vividness of the description makes one feel that the account was written by someone who had actually witnessed the performance of such actions. The song also sounds like an accompaniment for certain actions, as if it were an element in an opera or dance-drama." Thus, the three-part change of clothing can both be part of the narrative buildup or a description of costume changes in the accompanying dance. (Other examples of poems/songs as descriptions of their ritual frames appear on pp. 54 ["A Shaman Climbs Up the Sky"] & 314 ["The Shaman & the Red God"].)

Page 293   A SONG OF THE SPIDER GODDESS

Source: Donald L. Philippi, *Songs of Gods, Songs of Humans: The Epic Tradition of the Ainu* (North Point Press, 1982; University of Tokyo Press, 1979), pp. 78–82.

The Ainu—native non-Japanese population of Hokkaido Island—until recently maintained a rich tradition of oral narrative & poetry. Largely the work of female reciters (almost all Ainu shamans also were women), the story-poems involve a kind of projective first-person narration, in which the reciter-poet acts as a conduit for the personage (god, animal, or human) issuing through her. This sense of being-spoken-through is taken by Philippi & others as indications of the poetry's origins in shamanistic trance-possessions. While the "epics" themselves don't involve trance, what survives clearly is "a form of inter-species communication in which gods or humans speak of their experience to members of their own or other species." Though some of the force of that survives even in written transcription, "the epic tradition itself," writes Philippi, "has died out with the death of the last reciters."

As verse, the songs follow a flexible structure of (usually) four to six syllables per line, sometimes as many as seven or eight. "In actual performance, each verse is usually followed by a short pause, and in the mythic epics a [single-word] burden is interjected, sometimes after every verse and sometimes sporadically between verses. A verse which is too long can be sung rapidly, and one having too few syllables can be drawn out in singing, or additional sounds or syllables can be added." And further: "The singing of the epic would begin by the fireside in the early evening. The reciter would sit by the fireplace, beating time on the hearth frame with his *repni* (block of wood). The listeners would also each hold a *repni* in their hands, beating time on the hearth frame or on the wooden floor. From time to time, the audience would interject rhythmical exclamations of *het! het!* at certain points in the narrative. In this manner, a striking choral effect would be achieved. The reciter and his audience would be fused into a unity of experience, and the performance would engage the audience's attention so closely that they would scarcely notice the coming of the dawn. It was by no means unusual for the recitation to be still in progress in the morning." (Philippi, p. 25)

More discussion of Ainu poetics appears in *Symposium of the Whole*, pp. 155–158.

Page 301   THINGS SEEN BY THE SHAMAN KARAWE

Source: Barbara Einzig's translation from a Russian version in Waldemar Bogoras, *Materiali po izucheniyu chukotskavo yazyka i folklora* [Materials for the Study of the Chukchee Language & Folklore] (St. Petersburg, 1900). Told by the shaman Karawe on the Poginden River in 1896.

The shaman's "powers"—of vision, of flight, of control over animals & things-come-alive—manifest here in the shadow of the Russian overlords. Among the northeastern Siberian shamans, as elsewhere, the struggle with outside forces was to maintain such powers (& that of vision foremost) against all efforts to reduce them. Compare, e.g., the use of the "blood river" as a political metaphor with its "traditional" use in the Nenets poem on p. 359.

The narrative included here is one of several shamanic *videnies*—"visions" or "things seen"—collected by Bogoras as he traveled with the St. Petersburg Imperial Academy of Sciences expedition toward the turn of the century.

Addenda.   (1)   "I have made myself see. *I have seen*. And I was surprised and enamored with what I *saw*, wishing to identify myself with it.

"In a country the color of a *pigeon's breast* I acclaimed the flight of *1,000,000 doves*. I saw them invade the *forests*, black with desires, and the *walls* and *seas* without end.

"*A string lying on my table* made me see a number of *young men trampling upon their mother*, while several *young girls* amused themselves with *beautiful poses*.

"*Some exceedingly beautiful women cross a river, crying. A man, walking on the water, takes a young girl by the hand and jostles another*. Some persons of a rather reassuring aspect—in fact, *they had lain too long in the forest*—made their *savage gestures* only *to be charming*. Someone said: '*The immobile father.*'

"It was then that I saw myself, *showing my father's head to a young girl*. The earth quaked only slightly.

"I decided to erect a *monument to the birds*."

(Max Ernst, *Beyond Painting*, c. 1948)

(2)   "I don't have to go nowhere to see,
    "Visions are everywhere."

(Essie Parish, Pomo Indian shaman)

Page 303 PRAISE SONG OF THE BUCK-HARE

Source: Ezra Pound, *Guide to Kulchur* (New Directions, New York, [1938], 1970), pp. 211–213. Pound's working is from the German of Eckart von Sydow, *Dichtungen der Naturvoelker* (Phaidon Verlag, Vienna) & an earlier Russian version by Wilhelm Radloff (1866).

The translation given here is one of Pound's rare shots at a tribal-oral culture outside the boundaries of the "high" civilizations. But his contributions to the opening of other-than-Western & ancient poetries (Chinese, Greek, Egyptian, etc.) have already been noted in these pages.

Page 305 SETCHIN THE SINGER

Source: J. R.'s translation from the French version in Peter Domokos & Jean-Luc Moreau, *Le pouvoir du chant: anthologie de la poésie ouralienne* (Corvino Kiadó, Budapest, 1980), pp. 58–62.

In spite of early & late Russifications, a shamanistic poetics & religion survive among the Voguls of northeast Russia & western Siberia. Along with this shamanism are the remnants of that "circumpolar bear cult" that once figured so large in the imaginal life of three continents. For the Voguls, Bear was the son—sometimes the daughter—of the sky god, Numi Torem, & became the ruler & judge of life on earth. But he was also a prime source of meat & fur, a person therefore whose death required great feasts of reconciliation. Such feasts or wakes were the occasions for extended bear-chants & for personal accountings (= "fate-songs") on the part of hunters & shamans. In the present poem, the newly murdered bear is present & addressed, then himself becomes a speaker in the last two sections of the narrative of the hunter-shaman-singer who tracks him down with food, songs, & a final display of dancing marionettes. The musical instrument here isn't the typical shaman's drum but a kind of myth-sized harp fitted with strings of wolf-gut.

Page 309 MANTRA FOR BINDING A WITCH

Source: Verrier Elwin, *The Baiga* (John Murray, London, 1939), pp. 390–391.

Writing of Baiga poetry, Elwin's workings, etc., W. G. Archer describes a basic type of Baiga poem called a *dadaria*, which involves "the pairing of one image with another, the vitally important but latent link." Sometimes the process is one of simple juxtaposition, of placing the images together: "it is their compression into a dadaria which causes them to fuse and gives the incandescence of poetry." All this is part of a general "Baiga attitude to images. . . . An image of an object is regarded not only as vivid in itself but as capable of the most powerful associations with other images. The object can, as it were, exist not only as itself but also as the other objects which it resembles. A snake is not only a snake but a stick. A deer is not only a deer but a girl. An arrow is not only an arrow but a phallus. And it is the vivid collocation of these images which is the basis of the poetry."

Most of the combinations Archer cites, however remote they get, have a more or less precise (i.e., fixed) reference, but "in Baiga mantras, on the other hand, the relation continues, but *it is as if the effort is to make it completely obscure.* Images follow one another, all directed, it may be, at binding a witch. . . . 'The sharp end of a knife,' 'the glow-worm of a virgin,' 'the nail of a bone,' 'the lamp of flesh,'—all these are probably, at bottom, sexual symbols, but *it is the strained insistence on the image, the remoteness of the reference, the strange adequacy which gives the mantra its mysterious force.* In these mantra, Baiga poetry reaches the limit of its power." (*Man in India* XXIII [1943]: 59)

The process is, of course, fundamental to the language of magic & ecstasy, & is a key link between primitive & modern poetry—for which see pp. 453–459.

Page 310   *THE PIG*

Source: Verrier Elwin, ibid., pp. 406–407.

bewar—forest land cleared & burnt for cultivation.
Laru—the Laru-kaj, or pig-sacrificing event (see below).
phulera—a sort of swing in which are placed the leaf-wrapped head & liver of the pig.

The ceremony is called the Laru-kaj & is "probably the most ancient of all Baiga rituals." It appeases a demon of disease (Narayan deo) after he's been lured out of the patient's body with a bribe of pig. The pig is given rice to eat, its phallus is scalded with boiling water, then "three men, holding the pig by its two hind legs & buttocks, push the pig's head into [a] hole . . . half full of water. . . . Then the men begin to bump it up & down in the hole . . . [but] death . . . is due to suffocation." As an alternative the pig may be crushed by half a dozen men sitting or standing on the ends of a plank laid across the pig's stomach "while the fore and hind feet of the pig are pulled backwards and forwards alternately over the plank until it is crushed to death." This is the action accompanying the first poem. The second marks the washing, singeing & bloodletting, while the third coincides with the demon's appearance to receive his share of pig. And

> it was plain that pig had
> nothing on his mind. For
> Christ's sake didnt he
> know what was happening
> to him when one held him
> by the flanks? No, nor the other
> making click click, spin
> spin noises, clearing his throat

writes Robert Kelly of another pig, another place. But the indifference ("coolness") of the songs here seems deliberate.

Page 312 TWO COSMOLOGIES

Source: W. S. Merwin & J. Moussaieff Masson, *Sanskrit Love Poetry* (Columbia University Press, New York, 1977), pp. 111, 118; reprinted in W. S. M., *The Peacock's Egg* (North Point Press, Berkeley, California).

The accounts, as given here, of Vishnu & Krishna turn up in different versions throughout India. Writes Masson: "Vishnu is often represented as the cosmos. His right eye is the sun. When the sun sets, lotuses close their petals and Brahma will thereby disappear." And the eleventh-century compiler, Mammata: "When this happens, since [Laksmi's] hidden parts are no longer visible, her wild love-making can be unrestrained."

Authorship of the second poem is ascribed to one Candaka.

Page 314 From THE GUIDE TO LORD MURUKAN

Source: A. K. Ramanujan, *Hymns for the Drowning* (Princeton University Press, 1981), pp. 112–115.

A germinal poetic & religious movement between the sixth & ninth centuries A.D., *bhakti* signaled "a return, a creative regression" to the experience of Vedic seers & those earlier shamanisms still present in "oral & village folk traditions" throughout India. Like other such outcroppings "then" & "now," it moved through the work of its founding "poet-saints" toward an immediacy of experience—trance, ecstasy, possession—by means of "all the arts" (but especially poetry & dance) transformed but brought back to their oldest functions. Here the poem "evokes the primal, the essential experience of bhakti: not ecstasy, not enstasy, but an embodiment . . . a partaking of the god. [The bhakta] may pass through enstasy (withdrawal) and ecstasy (out-of-body experiences) as stages . . . [but] he needs also to sing, to dance: to make poetry, painting, shrines, sculpture; to embody [the god] in every possible way. In bhakti, all the arts become also 'techniques of ecstasy,' incitements to possession." (Ramanujan, pp. 115–116)

Toward such ends, the poetry comes into conflict with its more literary counterparts (here "the imperial presence of Sanskrit"), & the poet-saint seeks out both new means (the freeing-up, e.g., of meter & of punctuation) & the (re)creation of what had always been there: the personal & local, the concrete, the ecstatic & erotic, the image of the poet as a saint & madman—but, above all, a new/old poetics of performance & of the living common tongue. Nakkirar's poem, above, is itself an account of such a (shamanistic) performance; but what's less clear in translation is the movement's center in a language: its turning from "the language of the fathers" (Sanskrit) to an immediacy of speech & mind, in which the god "is everywhere, accessible," like "one's own thoughts." In this view, Ramanujan writes, ". . . god lives inside us as a mother tongue does, and we live in god as we live in language—a language that was there before us, is all around us in the community, and will be there after us. To lose this first language is to lose one's beginnings, one's bearings, to be exiled into aphasia. . . . Thus the early poet-saints required and created a poetry and a poetics of the mother tongue" (p. 137).

The Tamil instance of bhakti is one among many in India, drawing in this case from a written literature as well as local traditions & forms. The poem printed here is transitional to all that: a sixth-century work that locates poesis among the shaman-poets (= *camiyati* = god-dancers) outside the literary tradition per se. Part of a longer poem that sets up a mystic & sacred topography to guide the initiate to the country of the god, the poem focuses on Murukan, the "red one," as god of the mountain & fertility, who enters into & becomes the dancer-poet. Like other shamanistic poems, its origin traces back to a sacred journey: a demon capturing the poet & keeping him imprisoned in a cave, there to be rescued (along with 999 others) by the Lord Murukan, who kills the demon & delivers this poem "written in the cave [&] said to have the power to save anyone who recites it."

Addenda. The resemblance of all this to contemporary work—at least at its most ambitious—should not be overlooked. Thus, Antonin Artaud, among a host of others:

> All these pages float around like pieces of ice in my mind. Excuse my absolute freedom. I refuse to make a distinction between any of the moments of myself. I do not recognize any structure in the mind.
>
> We must get rid of the Mind, just as we must get rid of literature. I say that the Mind and life communicate on all levels. I would like to write a Book which would drive men mad, which would be like an open door leading them where they would never have consented to go, in short, a door that opens into reality. (Translation by Helen Weaver)

And again: "I cannot conceive of a work that is detached from life."

Page 317 *FOR THE LORD OF CAVES*

Source: A. K. Ramanujan, *Speaking of Shiva* (Penguin Books Inc., 1973), pp. 151–152, 168.

The work of the Vacana (Virasaiva) poet-saints is another instance of the bhakti movement discussed in the preceding note. A turning, like its Tamil counterpart, away from the narrowly literary, it is marked, on its social side, by a leveling of caste & class, & on that of its poetics, by a deliberate breakdown of traditional metrics & a blurring of the boundaries between verse & prose. "The poetics of the vacana," writes Ramanujan, "is an oral poetics," with an emphasis on "the spontaneity of free verse" & a virtual "rejection of premeditated art [&] standard upper-class educated speech" in favor of (something like) the real language of men. The result, at its most intense, is no nostalgic simplicity but the creation of "a dark, ambiguous language of ciphers . . . baffling the rational intelligence to look through the glass darkly till it begins to see. . . . It is 'a process of destroying and reinventing language' till we find ourselves 'in a universe of analogies, homologies, and double meanings.'" But this complexity—as a return to the primal—should neither be surprising to readers of the present volume nor be taken as "mere" wordplay in a world of suns & caves in which "there can be no metaphor."

The Lord of Caves, to whom all of Allama's poems are spoken, is one of the names of Shiva, to which the poet, "obsessed with images of light &

darkness," is particularly drawn. As such, it goes back to his (actual) "experience of the secret underground, the cave-temple," in which he first achieved illumination. While the translator gives a symbolic gloss to many of Allama's images & visions, the editor, in deference to Allama's denial of metaphor, will take the reading no further than that already given.

Page 321 *THE CALENDAR*

Source: Alexander Marshack, "Upper Paleolithic Notation & Symbol," in *Science*, 24 November 1972.

Marshack's "readings" of the marks on paleolithic bone fragments has pushed the history of writing (written notation) back toward the beginnings of language itself. The present piece is a reconstruction, based on American Indian & Siberian (oral) models, of early European lunar notations & calendar namings. "The Upper Paleolithic notations . . . suggest that they were kept by some specialized person. Leona Cope, writing of the American Indian, states: '. . . the more complex and highly developed the ceremonialism . . . the more careful the determination of the solstices, the lunar phases, and the time reckoning.' . . . The compositions by Upper Paleolithic artists which illustrate or imply seasonal and other periodic ceremonies and rites suggest that at least some were 'scheduled' in the year as in the Siberian and American traditions."

What the work points to, then, in brief, is the invention & reinvention of language as a fundamental act of poetry from then to now.

Addenda. Among the Ojibwa, e.g., the months (moons) appear as follows: "1. long moon, spirit moon 2. moon of the suckers 3. moon of the crust on the snow 4. moon of the breaking of snow-shoes 5. moon of the flowers & blooms 6. moon of strawberries 7. moon of raspberries 8. moon of whortle berries 9. moon of gathering of wild rice 10. moon of the falling of leaves 11. moon of freezing 12. little moon of the spirit." (L. Cope, *Calendars of the Indians North of Mexico*)

Page 322 *THE VULVA SONG OF INANA*

Source: J. R.'s English version, translated after Bette Meador, from the Sumerian text & literal translations provided by Renata Leggit. Previously unpublished.

The poetry composed around the figures of Inana & Dumuzi (elsewhere Ishtar & Tammuz, etc.) was extensive, & the (symbolic) readings multi-leveled & contradictory in their development through time. In the fragment presented here, the direct celebration of female sexuality conjures a descent from the stone venuses & incised vulvas $\bigvee$ of an earlier time. (The accompanying yearly festival in Sumer & elsewhere was the so-called sacred marriage of the goddess & the "shepherd-king.") This use of poetry to arouse sexuality is both a value in itself & part of an approach to a universe in which—wrote ancient Empedocles, himself a "weather-shaman"—"everything that is born / feels & has a share of thought." Thus sex—like "nature" or like "death"—has been a power of poetry over a wide range of times & places—showing nowhere in the West as clearly or as concretely as in its Sumerian beginnings.

Further instances show up throughout this volume; but see especially, pp. 166, 379, 392, & the accompanying commentaries. An example of a contemporary awakening follows.

Addenda. "From my identification with the symbology of the female body I made the . . . assumption that carvings and sculptures of the serpent form were attributes of the Goddess and would have been made [in ancient cultures] by women worshippers (artists) as analogous to their own physical, sexual knowledge. I thought of the vagina in many ways—physically, conceptually: as a sculptural form, an architectural referent, the source of sacred knowledge, ecstacy, birth passage, transformation. I saw the vagina as a translucent chamber of which the serpent was an outward model: enlivened by its passage from the visible to the invisible, a spiraled coil ringed with the shape of desire and generative mysteries, attributes of both female and male sexual powers. This source of 'interior knowledge' would be symbolized as the primary index unifying spirit and flesh in Goddess worship. I related womb and vagina to 'primary knowledge'; with strokes and cuts on bone and rock by which I believed my ancestor measured her menstrual cycles, pregnancies, lunar observations, agricultural notations—the origins of time factoring, of mathematical equivalences, of abstract relations. I assumed the carved figurines and incised female shapes of Paleolithic, Mesolithic artifacts were carved by women—the visual-mythic transmutation of self-knowledge to its integral connection with a cosmic Mother—that the experience and complexity of her personal body was the source of conceptualizing, of interacting with materials, of imagining the world and composing its images." (Carolee Schneemann, 1979, from *More Than Meat Joy*)

Page 324 *THE BATTLE BETWEEN ANAT & THE*
FORCES OF MOT

Source: Translation from the Ugaritic by Harris Lenowitz, in Lenowitz & C. Doria, *Origins: Creation Texts from the Ancient Mediterranean* (Anchor Press/Doubleday, New York, 1976), pp. 278–280.

Anat, the Canaanite war-goddess, was sister of Baal (god of rain & fertility) whom she aided in his struggles with his counterpart Mot (god of death & sterility). The episodes involve the death & resurrection of Baal & remind us of the Egyptian myths of Isis, Osiris, & Set (see p. 520). But the fragment given here is a perfect depiction of the goddess' fury—made more fantastic perhaps by the loss of explanatory data, etc.

The Baal & Anat poems were written in Ugaritic, a Canaanite dialect spoken at Ras Shamra-Ugarit & closely related to Old Testament Hebrew. The texts date from the early fourteenth century B.C., though the matter is undoubtedly older. The work of uncovering goes back to 1929.

Addenda.   (1) "The Goddess is a lovely, slender woman with a hooked nose, deathly pale face, lips red as rowan-berries, startlingly blue eyes and long fair hair; she will suddenly transform herself into sow, mare, bitch, vixen, she-ass, weasel, serpent, owl, she-wolf, tigress, mermaid or loathsome hag. . . . The reason why the hairs stand on end, the skin crawls and a shiver runs down the spine when one writes or reads a true poem is that a true poem is necessarily an invocation of the White Goddess, or Muse, the Mother of All Living, the ancient power of fright and lust—the female spider or the queen-bee whose embrace is death." (R. Graves, *The White Goddess*, p. 10)
See also below, p. 601.

(2)   Denise Levertov
                    THE GODDESS

> She in whose lipservice
> I passed my time,
> whose name I knew, but not her face,
> came upon me where I lay in Lie Castle!
>
> Flung me across the room, and
> room after room (hitting the walls, re
> bounding—to the last
> sticky wall—wrenching away from it
> pulled hair out!)

till I lay
outside the outer walls!

There in cold air
lying still where her hand had thrown me,
I tasted the mud that splattered my lips:
the seeds of a forest were in it,
asleep and growing! I tasted
her power!

The silence was answering my silence,
a forest was pushing itself
out of sleep between my submerged fingers.

I bit on a seed and it spoke on my tongue
of day that shone already among stars
in the water-mirror of low ground,

and a wind rising ruffled the lights:
she passed near me returning from the encounter,
she who plucked me from the close rooms,

without whom nothing
flowers, fruits, sleeps in season,
without whom nothing
speaks in its own tongue, but returns
lie for lie!

Page 327 *From THE SONG OF ULLIKUMMI*

Source: Charles Olson, *Archaeologist of Morning* (Grossman Publishers, New York, 1973). Olson's principal source here is H. G. Güterbock's *The Song of Ullikummi*.

In the longer work, of which Olson's poem is as much evocation as translation, Kumarbi (father-of-the-gods) fucks the mountain to create a stone-man (Ullikummi), who will destroy the storm-god (Enlil). From this action, "stone gave birth to stone . . . who grew up / in the water / 9000 miles tall / like a tower raised," &, with his father, fought the other gods, or grew so unchecked (in Olson's view), so dangerous, "that they had to, themselves, do battle with him." The "song," then, "is actually the story of that battle and who could bring him down. Because he had a growth principle of his own, and it went against creation in the sense that nobody could stop him and nobody knew how far he might grow. . . . This diorite figure is the vertical, the growth principle of the Earth. He's just an objectionable child of Earth who has got no condition except earth, no condition but stone." (*Muthologos*, I.73) In saying which, Olson (in the oldest tradition of translation & poesis) projects his own fascination with the matter, as in the figure of himself "stand(ing) on Main Street like the Diorite / Stone," or as part of his obsession with a rockbound earth, who takes her hero & "only / after the grubs / had done him / . . . let(s) her robe / uncover and her part / take him in."

Page 329   From *THEOGONY [THE GODBIRTHS]*

Source: Excerpted from Charles Doria's translation from *The Theogony*, in C. Doria & Harris Lenowitz, *Origins: Creation Texts from the Ancient Mediterranean* (Anchor Press/Doubleday, New York, 1976), pp. 313–314, 315–317.

The energies of the old gods—as manifestation of the imaginal underworld & the "dark powers of the unconscious" (see p. 449)—persist in the wildness of Hesiod's poem-of-origin. A sense of the ferocity & strength of the other-than-human (wind, lightning, earthquake, vacuum, flood, etc.) & its expression through human brutalities, is by no means unique to the "European vision," which has often enough favored repression over exuberance (& its attendant terrors). The force of Doria's translation is in its ability to show all of that (including Hesiod's still audible connection to older oral poetries) & to suggest, by so doing, what it may mean to be living in a state-of-myth.

Other poems-of-origin can be found in the opening section & elsewhere in the present volume. The killing (& castration) of Sky is paralleled in Babylonian accounts of the killing of the primal water-god, Apsu (= abyss), by his grandson Ea, but also in the killing of the primal-[serpent-]mother Tiamat by Marduk.

Page 333   *SONG OF THE ARVAL BROTHERS*

Source: Charles Doria's English version in *Alcheringa*, old series, no. 5 (Spring-Summer 1973): 59–60. (Recorded in the third century A.D. but thought to go back to at least the sixth or seventh century B.C.)

Surviving songs of the Arval Brotherhood—a society of dancing priests of Mars, who made offerings every May to the field-Lares & the Semones (gods of sowing). (Arval, from *arvum*, a cultivated field, a farm; & Mars or Marmar still visible as a god of fertile powers.) The priests were also known as the Salii (= dancers or leapers) & performed "wild dances" in groups of twelve, their songs set to the rhythm of a three-step dance, in which the halves of each verse consisted of three rhythmical beats & corresponded to what H. W. Garrod describes as "the forward swing & recoil of the dance." Along with scattered remains of Latin charms & "magic dirges" chanted by professional "wise women" (= shamans), the Arval fragments are among the oldest records of oral poetry & ritual-events in Europe.

Page 335 BIRTH OF THE FIRE GOD

Source: Translation by Garbis Yessayan & Keith Bosley, in K. Bosley, ed., *The Elek Book of Oriental Verse* (Paul Elek, London, 1979), p. 191.

The figure depicted here is elsewhere identified as Vahakn (*vahagn* = bringer-of-fire), legendary god-king of the early Armenians, whose birth-song is given in the fifth-century history of Moses of Khorni. The contrary mix—of child & man—is, like the fire itself, a sign of power.

Page 336 THE ROUND DANCE OF JESUS

Source: J. R.'s redaction &/or working, based on versions by Edgar Hennecke, Max Pulver, & G. R. S. Mead from the third-century gnostic Acts of Saint John.

Gnosticism, as used here, is the catch-all term for those religions—contemporary with & often a part of early Christianity—that centered on the pursuit of *gnosis* (= "knowing") in the sense of "enlightenment" or "illumination." What presents itself to us (in the aftermath, that is, of the later Christian orthodoxy) is the last outburst of the about-to-be-subterranean pagan world: a sense of myth as process & conflict, & a virtual *clash* of symbols (P. Ricoeur) in contrast to the fixed imagery & single vision of orthodox thought, whether religious or scientific. Of the poetics of gnosticism Elaine Pagels writes:

> Like circles of artists today, gnostics considered original creative invention to be the mark of anyone who becomes spiritually alive. Each one, like students of a painter or writer, expected to express his own perceptions by revising & transforming what he was taught. . . . Like artists, they express their own insight—their

own *gnosis*—by creating new myths, poems, rituals, "dialogues" with Christ, revelations, and accounts of their visions. (*The Gnostic Gospels*, pp. 19–20)

In this sense, too, the Gnostics may be seen—at least at their most heated—as carrying forward the open field of earlier speculative poetry & religion. (See also *Symposium of the Whole*, pp. 217–224.)

The image of the dancing Christ (& of Jesus as trickster, if one takes it just a little further) resurfaces in the high creativity (poesis) of the Plains Indians' Ghost Dance; for which see p. 511. Strong enough in their own terms, such versions serve us as vehicles of defamiliarization, etc., allowing the living image to emerge.

Page 341   A SONG OF AMERGIN

Source: Nineteenth-century translation by Douglas Hyde in *Literary History of Ireland*, with variations by J. R. after the version (1897) by Kuno Meyer.

The search for origins & for a primal poetic language focused in eighteenth-century Europe on the ancient poetries of Wales & Ireland. While the best-known version, James Macpherson's workings from the legendary poet Ossian, proved excessive, what came to surface was a genuine bardic tradition (or a series of such) with roots into what Robert Graves calls "the ancient language of poetry." As a "magical language" more than a literary one per se, this poetry dominated neolithic thought & was later carried forward by a subterranean network of poets & seers. Writes Graves:

> . . . the ancient language survived purely enough in the secret Mystery-cults of Eleusis, Corinth, Samothrace and elsewhere; and when these were suppressed by the early Christian Emperors it was still taught in the poetic colleges of Ireland and Wales, and in the witch-covens of Western Europe. As a popular religious tradition it all but flickered out at the close of the seventeenth century; and though poetry of a magical quality is still occasionally written, even in industrialized Europe, this always results from an inspired, almost pathological, reversion to the original language—a wild Pentecostal "speaking with tongues"—rather than from a conscientious study of its grammar and vocabulary. (*The White Goddess*, p. 12)

While the present editor is likely more sympathetic to such exuberances, it seems clear that the ancient (bardic) poet (*fili* or "seer" in Irish, *derwydd* or "oak-seer" in Welsh) was, like his shaman predecessors, a master of both ecstasy & lore. The master-poet's learning, as described by Graves, was in fact immense; & this is in line too with the estimates (by Peter Furst & others) of the learning & vocabulary of shamans in oral cultures. As seers too, the Welsh & Irish poets probably engaged in shamanistic rituals of possession, & their practice of magical language involved displays of spontaneous composition—e.g., a form of improvised divination that issues from the poet's fingers. (See p. 429.)

"A Song of Amergin," whose legendary dating would place it a millennium or more before Christ, comes to us in a later work called *Leabhar Gabhala*, or *Book of Invasions*. Said to contain the "first verses ever made in Ireland," it is a characteristic poem of the type in which the poet-speaker describes a series of self-transformations (metamorphoses) through a sequence of assertions following the pattern I-am-this, I-am-that, or I-have-been-this, I-have-been-that, etc. Other examples in the present volume can be found on pp. 62, 149, & 480, where they serve both to identify the (shaman)-poet & the power that speaks through him/her.

For more on poetry and metamorphosis, see p. 544.

Addenda.   Charles Stein
                From A BOOK OF CONFUSIONS (1981)

What the Gourd Man said
When the Gourd Man spoke
was:

I make a space
between me and this room.

What I feel of my old sadness is
a shining blue-like
body
in my body.

I am stopped up hotel clerk.
I keep check marks in a book.
I knock over gold birds.
I kick a rock.
I quarrel with Black Sun Demon.

I pick a fight with bone white fish.
I have never kept a lover and I eat steamed stones.
I make a space between me and my hook.
I pick up my club.
I make love in the posture called "Crossing the Great Fjords"
I make love in a little boat bound to the dock.
What I feel of my old joy is
a shining red-like body
in my body.

I reproduce myself endlessly causing

      little

       figures

with a club over all my shoulders
to hop about among heaped stones.

I reside in crystal.
I skirt the rim of winter weed jug.
I eat wool of milk stool.
I burn Name in leg of milk stool.

When blue light spot flashes on your keys
or in the soup
or blue light
the size of a stamp
flashes
I practice Night Hawk
I practice Panther
I practice Sludge
I practice Saw Blade
I practice Running Silk

When I came to an open space this side the Wallkill
two black horses
were lurking
by The Drum.

Page 342 *From THE RED BOOK OF HERGEST*

Source: Translation by D. Silvan Evans in William F. Skene, *The Four Ancient Books of Wales, Containing the Cymric Poems Attributed to the Bards of the Sixth Century* (Edmonston & Douglas, Edinburgh, 1868), Vol. I, pp. 569–571.

Like such seer-poets as Taliesin & Aneirin, the "real" Llywarch Hen may go back to the sixth century as a poet & warrior against the early English invaders. More likely, though, the poems in his name were the work of a Welsh court-poet between that time & the appearance, circa 1375, of the *Red Book of Hergest*. The figure emerging therein is that of an old man, who lives in isolation & in grief & anger over the deaths of his twenty-four sons & many companions—an image that colors all subsequent "biographies" of the poet whose last name means, literally, "the old one." But the poems, even if late, would seem to be spoken in Llywarch's voice to—& through—the poet who receives them: a "ritual of divination" of a kind well known in Irish & Welsh tradition. Writes Patrick K. Ford in a recent book on Llywarch:

> In the shaman-like trance which Giraldus Cambrensis described with regard to the *awenyddion* [inspired, in-breathing poets] of the twelfth century in Wales, the poets . . . go into a trance, their bodies taken over by some force . . . that apparently speaks through them. . . . The description of Celtic divination by Giraldus . . . suggests that we may think of the poet of the Llywarch poems as summoning knowledge that lay buried in the past, revealed in the person of Llywarch Hen, a denizen of that remoteness. (*The Poetry of Llywarch Hen*, pp. 58–59)

In that sense, the linking here is with a worldwide tradition of authorship that connects the Llywarch poems to the old shamans (see p. 485) & to the later assertions by, e.g., Blake that "the authors are in Eternity," or to Jack Spicer's sense of the poet as a receiver/retriever of messages not his own; of which he writes:

> We are irritable radio sets . . . but our poems write for each other, being full of their own purposes, no doubt no more mysterious in their universe than ours in ours. And our lips are not our lips. But are the lips of heads of poets. And should shout revolution.
> In silence.

Or Spicer again—to bring it home with a special finesse: "The poet is more like a catcher, but likes to think he's a pitcher."

Page 344   *TWO POEMS FOR ALL-HALLOWS' EVE*

Source: Trefor M. Owen, *Welsh Folk Customs* (National Museum of Wales, 1959, 1978), pp. 134, 124. Original texts in T. Gwynn Jones, *Welsh Folklore & Custom*, pp. 149–150, 146.

Of Christian festivals with Pagan (= country) carryovers, "All-Hallows' Eve," writes Trefor Owen, "was the weirdest. Spirits walked abroad. . . . In some parts of Wales the wandering ghosts took the form of a *ladi wen* (white lady), while in other parts . . . it was the *hwch ddu gwta* (the tailless black sow) which put terror into the hearts of men. The apparition of the black sow, in fact, was closely associated with one of the oldest *Calan gaeaf* [Winter's Eve] customs, namely that of lighting bonfires after dark. . . . To this end large quantities of fern, gorse, straw, and thornbushes were carted to the hill-top site of the fire, and ordinary work would be set aside on the occasion. When the bonfire was lit, often to the blowing of horns and other instruments, potatoes and apples were placed in it to roast; there would be dancing, shouting and leaping around the fire as it burned. The roasted apples and potatoes would be eaten by the light of the fire, and, according to some accounts, the participants would run round or through the fire and smoke, casting a stone into the flames. As the fire died down all would run off to escape [the black sow]" while shouting songs like the two presented here. (Owen, pp. 123–124)

Page 345   *THE FAIRY WOMAN'S LULLABY*

Source: Alexander Carmichael, *Carmina Gadelica: Hymns & Incantations* (Oliver & Boyd, Edinburgh, 1928), Vol. V, pp. 219–221. "Orally collected in the highlands & islands of Scotland & translated into English."

As underground, localized powers, the "faeries" (Scottish: *sith*, pl. *sithich*) represented, at some level, a world of "imaginal" beings, who come down to us as elves, leprechauns, & goblins, diminished into bright but feckless images from Disneyland, etc. What's lost—beyond the particulars & contradictions of a live tradition—is the sense of threat, even terror, in creatures whose name in English comes from the Latin *fata* (= the Fates) &

who were called, by their seventeenth-century chronicler, Robert Kirk, "the subterraneans." While that side of the tradition is probably as unsalvageable among the "folk" as elsewhere, it should be remembered that the "faeries" once functioned, like the Semitic Liliths (*lilin*), both as sexual lures & abductors of the newborn, connected at source with the fallen angels & the spirits of the dead. In testimonies gathered by Alexander Carmichael in the nineteenth century, such figures at their spookiest were described as "hosts" or swarms, "who had left heaven and had not reached hell, [but] flew into holes of the earth 'mar na famhlagan,' like the stormy petrels." A sense of marginality & exile is also strong here—as reflection of a "wilderness" (of place & mind [= spirit]) now out of reach. Writes Carmichael, again:

> According to one informant, the spirits fly about . . . in great clouds, up and down the face of the world like the starlings. . . . In bad nights, the hosts shelter themselves . . . behind little russet docken stems and yellow ragwort stalks. They fight battles in the air as men do on the earth. They may be heard and seen on clear frosty nights, advancing and retreating, retreating and advancing, against one another. After a battle, as I was told in Barra, their crimson blood may be seen staining rocks and stones. (II:357)

Of the context for the present piece, the reciter, James, son of Colin (James Campbell), crofter, Ceann Tangabhal, Barra, said, 26th September 1872: "MacLeod of Dunvegan got a child by the fairy woman; and because he would not receive herself, she sent the child home to him. But though she put him away, she was missing the child and she went to see him. The child was with MacLeod's foster-nurse, and the fairy woman seized hold of the child, and she was hushing and caressing and fondling and nursing and rocking him back and fore, intending to snatch him from her and to sweep him away with her to the fairy mound." The fuller work—of which this is a small excerpt—was known as "MacLeod's Lullaby" & existed thereafter in many versions.

Addenda. Western poets (Shakespeare, Spenser, Keats, etc.) have both promoted the attractive side of the faerie proposition &, less frequently, pointed at its darkness—as in Blake's vision, e.g., of the Fairies, Nymphs, Gnomes, & Genii standing "unforgiving & unalterable . . . four ravening deathlike Forms" at the gates of Golgonooza; or in more recent works by poets like Yeats & Duncan. And it's also worth noting that when Lorca calls his concept of a daemonic poetic force "duende," he has in mind a subterranean figure synonymous with "fairy" but of such a wildness as to make the Gypsy singer Manuel Torres say: "All that has black sounds has duende."

See also the discussion of the Serbian *vila*, p. 601, & of Blake's visions of the faerie world, p. 605.

Page 347 THE NINE HERBS CHARM

Source: Translation by David Antin from the Anglo-Saxon, previously unpublished.

Although it seems likely that such herbal charms were common in pre-Christian England & Europe, this is the only one with specific Pagan reference to survive the Church's roundups. Yet even here (in several lines omitted by the present translator) the later Christian reviser seems to have inserted a reference to the creation of two of the herbs by "the Wise Lord / holy in heaven as he hung"—though this, again, may not be Christ but Woden (= Odin) in the same charm-gathering account as that given above, p. 353 (commentary, p. 596). Used, they say, against snakebite, the poem leads into a virtual history of some of the herbs' past doings—much like the praises of the Ifa divination bones (see p. 536)—as displayed at real &/or imaginary places like Regenmeld, Alorford, etc. The poem, which may be a fragmented version of a longer, more symmetrical work in nine parts, ends with the directions for its performance: a language "event" that works through contact between the "magic words" & the object or person toward which they're directed. (See Malinowski's description—p. 443—of the physical nature of language in Trobriand magic & poetics.)

Page 350 *From* SHAKESPEARE'S LEAR

Source: William Shakespeare, *King Lear*, Act 3, Scene 4, first performed 26 December 1606.

In the depiction of madness, etc., as an entry to the primal world, Shakespear(e)—his name itself a praise-name—touches on that "magic" written of by Herman Melville in a note scrawled on the last flyleaf of his copy of the Shakespeare plays:

> Ego non baptizo te in nomine Patris et
> Filii et Spiritus Sancti—sed in nomine
> Diaboli.—madness is undefinable—

It & right reason extremes of one,
—not the (black art) Goetic but Theurgic magic—
seeks converse with the Intelligence, Power, the
Angel.

Nor is he an outsider to the traditions of this book but, as a master of oral soundings & of a lore still "in the air," is central himself to a Western *ethno*poetics that shares the intelligence & power of those seers & keepers-of-high-words presented elsewhere in these pages. It is this lore that goes back to the old shamans, etc., & breaks through, qua vision & madness, on the folk level as well—as in the song of Tom o' Bedlam that parallels Shakespeare's more "complex" (= "primitive") exploration:

> From the hag and hungry goblin
> That into rags would rend ye,
> > And the spirit that stands
> > By the naked man
> In the book of moons, defend ye,
> That of your five sound senses
> You never be forsaken,
> > Now wander from
> > Yourselves with Tom
> Abroad to beg your bacon.
>
> > While I do sing, "Any food, any feeding,
> > Feeding, drink, or clothing?
> > > Come, dame or maid,
> > > Be not afraid,
> > Poor Tom will injure nothing."

Or again, in the "archaic song of Dr. Tom the Shaman" among the latterday Nootka Indians of western Vancouver Island:

> I know thee. My name is Tom.
> I want to find thy sickness. I know thy sickness.
> I will take thy sickness. My name is Tom. I am a strong doctor.
> If I take thy sickness thou wilt see thy sickness.
> My name is Tom. I don't lie. My name is Tom. I don't talk shit.
> I am a doctor. Many days I haven't eaten.

Ten days I haven't eaten. I don't have my tools with me.
I don't have my sack with me. My name is Tom.
I will take thy sickness now & thou wilt see it.

(J. R.'s working, after James Teit)

See also the note on Rabelais, p. 602.

Page 353   ODIN'S SHAMAN SONG

Source: Translation by Gavin Selerie of strophes 138–145 from the
Hávamál (*Poetic Edda*), in G. Selerie, *Azimuth* (London, 1984).

Elder Edda—also called *Poetic Edda*, a late thirteenth-century gathering
of pre-Christian mythologies: multiple worlds & gods shared with other
northern European/Germanic peoples. Derived from oral sources & (re)-
composed circa 800-circa 1200 in Iceland &/or west Norway.

Odin—(elsewhere = Woden, Wotan = madman): chief god of the
Edda & remaining, as here, a (shamanic) god of poetry & of the dead. The
"fire-see" of the third line is an etymological rendering of the original's
"Oðni" (Oðinn).

Bolthorn—father of Odin's mother, *Bestla*, from whom comes the
power-of-poetry (*odrerir*).

Dain—king of the "elves"; *Dvalin*—king of the dwarves; *Asvid*—king
of the giants.

Thund—another of Odin's names.

(Writes the translator: "The 'beat' in the first line has a musical connota-
tion as well as the more obvious ones. The layout is exactly equivalent to the
Old Norse text. I have tried to limit the alliteration, rhyme, kennings, etc.,
while giving some sense of that order.")

Behind the present excerpt is the account of Odin's theft of the elixir-
(mead)-of-poetry—*odrerir*—& with it his own transformation into a virtual
god-of-language. As one grasps it here, that language is both voiced &
written in the form of runes, a magical alphabet in which each letter (rune)
stands for a charm, an incantation, toward specific ends. Odin's acquisition of
the runes follows an apparent self-immolation on his part—from a gallows-
tree in this account, from the world-tree Yggdrasil elsewhere—& ends with
the delivery to him, as ur-poet, of a range of runes & charms, both "white" &
"black." A widespread—if specialized—script before the coming of Christi-

anity, the runes (literally "mysteries, secrets") were closely tied to the old religion & suppressed along with it. The survival of the myth-poems, in their Eddic form, has a likely connection to the late arrival of Christianity in Iceland.

The magic/mysticism of letters & alphabets is otherwise a fact of poetry through large parts of the world—for which the reader may want to check out the reference on p. 465, & the other (nonalphabetic) examples of "magic" writing on pp. 26–31, 157, 205, 281.

Page 355 From KALEVALA

Source: Translated from the Finnish by Keith Bosley, in Matti Kuusi, K. Bosley, & Michael Branch, *Finnish Folk Poetry: Epic* (Finnish Literature Society, Helsinki, 1977), pp. 99–101. Collected 1839 by M. A. Castrén in Archangel Karelia (Russia), singer unknown.

Väinämöinen—central figure of the *Kalevala*, etc., who appears variously as god, hero, & shaman-poet.
Ilmarinen—wind-god & blacksmith-"culture hero."
Manala, Mana—the "otherworld," "underworld."
Lake Alue, Lake Alimo—"mythical primeval lake."
Ahti, Hirska—water-god.
Tuoni—underworld ruler; Death.

Another isolated group—like the Welsh & Icelanders (see pp. 588, 596)—the Balto-Finnish peoples maintained a "backwoods"/backwash culture in which the poetic tradition survived religious oppression & cultural "refinements" until recent times. Against that tradition the Reformation preacher Jacobus Finno wrote (1582) in his hymnbook:

> Because there were no sacred songs for the people to learn, they began to practice pagan rites and to sing shameful, lewd and foolish songs. . . . [They] sing them to pass the time at their festivals and on journeys, they hold contests with them, they defile and debauch the young with wicked thoughts and shameful speech, they tempt and encourage them to live a lewd and filthy life and to practice wicked ways. And because the devil, the source of all wickedness, also inspired his poets and singers into whose

minds he entered and in whose mouths he shaped the right
words, they were able to compose songs easily and quickly which
could be learned by others and remembered more quickly than
divine and Christian songs could be learned and remembered.
(Kuusi, p. 28)

In brief—some of the choicer adjectives aside—an active poetry still being
shaped & transmitted by those, like Blake's Milton, who were "true poet(s) &
of the Devil's party without knowing it," etc.

The collection & transcription of Finnish poetry began in the eighteenth
century & emerged in the work of Elias Lönnrot (1802–1884) & of later, more
"accurate" workers such as D. E. D. Europaeus. Lönnrot's great gatherings
were the *Kalevala*, an edition of fifty-plus "epic poems" published in final
form in 1849, & the *Kanteletar* (1840), an anthology of 625 "lyrical poems &
ballads." An example of "old ways" at the service of the emerging nation-
state, Lönnrot's *Kalevala* involved the rewriting, linking & expansion of
multiple individual pieces into a Homeric-sized collage, while often playing
down the older numinosities in favor of a more "rational" narrative structure.
(The gathering from which the present excerpt is taken is based on raw texts
compiled by Lönnrot & by others before & after him, rather than on his
Kalevala per se.)

What shows itself, as elsewhere, is a shamanistic performance poetry—
"not a heroic epic in the usual sense of the term," writes Felix Oinas, "but a
shamanistic [one] in which great deeds are accomplished, not by feats of
arms, but by magical means—by the power of words and incantations." As
ritual performance, the piece presented here survived, the editors tell us, "as
an incantation for treating burns. Its original function, however, is thought
to have been part of a seasonal fire-lighting [new fire] ritual . . . probably
performed in connection with burn-beat [slash & burn] cultivation . . . :
lighting the first fire in a new home or lighting a ritual bonfire at the summer
or winter solstice." (Kuusi, p. 524)

Although such functional poetry had likely ended by the time of the
collectors, nineteenth-century performing & re-collaging of earlier works
took many forms, including song-contests & a kind of double-voiced hand-
to-hand singing in which two (male) singers sat side by side, clasping each
other's right hands, & swaying back & forth to the beat of the songs. In so
doing, the one who acted as the lead singer started solo, then was joined
midway through the first line, after which the line was repeated by both, &

the singers went on in the same way to the second line, the third line, etc. In the women's song tradition, the role of second singer was taken over by a group.

Page 358 THE FOX

Source: J. R.'s translation from the French version in Peter Domokos & Jean-Luc Moreau, *Le pouvoir du chant: anthologie de la poésie populaire ouralienne* (Corvina Kiadó, Budapest, 1980), pp. 124–125.

Not evident from the translation, "The Fox" is an example of a type of improvised song called *yoïk* (*yuoigos*), whose performance exceeds the limits imposed by presentation of the words alone. As part of the Lapp hunting tradition, the yoïk was originally connected with animal magic & healing &, assisted by the (so-called) "magic drum," could lead the shaman-singer (*noidi*) into ecstasy, etc. Often sung without words or as a combination of words & untranslatable sounds, the yoïk became a complex form of improvisation on a wide range of Lapp concerns. In addition, gesture & imitative sound added to the evocation of the animal or object addressed.

Yet what's immediately striking, for all the emphasis on the poetics of sound, is the sharpness of detail in the presentation of the fox figure. While the fox as such is, in some sense, the European equivalent of Native American Coyote—i.e., as trickster-god—the Lapp poet's sense of the sheer animal particulars is also remarkable & should not be set aside as something less-than-mythic/mystic. (The reader might compare it, e.g., with the equally "realistic" Seri whale songs [p. 227] on the one hand, or with the humanized Coyote trickster narrative [p. 220] on the other.)

Page 359 BLOOD RIVER SHAMAN CHANT

Source: J. R.'s working from P. Simoncsics, "The Structure of a Nenets Magic Chant," in V. Dioszegi & M. Hoppal, *Shamanism in Siberia* (Akademiai Kiadó, Budapest, 1978), pp. 388–389. The song was collected in December 1842 by M. A. Castrén.

The "blood river" image here may refer to the shaman cutting himself with a knife at the midpoint of the ceremony, but Simoncsics also indicates a connection to the song's possible use in childbirth with its attendant bleeding. The key image for the latter part of the chant—the "iron tent" or home of the god, where the curing is resolved—is followed, he suggests, by a kind of faltering or break in coherence on the shaman's part. Of this he writes: "After the cutting, many a shaman lies speechless and motionless, almost like a corpse, while blood is trickling from his body. The shaman losing his power of speech while in trance, and lying like a *dead body* on the ground with the *blood* flowing from him, *taken all together*, reveal more of the great mystery of shamanism than any loquacious talk: the interdependence, the secret connection, of *life* and *death*. After this it is only natural that when the shaman prepares for this 'deep dive,' his speech should become broken and his words incoherent."

The Nenets are a Finno-Ugric speaking people, living on the tundra between northeastern Europe & northwestern Siberia.

Page 361 BALD MOUNTAIN ZAUM-POEMS

Source: Velimir Chlebnikov [Khlebnikov], *Werke 1: Poesie* (Rowohlt Taschenbuch Verlag, Reinbek bei Hamburg, 1972), p. 406. The original poems appeared in I. Sacharov's *Skazanija russkogo naroda* (Legends of the Russian People), St. Petersburg, 1836.

Among the early European experimental poets, the Russian "futurist," Velimir Khlebnikov, promoted a "transrational" language & poetry called *zaum*: an attempt to break through the limits of conventional syntax & meaning. Like others of his contemporaries (see p. 445 above), he saw the new work as a revival, in some sense, of a "folkloristic zaum-language"; & in a poem from 1912–1913, "A Night in Gallicia," he incorporated & cited elements from the pair of northern Russian (wordless) incantations ("The Song of the Witches on Bald Mountain" & "The Magic Song of the Nymphs") reprinted here. On the language of magic & its relation to poetry, he wrote elsewhere:

> Spells and incantations, what we call magic words, the sacred language of paganism, words like "shagadam, magadam, vigadam, pitz, patz, patzu" . . . are rows of mere syllables which the intellect can make no sense of, and they form a kind of beyondsense [zaum] language in folk speech. Nevertheless an enormous power over mankind is attributed to these incomprehensible and magic spells, a direct influence upon the fate of man. They contain powerful magic. They claim the power of controlling good and evil and influencing the hearts of lovers. The prayers of many nations are written in a language incomprehensible to those who pray. Does a Hindu understand the

Vedas? Russians do not understand Old Church Slavonic. Neither do Poles and Czechs understand Latin. But a prayer written in Latin works just as powerfully as [an ordinary] sign in the street. In the same way the language of magic spells and incantations rejects judgments made by everyday common sense. . . . The magic in a word remains magic even if it is not understood, and loses none of its power. Poems may be understandable or they may not, but they must be good, they must be truthful. [Translation from the Russian by Paul Schmidt]

For more on "magic words," etc., see p. 442, & *Symposium of the Whole*, pp. 107–112.

Page 362 *A POEM FOR THE GODDESS HER CITY & THE MARRIAGE OF HER SON & DAUGHTER*

Source: English translation by Jerome Rothenberg & Miodrag Pavlović, in M. Pavlović, ed., *Antologija Lirske Narodne Poesije* (Vuk Karadžić Publishing House, Belgrade, 1982), p. 192.

The figure presented herein is called *vila* (pl. *vile*) in Serbian & has been prominent up to (almost) the present in Yugoslavian oral poetry. Connected with mountains & rivers, the *vile* are usually described—by folklorists, etc.— as "fairy-like beings," but often enough there emerges a singular "white" *vila* with the attributes of the old goddesses & identified with Sun (a female in most Slavic traditions, where Moon is generally a male) &/or Morning Star. In this form she is something more than a localized being, credited with creation of the world-at-large, empowerment of the gods & saints (even of God himself for whom, elsewhere, she creates his "celestial mountain"), & with personal powers as a warrior &, as here, a master builder of great cities. In such poems, however far removed from their "pagan" sources, the description goes clearly beyond that of the faerie world (see p. 592) & touches the ferocity of ancient Anat & of that "White Goddess, or Muse, the Mother of All Living," cited elsewhere in these pages by R. Graves. (See p. 584.)

Page 364 *THE MESSAGE OF KING SAKIS & THE LEGEND OF THE TWELVE DREAMS HE HAD IN ONE NIGHT*

Source: Translation by Charles Simic in *Alcheringa*, old series, no. 1 (Autumn, 1970): 24–25.

Part of an ancient & worldwide tradition, the old mythological consciousness expresses itself in European dream-works & autochthonous surrealisms from "then" to "now." Writes poet Vasko Popa, editor of brilliant assemblages of Serbian folk-workings: "The only genuine bright tradition of folk poetry is in ceaseless invention and ceaseless discovery."

For more on dream, see pp. 463, 495.

Page 366   A LOVE POEM WITH WITCHES

Source: J. R.'s version from Spanish translation in Luis L. Cortés, *Antología de la poesía popular Rumana* (Universidad de Salamanca, 1955), pp. 127–129.

A type of charm called a *descântec*, it has, like magic language elsewhere, been a rich & constant source of poetry. What's notable here—beyond the clash of Christian & "pagan" symbols—is the expansion of charm into story: the charm-maker's depiction of herself in the act of conjuration. An example, too, of magic/poesis as self-reflection.

Page 368   THE DESCRIPTIONS OF KING LENT

Source: J. M. Cohen's translation in F. Rabelais, *The Histories of Gargantua & Pantagruel* (Penguin Books, Harmondsworth, England, 1957), pp. 516–519.

"This forest of dreams," Michelet called it & traced its power to Rabelais' knack for drawing from "popular *elemental* forces." But that was deceptive too, & Rabelais stood not so much outside all of that—as mere observer—but in the middle & a part of it himself. "Nonliterary," as Mikhail Bakhtin describes him: a primal poet whose images, etc., diverge from "the literary norms and canons" & assert their "undestroyable nonofficial nature." And further: "No dogma, no authoritarianism, no narrow-minded seriousness can coexist with Rabelaisian images; these images are opposed to all that is finished and polished, to all pomposity, to every ready-made solution in the sphere of thought and world outlook" (M. B., *Rabelais & His World*, pp. 2–3).

Rabelais' tradition, in specific, is what Bakhtin speaks of as "the folk-culture of humor"—but humor writ large as something wilder & more sacred than we had previously imagined & to which our own work has now, independently, returned. "A second world," says Bakhtin again, "and a second life outside officialdom," it manifested in carnival & market, where it reflected, in shadow of church & state, the energies of the "primitive"/ "primal"/"pagan" & "the ancient rituals of mocking at the deity" in the oldest of poetic/sacred traditions. By Rabelais' time, that comic life was subterranean but "deepened and rendered more complex in the process."

For which too it spoke its own language: "an extremely rich idiom [of forms & symbols] . . . opposed to all that was readymade and completed, to all pretense at immutability . . . a dynamic expression . . . ever changing, playful, undefined . . . [with] a characteristic logic, the peculiar logic of the 'inside out,' of the 'turnabout,' of a continual shifting from top to bottom, from front to rear, of numerous parodies and travesties, humiliations, profanations, comic crownings and uncrownings." The language of this "second world"—a world inside out—is that of the sacred clowns & of ritual laughter & sexuality: a descent into the body & a "degradation [that] here means coming down to earth, the contact with earth as an element that swallows up and gives birth at the same time." It is, as T. Rundle Clark described it for the ancient Egyptians, "obscene, brutal & inconsequential" (see p. 449), or as it turns up in the Jewish Gnostic image of creation:

> the 7 Laughs of GOD
> Hha Hha Hha Hha Hha Hha Hha
>
> each laugh he gave
> engendered the 7
> god god god god god god god
>
> the Fore-Appearers
> who clasp everything one

> > (4th-6th century A.D., translated by Charles Doria)

[N.B. To take it a step further, the reader might note that Bakhtin observes the primal push around "this half-forgotten idiom" in a range of European writers such as Shakespeare & Cervantes. If so, it should be possible to see their work as not only *influenced* by the language of that "second world" but, like Rabelais', as a manifestation & continuation of its energies. Not a backwash, then, but a vital center & a line whose re-emergence in the present is clear enough for all who care to see it.]

Page 372   *DEEP SONG*

Source: J. R.'s translation of Gypsy poems cited in Federico García Lorca, *Obras Completas* (Aguilar, Madrid, 1960), pp. 1524–1525.

Of the native Andalusian music called "deep song" (*cante hondo*), Lorca wrote: "It is a very rare specimen of primitive song, the oldest in all Europe, and its notes carry the naked, spine-tingling emotion of the first Oriental races." Its immediate source was the Gypsy *siguiriya*, a form older than flamenco, with filiations to Arab & Moorish songs &, beyond these, to the song & poetry of India. But what Lorca heard in it also—as a kind of "sung prose, [seeming to] destroy all sense of metric rhythm"—was something "deeper" & more ancient that blurred the distinction between "prose" & "verse" (really, between speech & song): "the reiterative, almost obsessive use of one same note, a procedure proper to certain formulas of incantation, including recited ones we might call prehistoric and which have made some people suppose that song is older than language." Finally, though, it was the *language* of the songs that drew him—finding in them not only a wildness but a more precise, "exact expression" for those poets "concerned with pruning and caring for the overluxuriant lyric tree left us by the Romantics and post-Romantics." With that much stripped away, he wrote, "deep song sings like a nightingale without eyes . . . [&] always in the night. It is a song without landscape, withdrawn into itself and terrible in the dark." (All prose quotes from Lorca's essay, "Deep Song," trans. Christopher Maurer, in Lorca, *Deep Song*, New Directions, 1980.)

The repercussion in Lorca's own work is not only impressive in itself but may lay claim to being a continuation of "deep song" by other means. (See above, p. 535.)

Page 374   *THE CANTICLE FOR BROTHER SUN*

Source: J. R.'s translation in *Pogamoggan*, no. 1 (1964): 86–87.

Where the expanding human settlement draws boundaries against the wilderness, a breed of saint arises whose career commences with a journey— heterodox & pagan—to the primal world outside the human. It is as if the saint's journey were the shaman's journey retold: a descent into the place of "magic words," in which, the Eskimo shaman tells us, "a person could become an animal if he wanted to / and an animal could become a human being . . . and there was no difference. / All spoke the same language." In the

case of Saint Francis, then, there are the matters of the meeting with—&
taming of—the wolf of Gubbio; the language of animals & plants he learned
to speak; & the creation (itself a recovery) of the song-for-all-beings trans-
lated here.

The reader can compare Francis's poem with the culturally distant (&
distinct) thanksgiving prayer of the Seneca Indians; e.g., the section in praise
of the sun, etc.:

> Now in the sky.
> He created two things.
> That they should be in the sky.
> They are the ones to give light.
> So the people could see where they are going.
> The people I created.
> Now this has happened.
> At this time of day.
> There is plenty of light.
> He has given authority.
> To the one who gives light for the days to have light.
> Now this time of day.
> We give thanks to our Brother the Sun.
> This is the way it should be in our minds.

> (Translation by J. R. & Richard Johnny John)

[For the complete translation, see the present editor's *Shaking the Pumpkin*,
original edition, pp. 4–11.]

Page 376   From *EUROPE A PROPHECY*

Source: William Blake, *The Poetry & Prose of William Blake* (Double-
day & Company, 1965), pp. 58–59.

A visionary himself, Blake was part of a by then occulted tradition of
poetry & vision, which he turned on its head in a series of extreme, often
comic, reversals & renamings, forcing it into a virtually new life. Of his
experience, e.g., of the faerie world, which the present poem explores in
implicitly sexual terms, he reported elsewhere:

> I was walking alone in my garden, there was great stillness among
> the branches and flowers and more than common sweetness in the

air; I heard a low and pleasant sound, and I knew not whence it came. At last I saw the broad leaf of a flower move, and underneath I saw a procession of creatures of the size and color of green and gray grasshoppers, bearing a body laid out on a rose leaf, which they buried with songs, and then disappeared. It was a fairy funeral. (Allan Cunningham, "Life of Blake," 1830)

But a darker image of that world—"unforgiving & unalterable"—appears in his masterwork, *Milton*, for which see above, p. 593.

Page 379   TWELVE KURA SONGS FROM TIKOPIA

Source: J. R.'s adaptation from Raymond Firth, "Privilege Ceremonials in Tikopia," *Oceania*, XXI (1950): 170–175. [Original reprinted in Firth, *Tikopia Ritual & Belief* (George Allen & Unwin, London, 1967).]

The *kura* is performed when "the eldest daughter of the elder . . . reaches maturity [and] becomes the *fafine ariki*," or chief female. She is then doomed to live apart from all men &, growing older, to commit suicide by swimming out to sea, dwelling after death among "the assembly of those who have made the *kura*."

The dance itself is said to have originated with the god Rata & his consort Nau Taufiti, both very fierce, both with more-than-human sex-hunger & -power. To tap this energy in the dance, "men and women face each other in pairs, and the songs are exchanged between the two parties. . . . It is so that the men are Rata and the women Nau Taufiti." The songs, like much sacred poetry, are expected to act as a sexual stimulant; their "black humor" is also clearly within the range of the sacred.

While *Kume* in Song 1 is likely a separate goddess from Nau Taufiti, the rest of the songs involve a series of exchanges (sexual abuse & praise) between Rata & his principal consort. The *One-Before-Us* is Faka-sautimu, adze-god, anterior & superior to Rata. In Song 4 *cherry* is literally the puka-berry & indicates that the woman's vulva is small & pink. The *black buttocks* in Song 8 come from rubbing them against the ground in (frequent) intercourse. The *cordyline root* of the final song is "carrot-shaped and several feet long, and when cooked in the oven gets very dark in color."

Page 382 TWO FOR THE GOD AIA

Source: Allan Natachee, trans., *Aia: Mekeo Songs* (Papua Pocket Poets, Port Moresby 1968).

This & the several Papuan poems that follow represent not only traditional & oral work in translation but an effort by Papuan poets to control the process & to create thereby a new English poetry in unbroken connection with the tribal past. The present translator—older than others of the emergent generation—writes of his own experience with the Mekeo poems he translates here: "When I was 3 or 4 years old I used to hear the older people singing. Then when they stopped singing, I used to sing just what they had done. They were very surprised in hearing me singing. I was very fond of smearing my body with red native paint. The song I first learned to sing was one of the war songs. It bears the name of the god Aia. . . . Then my poor mother died and I was taken to the nuns. There were no more war songs for me. . . ."

In the 1960s & 1970s the new movement showed itself in magazines such as *Kovave* ("New Guinea's first literary magazine") & *Gigibori*, as well as in the Papuan Pocket Poets, a series of small books edited by Ulli Beier. The two languages functioning as lingua franca are English & Papuan pidgin (see below).

Page 383 TOLAI SONGS

Source: Murray Russell, trans., *Kakaile Kakaile: Tolai Songs* (Papua Pocket Poets, Port Moresby, 1969).

S.D.A. = Seventh Day Adventists.

Song 2 is described by the translator as "a *bibolo*, a type of dance done by women." Performed with many repetitions.

The play of old & new begins in the native language & is carried into the English, where it serves as a model for a Papuan (New Guinean) "modernism" that draws power from its own past. The translators &/or collectors themselves are most often Papuan poets—thus exercising a control over their self-presentation & cultural continuities & transformations that hasn't always appeared in such a context. Writes Ulli Beier of the ethnopoetics at work here: "Poetry—if we may in fact apply our own term to this variety of forms and functions—is a *living* tradition in New Guinea. All the examples given here are *traditional* in the sense that they are part of a group of cultures whose roots go very far back and that they still use ancient forms. Many of them are *modern* in the sense that traditional forms are often used to describe or celebrate contemporary events." (*Words of Paradise*, p. 11)

Further examples of traditional forms adapted to new events & images appear throughout the present volume: a tendency toward the incorporation-of-the-new at least as widespread as that toward preservation-of-the-old.

Page 384 PIDGIN SONG

Source: Transcription by Leo Morgan in *Kovave: A Journal of New Guinea Literature* (Boroko, Papua-New Guinea, 1970), no. 1, p. 45.

Often classed as "marginal languages"—but this "marginality" may bring them closer to the language of our own poetries—*pidgins* & *creoles* have grown out of colonial encounters, etc., throughout history. Writes Dell Hymes of certain of the issues at stake here:

> . . . Pidgins arise as makeshift adaptations, reduced in structure and use, no one's first language; creoles are pidgins become primary languages. Both are marginal, in the circumstances of their origin, and in the attitudes towards them on the part of those who speak one of the languages from which they derive.
>
> Marginal, one might have also said, in terms of knowledge about them. These languages are of central importance to our understanding of language, and central too in the lives of some millions of people. Because of their origins, however, their association with poorer and darker members of a society, and through perpetuation of misleading stereotypes—such as that a pidgin is merely a broken or baby-talk version of another language— . . . these languages have been considered, not creative adaptations, but degenerations; not systems in their own right, but deviations from other systems. . . . Not the least of the crimes of colonialism has been to persuade the colonialized that they, or ways in which they differ, are inferior—to convince the stigmatized that the stigma is deserved. (D. H., *Pidginization & Creolization of Languages*, p. 3)

In New Guinea (Papua), the regional pidgin (Neo-Melanesian or *tok waitman*) has shown much expansion & development over the last several decades, including the appearance of an oral & written poetry. The preferred form of pidgin, under such circumstances, is that most distanced from the influence of English—i.e., an *active* language in the process, still, of *self-creation*. (With which the reader can compare the programs for a new language brought into early twentieth-century work by such marginal figures as Ball, Apollinaire, & Khlebnikov ([see pp. 445, 450, 600]).

Page 385 THE GUMAGABU SONG

Source: Bronislaw Malinowski, *Argonauts of the Western Pacific* (paper edition: E. P. Dutton & Co., New York, 1922, 1961), pp. 293–294.

Background: "Several generations ago, a canoe or two from Burakwa, in the island of Kayeula, made an exploring trip to the district of Gabu. . . . The natives in Gabu, receiving them at first with a show of interest, and pretending to enter into commercial relations, afterwards fell on them treacherously and slew the chief Toraya and all his companions. . . . The slain chief's younger brother (Tomakam) went to the Koya of Gabu and killed the head man of one of the villages, avenging thus his brother's death. He then composed a song and a dance which is performed to this day."

Malinowski adds, of the poem's non-euclidean structure & resemblance to modern poetry: "The character of this song is extremely elliptic, one might even say futuristic, since several scenes are crowded simultaneously into the picture . . . [and] a word or two indicates rather than describes whole scenes and incidents." Thus the opening strophe moves between the Gumagabu man on top of his mountain, Tomakam's pledge to go there, the women grieving for Toraya, the mountain again, the mist above Tomakam's home, lastly his mother crying for revenge. The second strophe starts with dream narrative, shifting suddenly to the expedition's arrival at Gabu & the ritual exchange of gifts. The third uses first-person narration to describe the killing. In the fourth (third-person again) there's description of a storm at sea, but in the fifth, without transition, the party is safe at home & the chief (Tomakam) holds up a basket containing the victim's head. The final strophe (description of a feast) slips back into first-person.

Thus the movement is complicated & very much alive—the gaps in sequence allowing that play-of-the-mind which is so highly developed a process among many "primitive" poets.

Page 387 *THREE DRUM POEMS*

Source: Ulli Beier, "A Note on the Drum Language of the Trobriand Islands," *Alcheringa*, new series, vol. 1, no. 1 (1975): 108–109.

A reversal, in effect, of African talking drums, the Trobriand usage is an imitation of drum rhythms by the human voice. "Though created as a memory aid or teaching aid," writes Ulli Beier, "the drum language has its own compelling beauty, like poetry in some archaic language." And he adds: "It is possible to 'speak' a whole drum sequence, just as the Yoruba people in Nigeria can drum a whole recitation of poetry." (See p. 529 above.)

All three examples given here are related to drum rhythms used for the *kesawaga* dance: a ceremony performed by four drums, the smallest of which "plays the complex rhythms that serve as instructions to the dancers and that can be identified and repeated in speech patterns." Similar methods of sounding turn up around the *canntaireachd* (wordless chants) associated with Scottish bagpipes & the meaningless refrains (*toti quiti toti totototo tiquiti tiquiti*, etc.) that punctuated old Aztec poetry like rhythmic markers. (The reader may also want to compare these drum poems with the sound-poems, etc., presented on pp. 8 & 361 of the present volume.)

Addenda.   Sonia Sanchez
           From *a/coltrane/poem*

(softly   da-dum-da da da da da da da da/da-dum-da
till it   da da da da da da da da da
builds   da-dum- da da da
up)   da-dum. da. da. da. this is a part of my
        favorite things.
        da dum da da da da da da
        da da da da
        da dum da da da da da da
        da da da da
            da dum da da da da
            da dum da da da da — — — — —
(to be   rise up blk / people
sung   de dum da da da da
slowly   move straight in yo / blkness
to tune   da dum da da da da
of my   step over the wite / ness

favorite	that is yesssss terrrrrr day
things.)	weeeeeeee are tooooooooday.
(f	da dum
a	da da da (stomp, stomp) da da da
s	da dum
t	da da da (stomp, stomp) da da da
e	da dum
r)	da da da (stomp) da da da dum (stomp)

```
                weeeeeeeee (stomp)
                      areeeeeeeee (stomp)
                            areeeeeeeee (stomp, stomp)
        tooooooday      (stomp.
              day      stomp.
              day         stomp.
              day            stomp.
              day               stomp!)
```

Page 388   SONGS & SPIRIT-SONGS

Source: Willard Trask, *The Unwritten Song: Poetry of the Primitive and Traditional Peoples of the World* (The Macmillan Company, New York, 1966), Vol. I, pp. 208–210. Translations from the German, after Börnstein, "Ethnographische Beiträge aus dem Bismarckarchipel," *Baessler-Archiv* (1916).

A concreteness of image & act distinguishes much of the tribal poetry that comes down to us—in line with one notable push in our own poetry since circa 1913, *viz* "direct treatment of the 'thing' whether subjective or objective." But "here" as well as "there," the mapping of said "thing" incorporates the *dream*world, *spirit*world, as well—or, in the life we really live, a world of *visions* somewhere in between.

Addenda.   (1) "The natural object is always the adequate symbol" (E. Pound, "A Retrospect," [1913], 1918).

(2)   Paul Blackburn
                    PLAZA REAL WITH PALMTREES

At seven in the summer evenings
they crowd the small stone benches

back to back
five and six to a bench;
young mothers
old men
workers on their way home stopping
off, their faces
poised in the tiredness and blankness
recouping
taking the evening coolness
five and six to a bench.
Children too young to walk,
on the knees of their mothers
                              make
seven and eight to a bench.

                    The older ones play immies
                         or chase each other
                            or pigeons.

Sun catches the roofs, one side
                         of the arcade;
the whole of the plaza in shadow between
seven and eight of an evening.

               The man with balloons
               rises above it almost
               his face deflated & quiet

                                        blank
               emptied of the city
                as the city is emptied of air.
               The strings wrapped to his hand
               go up and do not move.
               He stands at the edge of the square
               not calling or watching at all.
                              The cart
               with candy has food for the pigeons . . .
                                   A lull,
               a lull in the moving,
               a bay in the sea of this city
                    into which drift

five and six to a bench
seven and eight to a bench

> Now
> the air moves the palmtrees,
> faces.
> All of it gentle

Barcelona . 27 . VI . 55

Page 391   *THE DAYBREAK*

Source: R. M. & C. H. Berndt, *The World of the First Australians* (Ure Smith, Sydney, 1964; University of Chicago Press, 1965), p. 319.

[The translators write]: "Over the greater part of Aboriginal Australia, particularly in the Centre, most songs . . . are arranged in cycles, a few words to each song. . . . [In this] section from the sacred Dulngulg cycle of the Mudbara tribe, east of the Victoria River country, Northern Territory . . . each line represents one song, which is repeated over and over before the singers move on to the next."

Page 392   *SIGHTINGS: KUNAPIPI*

Source: Songs selected & arranged by J. R. from R. M. Berndt, *Kunapipi: A Study of an Australian Aboriginal Religious Cult* (International Universities Press, 1951), pp. 121–131.

Kunapipi is the name of a major fertility cult, which centers around "a Great Mother, expressed as either a single or dual personality, her power being extended to her daughters, the Wauwalak." In the myth, these (two) Wauwalak Sisters leave their home territory after the elder has incestuous relations with a clansman & becomes pregnant. At a sacred water-hole she gives birth to a child, blood from the afterbirth attracting a great python (Julunggul), who lives in the hole. Then, writes Berndt:

> . . . the sky was shut in with clouds: a storm broke, summoned by
> Julunggul. They washed the baby, to get rid of the smell of blood,
> but it was too late. Night had fallen. They crouched in the hut by
> the fire while the rain poured down outside, taking it in turns to

dance and to call ritually in an effort to drive away the storm.
When the elder sister danced . . . the rain dwindled to almost
nothing. When the younger sister did this, she could check the
storm only a little. Then they sang Kunapipi songs, and the storm
died down.

Later the sisters are swallowed & vomited up—thus the ancient pattern
of death & resurrection, etc.

But the relation of myth to ritual-event & song is complicated far beyond
the simple telling. The ceremonial ground is at once the place-of-the-snake &
womb-of-the-mother; & the myth is always a real presence behind the
Kunapipi songs, forming (on other ceremonial occasions) the basis of both
sacred & secular cycles with a clearly "narrative" quality. Here it's (mostly)
present through allusion, the songs' actual "content" consisting of descrip-
tions of accompanying ceremonial activities, particularly of ritual intercourse
between clansmen (fertility "magic" sanctioned by the elder sister's incest) &
of "fire-throwing" (djamala) that "symbolizes the lightning sent by Julung-
gul." Bullroarers of cypress bark reproduce the python's roaring in the storm;
also, the songs & dances are said to be those of the mythic beings them-
selves—the Sisters dancing to postpone the coming of the snake, etc.

Of the songs per se Berndt writes: "Like the majority of songs in
Aboriginal Australia, these consist of 'key' words, which seem to us to need
further explanation, but are usually understood by natives singing or partici-
pating in the ritual. These 'key' words, several of which constitute a song, are
really word pictures. . . . In short songs of this type in particular, the meaning
of a word usually depends entirely upon the context. . . . Moreover . . . a
song that is sung in one context, to a specific part of the rituals, may have one
meaning, while in another context it has a different meaning." There are also
different classes of words with the same "meaning": some open to the whole
community, some requiring special knowledge, some used only in singing,
etc.

Addenda. The editor, unlike the translator, is also interested in the
out-of-context "carry-over" of the songs, & has arranged this selection to
suggest the possibilities of a noncontextual reading. In doing so, he has taken
some songs in Berndt's literal renderings, some in his freer "general transla-
tions," & has patterned them after his own *Sightings* (see below).

o o o o o o o o

Jerome Rothenberg
SIGHTINGS (VI)

1. The earth shudders under the rain.

2. A hand.
   Five fingers.

3. Milkweed; was it that?

4. They add in rows.

5. Beginning from the waist, slip downwards; force
   a smile.

6. Perhaps a dish.
   A cup.

7. Horse   grey   knot
   fallen   throat   of-blood.

8. One thought, a thousand movements.

Page 395 From THE GOULBURN ISLAND CYCLE

Source: Ronald M. Berndt, *Love Songs of Arnhem Land* (The University of Chicago Press, 1976), pp. 56–67.

Complex in its presentation of multiple elements, the ritual poetry of the northeast Arnhem Landers brings together fertility in man (sexual, erotic) & nature (seasonal, monsoonal) as a matter of symbolic & ecological relationships. Sexuality is thus projected beyond the human, even the biological, & "onto the universe as a whole." But the terms are immediate, explicit, not mythic so much as physical & human—a narrative, writes Berndt, "about living persons who themselves act out a series of events, in a ritualized fashion, in order to achieve a desired result." And further: "As we have emphasized, Aboriginal man in this region, as in others, saw himself as part of nature, for he lived close to it and was wholly dependent upon its resources. Consequently, he humanized that environment and identified cause and effect in natural sequences, as having an internal logic that was relevant to himself and could be applied all around him. However, this materialism made up only part of the process he experienced himself and which he superimposed, through a complex mytho-ritual medium, on his environment" (Berndt, p. 76).

The ritual narrative as such follows the human actions & the slowly building movements of the storm: the summoning through the songs (but also the semen & blood) of the Lightning Snake (Yulunggul) in much the form in which he appears in the Kunapipi ritual, above. And this too is curiously distanced by setting the events on the Goulburn Islands in the west rather than at Yirkalla, where the actual rites are enacted. There, the songs tell us, the men & women "speak the western language," & the men are uncircumcised, therefore (derisively) described as "with long penes," etc. The approach is thus immediate & exotic at once—all of this natural enough to an art, a practice, in which "ordinary events mirror transcendental events" (or vice versa) & the Dreamtime emerges, precisely, in the here & now.

Correspondences.   Sexual symbolism is overt & not, it seems, a reading from outside; thus, Berndt: "From an oblique reference to sexual activity, coitus takes place in actuality, causing blood to flow. The scene is set for the coming monsoonal period, but the significance of the acts, viewed symbolically, must be sought in the Wawalag (and other) mythology. For example, spears = penes = snakes; fighting clubs = penes, placed to attract rain clouds = females = ball bags; clouds rise = females, joined by Lightning(s) = males; snakes writhe in the sky = copulation, resulting in rain = semen = blood, fertilizing the ground. These symbolic associations reaffirm the dual function of the cycle, underlining the relationship between the sexes and correlating human sexual intercourse with the intercourse of the elements" (p. 77).

Song Structure & Performance.   Berndt writes elsewhere: "The songs are usually sung straight through to a particular rhythm, and then repeated any number of times; so that the whole cycle . . . is rarely completed in one evening. . . . [There also seems to be] no defined punctuation in the actual singing; sentences and phrases may run from one to the other without an apparent break. . . ." (Compare this last point to modern practice.—J. R.) "[Songs of the northeast Arnhem Land region] are remarkable [also] for the fact that they are much longer than those in other areas of the Northern Territory. . . . [Finally] the traditional structure of [the] songs . . . has [not] stylized [the songmen's] art [or] stifled individual expression. On the contrary, the great song men add a touch of new mastery to the old rhythms, and extend or abbreviate the original versions as the mood seizes them."

And about the present sequence, viewing each line as a separate song, Berndt says: "Each poetic-song rendering, although it can stand alone, having its own internal consistency and its own intrinsic meaning, leads on to something else. The information it contains is extended or amplified when it is placed in relation to other songs within the same cycle. Further, sequentiality is quite strictly ordered, with one event being regarded as an outcome of what has preceded it. This method of verse construction demonstrates clearly explicit recognition of a relationship between cause and effect, a relationship that has a significant bearing on the song content. It is demonstrated too, not only in the unfolding of events from song to song, but in the complex cross-referent system between one song and the next as well as within a song, which spells out interconnectedness of past and future events" (pp. 143–144).

A complexity, in brief, that belies whatever notions of a "primitive mentality" may still survive among us.

Synopsis. Prior to the excerpt given here, the songs have described preparations for the rites that have already brought scattered storms & rain. Singing & dancing, relaxation, etc., while "the men and women paint their bodies, as well as their boomerangs and fighting sticks, with special designs representing rain. The men are uncircumcised. Around their necks hang ball bags, which they grip in their teeth when dancing, and they call invocations to the clouds. The storm reaches the mainland, lashing the waters of the billabong. . . . As the wind rushes through the trees, it calls out the names of places through which it must pass on its travels. The singing and dancing are stilled now, and the bags are hung up, since they have served their purpose— the storm has become a reality." Song eleven then begins with the intensification of the sexual rites, which will climax in the true arrival of the Lightning Snakes: "writh[ing] in the sky, copulating, twisting and turning among the clouds." The passages thereafter describe the winds & floods in the storm's wake, ending with a description of a seagull skimming the waters at night, hunting "with its sharp eyes, as a lover searches for his beloved. It sees the tracks of mice among the grass and foliage, swooping to catch one in its beak. The cry of the bird and the squeaking of mice echo into the sky and across the countryside."

Page 403   THE FIRST TRUCK AT TAMBREY

Source: C. G. von Brandenstein & A. P. Thomas, *Taruru: Aboriginal Song Poetry from the Pilbara* (University Press of Hawaii, 1975), pp. 21–24.

A major example, from the Pilbara section of Australia's northwest, of contemporary "tabi" singing, in which (as contrasted to group or corroboree style) "the poet sets his words to his own or a borrowed tune, and normally he alone sings his song." The payoff is a poetry of close observation & (often) fine detail, typical of old Aborigine practice & of twentieth-century (re)innovation—both at work here. The sense of locality & landscape, always essential to Aborigine ritual mappings (= "walkabouts"), conditions the response to a new technology—of railways, airplanes, dams, & mines, or (as here) the coming of the first trucks in the 1920s.

What's less clear at this distance is the verbal play & high-energy condensation ("gaps in sequence") that define the tabi-poet's art, along with a measure based on the repetition & variation of phrasal units in five-word lines & three-line stanzas. The maker of the present poem, Toby Wiliguru Pambardu, is described by the translators as "the greatest master of tabi-making in the Pilbara in this century." Concerning his artistry as displayed here, they write: "Considering the many songs Pambardu made, to make a song of such strict measuring without writing anything down is the sign of a really great bard, and of a superior individual. Unfortunately, little is known as yet of his personality. One peculiar habit has been reported: he used to sit alone listening intently to some imaginary person behind his shoulder, at the same time striking an imaginary mirrimba [wooden bow or scraper] on his forearm." Pambardu (also called "the blind") died in 1934, & the version sung & recorded thirty years later is by his friend & fellow poet, Gordon Mackay.

Page 407   NIGHT BIRTHS

Source: Martha Warren Beckwith, *The Kumulipo: A Hawaiian Creation Chant* (The University of Chicago Press, 1951), passim.

Kumu-(u)li-po—literally "Beginning-(in)-deep-darkness," but also the name of the first male god born from the Night, or *Po.*

Pimoe—"a shape-shifting being of uncertain sex, for whom in her feminine form legendary heroes go fishing."

Paliuli—"ever verdant land of the gods where abundant food grows without labor."

"The Hawaiian *Kumulipo*," writes the present translator, "is a genea-logical prayer chant linking the royal family to which it belonged not only to the primary gods . . . [&] to deified chiefs . . . within the family line, but to the stars in the heavens and the plants & animals useful to life on earth, who must also be named within the chain of birth and their representatives in the spirit world thus be brought into the service of their children who live to carry on the line in the world of mankind." Queen Lilu'uokalani, who first trans-lated the work in the 1890s, dated it from about 1700 & gave the author's name as Keaulumoku.

Further, the *Kumulipo* "consists in sixteen sections called *wa*, a word used for an interval in time or space. The first seven sections" (from which all excerpts in the present anthology are taken) "fall within a period called the *Po*, the next nine belong to the *Ao*, words generally explained as referring to the world of 'Night' before the advent of 'Day'; to 'Darkness' before 'Light'; or, as some say, to the 'Spirit world' in contrast to the 'World of living men.' . . . Of the over two thousand lines that make up the chant, more than a thousand are straight genealogies listing by pairs, male and female, the various branches . . . making up the family lines of descent. Thus, although the whole is strung together within a unified framework, it may in fact consist of a collection of independent family genealogies pieced together with name songs and hymns memorializing the gods venerated by different branches of the ancestral stock." The chant ends with the name of the chief's newly born son, whose claim to kingship it helps establish.

Addenda. (1) The "dog child" of the fourth excerpt is connected with "the hairless 'Olohe people . . . dog men with the mystical shape-shifting powers of the demigods." *Maloma* is "the place people go when they die"; the *Hula*, or dance wind, blows there.

(2) Beckwith points to the heavy punning of the original, in which "the use of double meaning in a word extends to whole passages." In addition "the Hawaiian genius for quick transition of thought, piling up suggested images without compulsion of persistency to any one of them, makes it difficult to translate consistently." Her own solution would lead to double renderings & much interpretive commentary; but the possibility that this Polynesian nightworld-dreamworld-punworld can be delivered through some form of Joycean translation oughtn't to be overlooked. Sounds from *Finnegan*, e.g.,

> . . . Dark hawks hear us. Night! Night! My ho head halls. I feel as
> heavy as yonder stone. Tell me of John or Shaun? Who were

Shem and Shaun the living sons or daughters of? Night now! Tell
me, tell me, tell me, elm! Night night! Telmetale of stem or stone.
Beside the rivering waters of, hitherandthithering waters of.
Night!

—or something like that as a way.

(3) For more on genealogies, composition-by-naming, etc., see the
notes on the Maori creation poem (p. 13), the Egyptian god names (p. 11;
commentary, p. 448), & the African praise-poems (commentary, p. 477).

Page 411 THE WOMAN WHO MARRIED A CATERPILLAR

Source: Armand Schwerner's working in *Alcheringa*, old series, no. 4
(Autumn, 1972): 34, based on *Hawaiian Stories and Wise Sayings* (Vassar
College Fieldwork in Folklore, 1923).

Kumuhea—identified elsewhere as "the god of cut-worms."

Kane—principal Hawaiian god of creation/procreation at the time of
the first missionaries.

A similar theme—but with a noteably different relationship & issue—
turns up in the Eskimo "Woman Who Took In a Larva to Nurse"
(pp. 265–266).

Page 412 THE BODY-SONG OF KIO

Source: J. Frank Stimson, *Tuamotuan Religion* (Bishop Museum
Bulletin No. 103, Honolulu, 1933), pp. 32–33.

Kio, or *Kiho*—supreme god & creator.
Oatea, or *Vatea*—overlord of the world of light.

"Ruea-a-raka" (the singer of the poem) "insists that the enumeration of
the parts of Kio's body was chanted by Kio to Oatea as part of the requisite
ritual, and finds nothing incompatible with the god's inherent dignity in its
wording; she explains that Kio, when conferring his mana upon Oatea, was
obliged thus to detail all of the various parts of his own body whose disparate
powers were consequently passed over respectively, and intact, to Oatea."

Page 413 FUNERAL EVA

Source: English version by David Rafael Wang, previously unpublished.

[Translator's note]: "The *eva* was attributed to Chief Koroneu, who composed it over the death of his son, Atiroa, who had died in bed of disease. The boy had been treated by Pangeivi, Tane's high priest.

"The performers of the *eva* blackened their faces with charcoal, shaved their heads, cut their skin to draw blood, and wore *pakoko*, filthy cloth dipped in mud."

Page 414 TOTA WAKA

Source: Translations by Pierre Joris from Tristan Tzara, *Poèmes Nègres*, as published in *Alcheringa*, vol. 2, no. 1 (1976): 86, 113. (Tzara's French in *Oeuvres Complètes*, Flammarion, Paris, 1975, Vol. 1.)

Although the present translation is by now at some remove from its original, it illustrates the contribution of Tzara & other European avant-gardists to the recovery of a primal poetry & what he himself called "the exalted source of the poetic function." By 1916 Tzara & Co. were chanting translations of African & Oceanic poems in Zurich's Cabaret Voltaire, & Tzara was compiling an anthology of such work—though never published in his lifetime. The Maori original of Tota Waka was performed by Tzara as a sound-poem—therefore its appearance here. Like the rest of his *Poèmes Nègres* ("discoveries & translations" he called them), it reflects the Dadaists' desire to break the stranglehold of European art—to search, as Hugo Ball wrote, for an art that "is the key to every former art: a Solomonic key that will open all the mysteries."

Page 417 THE LOVERS I & II

Source: Kenneth P. Emory, *Kapingamarangi: Social and Religious Life of a Polynesian Atoll* (Bishop Museum Bulletin No. 228, Honolulu), pp. 166–168.

Both dictated by Tomoki. The cunnilingus theme is explicit in the second poem but informs the first poem also. Emory writes of it: "The practice . . . of initiating intercourse by or limiting the sexual relations to cunnilingus . . . has such a prominent place in the chants that I suspect it functioned as a means of birth control, in the spacing of children. It was institutionalized to the extent that the hair-do of the men, the leaving of a point of hair on each side of the forehead . . . was consciously thought of as providing a grip for the women."

The first poem is exactly as Emory gives it; in the second the present editor has arranged Emory's prose translation in verse lines & made some minor changes to ease the reading. The *waka mara* is "a square beam used in setting up the warps in weaving."

Page 420   FLIGHT OF THE CHIEFS (SONG V)

Source: Buell H. Quain, *The Flight of the Chiefs: Epic Poetry of Fiji* (J. J. Augustin, New York, 1942), pp. 85–88.

Flight-of-the-Chiefs—legendary home of the ancestors of the present-day inhabitants of Bua Province, Fiji.

The-Eldest—the ruling chief at Flight-of-the-Chiefs; also called Sailing-the-Ocean.

Lady Song-of-Tonga—The-Eldest's chief wife.

Fruit-of-the-Distant-Sleep—The-Eldest's daughter, here a child but in the great Third Song (too long to reproduce here) the central figure.

Clapping-Out-of-Time—a dwarf of chiefly standing, brought to Flight-of-the-Chiefs long before The-Eldest's time, to amuse Sir Watcher-of-the-Land, who was then acting chief.

Nabosulu nabusele—the conventional closing for all epic songs.

The "composer" of this & fourteen of the fifteen songs in Quain's collection was Daubitu Velema who "[alone] among the descendants of his ancestral village (The-Place-of-the-Pandanus) . . . has inherited the right to practice [shamanistic] arts in his land-group and bears the sacred tokens. . . . When he was a small child, people knew he was destined to become a seer. It could be seen readily in his diffidence, his excitability and his curiosity about serious things." His mother's brother taught him & it is this uncle's "ancient war club and axe that give him power to compose epic songs, 'true songs.' . . . In trance or in sleep the songs come to him, taught him by his supernatural mentors (ancestors). He takes no personal credit for his compositions, does not even distinguish between those which he has composed himself and those old ones which his mother's brother must surely have taught him."

The Fijian poems are chanted by the individual composer, sometimes with the help of a chorus. "The rhythms implicit in the language are qualified by a musical style which can freely reduplicate syllables to change the stress in words. For instance, the word *cere* may become *ceyececeyere* to suit the rhythm of the chant." But though "the lines tend to be of equal length . . . no deliberate patterning of rhythm appears." Rhyme is very insistent, so that the lines of Songs I & II, e.g., end consistently in U-A. Gesture, or what Quain calls "posture language," accompanies the songs.

There's also an interesting narrative device imbedded in the language itself, which Quain indicates by shifting to first person & past tense from the "normal" third person present. "Fijian verbs in known dialects are (in fact) timeless." He writes of this:

> Frequently in formal songs action is recounted in the first person to distinguish it from direct discourse. I have indicated this change of person by italics. The person referred to is always the most recently mentioned. . . . A particle (*wa*) which occurs frequently but not always, in these sections, has been interpreted by missionary students to indicate imperfect tense. . . . At the Place-of-Pandanus it is not used in ordinary speech. In the songs it occurs always in the first line of direct narrative and nowhere else. To distinguish those passages which are direct narrative from those which are not, I have consistently translated the former as past tense throughout, although grammatical excuses for doing so are slight.

In short there's something going on that he can't put his finger on but knows to be there—like those devices described by Whorf & others in which the structure of a language determines the ways its users sense reality. However far from the linguistic solution Quain's intuition may be, the use of contrasting voices makes for meaningful movement in the English.

Compare the note on "Inatoipippiler" (p. 558) & the modern analogues mentioned in that commentary.

Page 423 *ANIMAL STORY X*

Source: Buell H. Quain, *The Flight of the Chiefs: Epic Poetry of Fiji* (J. J. Augustin, New York, 1942), p. 223.

Roko—highest native official of a province, under British regime.

Molau and *basina*—kinds of firewood; each has special function in Fijian fire-tending.

Quain further describes it as a "dance-song called *Village of the Animals* [which], though it makes but little sense . . . is filled with fine intralineal rhymes & bounding rhythms." Okay, but its making-but-little-sense didn't stop him from translating it, & having it now one feels an actual clarity about it: not necessarily in *what* it means (as some single equivalency) but in the positioning of the meaningful segments within it. It is very much what Rasmussen wrote of Iglulik Eskimo techniques:

> The Eskimo poet does not mind if here and there some item be omitted in the chain of his associations; as long as he is sure of being understood, he is careful to avoid all weakening.

Addenda. (1) For more on this last point, see, e.g., the commentary on Malinowski's translation of "The Gumagabu Song" (p. 609).

(2) Compare the poem's movement to the following, among many modern analogues:

Wallace Stevens
PLOUGHING ON SUNDAY

The white cock's tail
Tosses in the wind.
The turkey-cock's tail
Glitters in the sun.

Water in the fields.
The wind pours down.
The feathers flare
And bluster in the wind.

Remus, blow your horn!
I'm ploughing on Sunday,
Ploughing North America.
Blow your horn!

Tum-ti-tum,
Ti-tum-tum-tum!
The turkey-cock's tail
Spreads to the sun.

The white cock's tail
Streams to the moon.
Water in the fields.
The wind pours down.

Page 425   THE STATEMENTS

(1) Paul Radin, *The Road of Life and Death* (Bollingen Series V, Pantheon Books, New York, 1945), p. 6.

(2) Bronislaw Malinowski, *Argonauts of the Western Pacific* (E. P. Dutton, New York, [1922], 1961), pp. 408–409.

(3) Robert D. Scott, *The Thumb of Knowledge in Legends of Finn, Sigurd and Taliesin* (Publications of the Institute of French Studies, Inc., 1930), pp. 103–104. From a tenth-century text.

(4) Knud Rasmussen, *The Netsilik Eskimos* (Copenhagen, 1931), p. 321. For more on Orpingalik, see p. 563.

(5) W. H. I. Bleek & Lucy C. Lloyd, *Specimens of Bushman Folklore* (1911), pp. 303–305. (‖kábbo was the narrator of "Girl of the Early Race Who Made the Stars," see p. 32.)

(6) Edward S. Curtis, *The North American Indian: The Kwakiutl* (1915).

(7) English version by Denise Levertov in *O Taste and See* (New Directions, New York, 1964).

(8) Ezra Pound, *Confucius* (New Directions, New York, 1951), pp. 36–37. From the *Ta Hsio* (Great Digest), i.e., "Confucius' words as Tseng Tsze has handed them down." The statement here (really a group of quotes) takes the form of Tseng's later commentary.

(9) Alvaro Estrada, *María Sabina: Her Life and Chants* (Ross-Erikson Inc., Santa Barbara, 1981), pp. 47–48. See also p. 493, and Henry Munn's essay, "Writing in the Imagination of an Oral Poet," in Jerome & Diane Rothenberg, eds., *Symposium of the Whole*.

(10) The book of Daniel X:7–10.

P O S T - F A C E

WOULD-THAT-THEY-ALL-KNEW-THESE-SONGS is what I think of you.

It seems as if we were beginning to walk. It seems as if we were going as far as the earth is good.

ACKNOWLEDGMENTS

Grateful acknowledgment is made to the following publishers and individuals for material copyrighted by them and reprinted in *Technicians of the Sacred*.

Alcheringa, for material first published in *Alcheringa* and copyrighted by the editors.

George Allen & Unwin, Ltd., for excerpts from *The Nine Songs* by Arthur Waley.

Vito Acconci, for "Security Zone" by the author.

David Antin, for excerpts from "Definitions for Mendy" by the author, and for translations of "Free Union" by André Breton and "The Nine Herbs Charm." Reprinted by permission of David Antin.

Anvil Press Poetry, for "Spell Against Jaundice," from *The Golden Apple* by Vasko Popa, translated by Andrew Harvey and Anne Pennington, published in 1980 by Anvil Press Poetry, London.

J. J. Augustin, Inc., for excerpts from *Flight of the Chiefs* by Buell Quain.

Kofi Awoonor, for translation of "Abuse Poem" by Komi Ekpe. Reprinted by permission of Kofi Awoonor.

Amiri Baraka, for "Ka 'Ba" from *Selected Poetry of Amiri Baraka/LeRoi Jones*. Copyright 1979 by Amiri Baraka. Reprinted by permission of the author.

Ulli Beier, for excerpts from *Yoruba Poetry* by Ulli Beier and Bakare Gbadamosi and from *Black Orpheus*; and for "Three Drum Poems" by the author.

Ronald M. Berndt and the University of Chicago Press, for excerpts from *Love Songs of Arnhem Land* by Ronald M. Berndt, published by Nelson, Melbourne, 1976. Reprinted by permission of the author and publisher.

Ronald M. Berndt, for excerpts from *Djanggawul* and *Kunapipi* by the author.

Bernice P. Bishop Museum Press, for excerpts from *Kapingamarangi* (Bulletin 228) by Kenneth P. Emory; and for excerpts from *Tuamatoan Religion* (Bulletin 103) by J. Frank Stimson.

Joan Blackburn, for "Plaza Real with Palmtrees" by Paul Blackburn. Reprinted by permission of Joan Blackburn.

Robert Bly, for translation of "Ode to My Socks" by Pablo Neruda. Reprinted by permission of Robert Bly.

Keith Bosley, for "Fire" from *Finnish Folk Poetry: Epic* (1977). Translated from the Finnish by Keith Bosley.

George Brecht, for extracts from *Vicious Circles and Infinity* by George Brecht and Patrick Hughes.

George Brotherston, for "Poems for a Carnival." Translated from Quechua by the author.

University of California Press for "Horse" by Aimé Césaire, from *Aimé Césaire: The Collected Poetry*, translated by Clayton Eshleman and Annette Smith. Copyright © 1983 by the Regents of the University of California.

Augusto de Campos, for "Ôlho por Ôlho" by the author.

National Museums of Canada, for "How Isaac Tens Became a Shaman." Reproduced from *Medicine-Men on the North Pacific Coast* by Marius Barbeau, Bulletin No. 152, Anthropological Series No. 42, Ottawa, 1958, by permission of the National Museum of Man, National Museum of Canada.

Dr. P. Chakravarthi, for excerpts from the Papua Pocket Poets Series and *Kovave*.

Samuel Charters, for quotation from *Poetry of the Blues* by the author.

City Lights Books, for excerpts from *The Nine Songs* by Arthur Waley.

The University of Chicago Press, for excerpts from *The Kumulipo* by Martha W. Beckwith and from *The World of the First Australians* by R. M. and C. H. Berndt.

Clark Coolidge for "Wood" by the author.

Charles Doria, for translations from *Theogony* by Hesiod, "Song of the Arval Brothers," and "The Seven Laughs of God." Reprinted by permission of Charles Doria.

Dover Publications, for song from *The Gift To Be Simple* by Edward Deming Andrews, Dover Publications, Inc., New York, 1940, 1962. Used with the permission of the publisher.

Robert Duncan for excerpt from "Passages 24" by the author.

E. P. Dutton & Company, Inc., for excerpts from *The Last of the Seris* by Dane and Mary Roberts Coolidge. Copyright 1939 by Dane and Mary Roberts Coolidge. Renewal © 1966 by Coit Coolidge and Mrs. Calvin Gaines Coolidge. Reprinted by permission of the publisher.

George Economou, for translations of "Ioanna Raving" by Takis Sinopoulos and "The Train."

Munro S. Edmonson, for excerpts from *The Book of Counsel*, translated from the Mayan by the author.

Barbara Einzig, for "Things Seen by the Shaman Karawe" by the author. First published by Don Wellman in *O. ARS*.

Clayton Eshleman, for excerpt from his translation of "Alberto Rojas Jiménez Viene Volando" by Pablo Neruda.

Etnografiska Museet of Göteborg, Sweden, for excerpts from *Inatoipippiler*, translated by Nils M. Holmer and S. Henry Wassén (*Etnologiska Studier* No. 20, 1952).

Raymond Firth, for adaptations from *Tikopia Ritual and Belief* by the author. Reprinted by permission of Sir Raymond Firth.

Librairie Ernest Flammarion, for transcription and translation from *Oeuvres complètes*, volume I, by Tristan Tzara, © Flammarion 1975.

Stephen Fredman, for excerpt from translation of "Altazor" by Vicente Huidobro. Reprinted by permission of Stephen Fredman.

Peter Furst, for translation of Huichol poem in *Flesh of the Gods* by the author.

Gary Gach and C. H. Kwock, for translations from the Chinese by the authors. Reprinted by permission of Gary Gach.

Allen Ginsberg, for "Psalm IV" by Allen Ginsberg. Reprinted by permission of the author.

Judith Gleason, for translations of "Speaking the World," "Voice of the Karaw," and "Ika Meji" from *Leaf and Bone* and *A Recitation of Ifa* by the author.

Granada Publishing Limited, for "Birth of the Fire God" from *The Elek Book of Oriental Verse* edited by Keith Bosley.

David Guss, for quotation from the introduction to an interview with Eduardo Calderón by the author. Reprinted from *New Wilderness Letter*, number eleven, by permission of the editors.

Richard C. Higgins, for excerpt from *Clown's Way* by the author.

Houghton Mifflin Company, for excerpt from *The Navaho Indians* by Dane and Mary Roberts Coolidge.

Dell Hymes, for excerpts from the introduction to *Pidginization and Creolization*, edited by the author.

Indiana University Press and Peter Seitel, for "Little Leper of Munjolóbo" from *See So That We May See* by Peter Seitel.

Pierre Joris, for translation of "Tota Waka" by Tristan Tzara.

Allan Kaprow, for excerpt from *Some Recent Happenings* by Allan Kaprow.

Robert Kelly, for "To the God of Fire As a Horse" and excerpts from *Lunes* and "The Pig" by Robert Kelly.

Bengt af Klintberg, for excerpts from *Cursive Scandinavian Salve* by Bengt af Klintberg.

Alfred A. Knopf, Inc., for "Ploughing on Sunday" by Wallace Stevens. Copyright 1923 and renewed 1951 by Wallace Stevens. Reprinted from *The Collected Poems of Wallace Stevens*, by permission of Alfred A. Knopf, Inc.

Alison Knowles, for "Giveaway Construction" from *By Alison Knowles* by Alison Knowles.

Kenneth Koch, for "In the Ranchouse at Dawn" by Kenneth Koch.

Suzanne Lacy, for "Ablutions 1972," a performance by Suzanne Lacy, Judy Chicago, Aviva Rahmani, and Sandra Orgel.

Harris Lenowitz, for translation of "The Battle Between Anat and the Forces of Mot" and "Psalm 137" by Harris Lenowitz.

Miguel León-Portilla, for excerpts from *Pre-Columbian Literatures of Mexico* and from *Native Mesoamerican Spirituality* by the author. Reprinted by permission of the author.

Tom Lowenstein, for translation of "My Breath" from *Eskimo Poems* by Tom Lowenstein. Reprinted by permission of the author.

Jackson Mac Low, for "1st Light Poem: for Iris—10 June 1962," included in *22 Light Poems* (Los Angeles: Black Sparrow Press, 1968), copyright © 1968 by Jackson Mac Low. Reprinted by permission of Jackson Mac Low.

Macmillan Publishing Co., Inc., for excerpt from *The Unwritten Song* by Willard Trask. Copyright © 1966 by Willard R. Trask. Reprinted with permission from Macmillan Publishing Company.

David P. McAllester, for translations from *Peyote Music* by David P. McAllester.

David P. McAllester, for translation of "War God's Horse Song II" by David P. McAllester.

Michael McClure, for excerpts from *Ghost Tantras* by Michael McClure.

David McKay Company, Inc., for excerpts from *The Pyramid Texts in Translation and Commentary* by S. A. B. Mercer.

W. S. Merwin, for translations of "Elegy for the Great Inca Atawallpa" and "Three Quechua Poems" from *Selected Translations 1968–1978* by W. S. Merwin, published by Atheneum; and for translations by W. S. Merwin from *Sanskrit Love Poetry* by J. M. Masson, published by Columbia University Press, and *A Peacock's Egg*, published by North Point Press.

Linda Montano, for "Mitchell's Death" by the author.

Henry Munn, for translation of excerpts from "I Am the Woman of the Principal Fountain" by María Sabina, as published in *New Wilderness Letter*, number 5/6. Reprinted by permission of Henry Munn.

John Murray (Publishers) Ltd., for excerpts from *The Message of Milarepa* by Sir Humphrey Clarke; and for excerpts from *The Baiga* by Verrier Elwin. Reprinted by permission of the publisher.

The John G. Neihardt Trust and Hilda Neihardt Petri, for excerpts from *Black Elk Speaks* by John G. Neihardt, copyright John G. Neihardt Trust, published by Simon & Schuster Pocket Books and the University of Nebraska Press.

New Directions Publishing Corporation for "Air Baby" from Russell Edson, *The Very Thing That Happens*, copyright © 1960 by Russell Edson; "The Artist" and "The Goddess" from Denise Levertov, *Earlier Poems 1940–1960*, copyright © 1958, 1959 by Denise Levertov; "The Song Wants To Be Light" (trans. by James Wright) from Federico García Lorca, *Obras Completas*, copyright © Herederos de Federico García Lorca 1954; excerpts from Ezra Pound, *Love Poems of Ancient Egypt*, copyright © 1960 by Ezra Pound; "In letters of gold" from Ezra Pound, *Confucius*, copyright © 1947, 1950 by Ezra Pound; "Praise Song of the Buck-Hare" from Ezra Pound, *Guide to Kulchur*, copyright © 1970 by Ezra Pound, all rights reserved; "Papyrus" from Ezra Pound, *Personae*, copyright © 1926 by Ezra Pound; and "Canto I," "Canto III" (excerpt), and "Canto 113" (excerpt) from Ezra Pound, *Cantos of Ezra Pound*, copyright © 1934, 1962 by Ezra Pound.

Mrs. Kiyo Niikuni, for "river/sandbank" by Niikuni Seiichi.

Howard Norman, for selections from *The Wishing Bone Cycle* by Howard Norman, and for translation of "Going Out to Meet the Whales" by Paulé Barton. Reprinted by permission of the author.

George Butterick and the Estate of Charles Olson, for "Song of Ullikummi" by Charles Olson.

George Oppen, for "Psalm" by George Oppen.

Simon J. Ortiz, for excerpts from "Telling About Coyote" by the author.

Rochelle Owens, for "Words from Seven Magic Songs" and "Song of Meat, Madness and Travel" by the author.

Penguin Books Ltd., for extract from *The Epic of Gilgamesh*, tr. N. K. Sandars (Penguin Classics, Revised Edition 1972), pages 91–93. Copyright © N. K. Sandars, 1960, 1964, 1972. Reprinted by permission of Penguin Books Ltd.

Penguin Books Ltd., for extract from *Rabelais: Gargantua & Panta-*

Carolee Schneemann, for excerpt from "Meat Joy" by Carolee Schneemann.

Armand Schwerner, for "What the Informant Told Franz Boas," "The Machi Exorcises the Spirit Huecuve," "The Woman Who Married a Caterpillar," and excerpt from *The Tablets* by Armand Schwerner.

Charles Scribner's Sons, for Robert Creeley, "I Know a Man" from *For Love: Poems 1950–1960*. Copyright © 1962 by Robert Creeley. Reprinted with the permission of Charles Scribner's Sons.

Gavin Selerie, for "Odin's Shaman Song" from *Azimuth* by Gavin Selerie.

F. Kaye Sharon, for translation of excerpts from *Eduardo el Curandero* by Eduardo Calderón.

Leslie Silko, for "Si'ahh Aash' " and "Mesita Men" by Leslie Marmon Silko.

Charles Simic, for translation of "The Message of King Sakis" from *Alcheringa*, number one. Reprinted by permission of Charles Simic.

Gary Snyder, for "First Shaman Song" and excerpt from "The Hump-Backed Flute Player" by Gary Snyder.

Charles Stein, for excerpt from *A Book of Confusions* by Charles Stein.

Calman A. Levin and the Estate of Gertrude Stein, for excerpt from "Listen to Me" in *Last Operas and Plays* by Gertrude Stein.

Studia Instituti Anthropos, for excerpts from Joseph F. Rock's *The Zhi mä Funeral Ceremony of the Na-Khi of Southwest China*.

Dennis Tedlock, for translation of "Coyote and Junco" from *Finding the Center* by Dennis Tedlock.

University of Texas Press and Allan F. Burns, for "Three Mayan Definitions" from *An Epoch of Miracles: Oral Literature of the Yucatec Maya*, ed. and trans. Allan F. Burns (Austin, 1983). Reprinted by permission of the University of Texas Press.

University of Utah Press, for excerpts from *Florentine Codex* by Charles Dibble and Arthur J. O. Anderson, co-published with the School of American Research.

Viking Penguin Inc., for selections from *Book of the Hopi* by Frank Waters. Drawings and source material recorded by Oswald White Bear Fredericks. Copyright © 1963 by Frank Waters. Reprinted by permission of Viking Penguin Inc.

Diane Wakoski, for "Blue Monday" by Diane Wakoski.

Anne Waldman, for excerpts from *Fast Speaking Woman* by Anne Waldman, City Lights Pocket Poets No. 33, 1978.

David R. Wang, for translation of "Funeral Eva," translated by David Rafael Wang.

Barrett Watten, for excerpt from *Complete Thought* by Barrett Watten (Berkeley: Tuumba Press, 1982). Copyright © 1982 by Barrett Watten.

Hannah Weiner, for "Persons indicated present their compliments to" from *Code Poems* by Hannah Weiner.

Emmett Williams, for selection from "5000 New Ways" by Emmett Williams.

Wittenborn Art books, Inc. for excerpts from *The Dada Painters and Poets* by Robert Motherwell and from *Beyond Painting* by Max Ernst.

Witwatersrand University Press, for excerpts reprinted from D. F. Bleek, "Special Speech of animals and moon used by the ǀxam Bushmen" in *Bantu Studies* 10. Copyright © 1936 by Witwatersrand University Press.

Yale University Publications in Anthropology, for excerpts from *Origin Legend of the Enemy Way* by Berard Haile. Reprinted by permission of the publisher.

Nina Yankowitz, for "Filmic Frieze" by Nina Yankowitz.

Karl Young, for "The Origin of the Mexica Aztecs" by the author.

La Monte Young, for "Composition 1960 #15" by the author. Copyright © 1963 by La Monte Young.

Jerome Rothenberg is the author of over forty other books of poetry and translation, of whom Kenneth Rexroth wrote: "[He] is one of the truly contemporary American poets who has returned U.S. poetry to the mainstream of international modern literature. . . . No one writing today has dug deeper into the roots of poetry." Described as a "master anthologist" by Richard Kostelanetz, his assemblages, besides *Technicians of the Sacred*, include such works as *Shaking the Pumpkin* and, with Diane Rothenberg, *Symposium of the Whole: A Range of Discourse Toward an Ethnopoetics* (U.C. Press, 1983). He has taught for many years at the University of California, San Diego, and recently held the Aerol Arnold Chair in Literature at the University of Southern California. His *Pre-Faces* (1982) received the Before Columbus Foundation American Book Award.

Designer: Kitty Maryatt
Compositor: Trend Western
Printer: Vail-Ballou
Binder: Vail-Ballou
Text: 11/15 Galliard
Display: Galliard